DATE DUE

HIGHSMITH #45115

THE AUTHOR'S DIMENSION

CHRISTA WOLF

The Author's Dimension

Selected Essays

—

INTRODUCTION BY GRACE PALEY

EDITED BY ALEXANDER STEPHAN

TRANSLATED BY JAN VAN HEURCK

Farrar, Straus and Giroux

NEW YORK

Contents

———

Introduction

———

About ten or twelve years ago I visited my friend Marianne Frisch in West Berlin. I asked her if I could somehow meet the writer Christa Wolf. Yes, they were friends, Marianne said, and took me by way of Checkpoint Charlie through the Wall past the taciturn, well, hostile guards into that other country, the German Democratic Republic.

Christa Wolf is the second writer I've ever sought out; the first was W. H. Auden, in New York in 1939, the year, maybe the day, that ten-year-old Christa stood watching the SS march through her town, bayonets pointing toward Poland. She remembers that day, sharp as a wood carving, and tells about it in one of these essays.

Why did I want to see her? I had read *The Quest for Christa T.* and *Patterns of Childhood.* I thought we would talk for hours, this pacifist feminist who would never describe herself like that. What interested me was the woman, the writer who had a passionate commitment to literature and believed at the same time that she had to have a working relationship with society—and a responsibility as well. She seemed to be exactly the writer I wanted to know—not too many like her, though some are dear to me anyway.

And so we came to her apartment in East Berlin on Friedrichstrasse, trolleys rumbling by. I wanted to cry out—don't give up the trolley for the bus; your cars are bad enough. But of course my German was only a failed street Yiddish of about twenty words and her English had just begun. Still we became friends. For me, a lucky mystery.

When you read these transcribed talks, essays, interviews, you'll be reading Christa Wolf's political and literary history in the country which, after Allied shaping, became, in 1949, the German Democratic Republic, the special concern of the U.S.S.R. Berlin, itself divided, was stuck in the GDR's chest. Eventually the Wall was built, graffiti on one side, soldiers with guns on the other.

Between 1949 and 1959, Christa Wolf studied German literature in Leipzig and Jena, married Gerhard Wolf, a critic and poet, had two daughters, worked in a factory in industrial Halle, hoping to become the worker-artist the First Bitterfeld Conference wanted her (and all other artists) to become (described at the end of her talk at the Second Bitterfeld Conference). She worked for the GDR Writers' Union and edited *Neue Deutsche Literatur* and several contemporary anthologies.

Then what? How does a person, a young woman, learn enough, live enough, read and listen enough to finally become one of the most important European writers, to break through the walls of her own early understanding and narrow education in "the snares of theory," as she writes. Of course she was by nature thoughtful, interested, loved her native language and its speakers. She also hated not to be truthful, not to know what had really happened.

It's a vital fact that she was a citizen of a small country, its history fractured right at the decisive years of her entrance into young womanhood. She was needed—an experience most American writers don't have too often. The country was poor but lively with direction, socialist direction, newness happening all around her among the ruins, idealism, and a way to turn away from a shameful national past. In a review of Fred Wander's book *The Seventh Well*, she says, "After the war, we had to learn to live under the eyes of nations that shuddered at our name."

At the Second Bitterfeld Conference in 1966, she began her talk by discussing at some length the values of art in a socialist art-valuing society. She described the envy of West German youth at the breadth of the GDR literary themes. Having put participants at a certain smug ease, she offered a couple of harsh stories of repressive narrow-mindedness in the GDR, one about a writer sent to talk to a work-crew leader, in which the true facts of the worker's life censor him out of the story; the second about a schoolboy who notices the deadly imposition of stereotypes and falsifications in his textbooks. She urged her audience to be more self-critical, the writers to be less fearful.

She must have been thinking of her next book, *The Quest for Christa T.*, which was published in 1968. It's about a young woman who cannot, will not, live the rhythm of that society (and dies young). It's an exploration for Christa Wolf, through Christa T., of what it means to say, to be "I," "the difficulty of saying 'I.' " In "Interview with Myself," she asks: Will others be interested? She's not sure, but trusts that her whole life and experience, which grow out of an intense concern for the development of her society, will evoke problems and questions in *her* that are important to others. "My questions are what structure the book—not events." The book did provoke discussion, criticism, and censorship.

Another question she asks herself: "So, while working on this book, you have found out how you ought to write in the future?" She answers: "On the contrary. I have tried out one road, which I cannot take a second time . . . I have discovered that one must try at all costs to break out of the ring of what we know or think we know about ourselves, and go beyond it."

This "Interview with Myself" is only one example of Wolf's need to demystify the artist and her work. In essays and interviews over the years, she offers explications and meditations that may be useful to herself and her readers. Doing so probably frees her to make her novels as complex as they need to be and still feel she has included the reader. I like her solution. I think it's right to say whenever possible, and if asked: This is the way I journeyed into the unknown individual soul, bumping into history, society, and *myself* at every turn.

Patterns of Childhood was published in 1976. It is another fictional autobiographical journey, this time to the near, unspoken, hardly-to-be-borne German past, in which the child who saw, who knew, is hidden. The adult who pushed her aside, forgot and suppressed her, now must find and know her. Wolf called this kind of labor "subjective authenticity," in which "authenticity" makes the word "truthfulness" look like a barely scratched surface. How hard that must have been to write, how much harder life itself became.

In that year, Wolf Bierman, a popular singer and composer, was allowed to travel to an engagement in West Berlin. He was not allowed to return. Wolf wrote: "1976 was a caesura in cultural policy development in our country, outwardly indicated by Wolf Biermann's expatriation . . . A group of authors became aware that their direct collaboration, the kind they themselves could answer for and thought was right, was no longer needed. We are socialists, after all. We lived as socialists in the GDR because that's where we wanted to be involved. To be utterly cast back on literature brought about a crisis for the individual, an existential crisis." It must have been a political crisis, too. As one of the signers of a protest letter to the government, Wolf was dismissed from the executive board of the Berlin section of the Writers' Union. In a 1983 interview, she agreed with me that she had been stopped by that experience and the repression that followed.

In another place she wrote: "It was the origin for me among others of working with the material of such lives as Günderrode's and Kleist's."

These conflicts, this falling back on literature, became *No Place on Earth*, which I think of as a play of mourning for the Romantic writers of the early nineteenth century—Günderrode, Kleist, Büchner—who were sentenced to suicide and madness. "They wrote hymns to their country," Anna Seghers said, "against the walls of whose society they beat their heads." *No Place on Earth* is the wonderfully invented work in which the characters speak their own words from their letters and poems. The silencing of Biermann's expatriation had given Wolf the gift of new form.

There are several essays on Karoline von Günderrode and Bettina von Arnim in *The Author's Dimension*. Wolf examines their lives and work almost as if they could be our teachers if only we would pay attention to their personal pain in the historic moment. But it is the hard-squeezed lives of Günderrode in the early nineteenth century and Ingeborg Bachmann in the twentieth that lie heaviest on Christa Wolf's good mind.

Heaviest . . . As much as she cared about her contemporaries and her elders like Anna Seghers or Bertolt Brecht, it was the weight of Ingeborg Bachmann's work, its difficulty and mystery, its social consciousness trapped with no way to turn but death, that influenced her most. It made her think back to the other Germans a hundred and fifty, two hundred years earlier, walled in their particular German geography and culture; it made her decide not to die—or leave the GDR, her country, its walls. She and Gerhard would remain. She would struggle on her own terms and answer through work, her literary work, since she and others were prevented from speaking on radio or television and from political reporting.

When she presented the Kleist Prize to Thomas Brasch in 1987, she remembered how she had failed to persuade him to remain in the GDR in 1976. She said: "Contradiction is too cozy a word for the permanent friction forced on writers of the modern era . . . Brasch stands between two systems of value both of which confront him with false alternative values."

Wolf's fear of coming holocausts to bury all holocausts, a fear normal to any European who had lived through one or two twentieth-century world wars, culminated in the important work *Cassandra*, accompanied by four essays, accounts of reading and travel with Gerhard Wolf to Athens and Crete, methodology, and history. There is a determination to go back in time, to get under it all, that place, that time, ancient Greece, which offered to literature forever, by way of great Homer's song, war and a trivialization of ordinary life and, of course, female life.

I think that one of the aspects of Wolf's work that bothers—I mean enrages—the male critics of West Germany, apart from her disinterest in Hemingway, is her criticism of male hierarchical modes, her disinterest in the hero. "As long as there are victors," there's not too much hope for the world. The only hero is the anti-heroine Cassandra, who sees how decent Aeneas will finally, going forth, only re-create the same patriarchal system. "We have no chance against a time that needs heroes." Cassandra sees her death before her, and all the other deaths. She can't do much, but she can *see*. That is her task on earth, to see, to teach seeing, to tell.

I have not talked about *Accident*, a book I admire. It's about Chernobyl, a brother's brain operation, a woman's ordinary anxious day, "the significance of daily structure," which Christa Wolf says she learned, little by little, by living in the country for half of each year. It's a short book that moves gracefully from newscast to the garden vegetables, to the children on the phone, to the hospital operating room.

And then *What Remains*: a collection of older stories, including a novella describing Wolf's surveillance by the East German secret police a number of years ago. This story infuriated West German critics, who thought she should have published it much earlier. It was a jumping-off point for a scapegoating attack on Christa Wolf which held her responsible for all GDR corruption, bureaucratic crime, and political repression. This campaign chose to disregard Wolf's work which, in fiction and talk and interview, dealt with the life of the individual in a stultifying society, the pathetic condition of education, which she pointed out prepared young people for a life of dependent thinking, the untold stories of German literary history, as well as German difficulties in facing the Nazi past and the complicity of those still alive—her own generation.

The last part of this collection includes some short pieces, a report on a reading in Mecklenburg, "We Don't Know How . . . to think directly, to tell, we never learned in school." I'd like to quote from another essay, "Momentary Interruption":

> November 4, 1989, in Alexander Square in East Berlin was the moment when artists, intellectuals, and other groups in our society came together . . . That moment was by no means just a fortunate accident, as amazed Western reporters interpreted it. It was the . . . climax of a long process in which literary and theater people, peace groups, and other groups had been coming together under the aegis of the Church,

to meet and share talk . . . and drew encouragement for action. For years we addressed certain tasks in what we intended as our opposition literature: to name the conflicts which for a long time were expressed nowhere else, and thus to generate or strengthen a critical attitude in readers; to encourage them to resist lies, hypocrisy . . . to keep alive our language and the other traditions of German literature and history from which attempts were made to cut us off . . .

This talk was given at the University of Hildesheim when Wolf received an honorary doctorate in January 1990. In it there is also the sad sentence: "Our uprising appears to have come years too late."

Yes. As the young people ran laughing through Hungary into the West and the Wall corridors were opened and the Wall taken down, crumb by stony crumb, and the German election approached, and the currency changed, it was clear that an autonomous free democratic socialist East German nation would not be born. Certainly, when the cry "We are the people" changed to "We are one people," the heady hopeful weeks in East Berlin and Leipzig, the long candlelight vigils, talk, argument, dissent, and planning ended. Freedom, unemployment, and colonization of East Germany began. As Christa Wolf writes:

> [The] politicians, economic managers, and party officials need a fatherland to carry on their enterprises. There is no motherland in sight, no more than before.

—GRACE PALEY

THE READER

AND THE WRITER

—

Contribution to

the Second Bitterfeld

Conference*

All our public discussions in the past months, the Party's decisions about various spheres of our life, have a common center. The question is how to make better use of the possibilities our society offers in its present stage; to create the necessary conditions so that the acknowledged laws of socialism can be consciously applied in the economy, in science, in education. What, in our society, are the possibilities for art?

Sometimes we are still offered clichés: material support, industrial contracts, public honor paid to artists. That is something, but it is not the essential. What is essential becomes apparent at once if you do what I did recently: spend a few days in West Germany. The people I talked with there were mostly young people, fed up with the shallow anti-Communism of their official propaganda, with a burning desire to know the real facts about the GDR. You could see that the young are especially sensitive in their reactions, now that West Germans are waking up from the spell which the so-called economic miracle cast over many of them for years. Today they find themselves standing in front of this impressive store window full of merchandise and asking themselves: What now? And they are asking us: Do you know something better? They are looking to us for well-thought-out, practical, useful answers. They are also reading our books. They are

---

* Conference held in Bitterfeld, near Halle, in 1959, to establish a program to develop socialist art in East Germany. It encouraged artists to join actively in building socialism and to bring workers into all aspects of the arts. The second conference was held in 1964 to reexamine the program, as it had not lived up to expectations. (Text based on shorthand notes of Wolf's speech.)

3

not looking for trite replies or evasions. They can tolerate problems, too.

They are surprised by our themes; I was particularly struck by that. They tell us: "The things you write about over there are things that West German writers do not consider appropriate material for literature"—the real everyday conflicts of young people, the daily life of millions, the vast theme of the worker in a highly developed industrial society, the militant demonstrations like the Easter protest marches, for instance, which have a great moral significance for every person taking part, aside from their political content. In a sphere of formalized, very limited possibility for social action, they offer the opportunity for action, for initiative, for daring, for creative ideas, for personality development in general—not to mention the furtherance of artistic talents.

[In West Germany] we took part in an Easter protest march revue, where we heard songs with witty, impudent lyrics sung and accompanied by nonprofessionals, which would do credit to any evening performance the FDJ* puts on to promote young talent. There was one song lyric, for instance—over there the police have to be notified about any demonstration, and accompany the demonstrators in jeeps at the front and rear: "Dear police, to you/ an Easter egg is due,/ for you are all here, too./ Our friend and helper dear,/ police again this year/ so glad to see you're here." You can imagine the tone in which they sing that! We sang along with them. These young people have the same need we all have to see themselves expressed in art, and they feel—this was one of the most interesting and unexpected things we observed—that West German literature has let them down. They said to us: "One of you really must come over here, learn what things are like and write about it." It's not that they wanted Communist books, but they felt confident that we would pay attention to the areas of life that concern them. Of course, we had very different opinions on a great many points; there is no doubt about that.

They see that they can talk with us not only about aesthetics but also about economics, politics, sociology, psychology. They spontaneously agreed with us that a writer must know a lot to be able to get inside the complex organism of modern society; and, very naturally, they look in our books for a picture of our society, our ideals, our image of man.

We, too, have something to learn from talking with them. We have to get used to the fact that many things we take for granted are completely new to them. They have never heard these things said this

---

* East German youth organization.

way before. Questions they ask may seem silly, but are not always meant to be provocative. I already knew that we have a responsibility for West Germany; I now feel responsible for particular people. I now feel that everything I don't do well enough or that all of us together aren't wise and aggressive enough about—it seems to me we ought to take much more of an offensive role, produce more positive facts when we confront mistaken views, instead of going on the defensive—that whenever we don't progress fast enough, when we don't consistently overcome obstacles we have already recognized—I am angered, not only for us but also for them, for those young West Germans. Because even if they do not know it, they are dependent on us and we on them.

Naturally, the West German newspapers are suspicious. They ring alarm bells, including so-called critical reviews of our books. If you compare the reviews, you get the impression that some kind of computer has been fed two contradictory and incompatible pieces of information, which have thrown it out of whack. One piece of information is: There is no other Germany; therefore, there is no other German literature. The second piece is: In that other Germany which does not exist, conditions of extreme oppression prevail; and under these conditions, literature is being born. The literature examines social conditions in that nation, is part of the conditions, and works actively to help produce them, yet not only is read by vast numbers of the oppressed citizens but also is the subject of heated debate there. Different views are expressed about it; camps are violently opposed—yet literature continues to be.

Now, every West German reviewer, depending on his character, the political hue of his publication, the financial situation, and the degree of his misinformation about us, can work out his own scheme for turning these two incompatible axioms into a form of literary criticism. Some give way to wishful thinking—"Revolt against the regime"—while others warn against our "particularly refined Communist propaganda." Mistaken praise is handed out to flatter us, mistaken blame to intimidate us. A prominent role is played by the brotherhood of "experts on East Germany"—people who a couple of years ago were still living over here with us, looking very much like socialists. But as Tucholsky* would say, they haven't a clue to what is really going on. That would require solid information, dialectical thinking, a grasp of historical processes. The class barrier falls and the computer goes on the blink. The motor idles, the machine does nothing but chew at a couple of indigestible facts. One feels like

---

* German journalist and writer (1890–1935) opposed to National Socialism.

telling them: "Spare yourselves the trouble! Don't count on us!" But since they will not believe that socialism, in just under two decades, has become a constructive force in our country which millions of people work every day to produce, they are not likely to accept this well-meant advice either.

There are people who can get used to it when they see an apple fall to the ground and hear someone calmly and incessantly repeat: "It's not falling." People like that can be found over here, too, but conditions are less favorable for them in the long run. There are artists who consider the quarrel about the apple unimportant, or who do not see any apple but, for example, only empty space. In Frankfurt am Main we went to the Bergman film *The Silence*, which was causing a great stir, to the point that questions were raised about it in the Bundestag. In the afternoon of the same day, we attended the Nazi war trials, during a session in which the court concentrated on accusing the expert witness, Professor Kuczynski, of bias, instead of examining the truth of his evidence about the links between giant chemical corporations and the Fascist state. We left both places—the film and the trial—with the same feelings of apprehension. We could not escape the impression that the two events were related, albeit in a roundabout, indirect way: the depressing, sterile, bureaucratic atmosphere of the trial; the depressing, sterile emptiness, loneliness, and despair of the film. An art which leaves man alone in such a world as this and which does no more than record symptoms while renouncing any interpretation, which leaves no real alternative but suicide—an art like that abandons man, suggests to him the relativity of all moral values, and ultimately connives to leave him defenseless against Auschwitz, too.

Imagine the sensation it causes, in this atmosphere and in this same city, to hear a simple truth expounded on the stage. Someone stands up and says what everyone knows: The apple is falling. Just to show you how contradictory things are over there, the day after the Nazi war trial session, we saw a performance of Hochhuth's *The Deputy*, which contained the following dialogue between the representative of the Catholic Church and an Auschwitz doctor. The representative of the Church says: "*People* are being burned here . . ./ The smell of burning flesh and hair." To which the doctor from Auschwitz replies:

> *What foolish ideas you have.*
> *What you see here is only industry.*
> *The smell comes from lubricating oil and horsehair,*
> *drugs and nitrates, rubber and sulphur.*

6

A second Ruhr is growing up.
I. G. Farben, Buna, have built branches here.
Krupp will be coming soon.
Air raids don't bother us.
*Labor is cheap.**

I will return to my initial question: What are the advantages for art in a socialist society? We, as citizens of the GDR, were able to attend the war trial with different feelings than our young companions, who were citizens of the Federal Republic. And they pointed out something we had not noticed. While we were talking with them, we kept using the phrase "For us in the GDR . . ." One of them said to me: "I wouldn't dream of saying 'For us in the Federal Republic'; I would not identify myself with this nation enough to say even that much."

For art, the advantages of our society lie in the fact that by nature it is in tune with the objective laws of social development, with the objective interests of human beings. That is, it does not want to appear to people as something mystical and incomprehensible. It can be known, with a little work: its complex structure, its open and secret origins, its inconsistencies. To spread the truth about it does not hurt it but helps it. For the first time in human history, society no longer presents an unbridgeable contradiction to the humanism of art.

I believe we are all agreed on that much. But most of the questions which lately have led to disagreement, arise at a later stage. Differing views emerge when we get down to the concrete: What is the truth? And what is the truth of art—its statistical truth, its sociological truth, its truth as a tool of political agitation? What problems and conflicts can we attribute to our readers?

I'll give you an example, a story told to me by another writer. He was sent as a reporter to see the leader of an engineering crew, a man with a very good reputation who had recently joined the Party and whose picture was all over the newspapers. The reporter was told to gather an authentic, true-to-life story on this man to go with the picture. He went to the crew leader and found him a very open individual. He immediately invited the reporter to come home with him and revealed all about himself, starting as they drove to his apartment. The writer said: "How nice that you are taking me home to meet your family!"

"Oh God, family. My wife and I are getting a divorce."

"But you have children?"

* New York: Grove Press, 1964.

7

"Oh, well, children . . ." said the crew leader. "My son is doing time right now for trying to flee the country."

Then the writer asked: "But you joined the Party because you believed in it, didn't you?"

The man answered candidly: "I did, honest. It happened like this. Our work crew was having a terrible struggle; the work was poorly organized and there were all sorts of shortages and defects. And we couldn't get what we needed, even with my persuasive abilities. Then my buddies said: 'The only thing that will help is if one of us joins the Party; then he'll be in a better position to put his foot down.' I was the one chosen since I'm the leader, so I joined the Party."

The writer fell silent, somewhat disconcerted. After a while the crew leader said: "Don't worry. It's okay for me to be in the Party, I've seen that since I joined."

The writer wrote the story. Then the horse-trading began. I didn't make this up, that's why I'm telling it to you. In made-up stories, things get even more complicated.

It started: "Does he *have* to be getting a divorce?"

"Well," the writer said, "I don't know whether he *has* to, but he is."

"Can't you leave out that bit?"

"Okay, but then there would be no family. And to have no family life isn't typical of socialist man either."

"Then at least leave out that thing about the son!"

"But the people who know the crew leader know his son, too!" said the writer, and added: "Listen, you guys are the ones who sent me to him; I didn't find him on my own."

It turned out that they knew of another crew leader and they decided to put a story about *him* in the newspaper.

The story wasn't printed, but they paid the writer his fee, so in that sense the thing ended peaceably. Yesterday we heard a discussion about how authors work cooperatively with our press. Just imagine two, three, or four experiences like the one I just described, and any writer would pack up his notebook and try his luck somewhere else.

Last week I visited an eighth-grade class in a school where I was supposed to speak at a dedication ceremony,* and I tried to get to know the children a little bit beforehand. I talked about literature. A fourteen-year-old boy raised his hand and said: "Mrs. Wolf, recently I've read four books for young people. In all four there was an FDJ member who was absolutely sure of his convictions, who had all the

* A ceremony in which young people dedicate their lives to socialist principles.

8

positive qualities in the world, and who convinced his friends, who weren't nearly as good as he was, to believe the same. Do you think that's right?"

I was diplomatic and asked him: "What is it like in real life?"

He answered laconically: "Different."

I really did not have the heart to explain to this boy the rules concerning the Type in Literature. Instead, I said: "Somebody ought to write about how it's different."

People like the newspaper staff I described earlier sometimes seem to have the feeling—probably it's perfectly sincere—that we are all here sitting cozily on a sleigh, or in a jet plane, traveling toward socialism together. Then they observe a few writers and artists fiddling around with the bars and levers and drilling a hole someplace. And they sound the alarm: "Those people are drilling holes in the tank!" So we are forced into debating where the tank is, because these people do not always have a blueprint showing the plane's design. I am not claiming that writers and artists always have the blueprint; but it does happen sometimes, because, like everyone else, we have been living in this republic of ours for fifteen years and we have absorbed some basic impressions and education. Well, they sound the alarm; giant emergency crews are sent out which not only stop us but stop other people from getting on with their work. We have to keep fending them off with one hand, saying: "Let us go, let us go, that isn't the tank!" But the battle goes on and on. When the plane has been flying for years without crashing and maybe even increased its speed despite our drilling, only then are they ready to talk with us about the plane's design. Even so, a long time afterward we still hear whispering behind our backs when we walk through the room: "Those were the ones who . . . back then, you know . . . the tank!" You all can laugh about it now, and I can tell jokes. Six months ago I would not have told any jokes, and maybe you would not have laughed. That's a part of our history you could call "Conflict and Resolution."

The way those people have of drilling into *us* prevents us from recognizing the ones who are really drilling the holes. We should give that some thought. They also prevent us from being unrelentingly self-critical at the right moments, and with the required speed, even though it is absolutely essential for us. Perhaps even more than other people, we need to form as quickly as possible a self-critical, genuinely critical relationship to our own work as artists. Interestingly, in the past year what helped me with this was, by and large, not official criticism but the talks I had with "ordinary" readers. They didn't give me polemics! Actually, in the past year all the conflicts, or at least the important conflicts, which are evident in our present stage of cultural development, have been brought out into the open. In all these discussions, our concern has not been literature alone but all the problems of our life.

Who could say that we did not have a lot to learn from these talks! For instance, I have attended FDJ rallies where suddenly, without any prior hint, people talked about the idea of "homeland." I learned more than the young people taking part in the discussion. The FDJ secretary came to me afterward and said, "Actually the theme of 'homeland,' 'GDR,' and so on, wasn't scheduled until *next* week.' He was a bit confused. Many times at teachers' meetings— where, even in the past, people would talk quite openly about problems which now have been addressed in the new education system —I used to think: "If only the school inspector in charge could hear this!"

I have little more to say about the role which literary criticism might but doesn't play in our society. Taste, judgment, and the emotional capabilities of readers have advanced far more than literary criticism. They can no longer be contained within the stereotyped, old-fashioned schematic discourse on literature. I studied German literature myself and do not like to scold my colleagues. But I have been thinking: Why is it, really, that critical reviews are so lifeless and schematic? I sometimes have the impression that many reviews are not written for the people who will read them, or for the author, but for some authority figure who is present only in the imagination, with the hope that he will offer a favorable comment. This tendency to exaggerated caution, even to fear, harks back to a time when independent thinking and responsibility were not yet the self-evident values they are today.

I believe that a trapeze artist has to work with a rope, a safety belt, and a net. But a writer, in whatever field, cannot work with a net. He simply has to accept a little risk, tempered by responsibility.

April 1964

A Few Notes about

My Work as a Writer

—

My young daughter confessed to me recently that she has a remarkable habit. In bed at night she transforms herself into a princess and goes through the strangest adventures in her magnificent castle, where she is visited by a prince intent on rescuing her, and where a horde of animals is specially engaged to serve her. (It goes against her sense of social propriety to employ people as servants, even in her imagination.) Anything that her happy, busy child's life does not give her, she puts into this dream. In the daytime she makes bright watercolor paintings of her nighttime experiences.

The longing to produce a double, to express oneself, to pack various lives into this one, to be able to be in several places at once, is, I believe, one of the most powerful and least regarded impulses behind writing. My childhood dreams often had to do with transformations, too. Sometimes I wanted the transformations, sometimes I feared them: what if one morning I woke up as the child of different parents, as a different person? At a young age I started trying to achieve the transformation on a sheet of white paper. The pain at life's uniqueness and unrepeatability could be eased. Later we forget too quickly what as children we already grieved for . . .

I cannot forget how, at the start of the war, when the children of my generation were ten years old, the attempt was made to inject us with false grief, false love, false hate; how it almost succeeded; what effort it cost to break out of that net; how much help we needed from so many people; how much reflection, how much serious work, how many heated debates, how we also had to think back to the old dreams we had known as children.

I grew up in a medium-sized town—more small than medium, really—east of the Oder. I was attached to my surroundings, to the view out my window, from which I could see the whole town and the river; to the lakes, the pine woods, to the landscape, which perhaps was barren, overall. I could not picture any other background for my life. As a child I never traveled as far as I did at the age of fifteen turning sixteen, during the evacuation. I had never seen the war so close up before. I learned that watching dead, mangled "enemies" on a movie screen is different from personally holding an infant who has frozen stiff and having to hand him over to his mother; that hearing the word "Communist"—always in a whisper and always combined with the word "criminal"—is different from sitting by a fire one cold night next to a German Communist in concentration-camp clothing, after many weeks on the road and after seeing many images one would never have believed possible.

In the next few years we found out how much easier it is to say no than to say yes again, if the choice is to be based on knowledge instead of on more fallacies and illusions; how much easier it is to be ashamed of one's people when one has learned the whole truth than it is to learn to love them again. For our generation, it was difficult to formulate a valid literary statement of our fundamental experience in the early days. To begin with, we had to supplement this basic experience of our youth with a new and no less intensive experience which was not assigned or forced upon us like the first. This one we had to create for ourselves. Our situation was unique in that our path into adulthood, our search for our appropriate place in life, coincided with the rise of a new society, with its quest for forms of existence, with its growth, its mistakes, its consolidation. Since we learned to move around freely and securely in this society, to identify with it and at the same time stay critical as one can be only toward one's own work—since that time we have turned thirty or thirty-five and our books have become more vivid, more truthful, and filled with reality. This includes books which deal with the end of the war.

What about my own life? Since 1945, I have lived in nine different towns of our republic. First I worked as secretary assistant to the mayor of a small village. After finishing school, I studied German philology in Jena and Leipzig. I was an academic assistant in the East German Writers' Union; I worked as an editor at various publishing houses, as an editor of the periodical *Neue Deutsche Lit-*

eratur. I wrote criticism and essays on our new literature, a number of them with my husband, who is also an editor and a critic. We have two children, girls, who criticize our frequent absences.

Many people believe that there is a road leading directly from German philology and literary criticism to the "right kind" of literature. I will not deny that knowing how literature evolved and having a detailed insight into the problems of developing writers have been useful to me. On the other hand, the longer you occupy yourself with literature professionally, the harder it becomes to publish something yourself. For me, the best thing about all those years of work is that they brought me into contact with many different people, that they introduced me to all levels of the new society which was just then forming. Firsthand knowledge of the transitional forms between the old society and the new—the forms which were still "raw" and "in flux"—has a value which it is impossible to overestimate.

I always knew that what I really wanted to do was write, and write I did. Today I am glad that all those manuscripts fell victim to my personal censor. The first thing I let pass was *Moskauer Novelle (Moscow Novella)*, a not very voluminous tale which was published in 1961. I wrote it after my second stay in Moscow. The impulses behind it had kept me busy for a long time and were activated by new events and experiences, especially by the desire to replicate myself, to have the power to be in two places at once. I tried to capture some of the postwar problems of our two peoples in the story of the conflict-ridden love between a German woman and a Russian man, a former front-line officer: two people who a decade and a half after their first meeting meet again under different circumstances and must decide once more how they want to live their lives.

When I wrote the novel *Divided Heaven*, we were living in Halle, a thousand-year-old city which at one time was a crossroads of trade and a saltmakers' colony and today is one of our largest centers for the chemical and machine-building industries. A city with many layers, a restless medley of tradition and the contemporary; sooty, ugly at first glance, the junction of manifold contradictions. I tried to describe a lot of that in my book, to the extent that I myself had gradually become aware of it. It was and is clear to me that only exact information can enable us to get to the heart of the interesting events which caused rapid changes in human relationships during these years. At first I got lost in the apparent confusion, was drawn into questions which were quite new to me, met many new people and became friends with some. Through them, I discovered my interest in the sober science of economics, which influenced the lives of my new acquaintances so directly and which became the key to many human dramas, to many conflicts, to laments and struggles, successes and defeats. We huddled together over columns of figures and articles, over appeals, formal complaints, and financial statements. Sometimes I did not understand why it was so hard to put into practice ideas which everyone surely must realize made good sense.

Back then, no thoughtful person could avoid noticing that the key to the solution of many problems in every firm lay in increasing our productivity. My experiences with people in complex situations showed me that, fifteen years after the defeat of German Fascism, socialism in our country had become a reality of everyday life for millions, the goal they had been working for. In this part of Germany, it became a constructive power in people's lives. This is what gives us the security to interact freely with our material, to make increasingly better use of the advantages which our society offers to the writer: it places him in a position to acquire the knowledge and experiences he needs to get a total picture of what a modern, complex industrial society is like. He does not have to content himself—like a great many writers of bourgeois literature today—with marginal phenomena, but is driven toward the essential.

I am talking so much about the objective preconditions for writing because my genre is fiction and basically will continue to be fiction (although I am also attracted to film and drama). I feel certain that the writer's subjective qualities play a great role in prose writing, too; but the socialist prose writer is, it seems to me, obligated to expand his subjectivity as much as possible, to embrace as broad a range as he can, as accurately as he is able, continually to renew his effort to examine life's facts and to interpret them.

A scientific world view should form the basis for his work, for this will allow him to express himself by the subtlest and most subjective devices, without becoming capricious or mannered.

I admire contemporary novelists who have managed to give an overall picture of their society: like [Louis] Aragon, Anna Seghers, Thomas Wolfe. The great theme of our time is how a new world arises out of the old. That process could hardly be more astonishing, more trenchant, more conflict-ridden than here in our country. As a writer, one has only to see it.

It looks as though I have lost sight of the original impulse behind my writing—the longing for self-transformation, for self-replication —and switched over to quite sober, commonplace motives: economic, political, philosophical. True, grownups do not go on forever running into enchanted princesses and the other everyday citizens of a child's world. Yet, even today, I secretly think that many people behave as

14

if they are under a spell, and I often wish that literature, like a magic wand, could rescue them all: wake the dead souls to life, infuse them with the courage to be themselves and to acknowledge their often unconscious dreams, longings, and abilities.

1965

Interview with Myself

QUESTION: What are you reading?
ANSWER: I'm reading the first pages of a new novel which I may be working on for some time. I will probably call it *The Quest for Christa T.*
Q.: Can you say something about the subject of this novel?
A.: That's not so easy. There was no "subject" I felt moved to portray. There is no "sphere of life" that I could call its milieu; there is no "content," no "plot" that I could sum up in a few sentences. I have to confess that my motive is entirely subjective. Someone close to me died, died too young. I don't accept this death. I am searching for an effective means to resist it. As I write, I search. This very search is what I must record, as honestly, as exactly as possible.
Q.: All right, but what is the topic of this quest? What will fill the pages of your manuscript?
A.: I enter into the past world of this dead woman whom I believed I knew and whom I can hold on to only if I set out to *really* know her. I don't rely simply on treacherous memory but on evidence, too: Christa T.'s diaries, letters, sketches, which I was allowed to look at after her death. Concrete episodes float like small islands within the stream of my thoughts: that is the structure of the novel.
Q.: So you are writing a sort of posthumous résumé of her life . . .
A.: That's what I thought at first. Later I noticed that the focus of my tale was not, or was no longer, Christa T.—not in a clear-cut way. Suddenly it was *myself* I was confronting. I had not foreseen that. The relationship between "us"—between Christa T. and the narrator "I"—moved of its own accord into the center: the differences between

16

the two characters and their points of contact, the tensions between "us" and the way they were resolved, or failed to be resolved. If I were a mathematician I would probably speak of a "function": something which is not tangible, visible, material, but tremendously effective.

Q.: At least you have now conceded that two authentic characters appear: Christa T. and an "I."

A.: Have I conceded that? You would be right if both characters were not basically fictional inventions . . .

Q.: You talked about using documentary material. About memories.

A.: I treated that material as I saw fit. I supplemented memory with invention. I placed no value on sticking to documented facts. I wanted to match the image of Christa T. I had made for myself. All this changed her, and the "I" whom I could not manage without.

Q.: You are emphasizing the subjective elements. Can you give a general idea of the novel?

A.: I had already begun to work, I had familiarized myself with the material, the facts, and lost touch with them again; and then gradually I saw—not so much an idea as a sort of motto. I found it formulated in a line of Becher's* which I mean to quote at the start of my work: "For this deep unrest of the human soul is nothing but the faculty to sense and to divine that man has not yet come to himself. This coming-to-oneself—what is it?"

That is a great thought—that man does not rest until he has found himself. I see a deep-seated accord between genuine literature and socialist society, which is rooted in this very feature: both aim to help man arrive at self-realization. Like our society, literature takes up the cause of the restless. It seems to me rather boring and unproductive to portray people who are strangers to this restlessness: complacent, ordinary types who are all too able to adapt themselves. But it can be necessary all the same—for instance, to show the background against which a restless, productive person stands out, or to highlight the special quality of his unrest. Or to discover why his restlessness stagnates, if that happens: why it is unable to emerge and realize itself fully.

Q.: I suppose that that is the case with Christa T.?

A.: You mean because she died so young? Because the purpose of her life is not easy to assess? No. I found that she lived a full life in the time allotted to her.

Q.: So there is no mourning?

---

* German Expressionist poet, 1891–1958. The sentence which Wolf used as the epigraph for *The Quest for Christa T.* is taken from the Middleton translation of Wolf's novel.

A.: On the contrary, there is mourning. But not despair or resignation. I consider it the extreme of anti-resignation not to put up with death, to rebel against it.

Q.: So, in the process of writing, you were trying to learn something that you did not know beforehand?

A.: Yes.

Q.: What makes you think it would interest other people, too?

A.: I am never sure about that. All I can do is try hard to ask the right questions. All I can do is trust that my whole life, my experience, which grows out of an intense concern for the development of our society, will evoke problems and questions in me which are important to other people, too—maybe even matters of life and death, although I do not dare to predict that.

Q.: You consider literature a matter of life and death?

A.: I don't believe that humanity would have gone on for thousands of years making the enormous exertion we call art, and expended resources on it in times of the greatest material hardship, if art did not add something to life which is essential and new. Not necessarily something material, although I wonder if Anna Karenina has not achieved what is tantamount to a material existence . . .

Q.: You know that people today have a rage for science, for documentary evidence.

A.: I know and value it, and I share it. But if art does not rouse itself to ask large questions of the people it is addressing, and does not keep up its demands on us, then this scientific age of ours will not become what it could and must be if we are to avoid a catastrophe the like of which has never been seen before. Art must encourage us to become who we are; that is, to transform ourselves by creative work throughout our lives.

Q.: Isn't this goal of yours inconsistent with the actual result? Can you apply this standard to the sometimes very intimate and private conflicts of Christa T.?

A.: I know what you're thinking: Are there signs of some sort of retreat into inwardness, an escape into private life? I believe not. No one supports any longer the ridiculous notion that socialist literature is not up to handling refined nuances of emotion, or individual differences of character: the idea that it depends on creating types who move along prescribed sociological paths. The years when we set up the conditions for socialist production, laying the practical foundations for the individual to realize himself, are in the past. Our society is becoming ever more differentiated. The questions its members ask are becoming more differentiated, too, including those asked in the form of art. Many people are increasingly responsive to finely shaded answers. The individual is living an ever more sovereign existence within his society, which he experiences as his own handiwork.

Q.: So you are advocating a literature of sensitivity? How will the younger generation react to that, given their preference for hardheaded thinking?

A.: Sensitivity is not the same as sentimentality. Apart from its other effects, one traditional aim of literature has always been to intensify man's acuteness of feeling. Young people do not reject genuine feelings. Why not call to mind that old watchword: "Feel with thought and think with feeling"?

Q.: So, while working on this book, you have found out how you ought to write in the future?

A.: On the contrary. I have tried out one road, which I cannot take a second time. Obviously, other writers will find it does not suit them. But I have discovered that one must try at all costs to break out of the ring of what we know or think we know about ourselves, and go beyond it.

1966

Reading and Writing

———

Observation

The need to write in a new way follows a new way of living in the world, although there may be a delay. At intervals which seem to shorten as time goes by, we start to hear, see, smell, and taste "differently" than we had just a short while ago. Our perception of everything has changed, transforming even memory, which had seemed inviolable. Once again we see the world—what *is* "the world," anyway?—in a different light. These days, even basic emotions seem less durable than in past ages; there is a great sense of unrest.

The need to articulate the unrest is a powerful force, more powerful in the long run than the temptation to ignore it. Can it all of a sudden no longer seem worthwhile to talk about familiar things in the time-honored way? Can tried-and-true methods really have become unworkable overnight, and the conclusions they turned up become false or pointless? For a time we can explain away the embarrassing drama where with grand gestures we clutch at thin air. Glossing over our own failure, we can announce in a tearful or an artfully detached voice that the death of prose as a literary genre is nigh.

The alternative is "honestly" to admit our failure and act accordingly by lapsing into silence, by owning up that words fail us—for a reason which is to be kept as indefinite as possible: any attempt to define it would mean writing again. This attitude—like any based on *not* doing something—will go largely unnoticed and very likely will soon harden into a pose. Once someone begins to give something up, he commits himself to injustice. He must keep finding reasons to justify his continued renunciation. His honesty is now a thing of the past.

A third possibility remains: to try to stand one's ground, by continuing to produce. To stand one's ground against whom? And why?

By chance, that unrest which thickens until it becomes expressible has guided me to a place which I neither expected nor wished to see: because you cannot wish for what you know nothing about. But what ignorance kept me from wanting at the start, I now feel I could not do without: the city of Gorky on the Volga. The Russia Hotel, this room painted a light green, with its dusty desk and the two windows which—like the balcony where I am standing—show me a view of the Volga plain. I wonder why today, my second day here, this view is no longer the same one I saw yesterday right after my arrival. It's impossible to describe it. All I can say is that the weather has not changed—the heat still shimmers unabated over the river and the vast plain beyond—and neither have the colors. Not one feature of the landscape is new, and not even the fussiest eye doctor could find any change in my eyesight.

So, has a mirage slipped between my eyes and the river? No, only time, just a little time: an afternoon, a night, and a morning. The young interpreter, struggling in vain with her microphone, who showed us the sights of the city from the bus; the ikon nook in the household of Gorky's grandparents, the Kashirins, where his grandmother used to kneel for hours on end; the clothes chest from which Gorky—then a young boy called Alexei Peshkov—used to watch her, terrified that the big clock might fall on him; the pairs of lovers who keep winding up the park road as if they are riding a conveyor belt, while we sit at the side of the road under the open sky in the evening, listening to a singer breathtakingly laced into a shiny gold dress; the gaze of the journalist—formerly an officer with the Russian troops who occupied Mecklenburg—as he tells us the name of a woman we ought to look up: Berta Kopp, he says; the woman with tucked-up skirt and bare legs, doing laundry by the pump outside her house. Of all these things, none has vanished without leaving a trace. Not even the little church with the gilded onion-shaped domes which we try to reach through the tangle of streets but never find; and not even the multitude of gray dogs which dart out of wooden gateways, all looking like descendants of the same original pair. Each has left its imprint on me (how appropriate is that word "imprint"!), as if someone had pronounced his "None shall be lost!" over them; so that now, standing in the same spot in front of the same landscape—in past centuries they would have said it had "grandeur"—I *see* it all differently.

We use this sentence often, without "getting to the bottom" of it. To get to the bottom we would have to have the courage to close our eyes, to let ourselves go. So the banks of the Volga are still there, moving past slowly and steadily. The ship's engine shudders gently underfoot. I am riding the steamer. I have not yet arrived in the foreign city but already I know what it will be like: the arrival, this view from a hotel balcony, the pairs of lovers. And I know what it will be like to leave again, forgetting many things but certainly not this moment when, feeling back into the past and forward into the future, I ensure that I will remember it later, and accept the slight dizziness: the familiar sense of weightlessness and of free-floating in space and time. Then, pushing off, I let myself sink deeper into what we are temporarily calling "the past," and so I arrive at other moments which are similar; I discover a pattern in my experience, trace it back to its beginning perhaps, compare it with other familiar patterns, and possibly learn something about myself that I do not yet know.

I have gotten to the bottom of my sentence.

Instinctively, I am drawing parallels with the work of a deep-sea diver. This indicates problems of "depth"—no matter if some who have theorized about the novel not only despise but detest the term, due to the vagueness and abuse it has endured. And quite right, depth is not a property of things themselves: its experience is dependent on human consciousness. I am reminded of the can of condensed milk which baffled me as a child. The smiling nurse on the label held out her palm with another can of condensed milk on it, and this can had the same confounded nurse on *its* label, very tiny now, holding yet another downward-spiraling can. And so on, ad infinitum, until nothing could be seen, and yet—so the perfidious image suggested—increasingly minuscule nurses went on forever offering consumers cans of condensed milk. This notion disturbed me deeply, because the whole effort of imagination leads nowhere: the funnel you have forced your fantasy to creep inside runs out at last into a void.

I am writing this at the dusty desk of the Russia Hotel in Gorky, groping my way along a chain of associations. Aware of the *present* —for instance, the river down there with all the real and imagined experiences it represents—I am writing about an event in the *past* when I was remembering still earlier events, not only events but past thoughts and *memories*, and to top it all off, it occurred to me then that, one day in the *future* (which this moment has become the present), everything I was remembering might become meaningful in some way. For instance: if I described it in writing.

This is no farfetched claim but an observation which can be verified by anyone; not especially unusual, not especially complex. It is an everyday situation of the modern psyche—a relativizing and temporary suspension of objective time, a normal recognition that the moment is almost infinitely extensible, that it contains a vast number of potential experiences, each with any number of layers—and yet five minutes stay five minutes for all that.

Our brain is differentiated enough that by memory and foresight we can deepen the linear dimension of time—its surface, we could say—almost to infinity. This faculty is so widespread that, when society is unable to make adequate use of it, we get bored. The result is not merely boring but is cause for concern.

So, since depth is not a property of the material world, it must be a human experience, an ability acquired through the ages which man not only retained but developed further because it proved useful to him in his life in society. Depth thus depends on us: subjective individuals living in objective circumstances. It is the product of unsatisfied needs, of the tensions and conflicts arising from them, and of man's unparalleled efforts to grow beyond himself, or perhaps to reach himself. Such may be the meaning and purpose of depth in our consciousness, so we must not sacrifice it in favor of superficiality.

My five minutes are over. I do not have the time on my trip to describe them adequately in a piece of prose. All I can record is an observation, a partial answer to the question of what makes a person produce literature. Apparently, the writer waits for his hand successfully to trace a curve which is stronger, brighter, and truer to life than the curve of his life with its many deviations.

And since people have never completely abandoned the labor of writing even in the hardest times, it appears that mere life—life undescribed, untransmitted, uninterpreted, uncontemplated—cannot come to terms with itself directly.

Lamentation

Assuming that this was true once—is it still true today? Because today we are awash in descriptions, transmissions, interpretations, and reflections outside and beyond literature. The doubts which writers feel about the future prospects of prose reflect their suspicion that they are now anachronisms. Prose is under siege, and writers know it. And their position becomes increasingly precarious the more firmly they reject the role of esoteric outsiders or of trivial entertainers and insist that they have something to say.

Newspapers probably dealt the first blow by creating a distinction between prose and information. Later, modern information technology created super-information, whose essence is speed. The ups and downs of the Trojan War may still have counted as newsworthy years after they happened, to people in outlying regions of the then known world. But today news of fresher atrocities would overshadow a massacre on that scale within hours, in the remotest village. Prose, which is somewhat slow and ponderous, suffered no ill effects when it was liberated from its duties as a news informant. Likewise, it survived its parting from historical writing when history became a special field and office, and went on its way the poorer for shedding the guild of chroniclers. Now, a bit shorn but all the trimmer, suppler, and more elegant, it enters its bourgeois phase, where in its first exuberance it finds fresh possibilities by tending to the needs of that new discovery, the subjective individual. And then, waking up to the hangover that follows the high, it gradually learns to question its own right to exist.

Because now technology and science move up their forces one after another: radio, film, and television take over the job of instructing, entertaining, and distracting a public which, on the one hand, is thirsty for knowledge and, on the other, is prone to boredom. Whatever their other achievements, the moving images on the film and TV screens put no strain on our imagination or conceptual ability, as do the tiny abstract symbols on the pages of a book. Man's primordial interest in stories that "could happen to you and me"—the interest to which Homer owed his popularity—is now satisfied, even glutted, in a neat and systematic manner. Every day, trained technicians stand ready to gratify more curiosity than any person can continue to generate nonstop. The danger looms that the traveler, cut off for a few hours from the mass media, will read nothing but a crime novel he picks up at the railroad station bookstand, because that is all he is used to.

But that is not what we mean by prose here.

The sciences, too, are gaining ground at the expense of prose literature. The appetite which the promises of science engender has no easy substitute. What can literature offer that is equally tangible, equally sensational? The cornucopia of fantastic gifts which we are told will be showered on us by the end of the century has turned the year 2000 into a magic number. I do not like to think that on New Year's Eve 1999 we might all end up in the same fix I found myself in one Christmas when I was a child. My main present, an accordion, lay there under the tree big as life. But a talkative relative had long since spoiled the surprise for me, and anticipation plus guilt had consumed all my pleasure beforehand. Moreover, the moment I saw it I realized that it was not my love of music which had made me want the instrument, and that I would never learn to play it with ease. Yet I owed it to myself and to the others to pretend I was surprised, and even to exaggerate my fake enthusiasm.

An unsuitable analogy. For aren't we adult human beings capable of deciding which presents we want to give ourselves and of waiting for the moment when we are able to "play" them?

That's just it: *are* we? Who—apart from a small group of physicists—was in a position to wish for nuclear fission when it came along? Do we really long for the day when biologists will help determine the traits of our children by manipulating gene structure? Are we really champing at the bit for the perfect mechanical model of the human brain which cybernetics experts dream of? For the fifty added years of life which medical researchers intend to bestow on us? For the drugs which can artificially create happiness and misery? For the time when people will be frozen and stored away for long periods?

This list of questions was compiled with a negative bias. Even so, the honest will be hard put to answer a clear-cut no. Reluctantly, we find ourselves fascinated by the miraculous benefits which await us and sympathetic to the idea that what *can* be invented *will* be invented, what *can* be made *will* be made. We are forced to recognize that technological inquisitiveness cannot be eradicated, and we see the futility of a lamentation which looks more anachronistic every day. Everyone and everything that is not prepared to accompany mankind into its scientific future will fall by the wayside.

And so we eagerly devour popular-science articles from various fields, schemes for technological utopias, documentary studies, reports from labs and operating rooms; we take an interest in psychiatric case histories, sociological investigations, historical monographs, economic predictions. Who knows better than our generation that philosophical pamphlets can stir up more emotion than any other kind of reading material? Even social analysis—once the preserve of the novelist—is now carried on systematically by whole committees of scientists. In fact, there probably is no other way it could still be done—unless the ruling class of a society had an interest in keeping the social sciences in an undeveloped state, in which case the prose writer would have to take over the social scientist's function. (However, he would no doubt find himself in the same fix as anyone today who does not have access to the exact methods and abundant data of the expert.)

The last straw for the prose writer in this century is that reality itself is turning against him. Reality now is more fantastic than any product of the imagination. No fiction can surpass its cruelties and its marvels. So, those who want to read "the truth"—how things really happened—turn to factual reports, biographies, assemblies of documents, diaries, memoirs.

The "reality cake" from which prose writers of the past used to cut themselves slice after slice has now been fully parceled out. It is sour grapes to claim that those who got their slice did not deserve it. Meanwhile, well-organized teams of sharp-witted, clear-eyed researchers who can easily verify their own usefulness are busy tearing pieces of cake out of each other's hands and fighting over the crumbs.

What can prose possibly have to say to these sober individuals who are proceeding forward by the straightest route?

The prose writer, the "murmuring conjuror of the past tense" who is accustomed to regard the struggles, victory, or defeat of the sacrosanct human personality as the be-all and end-all—what can he say to his contemporaries building the streamlined man who is adaptable to all of civilization's demands? What can he say to people who are already conversant with the thought that not even individual identity will be guaranteed in our future, and who allow for the possibility that man as a species may become extinct—not in the unimaginably distant future when our planet cools off, but in our own lifetimes, and as a result, not of natural forces, but of our own actions?

Compared to that vision of the future, the ebb and flow of a literary genre looks like child's play. So why shouldn't we confront head-on the possibility that prose may be swallowed up by the history that gave it birth? Undeniably, these are tough times for fiction writers (though these times may pass). We look on indulgently at what today tries to pass itself off as prose literature: see it fighting for its life in the guise of the detective story, the best-seller. It has tasted the poison of self-surrender. Its only real hope of survival lies in its developing the ability to do something beyond the power of all the rivals which are pressing it so hard. It would truly be saved only if we realize that we need prose and that it may be a matter of life and death for us to get to where only prose can take us.

The question is, will we encourage prose to *want* to do what it *can* do?

And here of course ends our lamentation.

The Reader and the Writer

Tabula rasa

Let's beware of extravagant notions. "Prose," after all, is simply an idea, a concept, an abstraction. Its material incarnation is the book, which is traded in the marketplace like any other piece of goods. The smoothly functioning trade in books is not greeted with the wonder it deserves. We have grown accustomed to people offering to sell us products whose practical usefulness is doubtful, if not positively ruled out. Some people have the temerity to base their livelihood on this frivolous practice. Not only publishers, printers, book dealers, and publicists take the liberty—even authors do.

Let's try a mental experiment. Let's suppose that an undefined force has managed, by a stroke of magic, to wipe out every trace left in my brain from reading books of prose literature.

What would I be missing?

To answer is not just murderous; it is impossible. But if it *were* possible, we would have more exact information about how literature affects us.

Suppose I begin by killing off inside me the pure, innocently suffering Snow-White and her wicked stepmother, who at the end is forced to dance around in red-hot metal slippers: I am destroying an archetype, the vital, fundamental belief in the inevitable victory of good over evil. And next I get rid of the legends. I have never wanted to stand up to the dragon by the side of the invulnerable Siegfried; I have never been startled by a rustling in the dark woods: it's Rübezahl the mountain sprite! Never having read animal fables, I no longer understand the meaning of phrases like "sly as a fox," "brave as a lion." Now that I no longer know Tyll Eulenspiegel, I have never laughed at the tricks by which the weak overcome the powerful. The Seven Swabians, the Wise Men of Gotham, Don Quixote, Gulliver, the beautiful princess Magelone—away with them all. Away with impotently thundering Zeus and the cosmic ash tree Yggdrasill; away with Adam and Eve and Paradise. Never was a city named Troy besieged and captured for a woman's sake. Never has Doctor Faust fought the Devil for his soul.

I enter my tenth year poor, robbed of all I own, naked and defenseless. Burning tears have gone unwept. The eyes of the witch in my fairy-tale book have not been scratched out. I have not learned to know the joyful relief when a hero is rescued. I have never been inspired to tell myself fantastic dreams in the dark. I do not know that people of different nationalities are different and yet alike. My moral code is undeveloped, I am wasting away intellectually, my imagination is withered. I find it hard to draw comparisons, to make judgments. Beautiful and ugly, good and evil are wavering, uncertain concepts.

I'm in bad shape.

How could I guess that the world I live in is dense, colorful, abundant, peopled by the most remarkable characters? That it is brimful of adventures which have been waiting especially for me?

In short: I have not, like Faust, walked the primal path to the Mothers, have not drunk from the wellsprings, the standard for men and things has not been set. You cannot make up later for the emotional storms you missed out on. A world which was not enchanted and dark at the right time will not grow bright when knowledge grows, but only dry. Flat and barren are the wonders you dissect before being allowed to believe in them.

Irreplaceable, above all, is the knowledge that life's abundance is not exhausted by the few actions which chance permits us to perform.

Unspeakably desolate is the existence of one who cannot treat it as a metaphor, comparing it to the lives of others, and which he cannot assign to its place in mankind's unparalleled trek out of the jungle into longed-for order; let's call the order by the venerable name "civilization."

So, uncivilized in the deepest sense of the word, I find myself standing on the brink of a thorny period in my life. The experiment which we rightly shrank from performing in our thoughts has in fact already been carried out in reality, on the German children of my generation. It would be hard to imagine a more complete sequestration from the literature of one's own time than we suffered up to the age of sixteen. Quite possibly the conspicuous slowness of my generation to mature into independent adults was more than a little due to the reading material we were given: a "prose literature" which we devoured in huge chunks but which I have almost forgotten, as if it had involuntarily blotted itself from my memory—although that says nothing about its hidden effects. On the surface it was all chauvinism, war fever, and a thoroughly perverted image of history (the books I borrowed from the school library were mostly monstrously deformed volumes of history), but at a deeper level I am sure it also inhibited the process of growing up, the ripening of the critical faculties and of rational emotions which had not been crippled by the worst prejudices and grudges.

The past—what used to be—was shrouded in a horrible fog. The present—what exists now—was viewed through frightful distorting spectacles. At such times in history, the sober gaze of the storyteller is nonexistent. There was no one to whom we could have listened. The terrible abandonment of that generation of children has yet to be described. They were abandoned to the horde of little scale-model thrills tailor-made for them by government-employed magicians, and the greatest of them all was the thrill of death. The individual was nothing; immortal was the myth which the books we read called "the German people."

I often wonder what stopped the very worst from happening. Moral instincts are not innate, after all, and we had been deprived of any contact with a morally evolved culture. So why wasn't every human impulse rooted out of us? Whence came that recoil on just a few occasions, sharply etched in the memory, which today I think was decisive? When everything around me kept silent, what caused this disquieting warning from within which came to me three or four times, which I did not want to look at more closely, and which could be summed up in two words: Not that!

Once it happened when I was reading a book called *Christine Torstensen*. A girl of the valuable Nordic race, a fanatic of the Thirty Years' War, kisses and embraces the corpses of plague victims in her own camp, then steals off to offer herself to the enemy, using her own body and lips to infect him with the plague. A heroine, an example to us all. I read it and thought: Not that.

So maybe those childhood legends and fairy tales which I just wiped from my memory gave me a foundation, after all. Along with them, I will now extinguish all those other books, by the Bindings and Jelusichs and Johsts and Grimms,* for they deserve it; but not without hesitation, for those who do not die of their poison are made immune to even its most rarefied solutions.

Far harder to make the next sacrifices, Storm and Fontane. And I am truly reluctant to part with a damp-stained paperback which lay on my grandmother's bureau—an eternal riddle, for she never read books. It was called *All Quiet on the Western Front*, and, like everything interesting, it was deemed "nothing to interest you." I read it on my grandparents' sofa and I can still feel the worn patch where my sweating hand gripped the upholstered arm. I read how in wartime even a German could die a miserable death with a bullet in his gut. This dead man may have been the first whose fate led me to revolt instinctively. Heavyhearted, I command this book to leave me, too.

I see that from now on, I can no longer list all the victims by name. Now, Green Henry, Werther, and Wilhelm Meister have never

---

* Rudolf Binding (1867–1938), Mirko Jelusich (1886–1969), Hanns Johst (1890–1978), and Hans Grimm (1875–1959) wrote in a nationalistic style. Their ideas led into National Socialism; some became Nazis.

crossed my path. I have never met Julien Sorel or Madame Bovary or Anna Karenina—no, I can't go on. One day, someone must write the queer, erratic history of my generation's reading. It might give a clue to imbalances and insecurities which almost defy explanation.

But I, as a nonreader, of course have not experienced the need to "make up for lost time" after the war. I have not stood stunned before lists of authors and titles I knew nothing about. I have not gnawed my way into the badly printed paperbacks of the postwar years. So what *have* I done—in the thousands of hours which I now have on my hands retroactively because I did not fill them with reading books? They are empty of the shocks and insights which in those days were synonymous with "reading." (This shock may explain why we have held on to our seriousness about books.) That railroad bench is missing where reluctantly I read one of the shocking new books and understood at last that what it described must be *true*.

Next to go is a great stack of early Soviet literature: a unique signal flare lighting up possibilities which would never cease to fascinate me—if only I had read them. Gone, too, are those mere corpses of books, the deadweight of many years: mostly big fat volumes which were concessions to insincerity and bad taste. After them I send the vast jumble of reading matter from my university years, from studying German literature—the things I studied for examinations, the things I studied for life: it has never been easy to tell the difference.

Tabula rasa. I am finished. Torn out by the roots. One of the great adventures we can have in life—to compare, examine, define our limits and gradually learn to see ourselves, to measure ourselves against the most well-defined figures of all time—is extinct in me. I know nothing about it. My sense of time is faded, having never really been awakened. My own contours, instead of growing sharper, are dissolving; my awareness, instead of getting clearer, is blurring.

My return to savagery has only begun.

Because now we must move on to the next steps, wipe out the more delicate, almost undemonstrable effects of long-term association with books: the exercise and differentiation of our psychical equipment; the sharpening of our senses; the awakening of the pleasure of observation, of the ability to perceive the comedy and tragedy in situations and draw serenity from comparisons with the past; to appreciate the heroic as the exception it is, while calmly acknowledging, perhaps even loving, the unexceptional which we see every day. But above all: to be amazed—to be unendingly amazed at oneself and at others like oneself.

But *I have not read*.

Not only is my past suddenly transformed: my present is no

longer the same, either. One last thing remains to be done: to sacrifice the future, too. I will never read a book. The terror of this sentence leaves me, the nonreader, unmoved.

Because, without books, I am not I.

Commemorative Medallions

Apparently, the approval and support of imagination is something we need in our lives. In other words, we need to be able to play with the possibilities left open. But at the same time something else is going on in us, every day, every hour—a creeping, inevitable process of hardening, petrifaction, habit. Its particular target is memory.

Everyone carries around a collection of colored medallions bearing captions which are partly funny, partly gruesome. On occasion we take them out and show them to people because we need them to confirm the reassuringly unambiguous feelings we have that the past events they commemorate were beautiful or ugly, good or evil. These medallions are to memory what ossified lung tissue is to a tubercular patient, or prejudices are to morality: once there was life there, activity, but now they are encapsulated, shut down. Once you were afraid to touch them, you burned your fingers on them; now they are cool and smooth. Some have been skillfully polished; some especially valuable pieces have cost years of work, because there is a lot you have to forget, a lot you have to rethink and reinterpret before you can present yourself to advantage on each and every occasion: that's what we need medallions for. I expect you know what I mean.

"Memory" is the name we commonly use when we take out these prettily made craft items and pass them off to people as the genuine article so that we can learn their market value, compare them to what is currently on offer and—assuming they match it—hear them pronounced the real thing.

I, too, have my medallions. One item—especially convenient and plausible—is actually a short movie reel. The camera must have started shooting in my parents' bedroom, stationed near the night table. The lighting technicians saved on electricity; it was early one winter morning, and the blackout was on. As the scene starts, we hear an excited voice from the radio in the living room. It tells us the date; we recognize this as the last year of the war. We see packed suitcases, bags stuffed with bedding. The silver fox fur is weighed appraisingly in someone's hand and then thrown back into the wardrobe; it's now just a meaningless symbol. The radio voice from the living room advises in an urgent and aggrieved tone that all civilians must leave the city: the enemy is at the gates. The grownups irritably prod everyone to hurry. In the midst of the confusion we see a clumsy figure, taken by surprise again, unable to move, from sheer disbelief: I guess I'll have to call her "I." "I" is getting pushed around.

Change of scene, take two. Camera positioned at the foot of the stairs leading to the house of "I." Pan shot out to a truck on the road. The suitcases and bags which we just saw packed indoors are loaded on the truck; then the people from the bedroom are pushed, shoved, and lifted inside, including "I." Quarreling voices, complaints, sobs. Questions, answers. Tears, hands waving goodbye. The truck starts, leaving behind a few neighbors.

That's how childhoods ended in those days, or so everyone believes. The tale gets told over and over until it's shiny-bright. What a nice sad story: it gets a place of honor in the medallion cupboard, with an inscription that reads "Childhood's End."

Interesting: you don't have to change a thing to make it filmable; all you have to do is leave out a couple of details which your memory didn't really want to preserve, anyway: how amazed you were to see the grayness of the city where you had lived such a colorful life that you saw no point in ever getting to know any other. How you realized you'd never set eyes on this place again. It struck you like a spark off one of those same gray walls of a house on the Fisher's Walk, and after that, it traveled with you and made you lonely among the crowd of crazy people waiting for a miracle. And so I stopped waiting before I had even begun.

Maybe one day I will know where that irrational thought came from. Probably it would lead me back deep into childhood, into areas which people avoid when they are making medallions, and where it seems the film camera could not follow. But I *do* hope language can follow me, can follow me anywhere I one day have the courage to go: for from that trust I live.

Remembering—like writing—means swimming against the stream: against the apparently natural stream of forgetting. It is movement, exertion. Where is this movement headed? I see a barely familiar landscape, uncertain colors which gradually make up their minds: blue of the kind you see in a midsummer sky, to keep you from ever forgetting what is meant by the word "blue." Potato plants on either side of me; the sun-warmed sand of the furrow under my body, most beautiful, most desirable of beds. Heat. Why am I lying here? I don't know. I don't know why I have violently suppressed the habit of obedience, why I have not answered the calls from the house. Stillness at last. And then, after a while, a lizard sunning itself on my belly. I hold my breath. I am happy now, I know that I am not

supposed to be happy and that I will always remember it. There will
be an air-raid alert tonight. I force myself to think of the people who
are being killed this very minute. Guiltily I admit that I am unable
to feel guilty about being happy: the innocent forerunner of those
mixed feelings which, more than all else, are the signs of adulthood.

This is not a very useful scene and it has no caption. There is
no material here for a medallion, and nothing the camera could photograph. Any film director who wished to get along without interior
monologue would give up in despair—just as he would have had to
turn away from that balcony scene by the banks of the Volga.

But what about the storyteller? She is lying with me in the furrow
in the potato field. Shrunk down to the size of a fourteen-year-old
girl, she is watching the potato plants to the left and right, and the
vast sky overhead. She is startled by the lizard and holds her breath;
but at the same time she is a grownup looking down at the fourteen-
year-old girl. Twenty-five years later, she decides it is worth the effort
to remember: I was happy then and I wasn't supposed to be. She sets
out to write a faithful account and discovers that the twenty-five
intervening years have affected not only her but also that scene from
the past. She is forced to admit she did not tell the story
"objectively"—that isn't possible. She is not discouraged. She decides to tell it; that is, to invent something faithful to the truth, based
on her own experience.

Prose should strive to be unfilmable. It should give up the dangerous trade of circulating medallions, and of assembling prefabricated parts. It should have the integrity to insist on the unique
experience. It should not be lured into invading the experience of
others, but should encourage others to have their own experiences.

How can all this help us?

Celestial Mechanics

Right at this point I would like to find a sufficiently slanted example
of what we mean by the beautiful phrase "like a novel." Let's allow
the phrase to vibrate in unison with the following quotation:

> I sprawled politely with my elbow on the reception desk and peered
> into the face of a cheerful-looking young guy wearing a polka-dot bow
> tie. From him I turned my gaze to the girl at the switchboard on the
> side wall. She was an outdoorsy type with gleaming makeup and a
> blond ponytail. She had beautiful big soft eyes which shone when she

looked at the young reception clerk. Swinging her ponytail in an arc, she bestowed a glance on me, too.

Sometimes the most depraved specimens give the best clue to the underlying weakness of a whole genre. Respect and fairness to reputable practitioners of the novel cannot stop me from reading a meaning into these lines from some detective story, it doesn't matter which. So these are the depths, this is the cesspool to which they have dragged down the discoveries of the genius Balzac. Every small-time hack now cobbles novels out of the same four or five basic plot elements that caused a scandal back when they were first used: No, no, real life's not like that!

But it seems to have gotten like that in the meantime, judging by all the plot lines. Every John and Mary Smith have agreed to construct their lives as romantic triangles, or four-cornered affairs. They cannot resist feeling angry and hurt when they are betrayed, and blissfully happy when they are loved—what *they* call love. Time after time we see a father disown his daughter and a misguided young man thoroughly transformed by ennobling influences. Only the opinions which people dutifully utter on such occasions are, at least in part, assembled out of different words.

No mockery will stop novels like these from being turned out by the cartload, nor will any get-tough attitude: but since no one will be affected anyway, I can afford to go ahead and preach. One hundred and forty years ago—hard as it is to believe now—these very same tales were a way of taming a fairly savage world. It must have taken daring to force neatly unfolding plots into uncouth brains. Let us not forget that, in their day, Eugénie Grandet and Madame Bovary were startling apparitions.

Of course, no one author or century should be deemed to have invented the plot: it was in the air. Once you get used to thinking in terms of Newton's celestial mechanics, sooner or later you are bound to feel it is natural for social mechanics to function in a similar way. Solid objects keep up a continuous motion along mathematically de-termined orbits, and influence each other in accordance with deter-minable laws: they repel, they attract, and sometimes—as in heavenly catastrophes—they destroy each other. Under the circumstances, a novelist cannot help but light on the notion of using the novel as a means to propel certain objects—the heroes of literature—through space and time. Today we are still bound to admire the rules which the inventors of the novel devised for themselves, because these rules deviated so much from the norms that actually governed human life in their times and yet they managed for decades to come to evoke in the reader the fiction that they were "natural." In fact, in the end they turned into clichés, usable by social strata who lacked self-confidence as models for their behavior. That is, they created the possibility of living as quotations.

The foundation on which the newly created novel rested was extremely solid. How solid it was is most evident in those plots which ended in tragedy, as the bourgeois novel typically did. For even as the hero was overtaken by death, he would bequeath indubitable constants to his heirs: reality—however you might like to define that—and its immovable coordinates, space and time. The unparalleled optimism of this mechanics—a system which was never called into question even by those it pulverized—is obvious: *I* am dying, but *it* remains and continues to operate. The novel, thus constituted, was functional, encouraged learning and imagination, stimulated efficiency, and opened up conflicts without threatening the solid substance underneath. It produced reality.

Today this same system of celestial mechanics goes on turning like a big beautiful bucket wheel which no longer brings up any water; or we have been desensitized, so it no longer tastes like water. Those stock plots which obey the antiquated laws of Newtonian dramaturgy meet no resistance as they slide along their rinsed-out tracks into our innards. To regain its effectiveness, prose has had to tackle a new reality in a new way. For one thing, it has been forced to start separating from the old-style "plot line," manufactured out of portable stage scenery, which had hardened into cliché. It has had to try to abandon its mechanical approach to the world, in favor of a dialectical approach; and it still faces that task. The process of change has itself become a subject of the novel, and proved able to generate new, surprising plots. But it can also lead to contradictions, if it is interpreted in purely technical terms. One such contradiction is, I believe, the *nouveau roman* and its theory as formulated by the French author Alain Robbe-Grillet.

Keenly aware of the problems facing the genre, he turns the "crisis of the novel" into a crisis of the novelists. He accuses them of having so far lived off the arrogant presumption that they were omniscient and omnipotent gods who could do as they liked within the confines of their own self-created universes; whereas actually the objectivity of the author is an illusion.

Admittedly, the question of objectivity does stir undefined guilt feelings in the novelist which might be summed up in his suspicion: I gave you stones instead of bread. Robbe-Grillet's observations about this guilt are fine, satisfying, and pertinent. He has a horror of the stereotype bourgeois novel, whose present dilemma he diagnoses—I believe correctly—as due to the fact that "the world is no longer private property which can be inherited and converted into money," "the kind of prey which it was more important to conquer than to know." But in this sentence a glaring error stands out: the use of the past tense. "The world" on which Robbe-Grillet bases his argument is most definitely *still* private property, and prey. The revolution to abolish private ownership of the means of production has not taken place. Robbe-Grillet ignores this fact, and from his perhaps unconscious manipulation spring the more blatant contradictions in his theory: he returns by an indirect route to the method which he set out to combat.

For the new model he proposes is as much a cliché as the old one was. "Maybe it isn't progress," he says, "but certain it is that the present age is the age of identification numbers." After pushing off so energetically from the ancient banks of bourgeois art, he ends up back in the river of weary resignation: because it *is* resignation, retreat from the battle line, which hides behind his seemingly matter-of-fact judgment. Planning a "new novel" which would "found reality," he finishes, in practice, by giving a minute description of an object-world from which man—a mere ID number rather than a resisting, rebelling individual—can scarcely any longer be distinguished. As if the mere existence of "things," unaccompanied by commentary, were possible and desirable in the novel; as if art did not require the mediation of the artist who—with his fate and his conflict—stands between "reality" and the empty page, and has no choice of how to fill this page, but to project onto it the argument between the world and himself.

To deny this mediation means to install a new celestial mechanics in place of the old worn-out one. It means surrendering positions from which reality can be mastered. It means giving in to the domination of "ID numbers." It means, once again, the end of the novel: for how can ID numbers possibly write novels?

So, does the writer, with his indomitable passion to write, does *he* at least stand out from the mass where he sees nothing but ID numbers—but which he depends on all the same, because it supplies him with his readers? Does the same thing apply to him that applies to all the rest? Or is he alone, fighting to defend his own personality as he writes, sending out signals which no longer find any echoes outside him? But what, then, is the point of inventing a "new novel" if it is to be as ineffectual as the old one?

Yet, truly new ways of telling stories *have* been found; they were found long ago.

Models of the World

Georg Büchner—familiar with mechanistic materialism through his brother,* with the scientific theory of evolution through his medical studies, with the common people and contemporary social issues in Germany through his revolutionary activities—found a beginning more than a hundred years ago and we can say without qualifications that he established a peak in modern German prose. Granted, in his short novel *Lenz*† he drew in the most shamelessly outspoken manner on Pastor Oberlin's case history, and the way he managed to transform this material into art savors of witchcraft—until you realize that the storyteller has put everything he has into his work. With "few means" he has added himself, the insoluble conflict of his life, his personal peril, of which he is well aware. His conflict—that of the writer facing the choice of adapting to intolerable circumstances and ruining his talent, or suffering physical destruction—mirrors in magnified form the thousandfold threat to people hungry for progress and craving truth in reactionary times.

A variant of madness—of Lenz—cannot have been a completely unknown quantity to Büchner, who was born of a later generation, and he may have worked it through in a story as a means to escape it. The medical case history offered him the detachment of a cool-headed observer, which must have suited him: he did not want self-exposure. It is all very well to say he may have mimicked the case-history style. But we should not continue to overlook his discovery as his contemporaries and descendants did: that narrative space has four dimensions—the three fictive coordinates of the invented characters, and the fourth, "real" coordinate, the narrator. This is the coordinate which supplies depth, contemporaneity, unavoidable commitment, which determines not only the writer's choice of subject but also its characteristic coloration. The conscious manipulation of the narrator's role is a staple of modern prose. The complex narrative structures which result no more reflect caprice than Georg Büchner's deliberate practice of shifting pronouns abruptly—going from "he" to "I"—between one sentence and the next, a technique which even today readers find disconcerting.

Büchner's short novel *Lenz* towers above the dreary stream of conventional prose turned out in German since then. It stands fresh

---

* Ludwig Büchner (1824–99), a physician and a Darwinist, wrote *Energy and Matter*, a discussion of materialist theory.

† German poet and dramatist (1751–92) of the Sturm und Drang period; died poor and insane.

and daring as the day it was written. Unrecognized in its own day, it remained lost for many years, for reasons which can be explained, if not approved. Now everyone is free to evaluate it and to admire a man who was poet, scientist, and revolutionary in one, and who wrote this novella at the age of twenty-two, just two years before his death. For such a man it would have been absurd to invent traditional stories of the sort which can be made to measure at any time, with more or less artistry and technique. For Büchner, writing was the means of fusing with his times at the moment when the two were converging at the point of maximum pain and maximum conflict. Sizable energy must be produced to achieve the melting temperature for such a fusion. Nothing less is required than the total commitment of one's personal moral existence; and the same must be offered anew each time. Here lies the seriousness behind the play of art. Büchner gives us everything, all the prose of daily life—situation, circumstances, psychology, analysis—and transforms it by adding the vision on which he lives and from which he suffers, even if that is evident only in the tone of the incomparable last sentence of Lenz, which it may seem that mankind has been struggling to refute ever since: "So his life dragged on."

Swept away is the smoke screen which had blurred the horde of fictitious emotions. Insight reigns, sobriety and awareness, combined with a heightened capacity to feel: realism. Not dryness of construction, or naturalism; nor the excess of overheated emotions.

But, instead, visionary precision.

You get the feeling you have run into the same thing somewhere else. Unless I'm wrong, it is in the reports of physicists. Maybe it is easier for them than for writers to define the goal of their work: they want to discover what the world is made of. But strangely enough— because the smaller the particles they work with, the harder it gets to measure them accurately—physicists, by their own admission, need a quality which is not measurable: creative imagination. Who knows if in their most secret hours they do not succumb to the blasphemous thought that actually they are the ones who invent the world; anyway, it would not be surprising if they think that. And isn't there more than a mechanical parallel between the upheaval that has overtaken the traditional prose writer and the revolutions in the thinking of physicists? Einstein's space-time continuum must have been a devastating psychological blow to many. The stable coordinates of space and time turned relative; the illuminated ether laboriously generated by their thoughts dissolved into nothing; the brain which seemed created to understand the world in three-dimensional terms and to be incapable of grasping anything else no longer knew if it could trust its own findings.

It is not unexciting to hear a scientist like Heisenberg say: "In modern physics, it is no longer possible to describe all processes with exactness in the received language . . . But we *must* talk about atoms and elementary particles, because otherwise we cannot understand our experiments." The secret cause for the excitement I feel on reading such statements may be that I sense the link to the trickiest and hardest-to-formulate questions of my own work. Writers, too, face the necessity of talking about hunches which can become certainties only if they are articulated and discussed. Despite his resistance, the writer is forced to penetrate that unexplored region where the moral universe of man in society has not yet acquired a definite shape. Perhaps he feels very like the atomic scientists, groping cautiously as they dare to evolve provisional models of events within the atom. We have reason to be fascinated by their adventure, which outwardly takes the form of extremely exact, refined, repetitive, and thus probably monotonous measurements: for we are told the point has been reached when the ancient language of classical physics no longer has anything pertinent to say about the world. Now the scientist must "use a variety of alternating, contradictory graphic images to describe the smallest particles of matter." Heisenberg calls these images "word paintings" and says it is their task "by picture and metaphor to evoke in the listener's mind certain associations which point in the desired direction without trying to force him, through definite formulations, to specify a particular train of thought."

"The way poems do," he adds.

Probably there was no need to issue so explicit a challenge to literature. Brecht tried to establish a path to the scientific age inside the heads of theatergoers. His invention, which he called "epic theater," has perhaps been imitated more often than understood, and because it aimed to produce models for dialectical thinking, it deserved least of all to be made a stock technique and passed on to others.

The idea of writing "epic prose" along similar lines sounds like nonsense, and yet I have a feeling that something of the kind ought to exist. A genre with the courage to look on itself as an instrument: sharp, exact, arresting, variable, which would treat itself as a means, not an end, a means of pushing the future forward into the present, with all its individual detail; because prose is read by an individual who disregards all the seductions of modern technology in order to withdraw and be alone with a book.

Epic prose should be a genre which aims to penetrate this individual, the prose reader, along trails which have not yet been blazed. It must get through to his innermost core, the nucleus where the personality is formed and made solid. (Like the atomic scientist, we resort to picturesque paraphrases which are not "correct" but are necessary to make the reader understand.) This region is accessible to the voice of another human being; prose can reach it; language can touch it and open it up—not to take control of it, but to free psychic energies whose power is comparable to those locked in the atom.

This means that prose can join forces only with intellectual trends and social movements which give mankind a future, which are free of the age-old and brand-new magic spells of manipulation, and which do not shy away from experiment. I see a deep-seated accord between this approach to writing and socialist society. Exploiter societies have proved incapable of guaranteeing mankind a future worthy of the name. An American writer who uses American weapons against Vietnamese liberation fighters has not only betrayed the ethics of his profession; he has also demonstrated an inability to think which is harmful to his profession.

Consequently, it would be advisable to confirm what is stable in the world, before we try to transfer the scientific concept of "relativity" to the social domain. The question is, doesn't the start of a new type of society call for radically different achievements from the writer who is consciously committed to this society than just to modify the content of literature while clothing it in the same traditional models? Isn't he required to ask penetrating, radical questions whose answers at first would be provisional and hard to formulate, like those of physics? As for those hackneyed utterances which no longer do anything but light up a tiny lamp labeled "right" or "wrong" in the reader's mind—shouldn't they be removed from the realm of literature altogether? Whereas literature—that is, prose, which is the form we are talking about here—must have the courage to go in for investigation.

As yet we are shunning this adventure. We cling to the conventions; we devote ourselves to strengthening old ideas more than to looking for new ones. We soothe where we ought to alarm and stir to action. Prose, it would seem, has not yet arrived at the age of science. *That*—and not the possible death of the novel—is the real cause for lament: because the only things that perish are things which are not really used.

What we need is an unbribable yet sympathetic guide for this daring and hazardous expedition.

Realities

To begin writing, you must first be someone to whom reality is no longer self-evident.

Reality? It is a good sign that novelists do not agree about the aim of their endeavor, which in fact really is not as easy to define as the object of physicists' research. And yet, where effects are seen, we know there is some cause acting to produce them: and we still see people who are moved, touched, influenced by literature. The factor operating upon them is neither "life itself" nor factual information, yet it has to do with truth.

There is a truth outside the important world of facts. Here literature's affinity to the sciences ends. The storyteller can know and use their findings, but what he personally discovers in his search for the nature of man within society, though it may qualify as "true," need not be proved "correct," as must any conclusion of science.

So, would it be right to say that when we write we have to reinvent the world?

Not long ago I spent a long rainy afternoon in the world of Dostoevsky's Raskolnikov. You can uncover it like an archaeological stratum when you walk through certain districts of modern Leningrad. The moneylender's house is still standing. "This staircase is the very one that Raskolnikov climbed many a time," said the old man who acted as our guide: he was Dostoevsky's grandson. Apprehensively we tracked his footsteps in our own dusty shoes. "Here," said our guide. "He hesitated on this landing, as you know. Luckily for him —because he had to hide later—painters were working in this apartment on the right, and this one on the left was unoccupied, too. You could say that fortune favored his plans."

The grisly deed seemed on the point of being committed again, as we slowly climbed another floor.

"Here's where it happened," Dostoevsky's grandson said severely, and rang the handbell which Raskolnikov had pulled that unfortunate day. The apartment we asked to see is today marked number 72. A youngish woman, seeing nothing strange in our request, invited us in. They told us that we would no longer find the narrow hall which Dostoevsky describes; the wall dividing it from the kitchen had since been torn down.

We were led through the kitchen into the bedroom. The young woman's white bed, piled high with bedding, her clothes' wardrobe —what business had we to be here? I walked over to the window. "Right there where you're standing now is where the moneylender

41

stood when Raskolnikov delivered the blow." Involuntarily I retreated
a step and so betrayed myself: I had gotten caught up in the tangle
of reality and fiction. "Don't you find it spooky living here?" we asked
the young woman. No stranger to such questions, she replied indif-
ferently: "It's all right. You get used to it."

As if a pool of blood had ever *really* stood on the spot where her
bedside rug now lies.

Silently we descended the two flights of stairs, crossed the court-
yard, exited through the old gateway, and walked into the street. Our
guide offered to demonstrate to us that Raskolnikov gave a false
address to the porter whose suspicions he had aroused. "You remember, like every murderer he had to return to the scene of his crime.
The porter asked his name and address. Raskolnikov, caught by
surprise, gave his name but had the presence of mind to give a false
address: 'I live in the Schill House not far from here, in the cross
street, Apartment 14.' "

So we are going to prove that Raskolnikov lied, something which
Dostoevsky did not deem it necessary to do in the novel. We go to
the cross street, find the Schill House. It strikes us as a bit eerie
when we make the irrational suggestion that the fictional character
Raskolnikov might "really" have lived here and Dostoevsky's grandson
makes no reply but a contemptuous wave of the hand. Because now
he paces out with us the same 730 steps that Raskolnikov needed to
go from his apartment to the house of the murdered woman. They
take us way past the Schill House to an intersection, to a corner house
marked with inscriptions in German and Russian commemorating an
ancient flood, and in the gateway our guide points out a simple wooden
door which once—in Raskolnikov's time—opened on the other side.
Do you remember? Here is where the woodpile stood and where
Raskolnikov, having failed to get hold of a murder weapon the way
he had intended, quite unexpectedly saw the gleam of the ax!

More stone stairs. At last we are standing at the foot of those
thirteen wooden steps which must have led up to Raskolnikov's attic
room—although the room has long since been incorporated into the
main loft. "Here," says the old man, who is not so much guiding as
driving us forward. "Of all the houses in the neighborhood, this is
the only one where you have these kitchen windows which open onto
the corridor and which, as you know, Raskolnikov had to sneak past
to avoid his landlady, who was always dunning him to pay what he
owed her."

But right here, at the foot of these steps, the different levels of
reality among which we had traveled dizzily back and forth for hours
came together at last to form a unity that was complex and unmis-

takable. For the grandson's investigations left no doubt that Dostoevsky himself had sought refuge from his creditors here, in Raskolnikov's attic, while he worked like a demon on his book. Once again we felt solid ground under our feet. A certifiably real author, a historical figure and flesh-and-blood human being, had lived here a century ago, and saw no other escape from the trouble that assailed him within and without than to project his conflict onto an invented character. This character (should we still call him invented?) lived with him in the same miserable room, took the possessions of both to the same woman pawnbroker, and was able to carry out the act which must have begun as a grisly mental experiment in the brain of the author: the murder of a creature who in the sick mind of the murderer was inferior, loathsome, deserving of destruction—while the author was spared the need to perform it in reality because he shifted it forcibly onto his substitute, the shadow man.

The fusion of "author" and "subject" can get no deeper than this, nor more uncanny. This fusion, once achieved, generates a third element, the new reality of the book, which effortlessly implies "real" houses, streets, apartments, and staircases, without needing to prove, of course, that these particular houses and rooms can be found in the world in the exact form in which the book describes them. The reality of *Crime and Punishment* goes beyond the topography of a city. It is certainly St. Petersburg. But can anyone doubt that the Petersburg we think we know—this dreary human Babylon—would never have existed if the overheated imagination of an unhappy writer had not seen it? His temperament, his harrowing life story, his almost morbid sensitivity to the moral conflicts of his time—these were what compelled him to project a Raskolnikov out of himself, to build a world around him which only appears to be assembled out of components from the material world: a reality in which he, Dostoevsky, can play like a madman with his shadow figures and to a certain degree can overcome what in the "real" world has driven him to the brink of destruction or self-destruction.

Subjects like these are what prose writers write about. There are no such things as theme banks where subjects are stored so that any author who wants to can draw one out and take it home with him: the subjects are lying out on the street. One writer can have only one subject at any given moment. If he is hardworking and knows his subject, he will find the material he needs to describe it; if he is obsessed enough, he will know how to organize the material, and the degree of his talent will decide the intensity with which he simulates a new reality. If his vision is bold and his imagination inventive, exciting, and "true" enough, he will find readers willing to share it, actively to help create it as they read, to bring the whole of their personalities to bear on it, and to make more firm, secure, and permanent the flimsy threads which link reality to invention and which previously lay in the hand of the doubting author alone. Who would deny that Raskolnikov, Anna Karenina, and Julien Sorel are as much our companions in this world as are Napoleon or Lenin?

Drab inventions, pale and timid visions incapable of really going beyond reality, earn a drab and short-lived response. The events of everyday life always surpass them.

Let's let mirrors do what they were made to do: to mirror. That's all they *can* do. Literature and reality do not stand to each other in the relation of mirror to what is mirrored. They are fused within the mind of the writer.

The writer, you see, is an important person.

Thumbnail Sketch of a Writer

Unlike other genres of literature, prose continues to be written by individuals. This is not the self-evident fact which habit makes it appear. For instance, Walter Benjamin predicted without regret after visiting the Soviet Union in the 1920s that the age of the individual producer of literature would soon be over; like the small manufacturer, he would be crushed between the institutions carrying on mass production. But time has proved that analogies between economic and intellectual processes do not always apply.

Nonetheless, the position of the individual producer of literature in the societies of the present and the future remains problematic. The tax office lists the writer as freelance. The product he manufactures—using the "easiest available means" and, incidentally, the cheapest equipment: paper and a typewriter—is taken off his hands by a publishing house, which retails it for him and gives him the smallest percentage of the take. The stratum to which he belongs, for better or worse, counts for nothing sociologically. The insecurity of his position frequently makes him insecure, too. People say that writing is a job like any other. But the very fact that they need to say it proves it isn't true. No one would use that line to comfort an engineer or a metalworker. Consequently, almost all writers think often about changing their profession. It is rare that one makes good his threat; but a writer cannot hide from himself that he has no direct share in fulfilling the economic goals on which his society concentrates all its resources. In a time when measurable results seem to count for everything, he naturally questions his effectiveness.

Commonly, he is not a specialist in any field. His way of life radically distinguishes him from the majority of citizens in modern industrial nations, in that his work does not force him to be in a certain place at a certain time. His working conditions seem designed to isolate him.

How can he—this laboratory specimen whom we have created to get at the crux of the problem—how can he have anything to say which is universally valid and of interest to others?

No one, least of all the writer, can expect to find freedom outside the coordinates of space and time, above and beyond history. The writer is bound by his geographical location, which at the same time is a location in history. It would be both vain and unprofitable to ignore or deny this: why should he carelessly give up the advantage of living in a society which aims to achieve the self-realization of its members? The desire for self-realization is among the most vital prerequisites of literature. The writer's compulsion to write things down stems from the fact that this may be the only possibility he has of not missing his true self. And this explains the tenacity with which writers cling to their profession even in the most adverse circumstances.

So, the writer in our sketch uses the advantages of our society, the greatest of which is, for him, the fact that his thinking was not formed by life in an antagonistic class society. This means that he has an important freedom which should obligate him to project himself further into the future than can his fellow writer who lives in a class society. He should fully mine the advantage of his geographical and historical location and, as a person, expose himself to every feeling that a life of deep involvement can bring.

Thus, despite his unusual way of life, the writer we are talking about does not let himself be pushed into that role of an outsider which is loudly lamented by almost all bourgeois writers. The fact that there is no company doorman to stop him if he tries to walk into a big factory or a scientific institute reduces his risk of mental isolation. He is stimulated by the lively and demanding interest of a class of self-confident readers, yet he does not deceive himself that he is writing "for everyone."

He has to fight to make his own working conditions; no one will do that for him. He has to resist the imperceptible temptation to self-indulgence which comes when the public takes an interest in him. He helps to break down the barrier between art producers and art consumers. He is not and does not want to be anything more than a normal committed member of this society. He does not disown his responsibility to take it lightly, but neither does he exaggerate it to himself or feel inhibited by it. It is difficult to work on the basis of your own experience unwaveringly and with absolute truthfulness. This task is sometimes held up as a writer's test of conscience, but in fact it is pure self-interest, because any attempt by the writer to manipulate his experience would immediately cut him off from the living springs of inspiration and make him produce wild-eyed ghosts and monstrosities who speak with false tongues.

The writer we mean is deeply concerned about the future of mankind because he likes people. He loves being in the world and he loves the many shapes in which human life shows itself. He is clear-sighted and optimistic; otherwise, he would stop writing. His optimism can take the form of earnestness or anger, but not of indifference. Only if this is so, he knows, can he now and then claim the right to say "I." Consequently, "writing" is merely one event in a more complicated process for which we have the beautiful and simple word "life."

The situation calls for modesty. What can our writer wish for? Geniuses are rare; he will not exaggerate the chances that his name will outlive him. The radicalness of his questions will be important, and so will his productive relationship to his times and the intensity of his pleasure in life.

Besides this, what he needs as much as the intention to go to the limit is the tacit understanding that the most modest of his achievements—to be himself speaking with his own voice that is like no other—may turn out to be necessary to some other human being.

Remembered Future

Is it really the meaning of the world that it reveals to us who we are?

Of course not. The world does not have a meaning. It is our free choice to give it one, to give it this particular meaning. At least we can imagine the choice is free—until we realize that our survival as a species seems to depend on it.

To voice a dark suspicion of mine: Maybe the people alive today do not really care—or do not care enough—about surviving as a species. Maybe it is enough for them to be able to look forward to a relatively undisturbed existence in their own lifetime. And aren't most of our lives relatively undisturbed, provided that other peoples let themselves be murdered at a safe distance? Should we move a little closer to home, the border at which we begin to be disturbed? Why?

Humanism does not belong to the "nature of things" or to the biological "nature of man." It is not innate to us. No instinct forbids man to kill his own kind, as in most animal species. Each individual must relearn for himself that highest, hardest, riskiest achievement which society as a whole took thousands of years to arrive at. The cynical tendency of late bourgeois society to dismiss humanism as anachronistic and to claim that it functioned only in periods when the human population was so small that the race could have died out had it practiced uninhibited violence is dangerous. We have preserved a memory of past ages which afforded people a simple and serene way of living. This memory shapes our image of what we want for our future. But is this memory of the future real? Will the five or six billion individuals whom we expect to represent the human race in the unfathomable year 2000 find ways to live which deserve to be called by the old-fashioned word "brotherly"?

This digression leads us by an unexpected route straight back to our subject, prose. We set out originally not to ask questions about the fate of mankind but to find some justification for an activity which is not self-evident. We do not deny the most personal motives for this activity; indeed, we consider them the best motives because they can be counted on to work. It is just such personal motives, just such a personal interest in oneself, that the human race needs.

That is, it is what the individual needs, the person to whom prose is addressed. If our whole future depends on what types of social order exist to greet the new scientific and technological inventions, then we should remember that every Fascist "order" begins by eliminating the individual, that bourgeois ideology today stresses that any effect can be produced on any person, that it regards the "personality" as an obsolete ideal and considers it unavoidable to build a streamlined man who will be unresistant to technology, limitlessly adaptable and limitlessly replaceable—for whom joy and sorrow will flow from the mechanical stimulation of certain parts of the brain, for whom life itself will finally be accessible only in the form of a great "As If": consuming stereotypes, existing among artificial stimuli which he administers to himself.

This condition without history would at the same time mean the end of history, the end of everything which ties mankind to its roots and of every hope for a future. The socialist prose writer must work consciously and as effectively as possible to resist each of the above propositions, no matter what proofs he is offered in their support: for they are the kind of "truths" which become true only by getting inside people and scooping out everything they find there. One must not take part in this macabre business even with one word or one line.

Instead, prose should aim to keep people in touch with their roots, to shore up their self-esteem, which has become so fragile that in technologically developed nations many escape into suicide or the dead end of neurosis. One school of psychiatry believes the only treatment for this malady is "desensitization," a radical training program to adapt people to the norm. Others see a way out in going "back to nature," in a romantic irrationality which bans technology, even though this is the only means of feeding and clothing a human race which is growing by leaps and bounds. But a naïve attitude to life cannot be preserved artificially.

The only alternative left is the narrow path of reason, of growing up, of human awareness: the conscious step out of prehistory into history. What is left is the decision to become an adult. If pathfinders and guides are needed for this task, then we need not fear for the future of prose, for prose was born of that process by which man comes of age. It was a late development, specially designed to create and express differences. Prose creates people, in both senses. It breaks down deadly oversimplifications by showing all the possible ways there are to be human. It is a storehouse for experience and evaluates human social structures in the light of their productivity. It can speed up time and save time by playing through on paper the experiments which man confronts in reality. Here it meets the values of socialist society. The future will know how important it is for us to expand the space mankind has to play in. Prose can expand the limits of what we know about ourselves. It keeps alive in us the memory of a future which we cannot disown, on pain of destruction.

It supports the process by which man becomes a free individual.

It is revolutionary and realistic: it seduces and encourages us to do the impossible.

1968

The Sense and Non-sense

of Being Naïve*

———

Dear S.:

Simple as this request of yours may seem, it is giving me trouble. Maybe if I look for the reasons why, I can still comply. From the start, I felt no urge to write this little piece, but once I promised I would, you had the right to expect me to deliver it on time. Besides, as children we are taught that we ought sometimes to make ourselves do things we do not feel like doing, and I suppose I thought this was a good opportunity. The results—the usual mess of notes on my desk, the usual opening paragraphs stacked in piles of varying thickness all over the floor—did not this time give me a feeling of impatience and confidence, but rather of failure. The only thing that stopped me from calling off the job prematurely was the title I came up with—a title which is bound to strike you as odd as it does me—but which seemed to open a way for me to talk about my subject in general— hence, evasive—terms.

By then I had realized that you are after information which I am determined not to reveal to you, and that this discrepancy is the real source of my reluctance, and is bound to remain so. Have you really any idea what you are asking? Telling the story behind any work of literature means no more and no less than giving an account of the whole preceding period of one's life; tracing back to their origin the roots of themes one regards as peculiarly one's own, however timidly one may have broached them; indicating their development, sepa-

* Christa Wolf's contribution to an anthology of essays published in East Germany in 1974, and edited by Gerhard Schneider.

rating them from outside influences, and thus protecting the tracks which lead to one's own self. But who *could* and, above all, who would *want* to do that? The result would be hints, no more—we nearly always have to make do with them—and *then* how could they possibly be filtered out from the rest?

Besides, shouldn't certain things be kept under wraps out of love for one's fellow man? "Tell me about the first thing you wrote!" you asked me. In the first place, there is no such animal. Thinking back, one keeps remembering still earlier efforts, tried at still earlier ages—plans of novels and plays which were never more than half or three-quarters carried out, diaries, occasional verse on political and private themes, emotion-drenched letters exchanged with girlfriends, all the way back to the fairy tales one made up as a child, fantasies of revenge and other fantasies, daydreams and night dreams, and tall tales intended for practical use: those all-important preliminary forms of naïve artistic composition which it can be devastating for a child to be deprived of, and which sometimes can develop into a need to express oneself in writing. This still does not tell us much. You, as a reader for a publishing house, know that the need to express oneself in writing is quite widespread, as is the sensitivity to basic experiences of the sort everybody has to go through: feelings of weakness and helplessness, anxiety, pain, anger, shame, pride, pity, grief, happiness, despair, jubilation, triumph. Concerned parents do not mind your feeling these things but would prefer you not to feel them too intensely, lest as a result you become—God forbid!—permanently prone to fanciful notions and extravagant emotion.

But a childhood caught between the commonplace in private life and fanaticism in public may find no other outlet than a secret eccentricity and the effort to counteract it by choosing a straightforward profession: that of schoolteacher, for instance, which is what I used to list as my job when filling out forms, until I reached the age of twenty-one. After that, I spent years on the fringes of an occupation for which it never even occurred to me to presume I had the ability, due in part to the fact that the very young seldom are able to write prose. The true cause of my inhibition to write I may talk of on another occasion; of course it could not be overcome without deep turmoil, or overnight. You yourself must know how a lukewarm urge can evolve into a compulsion that sets itself above all the commandments— simply because it affords the means to be at least temporarily in harmony with oneself.

I had no thought of anyone reading my stuff. On the contrary, my early work was tucked away in a safe hiding place, for it involved highly intimate matters whose ambivalence was evident from the fact that they could neither be completely revealed nor remain unspoken. This shameful inner conflict—which was not as innocuous as it may sound—set off a perpetual-motion machine of the kind that produces, in an unascertainable percentage of cases, the product you referred to in your inquiry as "the first thing I wrote."

But the writer himself does not use that term, "my first work." If he did, his cause would already be lost: he would find himself precariously between two stages of naïveté and would have to be careful not to step down too heavily on a floor that might be incapable of supporting his weight. At this point he would also face the first in a long series of questions of conscience: whether this first work which had the luck or misfortune to get published was written with publication *in mind*, and whether this intention changed his attitude toward an activity he had been intimately familiar with in the past. In my case, the answer to both questions must be yes, and where the second is concerned, I say it with regret. The transition from amateur to professional changes an author. One change is a loss of naïveté in the sense of innocence. The later you notice the changes, the more dangerous they can get, and only by vigorous and ruthless countermeasures can you obviate them to some degree.

You can see for yourself what happens, the moment I even try to entertain thoughts of your request. There is no need for you to leap to your own defense. I understand perfectly well what you really want to know—the usual things: "What was your first published work?" (Answer: the *Moskauer Novelle* [*Moscow Novella*]—not counting book reviews and literary essays.) "When was it published?" (Answer: 1961.) "Where and in what circumstances was it written?" (In the East German town of Halle on the Saale River, on a quiet street called Amselweg, Blackbird Road, through which there wafted the stink of synthetic chemicals from the factories in Leuna and from the Buna rubber plants; at a light-colored desk which had been moved in front of a window to afford me a view of our balcony and a slightly rank garden where our children were playing noisily with the neighbors' children. I could tell you the names of the neighbors and the names of the children, and describe them to you as well, but I have forgotten what season of the year I saw outdoors when I looked up from the desk.) But your main question would be: "Where did you get the material for your story?" In other words, which parts are taken from "real life" and which are "invented"? Where can the curious reader find the "autobiographical nucleus": because everybody knows that, generally speaking, it is the author's own life which he forms into literature? This ploy to inveigle me into unwilling, unimportant, and misleading confessions I reject on the grounds that the labor of "forming things" is worthwhile only if the work cannot be destroyed later by someone carelessly spilling the beans. "Well then, can you at least tell us whether some of your characters had real-life models, and if so, which ones?" (No comment.) "How old were you when you wrote this story?" (Almost thirty.) "Were you familiar with Moscow?" (Not familiar enough, as you can easily tell from my story, provided you know Moscow better than I did—and in fact I now know it better myself, although I do not feel any urge to write about it.) "Then can you tell us a couple of your chief motives for writing this story?"

Your impertinent questions—even if I have only been imagining their impertinence—met a barrier so reliable that for days I could not think of a thing to say, and I was about to call it quits when, unfortunately, I got the idea of rereading that story I wrote fourteen years ago, which you are now asking me to talk about against my will. I need hardly tell you that it was as painful to read as I imagined it would be. Nor need I say that I do not propose, in this essay, to put myself through the justly grueling task of poking fun at my story for its obvious lack of formal skill—its awkward sentences, the images that do not come off, the wooden dialogue, the naturalistic descriptions—all the things that you run across even in good books and that people half correctly believe belong to the "craft of writing," which anyone who cares to can learn. What disturbed me more is a tendency to closedness and perfection in the formal structure, the way the characters are amalgamated into a plot that unfolds like clockwork—even though I know that the events and feelings which underlie parts of the tale could not be more violent and obscure.

This finished-off quality reveals something I had almost begun to forget: how well I had absorbed my university courses in German literature, and all those articles, which often covered the whole page without a break, about uses and disadvantages, realism and formalism, progress and decadence in literature and art—absorbed them so well that, without my realizing it, my vision was colored by them and I was moving far away from a realistic manner of seeing and writing.

Observing this, I began to feel interested in that first story of mine after all, quite independently of your question. How, I wondered, could a woman almost thirty years old who had been far from untouched and unmoved by the agitated and agitating events of this century write, nine years past its midpoint, a tract of this kind? I mean "tract" in the sense of a religious tract written to propagate a faith—because there is no denying that this story of a love affair between a German woman and a Russian man shows a certain pious naïveté in the way it stays neatly within prescribed borders and does not allow confusion to spread outside the psychological zone. Of course, renunciation is not something which merits our scorn; only it need not be given a moral motivation when the prevailing rules dictate it anyhow: remember, we are talking about 1959.

But do not be afraid this is going to turn into self-incrimination, or an attempt to get myself off the hook on the grounds of incompetence. Hermann Paul's dictionary defines the original meaning of the word "naïve" as "innate, natural"—and, indeed, that urge to express oneself by writing which I mentioned earlier may well be described as "natural" and "naïve." But the word "talent" (from Latin *talentum*, deriving in turn from the Greek) referred originally not to a quality but to a unit of weight and money. After its appearance in the parable in Matthew 25:14 where a man gives "talents" to his servants, "talent" took on the figurative meaning of a capital sum from which one is supposed to make a profit. Thus, it is up to the person himself—should even a few ounces of this talent have been "entrusted" to him—whether he lets it go to waste or makes it grow. Talent turns into a trial, a challenge, a thorn whose point can on occasion be broken off.

This, by the way, is what must have happened to my story. As it traveled down from my head through my arm, my hand, my pen, and my typewriter onto the paper, it seems to have undergone a transformation, as literature inevitably must—but a loss of energy as well. Apparently, my fear of dangerous explosives led to the use of controlling devices, building components which could be linked together to form a story. This is the birth of fable—fable in the ancient sense of "idle talk," as opposed to a truthful account. Fabulous creatures find a good home in it, a dry and reliable shelter, if they will take a little trouble to fit; and they learn to get on fabulously together and beget a convenient moral.

Of course, I would not deny the eminent relations between literature and social morality. But an author's social morality should not be limited to hiding from his society all he can of what he knows about it. I say this despite the fact that not so long ago—how quickly we forget!—a lot of carbon copies, produced from prefabricated formulas, were circulating under the label "sticking to the Party line." And we—by "we" I mean present company included—got in the habit of using the label "Party line" in a very careless way.

To get back to the subject at hand: Maybe I did not know any better than to write a "tract." In any case, it strikes me that my mixed feelings on rereading my story derived from the almost complete *absence* of mixed feelings in the text itself. Faith and fidelity, love, friendship, generosity, straightforwardness—aren't these the same pure, unequivocal emotions, unmenaced by hidden pits and hidden motives, which touch us in children but amuse us in adults, because they are signs of naïveté? Naïveté, that is, not as Friedrich Schiller uses the word* but in its plain sense, in the sense it most commonly has today: simplemindedness? But what is so shocking about this that I feel I must struggle to convert my hopeless dismay into a wholesome dismay?

It's shocking that I did not know better—anyhow, not *much* better—and that I *could* and *should* have known better. By 1959, after all, it was possible to turn up a few facts about the real background of life in a Soviet family, or the problematic relationship of two peoples, one of whom only fourteen years earlier was still trying to enslave, even exterminate, the other. It is not enough just to assign one side a bad conscience and make the other side look generous. In fact, conscience is not enough if it takes no other form than *bad* conscience—nor are the most pious intentions if they are presented as goals already achieved. Moreover, even in a love story you have to show more than a few idyllic glimpses of an event such as—for instance—the 20th Communist Party Congress in Moscow. I could go on with this unworkable attempt to crawl back inside my story and keep interrupting it with heckling cries, malicious remarks, and demands for improvement—if it were not that my knowledge of self-censorship has grown over the past fourteen years and would not let me sustain the tone.

Just "knowing better" is not enough. How simple it would be if extrinsic factors were all that hindered us from telling everything we know. But although it is true that people write in order to say what previously was unknown, every literature, including the work of great authors, proves the reverse as well: it is used to conceal. The writer's struggle with himself, which goes on between the lines and behind the sentences—this struggle to reach the limit of what he can say and perhaps cross beyond it at an unforeseeable point, only to discover that he cannot do it after all, that he is not *allowed* to because he is unable to violate with impunity a self-imposed taboo compared to which the dictates of outside censors seem insignificant: this tension is what gives writing its fascination and, once we have discovered it, gives reading its fascination, too, even if the reader does not have to be consciously aware of what moves him so deeply, beyond the fate of the characters.

So now we can tackle naïveté from another angle. A certain measure of self-deception—of naïveté—seems necessary to life; we

---

* Reference to Schiller's treatise *On Naïve and Sentimental Poetry* (1795–96).

continually draw on it as it is continually replenished. That this measure must be greater when we are young than later, when disillusionments—not regrettably—have sobered us, is something I cannot deny. *But* thirty is an age when one can no longer claim to be young, and I would give a lot to know some of the reasons why people of my generation took so long to grow up—a fact which I expect has escaped you no more than it has me.

Of course, I would have resisted that allegation fourteen years ago, but now I think I know what I am talking about. Just listen to the members of my generation sometime. Notice which topics they almost never bring up and which tend to trigger emotional outbursts when they do come up. This will tell you something about those deposits embedded in our life stories which we have not been able to come to terms with and which interfere with our becoming independent adults. Of course, when I wrote my story I believed what I said: that the inner "conversion" of my generation had now "come to pass." And it is quite true that our conscious ideas did undergo the radical change which necessarily was the first step in this conversion. The change was a deeply unsettling experience which encompassed the whole of the personality, and anyone who seriously bore in mind the atrocities we were all appointed to commit and barely escaped due to no merit of our own could easily have been destroyed by the aftershock, like the man who rode on horseback across Lake Constance and only afterward realized he could have fallen through the ice at any time. It is only to be expected that many of our generation carry a residue of deep insecurity, an almost ineradicable self-distrust—albeit often unconscious and glossed over by restless activity—which is bound to express itself in their social behavior, including their literature.

For our deep and persistent horror at the barbarism which emanated from our country and which we denied for so long is not enough to complete our conversion; nor is any new sobriety that applies only to past history. We may have recognized, repented, and amended the errors in our thinking, after much effort, and we may have radically altered our attitudes and opinions, our entire view of the world—and yet our *style* of thinking was not to be changed so quickly; still less, certain reaction and behavior patterns which have become ingrained in people as children and continue to structure the way their character relates to the surrounding world: the habit of trusting those in authority, for instance; the compulsion to idolize or submit to others, the tendency to deny reality, the tendency to zealous intolerance.

Of course, all this can be explained, but for once I would like to *read* the explanations. Our old overblown self-esteem, with a deep sense of inferiority at its root, was deservedly destroyed, and could not simply be replaced by a new, ready-made self-esteem. But in order to survive, people eagerly latched on to inadequate substitutes—a new blind religious zeal, for instance, and the arrogant claim that now they had found, once and for all, the only correct and only workable truth—at a time when, I need hardly tell you, dialectical thinking was what was really needed, especially from socialists. In fact, the *Moskauer Novelle*—which I am still discussing—bears witness to all this by the touching efforts it makes to use rationality to ward off the subterranean threats of passion or grief, and by claiming and presupposing changes which in fact it had yet to be proved had taken place. The story is not completely successful at either attempt, and thus produces those holes and ruptures which give cause for hope after all.

I am sure you will believe me when I say that what I am writing here is neither a complaint nor an accusation but more an exercise in self-communication—a preliminary, abstract formulation of problems which remain to be dealt with concretely in literature. Prose is one of those genres which depend on coolheadedness and self-command and which, thus, seem to have no use for naïveté. At the same time, like all so-called art, prose feeds off that store of primordial behavior whose groundwork is laid in our childhood. It requires spontaneous, direct, no-holds-barred reaction, thought, feeling, and action; an unself-conscious—that is, after all, a "naïve"—and unbroken connectedness to oneself and one's personal history—those very things which our generation has forfeited.

This contradiction is itself one of the things that determine how we live, and how we write, too. We can ignore or deny it, belittle or cover it up, brace ourselves against it, lament it or curse it. We can run away from it, taking refuge in the unproductive, mechanical processes of life, or we can be broken by it without even knowing it. Whatever tricks we put ourselves through, there is only one way to relate to our times in a creative and unforced manner, and that is by working through this conflict which affects more than one generation and thus provides the raw material for role models. Persistent, unflinching work is needed on those complexes, rooted in the past, which it hurts to touch: not so as to tie society's resources to the past unnecessarily, but to make them productive in the present. This task, if carried out consistently, could lead to literary discoveries of a kind we do not expect.

Fourteen years is only an accidental time span, after all. How can we guess how near or how far the day may be before we disbelieve the things we are saying today—for instance, what I have written in these pages? That is how it should be. If our hopes were destroyed the minute they arise, all production would stop, and with it, hope itself; whereas nowadays, when our every word must pass knottier and severer tests than in the past, our work indeed may be more arduous and wearisome, but by no means has it become impossible. New kinds of information require new resolutions and techniques, if they are to be brought into play effectively. So far, we are still left speechless when we hear on the news that the United States' twelve-year "military involvement" in Indochina simply "ended punctually at 5 a.m." one morning, after 6.6 million tons of bombs costing more than 30 billion marks had been dropped on Vietnam, Laos, and Cambodia, "with scant success." In a case like this, an old-fashioned word like "madness" is not much good to us, and it will take some hard work to get the quotation marks out of sentences like the above. Yet, to act decisively—in any way which goes beyond the merely mechanical—requires us to recover that basic trust in ourselves that we have lost.

And so I will end—to my surprise and yours—with a word in praise of folly. That folly I mean which has many faces, some of them perfectly consistent with insight and experience. That folly which nourishes great experiments but lets frivolousness, cynicism, and resignation wither away. Which enables us to build houses, plant trees, bring children into the world, write books—to *act*, as clumsily and imperfectly as ever we may. Such action, in any case, is wiser than surrender to the multiform, often hard-to-recognize, perfect techniques of destruction.

August 1973

A Sentence[*]

Ladies and Gentlemen:

Now would be the moment for me to say "I thank you." A simple sentence, appropriate to the occasion, with a subject, a predicate, and an object. So what is wrong with it—or with me? I don't know if you can hear it, too. It rattles. As if it had a fine crack running through it.

Now the thing is spreading. There are cracks in the words, fissures running through the sentences, fractures shooting across the pages, and the punctuation marks—periods, commas—are opening up like clefts and trenches. Not to mention the grimaces the question marks make, the mysterious way that the exclamation marks vanish into nothing. Language starts refusing to perform its customary services. What this indicates, what it stems from, and where it is leading I am not here to discuss. It is a tricky and long-winded subject, and for the present it cannot be talked about in words, anyway. But I have caught this one sentence in the act and put it under arrest—"I thank you"—and now I want to rake it over the coals—precisely because it doesn't look like a hard case—with the aid of the *Concise German Grammar*, which I have owned for a long time, although I rarely use it. Let's start at the first chapter, "The Sentence."

"Living language"—that's the first phrase I read, and it is not one I would have expected to find in a grammar book. "Living language is born out of a language situation; that is, out of a situation which

* Speech delivered in Bremen, West Germany, when Wolf was awarded the 1977 Bremen Prize for *Patterns of Childhood*.

58

due to certain internal and external conditions leads to a language utterance."

Excellent, we are making progress. Words like "situation," "conditions"—at least the "external conditions"—could hardly sound more compelling. Paging through the chapter, I learn that the shortest complete sentence in the German language is the second person imperative form of a verb, for instance: "Speak!"

"Living language." Okay, but what does that mean, exactly? Of course, I know. I still recognize it most easily in sentences like this one*: "No longer will I bind my heart and break it on the wheel, freely shall it stir its wings, unbridled shall it fly round its sun, dangerous though the flight may be like the moth's round the candle." That's Heinrich von Kleist. And we know where such language leads: to death—and likewise to certain follow-up sentences like this one: "There is no sadder spectacle than the sudden attraction to the absolute, in this world which is anything but." That's Johann Wolfgang Goethe, of course, and we know he is right, and we would prefer not to have to arbitrate between these two sentences, which obviously are not to be found in my grammar book—to which I now return.

Now we are back on solid ground, among solid paragraphs which ought to be capable of dispelling the doubt from the sentence I started with.

Paragraph 56. *The Subject*: "That which is placed beneath and is capable of tying up a verb." In the case of our sentence, the subject is the personal pronoun "I." The subject is placed beneath the sentence so as to support its weight. Although I am not so tasteless as to ask "Who am *I?*" I *will* ask "Who am *I* for *you?*" or rather, "Whom do *you* take me for? Do you know, or think you know, on whom you are conferring this prize?" And: "Would you still do it, if you really did know?"

Paragraph 63. *The Predicate*: "That which is publicly proclaimed." That's it, all right. But the ancient Latins from whom the word "predicate" derives did not have the mass media turning up in their nightmares. The "public" surrounding my sentence gives it a tough time. Morbid thrill-seeking and an unreserved zeal for interpretation destroy the conditions for speaking naturally.

The predicate in our sentence is "thank": a full verb, one of that class of verbs which express human behavior: to thank or to take offense; to concur or to contradict; to please or to displease; to desire

---

* German *Vor-satz*. A series of puns follow on the noun *der Satz* ("sentence") which have no direct equivalents in English. Kleist's sentences lead to suicide, whereas Goethe's allow for survival.

or to renounce; to benefit or to harm; to trust or to distrust; to respect or to revile; to yield or to resist; to help or to hurt. If only there were a single verb which contained an element of all those behaviors! But language is not equipped to express such contradictions.

Or is it? Friction, contra-diction, are contained not in individual words but in whole sentences. "God knows that often man has no choice but to do wrong," Kleist says. This is an agonizing example of contradiction, which is made to depend on the Highest Authority to save the sentence from dying of dread; and it also depends on a more complex sentence structure than our own little sentence does. For language, too, has its hierarchical order. Besides the main clause, there are other sentence parts, subordinate clauses which depend on it and which it governs as it likes, which it forces to submit, which it can tie up or set free according to rules which it seems to have a vested interest in reinforcing.

Paragraph 84. *The Object*: "That which receives the action." Not without guilt feelings, I allow the grammar book to throw some sentences at me. In these sentences—as in the modest sentence we are discussing—"an object meets the verb or is acted on by it." Examples: "The child obeys his parents." "The laws serve man." "He trusts his friend." Just between you and me, sentences like these rattle and clank at me like mad when I listen to them, but then maybe there is no need for me to make that confession. So let's stick to the "you," the dative object in my sentence, a "you" who—I don't mind telling you—is a complete stranger to me. I don't know you. In what sense—I would like to know—do "you" meet my thanks? In what other sense could it meet you? Do our attitudes and intentions meet, however fleetingly, within a word? I don't know, but I hope so. It may be that the subject and the object are not sure of each other. But the deeper cracks in sentences develop only when someone speaks in a way which *simulates* a sureness that is not there.

Now I've gotten stuck. Have I overtaxed the occasion, my sentence and the "language situation"? Don't we all feel very glad, frequently, when we can just let smooth sentences slide past one another? As for the disharmony between an occasion and our response to it—well, there is nothing new about that, surely. It's what we call having "mixed feelings." Anyway, it feels refreshing now and then to see someone experience *un*mixed contentment. Take the aged Wieland,* one of whose sentences my grammar book cites as an example: "I enjoy my wealth and others enjoy it with me." "How nice!" I feel like exclaiming.

* Christoph Martin Wieland, German poet (1733–1813).

But at least now we know why I find it hard just to rattle off a simple sentence: it's because I doubt if the sentence really matches the facts, or more precisely, the human behavior, the "internal conditions." "This above all: to thine own self be true" is another example of a sentence. But we have outgrown such juvenile precepts by now and learned to lie, which, after all, is one of the tactics of survival. Yet we are talking about literature here today and literature cannot in the long run be tactical if it is to survive. So are we to accept, and go on accepting, the sentence my grammar book quotes as an example of the variables of a complex sentence: "Everyone *hears* only what he *understands*"?

Or suppose that we vary this sentence to read: "Everyone reads only the meaning he wants to read"? Misjudged criticism, praise that distorts meaning, and worst of all, often it's done not with any bad or good intention but in "all sincerity"—just with no concern for the "internal conditions" that governed the other person. People don't get to know each other, and why? Their judgment is swallowed by the desire to prejudge, their thinking ability by the compulsion to think wishfully or in condemnation. We allow ourselves the pleasure of being unjust and scarcely even notice the price we pay: we don't really get to know ourselves, either. Things are not as they seem, but a host of public "predicants" want to make us believe that appearances are *not* deceptive. So, do we want to go on seeing, praising, censuring, and thanking each other in the same way we have been doing, and above all, is this how we want to find out about ourselves? "You don't have to travel around the world to understand that the sky is blue everywhere" is the sentence my grammar book offers as an example of the infinitive.

"I can promise to be sincere, but not to be impartial." A first-rate example of the compound sentence, taken from Goethe. If only everyone who is called on to speak in public knew this about himself and would say it occasionally! Also, this sentence has a "but" in it and I like sentences with "buts" in them because it is hard to turn them into senten-tious sentences, that is, into dogma.* Literature which does not pound in dictums but draws out contra-dictions can encourage us to say "but"—even at the risk of creating very noticeable cracks and big gaps in the principles and dogmas and making people unhappy. What has happened up to now is that every time somebody says "but," somebody else counters it with an "even so." "Even so, be not downcast. Even so, do not give up." This sentence comes from

---

* Another series of puns on "sentence" and "speech": *Lehr-Satz, Grund-Satz, Spruch,* and *Widerspruch*—"dogma," "principle," "dictum," "contra-diction."

the middle of the Thirty Years' War, back in the days when poets still used to supply people with rules for life. The poet in question was Paul Fleming, who in the same poem ventured on this incredible line: "What thou still canst hope shall yet be ever born."

That was three centuries ago. Of course! It's time itself that draws out doubt, draws it far out from its covert place, deeply buried in language, so that language—which actually is up to handling any circumstance, even the most complex or subtle—often, all too often, surrenders. But it is not the rattling and asthmatic sentences that are the dangerous ones; it's the ones that lull you to sleep, or are hammered flat and trite, or are worn down to the bone; the domineering and the flattering sentences are the ones that carry on the lies and deception, and thus the murder and the homicide. For instance—my grammar book, in whose labyrinth I got lost for a long while—shows a powerful yearning for participial clauses. "Fanatically standing up for his rights, Michael Kohlhaas turned into a tragic figure." Yes, he turned tragic after his rights had devoured his life and many other people's, so he could no longer ask himself what he was doing and why. Second example: "And searching more deeply I froze still more, and then, having died, I came here into the realm of Shades" (Brecht). Freezing, dying, and loss of self—are these really the things that happen to people when they "search more deeply"?

I am not surprised that we feel afraid to bend over the dark and hidden abyss of language which Wilhelm von Humboldt speaks of, and to interest ourselves in its fate: because it is so hard for us to take an interest in ourselves. Nonpersons are beyond the reach of anything people can say. The sentences they use to deal with each other are impersonal, noncommittal, geared to get results. Language that runs like an idling motor, that is an end instead of a means, is evil magic in a world where magic has been done away with.

Where we take no interest there is no memory and no literature. Where there is no hope of arousing interest there is no living language, only automatic punch-card talk. There are no quiet, straightforward declarative sentences because contention has taken the place of fact. There are no interrogative sentences: "What is the thing in us that lies, murders, steals?" (Büchner). There is no dialogue, only strict monologues. There are no frank avowals, due to fear of the jealous mob. There is no elegy: "Ah, life is growing ever more complicated and trust ever more difficult!" (Kleist). There is no word of compassion: "If your mother knew, it would break her heart." There is no language to follow or shore up the paths where our most essential and riskiest thoughts and feelings must travel. There is no sentence of wisdom or of kindness. And there is no sentence that stays open, open like a wound. Instead, we have an increase of sentences that stick in our throats, or are rammed back down them—which seem to depend on our increasing indifference. The sentences which are left unspoken are those for which there is not an urgent enough demand. Their place is taken, more and more often, by ersatz sentences, additive sentences, alloy sentences, whipped-up sentences, tune-in-next-week sentences.

What can we do about it? Get interested, talk, write. The book of mine which you found worthy of receiving this prize is a recollection—among other things—of a childhood spent in a Germany which I hope with all my heart is gone for good. Today, like then, children are growing up, in both the Germanys. So, are we serious enough when we ask the question: How will these children *talk* to each other when they are grown? What words will they say—in what kind of sentences—and what tone of voice will they use?

Ladies and gentlemen, I thank you.

January 1978

*Example without a Moral**

—

"Literature in disguise"? Isn't that phrase a tautology? So I thought
when I first heard it. Isn't disguise—or the outward garb at least—
the essence of literature, in the sense that it is not a primary but a
derived reality? In that case, doesn't the topic "Literature in Disguise"
offer too broad an umbrella, which would include every kind of problem that interests, troubles, or speaks to literary people today?
Or should a new reality require literature to put on new types of
disguise?

We rarely witness the moment when a person encounters a piece
of literature clothed in its disguise of metaphor and experiences it as
a basic clue to his or her own contradictory existence. Recently I was
lucky enough to witness such a moment. One night I sang my granddaughter, who is five and a half, the old folk song about the hunter,
and she challenged it for the first time. After each stanza she asked,
"Why?" In the version I know, the song goes like this:

> *A hunter blew into his horn*
> *and all he blew was lost and gone.*
>
> *Should all my blowing disappear,*
> *I'd rather be no hunter more.*
>
> *Over the bush he cast his net,*
> *a dark brown maid came out of it.*

* Wolf's contribution to the May 1978 PEN Congress in Stockholm. The assigned theme
of the Congress was "Literature in Disguise."

Ah maiden dark, leap not away!
I've hounds to fetch you if you stray.

I have no fear of your great hounds,
they have not seen my high, wide bounds.

They know your leaps so wide and high,
they know, too, that today you die.

If I die now, then I am dead,
so bury me under roses red.

His net he cast over her fair young life,
and she became the hunter's wife.

"Why?!"

I could see that her question was justified, and not at all easy
to answer. For the theme of this song—"love"—has been disguised
to the point that it is almost unrecognizable—at least to a child, I
thought. "Why was everything 'lost' when the hunter blew his horn?"
"Because no one was there to hear him." That seemed to fit. It also
seemed plausible that the dark brown maid had been listening to him
secretly while she was hiding in the bushes.

"Why did she listen?" "Maybe she liked the hunter." Okay, but
why does he threaten her with his dogs, with murder and mayhem?
At the risk of losing my credibility, I ventured to claim: "He loves
her, too." Silence. Then: "But he isn't very nice to her." I replied:
"Maybe he is very afraid that she will run away from him again."
And she: "Maybe he doesn't mean the dogs to really bite her to death?
And the girl didn't really want to run away and be buried?"

"Surely not."

I was silent, leaving her to wrestle with her experiences of love,
fear, aggression, masquerade, and self-pity, which we notice already
at the age of five or six. I also knew the limits of her experience, but
I could not "explain" anything. We are looking at a basic pattern
which each person either must accept and complete as well as he can
or must refuse. I waited in suspense to hear her next question. It
was: "But what did the girl look like?"

In other words, something in her had recognized and accepted
the pattern, alien and strange though it was. Something in her wanted
to identify more strongly with the girl. I was touched, but still on
guard. What did she want: for the girl to resemble her? It seemed
very likely. I mentioned the only phrase that describes the girl: "dark
brown." My granddaughter has brown hair, so the two of them looked
alike.

I missed the mark. What she wanted to know was: Did the girl have straight hair or curls!

I was in a fix. For my granddaughter, this is the most ticklish of all questions. You have to realize that she has brown curls which everyone thinks are charming except she herself. For reasons we will never know, she has an unshakable ideal, an inner image of a girl with long straight black hair, and I don't know what she would not be willing to do to look like this image. Thinking that I would humor her, I said I believed the girl in the song had curls like her. Then she gave an indescribably disappointed and disgusted groan and I realized that I was on the wrong track. She wanted the heroine to be "more beautiful" than she was.

Since I could not take back what I had said, I decided to try all or nothing. "Go ahead and picture the girl with long straight hair if you want to," I said.

"But what does she *really* look like?"

She would not let me off the hook. "*Really?* We don't know, the poet was thinking about the girl he loved the most. And anyone who sings the song can picture the girl *he* loves the most." "Really?" "You can believe it." To which she responded with relief, "That's okay, then."

Simple as it was, I found this incident moving. There was something right about it all. The metaphor—literature in disguise—was used as the key to understand a fundamental personal experience: that surrender also means destruction. The metaphor had revealed this meaning when it was decoded—not disenchanted. Its effect was in harmony with its means. The "purpose"—if such there was—was achieved: something along the lines of self-discovery. A tiny mark may have engraved itself in the child's memory, where it can be deepened by later encounters with art, provided that she does not stop confronting her experiences—even the painful ones—without disguises, without masks. To be sure, it seems to me that the confrontation with painful experience is becoming more frequent and that literature in the process is facing some new facts.

Yesterday—I am writing this on May 2, 1978—I read a report in a Scottish newspaper about a very young girl who tried to throw herself out the nineteenth-story window of an apartment building. A policewoman held on to her by her coat until two more officers arrived to assist her, and pulled the girl back inside. The rescued girl said she had nothing to live for.

Three or four weeks before this, I heard about a radio report from Sweden announcing that plans were being considered to set up clinics for would-be suicides: not to dissuade them, but to make it easier for them to kill themselves. How would they go about that, I thought: with the help of a medical staff? A person who instinctively grabs the coattails of someone who is trying to plunge into the abyss is to be replaced with "rational" and "humane" deliberations. No doubt these words were not used in the radio broadcast, but they must have been implied, because no plan which did not present itself as rational and humane would be allowed to challenge the Hippocratic oath. The report said that a person who wants to die should be able to die with dignity, and without endangering anyone else.

Within seconds, my imagination conjured up a fictional clinic, a business operation that ran like clockwork; hygienic, antiseptic, equipped with nurses, doctors, psychologists in white coats, with cooks, kitchen help, and cleaning women, a gardener, and an unusually large number of students studying anatomy: for this hospital would produce not health but death. The physician would get to know the patient, perhaps spend days trying unsuccessfully to dispel his longing for death, then leave a fast-acting tablet on the night table one evening and signal to the night nurse not to go into the room again; and she in turn would leave an order for two men to come with a stretcher the next morning.

Everything is functioning and everything is upside down.

I am very much afraid that this is a metaphor for the confusion of ends and means, which is a basic trait of the world we live and write in. The means of our preservation have degenerated into means to destroy our environment; the means for our defense into means of self-destruction; the "authentic" ends which our means once served have sunk beneath the threshold of our consciousness, and we are forced to substitute delusions for reason, to hide this condition from ourselves. When people despair of this beautiful world, we are more willing to hand over money to get rid of them fast and inconspicuously than we are to struggle to put our troubled civilization on a new footing.

And what happens to literature in such a world? Disguised by nature, now it encounters disguised people, "reality in disguise"; and readers who fail to read their doom, or to whom it may even appear to be "happiness." When I was a child, I scratched out the eyes of the witch in my book of fairy tales, the one who is offering the poisoned apple to Snow-White. The fairy tale could not protect me from biting into the poisoned side of the apple more than once in later life, and finding out how hard it is to get the poison out of one's system. But what if Snow-White, once she is poisoned, were to claim that she feels quite well? What if she explains that this is what she wanted all along: to lie in the glass coffin and have people weep for her? What if she sends away the prince who wants to love her, saying that she has no need of love?

The song of the hunter and his maiden would not be applicable to this Snow-White. If we were to tell her her own story, she would not understand it. She lies in her coffin "as if she were alive," smiling and very beautiful and beyond our reach inside her well-armored hiding place. Meanwhile, the Seven Dwarfs hand the tourists glossy leaflets in which scientists certify that there is nothing wrong with the girl.

You must feel—as do I—that my collection of anecdotes is still missing a moral that applies to us and to our theme. But I confess that I am finding it hard to provide one. Here, too, there is the risk of responding to deception with self-deception. And even a question may be posed in a false way. I will ask this one all the same: How can literature help to liberate reality—that is, its readers—who are trapped in the delusion of progress? Or, to put it perhaps more accurately, without the "how" at the beginning: *Can* literature help to liberate . . .

I don't know the answer. The situation calls for modesty. People who care for literature are no more immune than anyone else to delusion in all its forms, or to despondency, fear, or resignation. But provided that we are able to hold on, again and again, to our own sanity, and to keep up our courage, isn't it time to reconsider what kind of key is needed today to open up to people their locked reality, from which they are "alienated"? With so many masquerading to hide from themselves, should literature respond by wearing more and more masks of its own, by making itself unrecognizable, fleeing into costumes, working with images, metaphors, myths? Should it slip "in disguise" behind the defensive armor of its readers? Or should it, on the contrary, step forth undisguised, naked and bare, to combat the secret-coding of the world: point out the structures and tell in dry words what is there?

To ask such questions implies not knowing the answers. To me, it seems that any and all means are permitted, the old as well as the new, provided that we keep strict watch on ourselves to ensure that they do not serve manipulative ends: provided, that is, that we do not allow our work to be infected by that poisoned apple which makes ends disappear and turns abuses into means. The policewoman who held on to the would-be suicide could hear and feel the fabric of the girl's thin coat tearing, but she did not let go. Who can know whether next year, or ten years from now, this girl may not discover a meaning in her life? It seems to me that literature must behave like the tenacious policewoman. It must not let go.

May 1978

Illness and Love Deprivation:

Questions for Psychosomatic

Medicine*

So I am supposed to give a "celebration speech"? I guess that means we have something to celebrate? As I write these lines, it does not seem that way to me. Instead, I feel I am under pressure. Not only and not mainly the pressure of meeting a deadline. If my profession has taught me anything, it is that whenever I try to "get something down on paper" about a certain topic and am prevented by unusually tough, stubborn feelings of resistance, which at the same time are not clearly defined—the reason is always fear: most often the fear of insights which are too far-reaching in their implications, and/or the fear of breaking taboos.

As far as I can tell, two impulses lay behind my spontaneous agreement to talk here: the vain wish to do some good, and simple curiosity. I wanted to "do good" by expressing my approval of the little Work Group on Psychosomatic Gynecology, which I was amazed to find exists. I had not believed it was possible, and I wanted to support it. Second, I felt curious about the men and women—but especially the men—who had joined the Work Group, or who at least would attend this conference, and by doing so—this is how I looked at it—were registering doubt about the infallibility and the universal validity of "scientific medicine": that powerful and unquestionably very successful institution—that myth which a lot of people besides you and me have been afraid to question.

---

* Lecture delivered at a conference of the Work Group on Psychosomatic Gynecology, held in Magdeburg on November 2, 1984.

Childish as it may seem, it made me feel better to realize that you may have felt afraid in the beginning, too, that probably you, too, had to struggle before you could bring yourselves to use the word "psyche" to the head doctor in your department or to one of your other medical colleagues. Is a fear shared a fear halved, then? Is this question itself a "therapeutic question"—one that a practitioner of psychosomatic medicine ought to consider?

By the way, why is it that we say "psyche" but never "soul"? Even though we *do* hear the word "physique," and even more often "body," instead of "soma"? Isn't Psyche, in Greek myth, the wife of Eros, the god of love? Isn't the Greek word *psyche* translated as "breath, soul"? All right, so how does a contemporary German dictionary define the two concepts?

If we look in the *Dictionary of Contemporary German* from 1976, we find: "Soul, feminine noun: the total sphere of feeling and experience, especially of the emotions." Among the examples, a line from Musil is quoted: "A person can still claim to have a great, noble, cowardly, daring, or petty soul, but he cannot bring himself simply to say 'my soul.' " Aha, I thought when I read that: so Musil feels that way, too.

And now let's look at "psyche" in the same dictionary.

"Psyche, feminine noun: the totality of phenomena in an individual's perception of the surrounding world, mediated through the activity of the higher nervous system." Well, that sounds like a different story! And as examples I find: "To understand the child's psyche." "The woman's psyche." "The female psyche." "The psyche of the natives . . . as the European jargon expresses it" (Stefan Zweig). Also: "In his last novel the writer shows himself to be a great connoisseur of the human psyche (soul)." The male psyche does not seem to crop up, or does so only in an atypical form: "One must have a precise knowledge of the actor's psyche in order to . . ." and so on. But isn't a male actor often viewed as a man with feminine traits— the tendency to display feelings openly, for instance, and to be emotionally highstrung? And how is it that "the writer" is described as the connoisseur of the psyche, but not the scientist who claims expertise in that field?

The way we use language suggests to me that the words "psyche" and "psychical" are more scientific, closer to scientific attitudes, and easier to accept than the old-fashioned word "soul," which has been meekly turned over to the arts; but that both "psyche" and "soul" are regarded as not very "masculine," or not masculine at all. Whereas the stereotype is still in force that the sciences are very "masculine."

That is, they are unswayed by the disruptive factor of "emotions"; they are based on experiment, and on evidence which is made as convincing as possible by the use of numbers (statistics) and/or formulas; they are as free as possible from the impurities which stem from actual life processes in all their bewildering complexity; they avoid chance; aim to eliminate contradictions; are detached from the values which may apply in the nonscientific world made up of human beings.

This list is not intended to be either ironic or derogatory. What I mean by it is simply that there is a time and a place for everything. It seems to me that I always have known, and that everyone must always have known, that these traits, which may be valid if we are calculating the orbits of stars or the movements of atoms, are not valid when it comes to human illnesses. And *one* of the inhibitions I felt about giving this talk is that I simply do not understand an *exclusively* scientific and physiological approach to medicine. I feel better now that I have made this confession, and I assume that many of you agree with it. I am trying to think back in my own life to the first time that I clearly felt there was a connection between a person's illness and the circumstances of his life. I must have been eight or nine years old. One night when I was alone with my mother, she suffered a miscarriage, and although officially I was not supposed to know anything about conception, pregnancy, and birth, I understood everything that happened. And the reason that the actions and images of that night engraved themselves on me so deeply is that I also understood that my mother did not "want" any more children, and I understood why this was so—whatever the diagnosis of the gynecologist may have been.

I have steadily built up this kind of knowledge, which cannot be obtained by scientific methods and cannot be expressed in the language of the sciences. It has come to me mainly through simple self-observation. But not only are physicians today not taught the technique of self-observation; they are actually required to exclude their personal experience, their own illnesses and health, for the sake of a fetish known as "objectivity." So I ask myself, and I ask you, too—is this really appropriate? And isn't this ability to exclude oneself the most compelling reason why academic medicine concentrates almost exclusively on developing a steady stream of new machines, techniques, drugs, and computers? All these things deserve our praise too, no doubt about that. In the field of gynecology, such inventions have simply made superfluous whole libraries full of women's tragedies—unwanted pregnancy, for instance. All the same, I ask you

—maybe a little too directly, but I don't have much time!—whether the division of labor, the way all men are confined in this or that compartment of the work world, and also the objectification of thought, and the elimination and suppression of the emotions which increasingly go along with it, have created a mostly unconscious need in doctors (on the model of other scientists) to keep their distance from patients, to flee from close contact, both physical and psychical, into the apparently objective evidence and achievements of their equipment.

Many women willingly collaborated with me in this lecture, by contributing stories, letters, suggested reading lists, and criticism. They included some women doctors, one of whom—not a gynecologist—wrote to me: "You can't practice medicine without a knowledge of nature; that is, without science. But what is the science of nature, really?" Incidentally, I wonder whether the absurd way that we divide a person into body, mind, and psyche is not being made worse by terminology. When we use the term "natural science" to describe medicine, we are referring to the kind of medicine which is most prone to view its object, the patient, as a biological machine. But doesn't the "nature" of man consist in the very fact that—despite the specialization of the individual organs, including the brain—every single cell we can isolate under the microscope remains the cell of a particular *person*, not to mention *personality*, and behaves accordingly? "We can't get along without the equipment, it can help us a lot," wrote the woman doctor I quoted before. "Only it can't give us insight into the interrelatedness, the 'mysterious weave' on the inside."

You will not be surprised to hear that my own equipment, my machinery of association, fed me a quotation from Goethe's *Faust*. It is the scene in which Faust conjures up the Earth Spirit by the power of magic and makes it appear before him:

SPIRIT. *In flood of life, in action's storm*
I ply on my wave
With weaving motion
Birth and the grave,
A boundless ocean,
Ceaselessly giving
Weft of living,
Forms unending,
Glowing and blending.
So work I on the whirring loom
The life that clothes the deity sublime.

Faust, the investigator of nature, then goes on to soliloquize about the inadequacy of the research tools from which he had hoped for so much:

> *You instruments, you mock me to my face,*
> *With wheel and gimbal, cylinder and cog;*
> *You were my key to unlock the secret place:*
> *The wards are cunning, but the levers clog.*
> *For Nature keeps her veil inviolate,*
> *Mysterious still in open light of day,*
> *And where the spirit cannot penetrate*
> *Your screws and irons will never make a way.**

Nor, I presume to add, will obstetrical forceps and speculum open a way for you.

I want to quote that same woman doctor again. She told me how, during a crisis in her life, it helped her to pay attention to her dreams. "Know thyself!" she writes. "That's easy to say, of course, but evidently it is sometimes simpler in a dream than during the day. Only a few years ago, I would never have had the courage, as a physician and scientist, to say that among other things I also believe in dreams. I would have felt ashamed and kept to myself a lot of what I am sure constitutes my greatest talent, because I would no doubt have been labeled 'hysterical.' Isn't that silly? We frantically suppress a part of ourselves, merely because we might get a negative label!"

No doubt she *would* have been labeled hysterical, and many people would still call her hysterical today if she confessed to them that in quiet hours she tries to imagine an overall "picture" of this or that patient, and that she finds this more useful than wracking her brains for hours on end. People would say she is downright "crazy," in the sense that she sees things that are not there. The one thing I would really criticize about scientific and technological thinking is that it tends to regard only a certain type of fact as "real" and existing; namely, that which can be learned through scientific method and described in scientific terms. Faust fought on two fronts: against the charlatanry of magic, and against the new myth of "science" which he saw when it was just emerging. The nineteenth century, which was the century of the bourgeoisie and of capitalism, provided the fertile soil in which that myth could flourish. Then our own century linked the myth to technology, and with it replaced many values which had come to seem "obsolete." But gynecology, it appears to

* Goethe's *Faust: Part One*, "Night. Faust's Study."

me, does more than just mirror these tendencies toward objectivity and scientific method within medicine. Its history also reflects a long and deep-seated tradition of contempt for women, hostility toward women, in Western history.

Whenever I began to think about our topic, I was flooded with associations. Oddly enough, one of these associations in particular refused to go away. Again and again I thought of a taxi driver I met not long ago. He seemed really indignant when he told me how he and his fellow drivers hate to work on the evening of March 8, Women's Day, when they have to drive home women who have been out celebrating and have gotten "completely out of control." The last time, he said, one woman actually pinched the back of his neck from behind. He and the other drivers also got propositioned a lot, on that evening: they just weren't safe.

Aha! I thought. It's a modern variant on the ancient custom of setting aside days when people would reverse their usual roles in society. Then a signal fire lit up in me: "the wild woman!" And deep down inside the "well of the past" I saw women celebrating the Dionysian mysteries with their ecstatic, orgiastic rituals, at whose climax a man might be hunted down, torn apart, and devoured, as Euripides describes in *The Bacchae*—a reflection of that lengthy, probably very violent historical process which ended in man's victory over woman and in the installation of patriarchy. "The overthrow of matriarchy represented the defeat of the female sex in world history. The man seized control in the household, too; the woman was demoted, given menial status, made the slave of his pleasure and a mere tool for the procreation of children"—Friedrich Engels says in his *Origin of the Family, Private Property and the State* (1884). Wild outbursts from the otherwise subjugated women seem to have been taking place ever since and causing the ruling males to shy away from women's unbridled emotions. Nowhere does their fear express itself more clearly than in the legend of the Amazons, in the cautiously avoided figure of Penthesilea, who while in a frenzy—the frenzy of love?—causes her lover Achilles, who will not submit to her law, to be torn to pieces by dogs and then holds a ghastly banquet in which she joins the dogs in feasting on his flesh. Relations between the sexes turned into a life-and-death struggle which only one of them could win in each area, including medicine. I remember medallions from Minoan Crete which are inscribed with images of the goddess and of the women who performed acts of healing with her help. Women were especially active in all that concerned childbirth, which for thousands of years was left entirely in their hands. The serpent which winds around Aesculapius' staff is a primeval female symbol, and even after the dominant medicine came to be practiced exclusively by men, women continued for centuries to practice as nature healers, in the role of midwives and herb-wives. For generations they also passed on the secrets of how to interrupt a pregnancy, doing so behind the backs of institutional practitioners, who aimed unconditionally for propagation of the species. Men, male physicians included, harbored great fear, anger, and resentment toward women, but were forced to repress these emotions. The history of gynecology is not without charm, because men felt driven to philosophize about the phenomenon of "woman," and arrived at some very amusing conclusions. All the better if we can laugh at them today, men and women together. But there is a disturbing unanimity about the men's reflections.

Take Plato, for instance. Like the Bible, he regards woman as having derived from a male person, who was punished for misconduct in one incarnation by being saddled with a uterus in the next. And Aristotle said that all procreation aims to produce a man, so that by this standard woman is merely a freak, an "impotent man." This claim is interesting because it launches a whole series of later attempts to deny, or to restrict as much as possible, women's share even in *reproduction*, which was the sole function still remaining to them. The allegation that women were monsters shows that male attitudes were rooted in psychosis: men continued to feel that woman offered a threat to the patriarchy even after she had been completely tamed, redesigned, and deformed into a product of male culture. What people suppress, they come to fear. So women seemed uncanny to men; the conquered native peoples made their colonial masters uncomfortable; and we all feel uneasy about impermissible drives and impulses, irrational longings, and wild desires which we do not act upon but which—behind an emotionless, factual, objective, and scientific façade—influence our thought and behavior far more than we are willing to believe.

I find it interesting that in every period of history the quality which men said that women did not have was the same quality which men regarded as the most valuable at that time. In the age dominated by medieval Christianity, woman was said to lack the capacity for true faith. The word *femina* (woman) was itself interpreted to show this. It was made up, medieval etymologists claimed, of the words *fides* and *minor*, that is "of less faith." The question was asked whether women even have souls, and this led to heated debate among scholars. Today, when the soul no longer counts as a valued possession, it is attributed *only* to women. In the postmedieval centuries, women were said to lack intellect; and today the missing quality is said to be efficient functioning. Whatever women may have lacked, what men disliked and feared the most seems always to have been what women had *too much of*: female sexuality. We all know that at the beginning of the modern era women were burned at the stake in such numbers that many authors have been moved to compare the witch burnings to the Jewish Holocaust of our own century. But how much do we know about the reasons the inquisitors gave for these executions? Two noted authorities recorded their opinions in the notorious *Hammer of Witches* (the *Malleus Maleficarum*): women in reality are "imperfect animals"—the book says—and are completely delivered to "fleshly desire . . . which is insatiable in them . . . This is why they consort with demons, to satisfy their desire . . . No wonder if more women than men have been found to be polluted with the heresy of witch-craft." And the men must have experienced the threat emanating from these women as aimed directly against their potency: for the book says that the women could also afflict men with "sexual" disorders through witchcraft. (Incidentally, a West German newspaper recently carried a report of a gynecology symposium which found that the increasing sexual activity of women, which has resulted from their economic emancipation and their use of safe contraceptives, has been causing anxiety and conflicts in men, and impotence is said to be increasing among men, who have come to feel insecure.)

I believe that men's fear of impotence in a male-centered culture which demands that they be superpotent is something that must be taken very seriously; it may be a source of the growing violence and destructiveness in our male-governed world. Today, when the mass witch burnings lie three to five hundred years in the past, women writers are acknowledging the witch in woman's nature. Renate Apitz gives her novel *Time of Witches* a female protagonist who achieves supreme sexual ecstasies with her lover, and he experiences the same with her. But when he leaves her to resume his comfortable bourgeois life, she casts a spell on him, afflicting him with sexual impotence. I thought that I would ask you whether this freedom of women to acknowledge their dark side could not be regarded, partly or even chiefly, as an indication that we are making progress. Yet if women are achieving self-confidence at the expense of the men's self-confidence, that just gets us into new problems. But, to quote Fontane, this is too big a subject,* and it is not exactly the one we are discussing.

Back to history. Along with my mental images of the male taxi driver and the frenzied women at the Dionysian mysteries, I "saw"

* The last line of the nineteenth-century German novel *Effi Briest* by Theodor Fontane (1819–1898).

another image right away: several women who were part of the Romantic movement in Germany seated together reading Schiller's poem "Song of the Bell." Caroline Schlegel fell off her chair with laughter when they came to the verse: "And within doors reigns/the modest housewife." But soon after this incident came the Karlsbad Decrees [1819] with their reactionary attitudes, persecution from political demagogues, and Biedermeier style [1815–1848]—a time when the modest housewife indeed was consigned to reign indoors. That is when the women probably stopped laughing. Women started presenting new illnesses, and medicine, which had learned to dissect the human body with ever-increasing refinement, discovered the existence of nerves and devised names for women's "conditions." Women by the score were diagnosed as "neurasthenic" or "hysterical." Symptoms which are hardly ever seen any more today were considered typically female in the nineteenth century, because "only the immature, undeveloped nervous system found in a woman" showed a "tendency to hysterical reactions." Esther Fischer-Homberger, in her book *Woman as Disease* (1984), tells how the German neurologist Emil Kraepelin [1865–1926] classed hysteria as "closely linked to those natural, enduring characteristics of the female sex"; that is, as a "form of disease of undeveloped, naïve emotional life." And the quality which the nineteenth century admired most—intellect, reason—was said to exist in woman only in an atrophied form. The German neurologist Paul Julius Möbius [1853–1907] proposed the theory that "the circumference . . . of the head . . . grows along with intellectual powers," and used an instrument ordinarily employed in hatmaking to measure the circumferences of people's heads. Then he published a book on the supposed relationship between sex and head size, *Sex and Head Size* (1903), in which he listed the large head sizes of famous men, along with the smaller head sizes of anonymous women, making the women seem stunted by comparison. On the basis of these findings, Möbius diagnosed women as suffering from "congenital feeblemindedness."

This was the era which created the stereotypical bourgeois woman: weak, uninformed, dependent, constantly falling into a swoon, and resorting to the most ridiculous whims to get even with her jailer-husband. This same period saw medicine develop into a social agency for the supervision of women. Disease processes were rigorously defined, and strict rules were laid down for behavior during pregnancy and childbirth, and for infant care; the modern clinic was born, helping to promote specialized medicine which treated each organ separately; and a consultation with a senior specialist was considered, in all seriousness, as a tool of diagnosis. This was the time, moreover, when "scientific" thinking came to be regarded as the only realistic way to think, and as an inevitable result, scientific and artistic think-ing diverged to form two separate models, to coin two kinds of truth. One of the main reasons why I experienced feelings of resistance when I tried to work on this lecture is that I am keenly aware of this parting of the ways between art and science; because I know that you and I do not speak the same language; because I have seen how a scientist writing a paper will afterward translate it into incomprehensible gibberish so that his colleagues will accept it as "scientific"; because my incompetence in your field must jump out at you from each of my sentences. Nevertheless, throughout the last century, writers, calmly trusting in their own observation and experience, went right on describing over and over the connection between a woman's life situation, her character, and her illnesses.

Take Flaubert's *Madame Bovary*. Let's look not at Emma herself but at the laconic description of her husband's first wife, the woman who preceded her into the marriage bed of the provincial doctor, Charles Bovary. Héloïse, an aging widow whom Charles married for her money, loses her small property, and her fortune turns out to be a mere pittance. Here is the account of her death:

> She had lied, the good lady! In his exasperation, Monsieur Bovary the elder, smashing a chair on the stone floor, accused his wife of having caused the misfortune of their son by harnessing him to such a harridan, whose harness wasn't worth her hide. They came to Tostes. Explanations followed. There were scenes. Héloïse in tears, throwing her arms about her husband, conjured him to defend her from his parents. Charles tried to speak up for her. They grew angry and left the house.
>
> But "the blow had struck home." A week after, as she was hanging up some washing in her yard, she was seized with a spitting of blood, and the next day, while Charles had his back turned and was closing the window curtains, she said, "O God!" gave a sigh and fainted. She was dead! What a surprise!*

What a surprise! that Flaubert should be so clearly aware of the link between an emotional blow and a woman's illness. Emma herself has the misfortune to be a woman hungry for life but imprisoned in an extremely confining, provincial environment. Her step-by-step decline unfolds over a long period, as if in torturous slow motion, until in the end she delivers her own death blow, like Anna Karenina; and like Effi Briest from Prussia, who takes a roundabout route through tuberculosis. "Where will these unbridled passions lead!" one of

* *Madame Bovary*, Part One, Chapter II (New York and London: W. W. Norton, 1965).

Tolstoy's characters exclaims; and many nineteenth-century readers and reviewers echoed those sentiments. "He loves me?" Anna Karenina thought, referring to her husband. "As if he were capable of it!" Monologue phrases from women, repeated endlessly, over and over, for decades. They are scattered throughout the literature of the time. I am quoting them here because often, without realizing it, the women are stating the causes of their illness.

To these sentences I would like to add another, quoted not from literature but from a woman of our time, a bit of "firsthand testimony." For some unexplained reason, pus kept collecting in cysts in her abdomen, and she was forced to spend a lot of time lying in the hospital while it was drained. One day she asked a woman friend: "Can losing somebody's love make you sick?"

At this point you may feel like saying: "All right—but so what? Assuming that we doctors agreed that being deprived of love, or suppressed passions, or repressed joie de vivre, caused this woman's immune system to break down, and that the same kind of thing makes many other women sick, too, each in her own way—what change would this make in the therapy we offer? Would we, or should we, prescribe a different drug on that account, or perhaps a milder dose? The crucial question seems to be: Could we change this woman's life?"

There is no satisfactory answer, I know. But I would like to mull it over, using spontaneous associations, in the way you are used to by now. The first thing I would ask you to consider is: If this woman's illness were not a recurring abscess but a life-threatening depression, for example, then the one who treated her would not be you but your colleague in psychiatry, who would at least try to influence the way in which she is experiencing her misfortune—losing someone's love. Granted how problematic that is, how difficult, how rarely it succeeds, he would still try. But my point is: the nature of his profession requires the psychiatrist to enter into the language and the world of this woman, her mode of experience, in the attempt to understand her and to help her break out of the self-destructive cycle in which she is trapped. But the ordinary physician—a gynecologist, let's say—who uses the most modern instruments to diagnose her illness and the most up-to-date treatments to fight it, who each time she visits him asks about her temperature, her appetite, bowel movements, and how she feels in general—this doctor, who may be an outstanding specialist, is living in a different world from the woman who is lying there wondering if losing someone's love can make you sick. They do not inhabit the same reality. The world of the emotions is irrelevant, irrational, unreal to the true scientist, and to use them as a guide is irrational. For the

79

woman, the only thing that exists is her anxiety about her husband, who is withdrawing from her. The question Can the doctor change her life? was certainly too ambitious. It has now reduced itself to a different question, which looks more modest: How can this woman and her doctor talk the same language? How can they meet in the same reality?

Assuming that you agree with me that this is a desirable goal and very likely would help the treatment, then we may have arrived at one of the basic questions for psychosomatic medicine, which, if I understand it correctly, chooses not to reinforce the split between body and "psyche," which exists only in people's heads; and which therefore chooses not to split up treatment between an internist or gynecologist on the one hand and a psychologist on the other.

I expect you will have noticed that my talk is moving into the present day—only not along a straight path but along a path that is full of twists and meanders. Most of the associations that came over me when I started working on this lecture came from the present. I have mentioned several: the taxi driver, and the woman who asked if it can make you sick if someone stops loving you. A third example is a half-hour address by an Austrian sexologist which I heard a few years ago in Graz, where the traditional autumn program was devoted to the topic "The Language of Men—the Language of Women." The sexologist had asked Austrian gynecologists and their co-workers— I don't know whether he asked West German ones, too—what colloquial expressions they knew for women and women's genitals; and he got no dearth of answers. For twenty minutes or more, he plied us with vulgar, obscene, and contemptuous names for women and for those organs which the gynecologists—in their therapeutic role!— were especially concerned with. I still remember how, during this harangue, the audience—consisting of about two hundred men and women, mostly young—gradually stopped laughing, grew steadily quieter and more embarrassed, until at the end they were abashed and silent.

This is one possible answer to the question—I don't know, is anyone here asking himself this right now?—the question of why the waiting room outside a gynecologist's office has that special atmosphere of inhibition and fear. Many women who know nothing about the history of medicine, or the history of hostility toward women in the Western world—because they are never taught this kind of history in school anyway—nevertheless feel afraid in a gynecologist's office, afraid that they are going to experience a repetition of what they have been experiencing all their lives: being made an object of male contempt, disparagement, or even brutality. This is the reason, often unconscious, why many female patients prefer to have female gyne-cologists. The fact that today it is actually possible for them to have women doctors if they want them is one important example of the profound revolutions which have taken place in the lifetime of a single generation of women; and what is just as important, we are now able to take these changes for granted. With ninety percent of women working, we are unlikely to meet any woman walking forlornly along the streets of a provincial town day after day, as in the last century. The evidence and counterevidence of psychologists and biologists debating whether woman is "equal" to man are a thing of the past— although not the very distant past. If a woman is able and willing to do the same work as a man, and on the same terms, in a work world which was designed for men, then nowadays we permit her to perform tasks which go beyond the traditional women's professions—with a few exceptions, such as the top jobs in almost all institutions. Yet the standard and model in work life continues to be the man. The "special feature" of women—that they are able or even obligated to ensure the biological reproduction of society—is a weakness mea-sured by the standards of the work world, and requires special pro-tection: the laws protecting the rights of pregnant women and nursing mothers. And these laws, which guarantee women the prolonged leaves which they need after the birth of a child, in turn bar them from the highest achievements in the sciences and from moving into the top positions in sizable numbers, unless they are willing to re-nounce having children.

I am reminded of the face of a young woman with whom I talked for only a few minutes. She came to see me after one of my readings and asked if she might write to me. She was looking for someone she could communicate with, she said. She was a scientist, a chemist. Becoming a chemist had been her dream, and she had achieved everything she could in her field. And now, she said: "It's so cold, it's so empty." Unfortunately, she did not write to me. But I could quote letters from other women which I believe at least point to a conflict that is gradually taking shape. It affects the very women who have made the most progress, those who chose to enter the most "masculine" professions, the sciences. One woman who is now forty-three described to me how she became a scientist despite the diffi-culties of having two children while she was doing it. "With kindly support from other women, and through my own efforts, I reached a substantial managerial position. For a long time, problems of ad-justment and feelings of numbness had been eating away at me. I could no longer resist the urge to break away, which was reinforced when I had my second child." Giving up her scientific and managerial work, she "started over" in her "practical primary profession." "This concrete and directly useful job does me good. I find more opportunities to work creatively. Now that the burden of working within a framework has let up, I think and feel in a more impartial, spontaneous, and pleasurable way." I do not know whether, before she decided to change the direction of her life, this woman suffered symptoms of illness which made her visit a gynecologist or some other doctor. I do know that other women in similar situations have experienced symptoms. I cannot help wondering if this is what Dr. Franke expected me to say when he invited me here to talk about what his letter called "Woman in society, which of course is male- and achievement-oriented," or about "The conflicts women experience today," or about something that is "related to the changing role of women and how they view themselves."

Nothing about this subject can be supported or determined by statistics. We can find out about the double load which most women carry by looking into their second workplace, the household. Our findings are sobering. As you all know, symptoms of stress often result. The daily lives of working women have by now been described with laudable concreteness by women writers. I remember the opposition, in the early seventies, which greeted the publication of an anthology in which a number of authors, some male and some female, each described his or her own idea of what it would be like to change sex. I remember, and most of you will remember, the sensation which Maxie Wander caused in the mid-seventies when she recorded the testimony of women who could no longer refrain from speaking out about the new problems they experienced when they liberated themselves and worked their way into the professions. Maxie Wander told me that when she gave her first public readings she met strong defensive reactions from men, which once again were related particularly to the sexual demands of women.

A young woman sociologist with whom I talked about this lecture described the position of many women today as being "between a rock and a hard place." That reminded me of a passage in Virginia Woolf's famous essay "Three Guineas," which she wrote in 1938—the same year in which Dr. Leitner had to leave Hitler's Germany—while she was pondering what women could do to help prevent the war which she, too, saw looming on the horizon. Even today, after all the revolutionary changes in the circumstances of women, her essay is exciting to read because of the radical questions it asks. Probably this was the earliest moment in history when her questions *could* be asked, because, until then, not enough data had accumulated about working women. And not until women enter the work world, Virginia Woolf concludes, do they acquire the "weapon of independence" which alone can enable them to develop a will and ideas of their own. But then she pauses, stands on a bridge by the Thames in London, watches the procession of professional men going by, and finds that professional men appear to be losing their physical senses, their speech, their health. She ventures to ask whether the qualities which successful men must develop to replace those lost qualities do not lead directly to war. "[T]he enormous professional competence of the educated man has not brought about an altogether desirable state of things in the civilized world," she muses, and goes on: "Simply . . . we daughters of educated men are between the devil and the deep sea. Behind us lies the patriarchal system . . . Before us lies the public world, the professional system . . . It is a choice of evils . . . How can we enter the professions and yet remain civilized human beings; human beings, that is, who wish to prevent war?"*

She found no answer that sticks to the rules. About two years after the war began, Virginia Woolf committed suicide.

There *must* be an answer to her question that sticks to the rules. I am standing on the Weidendammer Bridge, walking down the Friedrichstrasse toward Unter den Linden. I watch the stream of men and women, whose appearance tells me about their working lives. I see girls who look like young men when glimpsed from behind; boys who have what seems to me a "feminine" look. In the afternoon hours, mothers impatiently drag their children along behind them. On a bench in front of a hotel, completely oblivious to his surroundings, a young father is feeding a bottle to his child, a tiny infant. Certain behavior, it seems, is no longer assigned clearly and exclusively to one sex, and I cannot help regarding this as a step forward, just like the new marital and family laws. But does this mean that Virginia Woolf's question no longer needs asking?

I don't think so. Thousands of liberated women are asking themselves the same question today, each one as an individual. They are asking themselves if they are ungrateful, if they are half monsters. Often the contradiction in which unconsciously or half-consciously they are living chooses to express itself in their bodies. What dreams women tell me they are having! One young woman who was expecting her second child dreamed that she had already given birth, that an atomic war had begun, and that all people, including her children, were suffering from burns and radiation sickness and were doomed to die. Since she had no other way to rescue her children from their torment, she killed them with a hammer. Then along with her husband

* Quoted from *Three Guineas* (London: Hogarth Press, 1986), pp. 85 and 86.

83

she searched for a means they could use to kill themselves, too. But there were no longer even any tall buildings left standing, for them to jump off.

I don't know if it would make any sense right now to debate the question of how "real" dreams are. That they can mirror a person's real fears seems indisputable; and real hopes, too. Without them, without the whole spectrum of the emotions and passions, perhaps the only thing left would be bodies, still functioning but in reality dead. At the moment, women still allow their emotions freedom, because they are less practiced than many men in the techniques of adapting, and of deadening their feelings; but I do not know how long this will last. A book was published in this country recently in which an author describes a woman doctor who stops feeling anything in order to avoid suffering and pain.* More than a hundred and fifty years ago, Rahel Varnhagen said that she had been "created to live the truth in this world." Today, women still seem to get sick more often, in a more direct way, or at least in a different way, when they are not able to do that. I believe that this need for the truth gives us all an opportunity—men and women both. What will happen if we do not make use of it?

Am I expecting too much of you? Maybe. But I do not intend to end my talk by making some kind of appeal. I am merely wondering whether it is not possible for a gynecologist and a female patient to have more meetings which do not produce detachment (not even out of habit), and where the old patterns of superiority on one side and subservience on the other are replaced by a relationship in which both parties are involved. A relationship which is not blocked by the selective gaze of a scientist who looks *only* at the woman's organs, or by the long-ingrained need that many women have for a hero, a savior, a god. (And getting rid of that need takes time, too!) Ideally, the therapy would develop out of this relationship, which of course would not rule out the application of the most modern medical discoveries. Whether the relationship ought then to be described as "psychosomatic medicine" or whether we ought to give it some other name is, I believe, a question of less importance.

October 1984

---

* Christoph Hein, *Der fremde Freund* (Berlin: Aufbau, 1982).

On Receiving

the Geschwister Scholl Prize

———

Ladies and gentlemen:
Since the day I learned that I had won this prize, it has not let me rest, because of the people for whom it is named. In the past few weeks, when I was looking for ways to approach this speech, many thoughts went through my mind. I had to ask myself if my own relationship to German Fascism has continued to change since I wrote about its effects on my childhood. I realized that the calamity of those twelve years has not left us; I feel as if it is coming closer all the time. Grief for the victims is growing; the dark rays emitted by the word Auschwitz are still gaining intensity. I notice how hard I still find it to picture in every detail certain moments from the life, and especially the death, of Sophie and Hans Scholl.* And the machinery of annihilation to which the victims were consigned haunts my imagination more often, not less. The forms of destructive rage and contempt for human beings that we are seeing now seem to me, in desolate moments, overwhelming. My writing—including the book which is being honored here today—is intended to combat them.

Recently, people once again have asked why an attitude of historical detachment has not been achieved about this period of the German past, as it has about other periods of history in which murders took place. Exaggerated importance has been given to this

———

* Sophie (1921–43) and Hans Scholl (1918–43), sister and brother, both university students in Munich, were the founding members and leaders of the Weisse Rose [White Rose] German resistance group, composed of students, scholars, and artists, who printed and distributed anti-Nazi leaflets in Munich in 1942–43. The leaders were imprisoned and executed in 1943.

question, and frankly, each of us ought to be able to answer it for himself.

This past is not past. To touch it arouses feelings of pain, shame, guilt. I found myself forced to return once more to the time of what Hans Scholl called "the most abominable tyranny our people ever endured"; to confront the images of those years again, including some with a look of normality about them which over the years has veered more and more into ghastliness. I remembered again the dread that haunted me for years when I realized the purpose for which I and my whole generation were reared and destined. I have never been able to feel "spared" because I was born too late; I was never able to feel exempted from responsibility, but only horrified at how a system of delusion can seduce people into hatred for mankind. At the age of fifteen or sixteen, we had to be born all over again. Certainly we were granted a favor, but above all, rebirth became our lifelong obligation. Seeing through the false teachings, the perverted ideology, proved faster and easier for us than overcoming our deep insecurity, our susceptibility to power, our leaning toward black-and-white thinking and closed systems of ideas. It seems to me that many of my generation—although differently shaped by the different offers and demands in East and West—retained some of their early imprints: the inclination to fit in and submit to others, the habit of functioning, the faith in authority, the craving to agree with others, and especially the fear of contradiction and rebellion, of conflict with the majority, and of exclusion from the group. We have had a hard time growing up, attaining independence, autonomy, and positive social attitudes. This experience is one of which I have intimate personal knowledge, and it has not yet been described in print; writing about it is a debt which has yet to be paid. The need to whet my conscience, the impulse to live more consistently in accord with my own insights and to pursue them in writing are what allow me to face the challenge of this hour.

As I read the letters and diaries of Sophie and Hans Scholl, I followed with deepening emotion the physical details of their everyday lives; I tried to retrace the road by which they arrived at their convictions. Along with their crucially important religious experiences, this road was marked, from childhood, by books and writers. Their obsession with literature, the earnestness with which they both drew intellectual nourishment from books which at the time, of course, were mostly forbidden, are bound to ease any doubts I may feel about whether other people can glean meaning from a writer's efforts to write out of his own innermost truth. A glaring example comes to mind of the ambivalent uses of literary texts, of how they can be misinterpreted and made to serve ends which they were never meant to serve. I remember how when we were fourteen our German teacher enlisted the line from Goethe, "Defy all powers to hold what's ours," to support National Socialism. The Scholls read a very different meaning into the same line and made it one of their slogans. Hans Scholl etched it on the wall of his death cell.

People are not aware enough, I believe, of the profound effect which the experience of Russia had on Hans Scholl and Alexander Schmorell. Scholl drew a parallel between Goethe and Dostoevsky and recognized that German poets and German culture needed to be defended from the Nazis, too. I would like to quote a note dated November 1941 in which he recorded his vision of what Germany would be like after the war:

> War will make us all very poor . . . To begin with, hunger and misery will not stir from our sides; people from destroyed cities, destroyed countries, destroyed and half-exterminated races will scour the rubble for indestructible diamonds buried there.
>
> Yet we do not ask that this cup may pass from us. We shall drink it to the dregs. Our enemies are not destined to be slain by roof tiles falling from above, or to vanish off the earth. Instead, they should collapse completely from their own incapacity and suffocate in their own mire.
>
> Only in this way will it be impossible for a false glorification of history to take place in the future.

The enemies Hans Scholl refers to did indeed suffer a complete military defeat; but hasn't a "false glorification" of them taken place here anyway, in certain circles? And doesn't it flare up again and again, because of a failure thoroughly to dispel the identification many Germans feel with National Socialism? Isn't there a danger that the younger generation may experience this identification? This is why I feel concerned when I see the attempts to muffle and obstruct the legacy left to us by the German resistance against Fascism, and if possible to wipe it out of the consciences of those who were present, and out of the consciousness of their children—by trying to make the unique crimes [of Fascism] look similar to other crimes; by mixing up cause and effect; and by condemning a straightforward anti-Fascist view of history.

In the GDR, we have worked from the start to promote an anti-Fascist attitude, for reasons of state, and not unsuccessfully. But I believe that at a certain point the government, in which many former resistance fighters occupied and still occupy positions of leadership, relieved our citizens of their compelling need to confront their own share in the guilt of the Nazi years, by delegating the past to the other German state. Also, my observations of young people lead me to fear that they regard portrayals of National Socialism as an empty ritual. There is in the GDR no actual movement to treat German Fascism as innocuous. During the past few years, we have even overcome our biased tendency to acknowledge only those German resistance fighters whose political attitudes were similar to ours, while ignoring groups with a different line of thought. Public tribute is now paid to the men of the 20th of July, the members of the Weisse Rose. I would just like to ask: Are members of the substantial Communist resistance movement similarly honored in the Federal Republic of West Germany?

Why have I brought up this subject? After their return from the Soviet Union, where they had served as soldiers, Hans Scholl and Alexander Schmorell began to forge links with other resistance circles and groups in Germany. They met Falk Harnack, the brother of Arvid Harnack, a member of the largely Communist resistance group Rote Kapelle.* One of the leaflets printed and distributed by the Weisse Rose may have been influenced by this meeting with Harnack. It says: "Don't believe the Nazi propaganda which pumps you full of the fear of Bolshevism!" Soon after that, the first members of the Weisse Rose were tracked down, captured, murdered. A germ cell of hope for the future was crushed.

"Unhappy is the land which has need of heroes," Brecht said. That line has come into my mind over and over as I discovered Sophie and Hans Scholl's zest for life, their capacity for friendship and love, their devotion to nature, to art, but also to insignificant everyday chores, to work in general. These young people had a rich, full life to fight for, a life they loved. It was the others who craved death: the ones who killed them, and whose humanity had been gravely injured. I am afraid that the industrial societies we live in force on many people a way of life which deprives them of this zest for life, this ability to love, and thus manipulate them into substitute needs which then can be satisfied, on the most mindless level, by the techniques of politicians, the media, and the consumer industry.

Naturally, I wonder how I, as a writer, can help to develop different, more productive needs of the kind which arise only in

---

* Rote Kapelle [Red Chapel] was the name given by the Gestapo to several anti-Fascist groups operating in Germany and the occupied countries. The groups were destroyed in 1941–42.

emotionally independent people who think critically and act responsibly. I am very concerned about what may be causing the destructive tendencies in our civilization. What Hitler wanted and did not fully achieve—the destruction of Europe—could perhaps be achieved today. But above all I want to hunt for alternatives to these steps toward ruin, however frail the alternatives may be, however utopian they may appear.

There is a lot of talk right now about "the new thinking," a phrase which is in danger of degenerating into a catch phrase. I would like to take the idea seriously. Not so many historic opportunities are left to us that we can afford to throw one away. For me, the new thinking is not, in its essence, economic, technical, or military in character; in fact, it is not any kind of pragmatic thinking, but is a challenge thoroughly to review the goals and values of our culture, to give the Western world an extra chance, by means of a spiritual, ethical concept. The little circle of Munich students who gathered around Hans Scholl arrived at that same conclusion in the 1940s, starting from a different vantage point.

I believe that we are at a critical moment in history, because hard-line positions and images of enemies are dissolving today, releasing fear and aggressiveness in groups and people whose stability depended on holding on to clearly defined camps. Those who try to mediate must prepare to be greeted with hatred and insults. But this is not the place to talk about all that. Prudent but undeterred, we should work with others in the society where we live, to bring about, as far as we are able, the changes needed to keep this earth habitable for the next thousand years. I regard my book as one voice in a greater dialogue which we must carry on despite all the doubts that assail us again and again.

In one of Hans Scholl's last letters, I came across some sentences which moved me. He writes: "For I still feel a certain aversion to writing. In conversation, by contrast, what one person says calls on the other to answer, and from question and statement, the other person's inner mental structure soon takes shape, becoming visible before our very eyes. —I expect you have already heard about the circle I have gathered together here. You would enjoy these faces, if you could see them. All the energy one expends in their direction flows back into one's own heart, undiminished . . ."

We know what "circle" he is referring to. These lines had a very personal meaning for me. Don't we all long to relate to each other in such a human way? And rediscover our own joy in the faces of others?

Thank you. The money part of this prize will go to a Chilean woman, Carmen Gloria Quintana. On July 2, 1986, during a strike in Santiago de Chile, she was beaten by security forces working for Pinochet's military junta, who then poured gasoline over her and set her on fire. Her male companion died of his injuries. She is now in Canada, recovering her health as far as that is possible.

November 1987

Pleading the Case:

Two Speeches for the Defense

Dear Fellow Writers:

Owing to other obligations, I am unable to attend the Writers' Congress, but I would like to convey, at least in synopsis form in this letter, the main points which I would otherwise have discussed in more detail.

In the last few years, the germs of a new way of thinking have come out of socialist countries, and from them derived the first concrete steps toward disarmament, the first grounds for hope for a livable future. Many of our writer colleagues recognize the significance of these processes. They are reflecting on novel forms of behavior, reexamining old positions, and wish to contribute to changes which would make relations among GDR authors more open, make literary life more open, and make literature more effective. In the history of the East German Writers' Union, events have occurred which I believe we must confront so that our work may become more productive. I am referring to what happened after petitions were signed in protest of the expatriation of Wolf Biermann in 1976,* and to the fact that a number of our colleagues were unjustifiably expelled from the Writ-

---

* West German songwriter and performer who moved to the GDR in 1953, where he sang and wrote ballads of social criticism. Although an avowed supporter of socialism, he was forbidden to perform in the GDR after 1965 and was expatriated in 1976 after a guest concert in Cologne.

ers' Union in 1979. Everyone who knows me knows that I have kept up my objection to these measures and have not modified it. At the time, I tried to ensure that comparable measures would be taken against those in the opposite political camp, on the grounds of equal entitlement. When I realized that this was not possible in the Writers' Union, I gave up my participation, explaining my reasons in a letter to the executive committee.

Ten years have passed since then. A large number of writers, among them writers of stature, have left the GDR. Younger writers have followed them, in part because the Writers' Union was not able to incorporate them into its ranks. I could not, and did not wish to, grow accustomed to this. I feel the absence of friends, of partners in dialogue and work; I miss their participation in our intellectual life, even where I do not share their attitudes. I am not speaking of those who chose to leave the GDR as enemies. I am speaking of the writers—not just the ones who left, but those who stayed, too—who have experienced conflicts, painful disappointments, and restrictions, and who up to now have seen hardly a trace of sympathy or of a willingness to begin a dialogue on the part of the organization whose duty it was to represent them. But, above all, I am speaking of the young writers who remain outside the Writers' Union, either because they have not been admitted or because they have found no place there for the open discussion of their problems.

Many things have changed in the past few years in the policy of publishing firms and in the media. The works of writers who formerly lived in the GDR and then moved to the West are being published here, or plans to publish them are under way. Isn't it time for the Writers' Union to lend stronger support to these encouraging starts? The first thing we must do to normalize relations with our colleagues who have left the GDR is to seek a dialogue with everyone who desires it. I believe it is the Union's task, if we are to keep step with the times, to air present and past problems frankly and thoroughly, and to investigate the causes of conflicts. Its proper concern is not to exclude but to include young critical writers. The valid requirements for the publication of literary works should be Brecht's: unrestricted publication, with the limitations we all know and approve.

The Reader and the Writer

Speech at the District Assembly of Berlin Writers,

March 1988

Dear Fellow Writers:

The thoughts which I would like to express here today begin with the letter I wrote to the Writers' Union. Probably the executive committee interpreted my letter as some kind of attack or provocation. Otherwise, I could hardly explain their obstinate resistance to having it read aloud, or the fact that Hermann Kant used more than double the time it took to read the letter to wage a polemic against the way it was sent to the Congress. This polemic, which certainly was spectacular and in my opinion demagogic in parts, achieved its purpose: to divert attention from the contents of my letter. It failed to convince me.

I was unable to be present at the Congress—that was no ruse. I did not and do not consider it arrogant or undemocratic that I chose to express certain thoughts in a letter. I did not anticipate that the letter would be regarded as sensational; that was not my intention. I will say no more about it. And since neither Hermann Kant nor Günter de Bruyn can be here today, it would be wrong to discuss the point any further.

What I wanted—and what I still want today—is to bring up incidents in the history of the Writers' Union which we are in danger of forgetting and which, in my opinion, are making it hard or completely impossible for us to do productive work in the present. Or isn't it part of the Union's history that since 1976 relatively large numbers of writers have left the GDR—some of them major authors, others little known or not at all, some members of the Union and some nonmembers? I have seen no public evidence that the East German Writers' Union recognizes or has even thought about the significance of this kind of event for a country, for a literature, for a professional union of writers; what the judgment of history will be, and what responsibility must be borne by those who deliberately choose to stay here, to work and to have an influence here. For a long time I have waited in vain to hear expressions of shock and grief at the loss of colleagues. I have waited especially for some collective reflection, a penetrating analysis of the causes of the resignation and despondency which in many cases preceded a writer's decision to leave the GDR.

Just the opposite has happened. In some cases the Union has actually encouraged writers to leave by expelling its members. Then, when the Berlin District Union met to vote—by the way, this was one of the things that moved me to write my letter to the Congress—

Hermann Kant spoke, for the first time as far as I know, about what happened in June 1979. He said: "The decision we made then, that a number of our colleagues should leave us, should be expelled—that doesn't have to be forever, of course." I noticed that more than a few of our members did not really seem to know what he was referring to. Some of those who were present [at the expulsion] have suffered a remarkable loss of memory, and those who were not present are completely uninformed about what went on. Hermann Kant used metaphors to paraphrase the facts: "We waged a life-and-death struggle here—for literary life and literary death. We experienced our own defeats and other people's. We bled inside." This chapter in the Union's history can perhaps be described in more sober and concrete terms. This is how I experienced it: In June 1979 the Berlin Writers' Union, in a disastrous meeting, voted by a large majority to expel nine of its members—unjustly, in my opinion, and in the opinion of some other members. The opposition votes were not counted, even though an express motion was made that they should be. Stephan Hermlin, who warned us against this mass expulsion, said at the time (and I agreed with him): "This will not be the end of our worries, but the start of the next turn of the screw." (I will venture to say that, under the new district administration of the United Socialist Party, I suspect, a meeting conducted in the spirit and style of that one would be unthinkable. That meeting made it impossible for me to stay in the Union.)

Five of our nine expelled colleagues left the GDR: Kurt Bartsch, Karl-Heinz Jakobs, Klaus Poche, Klaus Schlesinger, Joachim Seyppel. Four are living here: Adolf Endler, Stefan Heym, Rolf Schneider, Dieter Schubert.

I would like to make some proposals to help ensure that the "outstretched hand" which Hermann Kant also spoke of does not remain an empty gesture. I can picture a number of things we might do:

Next month Stefan Heym will be seventy-five years old. The Writers' Union should take this occasion to reestablish relations by beginning a dialogue with him, with the aim of readmitting him to the Union. This could be done, provided that a majority votes in favor of the measure, at a plenary session of the Berlin Union. I ask that we not wait long before taking this corrective measure.

At the same time, conversations should take place with the other three writers I mentioned, with the same goal. I am aware that these individuals have undergone a different development in the intervening time and that therefore our conversations with them may produce different results. It seems important to me that the Union should approach them, not with the intention of abandoning our own convictions, but prepared to reexamine earlier viewpoints and to retract hard-line attitudes; ready to listen with an open mind, and also to accept criticism and, where it is possible and necessary, to learn.

My third suggestion is: the Writers' Union should also try to approach those of its former members who today live in the West. I am fully aware of the difficulties of taking such a step. But we cannot, in the books we write, demand that people dismantle their enemy images unless we begin to do the same in our own area of special concern. At a time when, in the long run, we are entirely dependent on mutual understanding and communication—no matter what frictions exist—when we are dependent on dialogue even between the proponents of contrary views, writers ought to be able to start talking again to former members of their own union. At the peace conference set in motion by Stephan Hermlin, initial approaches were made to a few writers, but these were not followed up, and the Writers' Union did not pursue them either. I believe I know some reasons for that, including some which were the responsibility of our departed colleagues and which made follow-up difficult. I stick to my suggestion, and I persist in saying that even in cases like these we must ask the cause of their behavior.

On the other hand, there have been some positive developments. Books by Jurek Becker and Klaus Schlesinger are being published by East German publishing houses. Books by Günter Kunert and Sarah Kirsch are due to be published here soon. Hans Mayer was recently allowed to speak in the German Theater [in East Berlin] and received the press attention the occasion deserved. The Writers' Union could take its lead from signals like these; indeed, it would be in the Union's own interest to do so.

I believe that relations between the writers' unions in the two Germanys depend on relaxing our relations with our former GDR colleagues who today are members of the Writers' Association in the Federal Republic. Even more important, it seems to me the business of the Writers' Union to know the details and to analyze the reasons why our colleagues left—because those I named have been followed by a train of younger writers in the past few years—and then to work to help eliminate these causes so that the exodus of talented people will stop. Nothing else this country could produce can ever replace them.

So I am pleading for a wide range of meetings and dialogue with colleagues who today live in the West and who are ready to meet with us—ready for an intensive exchange of experiences, for rapprochement.

95

The events I have spoken about here today lead me also to make a second plea. I entreat the Writers' Union to put persistent effort into changing the system for obtaining permission to print books in this country. It should be changed along the lines which Christoph Hein and Günter de Bruyn discussed at the Congress.

I also plead—by the same token as all the rest, although it really deserves thorough treatment on its own—that the Writers' Union turn its attention to the young writers of this country, get to know all about their development, their ethical views, literary goals, living conditions, conflicts and difficulties, and represent their interests effectively.

I can already hear people telling me that I keep harping on the same old stories. These old stories are part of our history, whether we set them in motion, participated, or remained passive. Nothing that we do or leave undone in our lives is without its consequences, and one day we cannot help having to confront them. The less we remember and work on the mistakes, conflicts, and contradictions of the past—especially the painful and shameful ones—the more risk we run, as individuals (and as institutions, societies, and nations), of sinking into stagnation, of becoming unproductive, in our present lives. Whenever we disapprove, exclude, and suppress the thoughts, suggestions, rebellion, and criticism of others, we repress them at the same time in ourselves. Part of our thoughts and feelings become taboo; our creativity is curtailed—in some cases, completely shut down. Most writers will know what I am talking about. I wish I could find the words and the tone of urgency to convince you that the same fate can befall an institution, and that the more integrated and open the Writers' Union becomes, the better equipped it will be to play a creative role in society, as befits the powers of its members.

ON

OTHER AUTHORS

—

The Truth You Can Expect:

The Prose of

Ingeborg Bachmann*

1

*On this darkening star we inhabit, at the point of becoming mute,
in retreat from growing madness, vacating heartlands, about to
depart from thoughts and taking leave of so many feelings, who
would not suddenly realize—if it rang out again, if it rang out
for him!—what that is: a human voice?*
    —INGEBORG BACHMANN, *Music and Poetry*

When you get ready to read this prose, you should not expect to find
stories, descriptions of actions, information about events; neither characters in the ordinary sense of the word nor loud assertions. You will
hear a voice: daring and lamenting. A voice that suits the truth, that
is: talking about what is certain and uncertain, on the basis of personal
experience. And a voice that truthfully goes silent when it doesn't
know what to say.

Neither speaking nor keeping silent without cause, without standing on the cause of hope or of despair. It has scorned lesser motives
for speaking.

Daring? Where shall we find it—in her admitted retreat from
superior odds? In her admitted powerlessness toward a world which
is growing more alien? In the admissions themselves? Definitely:
because she does not offer them routinely, easily, or willingly. But
even more, we find it in her resistance. She does not back down

---

* Austrian novelist, essayist, and poet (1926–73).

without a fight, she does not go mute without talking back, she does not leave the field in resignation. To acknowledge what is true—to make true what ought to be true. Literature has never been able to set its sights higher than that.

Lamentation? She does not lament for trivial things and she is never pathetic. She grieves for the speechlessness which lies ahead. For that breakdown of communication between literature and society which no honest writer in a bourgeois environment can overlook. For a future of remaining alone with words ("The word will only draw other words after it, sentence will draw sentence"). For the eerie temptation to let herself adapt, go blind, consent; to let habit, deception, and betrayal lure her into complicity with the deadly dangers which threaten the world.

Bravery? She is wounded but not defeated, grief-stricken but without self-pity, suffering but not in love with pain. We stand facing a battlefield, watching the forces assemble. Lyric poetry, prose, essays advance in the same direction: away from the unquestionable toward the questionable, away from the commonplace toward the unfamiliar, away from the noncommittal toward commitment and connection; away from the inexact toward the authentic. "Words, follow me!" A kind of battle cry, brave enough, dignified enough.

The poet as representative of his age? Ingeborg Bachmann, proud as well as modest, dares lay claim to that title. She is bound to cause offense because modern writers have largely renounced the pretension to represent others. She goes further. "The poet who wants to change things"—she says, as if it were an accepted instead of a hotly contested fact in her part of the world that the poet wants to change things: "How much is he at liberty to do and how much not?" In other words, is the poet in her time and in her country still master of the effects she aims to achieve? She has no illusions about this, she keeps her integrity: "There is no response but this fatal applause." No response. So, does that mean that the poet has spoken in vain? Is the apathy irretrievable now, after the "many playful shocks" which the public has been given for years? But if so, what would poetry have to be to destroy the apathy—before doing anything else?

2

*Poetry like bread? This bread would have to be ground between
the teeth and to reawaken hunger before appeasing it. And this
poetry will have to be acrid with knowledge and bitter with longing, to have the power to trouble people's sleep. For we are sleeping, we are sleepers, out of fear of having to look at ourselves
and our world.*
　　　　　—INGEBORG BACHMANN, *The Frankfurt Lectures*

To become seeing, to make others see: that is a basic theme in the
works of Ingeborg Bachmann. The poem "To the Sun," her lecture
"Man Is Someone from Whom You Can Expect the Truth," and the
narrative "What I Saw and Heard in Rome," all treat this theme. We
saw how *she* begins to see; how her eyes are opened, how it takes
her breath away. She draws pride from what she has been able to see
("the pride of him who in the darkness of the world does not give up
and does not stop seeing to it that things are put right"); draws joy,
too ("Nothing more beautiful under the sun than being under the
sun"), and insight: "I heard that there is more time in the world than
sense, but that our eyes are given us to see with."

Seeing, understanding, gazing into the heart of: "Because it's
time to have understanding of man's voice, the voice of a captive who
is not quite able to say what he suffers." The classical view, "a god
made me able to say how I suffer,"* is here annulled, questioned,
disputed without polemics. "Not quite able"—a phrase that records
a different, later experience, a basic experience for Ingeborg Bachmann. As a writer her duty is to add her own true experience to the
sum of experience which is already in the world. She has to keep
producing anew the courage to have her own experience and to assert
it against the overwhelming bulk and the demoralizing power of empty,
meaningless, and ineffectual phrases. Self-assertion is a basic impulse
behind her works—not in the passive sense of self-defense, but in
the active sense of self-expansion, of movement directed toward a
goal. And in the sense of confronting things head-on, of showing what
she is made of, including her weakness; taking blows, getting up
again, making another attack on the enemy's vital center while constantly at risk of a blow to her own vitals . . . Self-assertion as a
procedure, clearly depicted in the narrative piece "What I Saw and
Heard in Rome," which rather strangely she includes among her
essays. An experiment—but then you could describe all her work

* Scene V,5 of Goethe's *Torquato Tasso* (1790).

that way. An attempt to assimilate a city. To reconquer a sovereignty lost by giving in. To become her own master, by naming things. To try out once more the magic of the precise and vital word: does it really still have the power to bind and to loose?

"In Rome I saw that the Tiber is not beautiful but is unconcerned about its docks, from which riverbanks walk and no one lays his hand on them." The first sentence sets the tone. Devout sobriety. The pathos of description with the tensions kept inside. Sentences murmured to oneself, the kind that issue from a deep attentiveness to the outside world and a great lack of prejudice on the inside. The caution of the doubter, and the gripping precision of one who knows. Sentences which continually refer to facts in reality but never pretend to reproduce or replace the reality. And yet the new reality which they produce merits our attention. Within its own surprising frame of reference, it is the product of an indomitable and insatiable desire to examine the natural and social environment in the light of humane values. It is like a path which someone is struggling to cut through the jungle: the naked wilderness of unthought reality keeps closing in ahead and behind him.

But this new reality remains intact: not injured by haste or by slowness, not by arrogance or by faintness. She focuses on it her reflective gaze, tolerant but not all-forgiving. Compelling but not obtrusive. A gaze which appears to dissolve what is rigid and all-too-solid, and to shore up the seemingly frail: "They sleep where the plane trees have pitched them a shadow and they pull the sky up over their heads." The words "poverty" and "freedom" are not needed to convey the feeling that these people are poor and endowed with the gift and right of freedom. The narrator-observer allows herself the liberty of sympathy so as to communicate and to share with us. The most intense subjectivity but not a hint of caprice—not even the caprice of compassion or exuberance—instead a genuineness rich with tension.

Elegy and hymn—lyrical categories typifying an attitude—both apply to her reality. Often, both can be found on the same page. Not excluding each other but not blending either. The old people in the Rome ghetto "remember their friends whose lives were bought with an equal weight of gold. When they had been ransomed the trucks drove up anyhow, and they did not come back." Then when her gaze rises: "I saw, where Rome's streets come out, the triumphal entry of the sky into the city." What merits praise is praised without breaching the gesture of measured, concentrated communication. There is no self-imposed demand to be spare. You could say this prose is "mood-drenched" if the word had not too often been used as a synonym for "vague." But here "mood" comes out of concrete relationships, it is produced before our eyes in the way the narrator's sensuousness links up to the sensuous glow of the city and the way she refrains from linking up to the city's wounds and the crimes it commits or allows. Overall, it takes the form of consent to Rome's miraculous existence.

Miraculously, too, the city *needs* the consent of this visitor, this inhabitant: lives off it. The magnificent courage and the matter-of-factness of the woman who enters the city is submerged in it, allows everything to happen that can happen to her here, does not close her eyes even when she feels like looking away; who resurfaces, knowing that this is just a breather, a spell in which to make sure of the ground under her feet. She stands there simply saying "I," without conceit, but holding her head high. The attitude of this person, the writer, makes her prose what it is, makes it concrete and yearning, keeps its tricky balance between demand and fulfillment, between reality and vision.

We see, too, that vision is not something to be ashamed of; it is nothing frivolous or contrived but rather is the sign that the writer's work on her material is completed—because the sign does not appear if the work has bogged down halfway or even one step before the goal. "Vision!" people scoff: "What's that, vision?" Suddenly we see what cannot be seen but must be there because it produces effects. We see the past within the present, for instance. Or the boundless desires we always suppress, which can gush out in anyone at any moment, though no one knows where they come from ("But dew falls around three in the morning. If only one could lie awake there letting it moisten one's lips!"). But, above all, vision means seeing the unity and meaning behind seemingly unrelated and meaningless events. The discovery of what animates them all, and of what really is destroying them—regardless of what they may pretend.

Serious and honest visions are the stuff from which every city makes its future, for by nature it depends on what is living and viable. It is dependent on the sleeping workers on the balustrades, the old people in the ghetto, the shouting market women; the child washing cups in the bar or the people saying goodbye to each other at Termini; and the boy who fishes out the coins at night from the fountain where they were thrown by departing travelers. Every one of these people is completely real, and more than real: visionary. For their sake and with their help, the visitor can ward off the feeling of destruction which comes over her in the city, and can ward off the temptation to be irresponsible which goes along with knowledge of her powerlessness. Both are parried and denied, if only for the duration of these pages. Instead, what emerges is the person of the visitor, who is not

miserly with the city and with nature and who greets their challenge
with her own claim to dignity.

3

*But change is indeed possible. And the transforming effect of
new works educates us to new perception, new feeling, new consciousness.*
———INGEBORG BACHMANN, *The Frankfurt Lectures*

Ingeborg Bachmann knows that "literature cannot be composed outside the historical situation." The historical situation is such that all
literature must have at its heart the question of man's possible moral
existence. This question is a major impulse behind Bachmann's prose.
Often it appears in bizarre disguises and is not immediately recog-
nizable. It can take the form of a subjective reflex, of fear, doubt,
the sense of menace: "Hanging on to the high-voltage current of the
present."

Ingeborg Bachmann is not a natural-born storyteller, if by that
you mean someone who can tell stories spontaneously, forgetting
herself while she does it. She does not report cases but reflects about
cases—about the "borderline case which lurks in every case." She
is true to the lyric poet in her. In her poetry, too, she reveals a person
who deserves to be known to future generations—because she is
willing and able to endure the conflicts of our own time.

From poetry to prose, another medium for the same questions.
"And in future let us ask them in a way that demands our commitment
again." It may be that she wanted the greater commitment of working
in prose as a chance to combat the flagrantly prosaic banality of her
own surroundings. She may feel the urge to overcome banality by
writing. Composition, a taut plot, an intricate dramatic construction,
stories in the strict sense, do not come her way. Behind her prose,
as behind her poetry, lies the compulsion to speak, a need which is
genuine and which legitimates her work. Often you will look in vain
for the depiction of concrete situations and social processes. These
are stories of feelings.

Like every writer, Ingeborg Bachmann is tortured by the problem
of truth, of how to tell the truth. Is it enough to "say exactly what
happened"? In the Wildermuth story, where there is a play of pronouns
from "he" to "you" to "I," she dissects the failure of an attempt to
replace truth with morbid exactness and a delirium of detail. Judge
Wildermuth, clearly entangled with the figure of the narrator, goes

to the ultimate limit of doubt after realizing that he has lost the stable criteria he once had. No longer knowing what is true, judging it impossible to find the truth, he finally loses his faith in its value: "But will truth enable me to move ahead? Where? To Buxtehude, to what's behind things, behind the curtains, to heaven, or just to behind the seven mountains? . . . I don't want to have to travel those distances, because I stopped believing long ago."

The story of a disillusionment which takes away the power of movement: paralysis through the seemingly inevitable loss of faith. A miniature model of an event which is typical in the lives of the bourgeois intelligentsia of this century, magnified by self-torment to the point of asking an absolute question. The only way out—action linked to the real processes of society—seems barred by a hopelessness which feeds nonstop off the alienation she feels when she observes real events. The circle is closed.

Ingeborg Bachmann, deeply conscious of the tradition to which she belongs, and of the range of problems she can draw on and to which she remains bound, is so convincingly, radically, and uniquely affected by her experience that she never seems to cover ground already covered by others. She does not play with despair, menace, and anguish: she *is* desperate, *is* menaced and anguished, and consequently truly wishes to be saved. The symptoms she presents—the pounding, the attempts to escape—are genuine. The efforts she makes spare neither others nor herself.

She is someone, a lyrical existence, who converts her inner experience into a theme of her prose, and who thus is compelled to return again and again to the problem of the writer in our times, as she has experienced it. She knows all the repetitive phrases about the doubtfulness of the writer's role in late bourgeois society, about the decline of literature to a moneymaking enterprise, about the allegedly inevitable compulsion of modern-day authors to rehash outworn styles and themes. She has tested it all. But she resists the temptation to give way to it and so succumb to self-deception. She goes back to asking simple questions: What is the point of writing, since "there is no longer a commission from on high and in fact there are no more commissions and none deceives people any longer. What to write for, for whom to express one's thoughts, and what is there to say to people in this world?"

She understands the guilt feelings, the self-accusations, the "leaps into silence," and even into death, which afflict writers of the past and present. She knows the pain when the world is not tuned in to the same note as oneself. She accepts these experiences but does not consent to them. Neither arrogance, snobbery, nor the purely formal pseudo-revolt now in fashion is a possible response for her. Cynicism—the razing of faith right down to the roots—is ruled out, too. Her essays record, more strongly than her prose fiction, her determination to resist: "If we put up with this 'L'art pour l'art' attitude, if we accept this insult which stands for all the rest—and if writers tolerate it and promote it by a lack of seriousness, and by deliberately breaking down their communication with society which is always fragile anyway—and if society avoids literature when it shows a serious, disruptive spirit that wants change—it would be tantamount to our declaring bankruptcy."

She defends "heartlands" rather than outlying districts. Man's claim to self-realization. His right to individuality and personality development. His longing for freedom. "Hungrier for knowledge, interpretation, and meaning" than others are, she is angry at the contrast between her life and the more easygoing, perhaps more colorful but run-of-the-mill existence of the plain citizen. As a young man, Thomas Mann could still feel nostalgia for the "blisses of the commonplace," but in this century these have turned into starting bases and preserves of crime which no longer attract us. Without doubt, the individual is exhausted by his revolt against the technological perfection of barbarous banality which is the only goal left in a capitalist society: "one performing-animal act on top of another." Revolt is exhausting due to the feeling of being an outsider, and to the suspicion that one has become an anachronism, which sometimes afflicts Bachmann.

And so the names and faces of the characters get lost, all the men are named "Moll," their behavior is stereotyped, it is no longer worthwhile to invent individuals to carry out the meager functions which remain to them. When the writer is left so alone, his normal exertion to keep penetrating new and harder areas of reality and to win them for consciousness turns to overexertion; the necessary tension between his abilities and the demands of his work turns to strain. His radical claim to freedom, if cut off from any corresponding movement in society, turns into a gnawing desire for an absolute, boundless, and unreal freedom. His complete despair about how to take the next few steps makes him lodge illusional demands: we must "found a new world" by "breaking up everything that now exists." And any move to abandon this radical position and to return to normal activities and attitudes is felt to be giving in to the enemy or—as in Bachmann's story "The Thirtieth Year"—it looks unmotivated, baseless: "I tell you: Stand up and walk! Not one of your bones is broken!" Self-confidence, which is a prerequisite of life, here becomes the product of solitary struggle.

Weariness of civilization and the doubt of progress are most intensely expressed in the story "Undine Goes." We see man totally alienated from himself and his species, and a romantic protest against this. The story is romantic not only in adopting the character Undine from Fouqué's fairy tale* but in its attitude, in the contrast it draws between bland utilitarian thinking and a "spirit appointed to no use." A spirit whose proper destiny would have been to be put to some humane use, to help with the understanding of "time and death."

An end-of-the-world feeling—yes. But no resignation. Again and again we see her faith in man, touching because it vastly intensifies vulnerability. Even Undine, female accuser of the masculine world who speaks with the thinly disguised voice of the female author, believes "absolutely" "that men are more than their weak, vain utterances, their shabby actions, their foolish insinuations." But she is condemned to say "you," to separate herself, to go away. She can see no way to put up a fight and so she retreats from the unreasonable demands of society in the hope of being able to preserve herself. But this kind of retreat invariably ends in giving up the self, because separation from society eats away at the individual's inner powers of resistance.

She makes attempts to escape. In the short story "Among Murderers and Madmen"—the prose work which comes closest to a concrete portrayal of relationships within society—Bachmann questions the meaning of sacrifice and consequently the meaning of resistance. The young male narrator is a perplexed, searching, fed-up individual, troubled by the frequent changes he has seen in social values: "Right after 1945, I also thought the world had been divided into good and evil for all time; but it keeps on being divided over and over and it comes out different each time." He is voicing a basic experience of his generation: the eerie resurrection of reactionary powers. But he no longer seems willing to feel surprised, confused, and "on no one's side but the victims'" over and over each time a new change comes. "That gets us nowhere, they don't show us a way." Apparently he is able to imagine the possibility of taking someone else's side, giving up his attitude of defenselessness, looking for a way within society, a concrete way, therefore governed by the laws of concrete reality. We see just a hint, a cautious question asked along the borders of that zone which cannot be changed by literature alone . . .

The intellectual achievement of Ingeborg Bachmann—one might almost say her human achievement—is most evident in her steadfast desire to bring about change. In her determination not to adapt herself

---

* Undine, the female water sprite, tried to acquire a human soul by marrying a mortal.

to "medium temperatures," not to allow everything to be "reduced to a question of giving in, of consenting." In her search for a "new language," for a "thought which aims at understanding and wants to achieve something with and through language: provisionally let's call it reality."

4

But a few drank the cup of hemlock unconditionally.
      —INGEBORG BACHMANN, "The Thirtieth Year"

She no longer sees any hope of change within the "framework of what is given." At this point she must ask to what extent she herself, as a writer, can be anything but an institution within this very same society which is in need of change. Is she not condemned to participate in educating people "half for dog-eat-dog practice and half for the theory of morality"? This is the most ruthless and terrible question a writer can ask herself. If the answer keeps going against her, it may give her cause to turn silent, especially if the solution to this cardinal question depends not on the writer alone but on social changes which would give her work a new basis and herself a new responsibility.

Ingeborg Bachmann has no hope of this type of change. She has never been able to attach herself to a progressive historical movement. Instead, she tends to exit from society—or lets her characters exit from it, to learn in despairing isolation the terms which their society dictates to the individual, to find out the price of just staying alive, which has to be paid a million times over. "But a few drank the cup of hemlock unconditionally." A few could not be bought, seduced, or blackmailed; they preferred the death of self-surrender so that they could go on living in their times and help shape the future. Ingeborg Bachmann apparently means to imitate their moral example. She seems to see it as the task of her writing to stand by their side.

Literature as a moral institution, the writer as the champion of new moral impulses which are struggling to express themselves in his times. She has to project herself forward into pleasure and pain, she has to go to the limit, and her distinguishing feature is the way she "takes a direction, is hurled onto a course to which nothing accidental in words or things can gain access anymore."

But the strictness and integrity of this idea does not hide the fact that the larger frame of reference within which the courses of individuals, however daring, alone have value remains undefined, probably unthought-of. Literature as utopia. But whose utopia? Utopia based on what real foundation? She offers a brave and deeply moving design for a new type of human being. But it is a solitary design, and gives no hint of the real steps to be taken to remove herself from the misery of the present, toward this vision of the future. Is there never anything more than the mind's own self-impelled movement?

Bachmann's writing enables us to arrive at these questions—questions which involve us deeply. But she herself seems to be totally surrounded by them. She occupies an embattled outpost of bourgeois literature today, in her attempt to defend humanistic values against the all-embracing destructive drive of late capitalist society. In our experience, the writer cannot escape from this encirclement on her own, not exclusively through literature. To challenge bourgeois society with all its questionable aspects requires first of all that one break out of the "framework of what is given." Only then—only on a new social foundation—can we really begin the "defense of poesy."

We read the prose of Ingeborg Bachmann through the filter of these experimental truths. Her prose is serious and genuine, and thus may gain an added dimension from our reading it this way which the author herself could not have foreseen. Because every reader helps write a book while he reads it. And Ingeborg Bachmann is one of those authors who expressly depend on the collaboration of their readers. She demands and she fulfills the demand to be contemporary.

December 1966

Shift of Meaning:

Thomas Mann

———

"What is it? Where are we? Whither has the dream snatched us? Twilight, rain, filth. Fiery glow of the overcast sky."* The scene, of course, is "the flat-land, it is the war," where, as we all know, we find Hans Castorp, "the genial sinner," undergoing his baptism of fire. Why did I feel shocked recently when a woman I am close to told me that at age eighteen, when she was a prisoner in Auschwitz, Thomas Mann of all writers had helped her to survive? She had adopted a line from the end of *The Magic Mountain* which said something like "It is not so important whether he survives." Filled with the realization that one must not regard oneself as so very important, she was able to look calmly—that is the word she used, "calmly"—at the small openings in the showerhead of the camp washroom while she waited to see which would come out: water or poison gas?

Thomas Mann could not have written that sentence, and in the meantime, of course, she had realized it, too. Together she and I hunted for the lines which she had adapted for her own purposes: "Farewell—and if thou livest or diest! Thy prospects are poor . . . we should not care to set a high stake on thy life by the time it ends. We even confess that it is without great concern that we leave the question open."

So it is true; once Castorp has served his purpose, the storyteller sends him out rather coolly into the chaos of battle while he himself, "shamed by the security of our shadowdom," does not share with his

* English from *The Magic Mountain* (New York: Alfred A. Knopf, 1977).

110

protagonist the latter's final, uttermost experience. He excuses himself by saying that he was "merely led hither by the spirit of our narrative," which can only mean by a rigorous and remorseless professional curiosity. It is unnecessary to point out that, since then, places have come into being which fundamentally resist the spirit of narrative and which absolutely prohibit the storyteller—who may have been snatched there by a dream but not in reality—to tell about them.

Nevertheless, it startled and deeply troubled me to see how, in just such a place as this, a Jewish girl raised on humanistic literature was forced to make so upside down a use of her education. That, under the fiery glow of the overcast sky, the interest in the individual, in his life and actions, which had been refined over centuries should shift into its opposite: into a strict lack of interest in oneself—as the precondition for physical and mental survival. The individual is not so important.

If this tale has a moral which can be put into words, then the moral is definitely *not* that a narrative writer ought to be indifferent to the individual. Instead, it is just the opposite: it behooves the writer to help bring about conditions which will create and compel the interest of the individual, in himself and in the rest of his species.

1974

Max Frisch, a Rereading, or: On Writing in the First Person*

At bottom, everything we write these days is nothing but a desperate self-defense which goes on continually and inevitably at the cost of truthfulness; for anyone who remained fundamentally truthful would never come back once he entered chaos—unless he had first transformed it.

In between, lies only the untruthful.

—MAX FRISCH, 1946

Assuming

that Frisch is right when he says: "Our effort, seemingly, is directed toward expressing all that is sayable." Assuming that every author is intent on perfection: that to become authentic in whatever way is possible to him is the goal of the devotions he takes on with his entrance into literature. Assuming this desire to be so fervent that it does not allow him to choose a less precarious existence: *then* the question is, What type of injury is it—what is the specific nature of the contradiction—which drives out of him that series of works which eventually we are compelled to call his "work"? Max Frisch considers it a sort of duty to inform us about his case.

"This is not the time for stories in the first person. And yet

---

* Reference is made to the following Frisch books: *Mein Name sei Gantenbein* (1964); *Gantenbein* (New York, Harcourt Brace Jovanovich, 1965); *Homo Faber* (1957), *Homo Faber* (New York: Harcourt Brace Jovanovich, 1971); *Tagebuch 1946–1949* (1950), *Sketchbook: 1946–1949* (New York: Harcourt Brace Jovanovich, 1977); *Tagebuch 1966–1971* (1972), *Sketchbook: 1966–1971* (New York: Harcourt Brace Jovanovich); and *Stiller* (1954), *I'm Not Stiller* (New York: Vintage Books, 1958).

human life makes or breaks itself in the individual, and nowhere else." Frisch is an author with the luck to have experienced personally a fundamental conflict of our times, and to be able to express it, while at the same time intensifying and making it comprehensible. This is the reason for his impact. His readers believe they find themselves mirrored in his books. I doubt that. Frisch's prose has a dimension which lies outside and beyond the plots it narrates. Bent on finding and concealing himself, he advances on himself from two directions, using language as a precision tool, with ever-increasing relentlessness. First, he hides the most personal of material in "fictional" stories, which as time goes on are less and less often fully worked out and more frequently left as mere sketches. Second, in his diaries he voices factual, political material, "the world." It goes without saying that the division was never absolute. But almost all his fictitious prose works are written in the first person. In his diaries, the word "I" becomes a rarity. No protagonist of his novels is a match for the "I" of the diaries, in spiritual range and cool command: they are obviously captured by their own egos, whereas the "I" of the diaries can also appear as "he," as "you," as "she." The author neither could nor wanted to invent a character who would be on a par with himself. "I would not want to be the self who lives my stories."

Frisch would not say that in his own person it is the character Gantenbein who says it, a man whose life consists in stories he imagines. Another of Frisch's characters, Homo Faber from the novel of that name and a Swiss like Frisch himself, is led by a chain of accidents to become the lover of his daughter, born, without his knowing, out of his affair with a German Jewess: a plot design which never really appealed to me much. In Frisch's diary we read "Reminiscence: 1936, when I wanted to marry a student from Berlin, a Jewess . . ." This, as a trial run for the impenetrable tangle of invention and biography, narrative and diary which makes up the roughly two thousand pages of Frisch's prose, gave me something to think about as I reread it all.

There is a peculiar logical consistency in the way Frisch makes the two lines of his work converge. Doesn't it stand to reason that a man who in fiction never stops "looking for the story of his experience" must one day stand before his own real history unveiled; that everything will be possible once again; that he will be free as he was at the outset, to define his authenticity however he chooses, and that he will test it now by how he masters the story of his own experience? The dislike of invention as a way of making things easy on oneself can grow to the point where it takes over completely and self-esteem depends on confronting one's readers face to face. "The writer can later find himself compelled to use a naked 'I' form, not because he now considers himself more important as a person, but because his disguise is used up," writes one of the He's in the diary.

His opposite temptation is that of complete disguise. "I think I might like to write fairy tales," he says in one of his letters.

Supposing

that an author makes the success of his life and of his work dependent on each other almost from the start. His confession that he practices his profession because he is "more successful at writing than at life" should be taken quite literally. He tells us that although other possibilities were open to him, he had to begin writing because this activity united the two conditions which at the time were necessary to his life: "to atone and to work." His deepest longing (he says) is not to produce a masterwork—though that, too, of course—but to stay alive. The compulsion to self-revelation clashes (he says) with a contrary impulse to shame. Forced into perpetual confession, he never enjoys the liberating feeling of absolution because his consciousness of sin is swiftly renewed. Though he strives fervently to be truthful, keen self-observation teaches him how to be "truthful to the point of exhibitionism, so as to avoid touching on the single sore point." He claims to suffer continually from the "basic fear of not measuring up." Directed toward himself, he nevertheless feels compelled to move out of the position in which he finds himself.

"Grand themes" are barred from his prose—his most intimate means of expression—for reasons of honesty: he has no experience of them. He claims that he only gradually learned to accept the writer's *social* responsibility, as a result, he says, of his success. By nature not inclined to represent political views, the citizen of a traditionally neutral country, and born in 1911, he did not join a political movement, yet felt a desperate yearning for purity which virtually ruled out political action and feared that trend to institutionalization which is inherent in all organizations; and so he was unable to attach himself to any political movement. He tries, I think, to learn to live without alternatives. "I regard the choices imposed on us at the moment as obsolete, that is, as unsuccessful" (Kürmann). And yet he lives a life of asking questions ("I ask," he says often); that is, he does not live without trust. His questions burgeon into urgent questionnaires: perhaps signs of his hope of contacting other questioners. This would seem to be his way of finding meaning. He can understand history and individual stories only as the sum of events and facts ("That's just how it is") and not as the outward form taken by an innate meaning put into them by God or by nature. And yet his attitude to life is not absurd or tragic.

He is no man of extremes but inhabits a zone of skepticism bordering on resignation; but out of shyness or embarrassment he does not allow himself to express this resignation openly ("Why are signs of resignation always indiscreet?")—and out of modesty, too: Who am I that I should be allowed to express resignation? His doubt is sincere: one of the things he doubts is his own competence.

Early in life he realized that "there is no more *terra incognita* for us today" (a feeling, by the way, which is not likely to be shared by authors in socialist countries whose predominant emotion is that they are no match for all that is unseen and unsaid)—"except Russia," he added parenthetically, because at that time he had not yet traveled in the Soviet Union. And so he felt compelled to ask: "So what is the point of storytelling?!"

As he works—as he writes, that is—Frisch then answers his question: The point of storytelling is to relate to his own existence—which among other things is a literary existence—and which he never forgets is a dubious enterprise that deserves his questioning. Down through the decades, the two lines of his prose are linked together by what amounts almost to a self-betrayal: by his repeated attempts to formulate his pain, which is a pain of discrepancy between his need to live a real life—that is, to experience reality—and the experience of a loss of reality, the draining of actuality into abstraction. Alienation—a feeling with which presumably he was familiar long before he met the word for it—is the root of that private drama to which he devotes all his "novels" and "tales": A man—a male person—feels deprived of experience; suffers a lack of connection, an inability to love and be loved; suffers an unbridgeable estrangement from other people, from women, whom he keeps at a distance by way of fear, guilt, adoration, jealousy.

Life as an "event without a present. What we can experience is anticipation or memory." The insoluble paradox: he can be authentic only when he is expressing his basic experience, which is the inability to be authentic.

The storyteller gives his attention to the "tension between statements." To him, "belles lettres" is a term of abuse.

Most of the heroes he invents die premature deaths.

The longest passage in a foreign language that he inserts into his 1966–71 diary comes from *The New York Times* and is about the right to die with dignity, about euthanasia.

He can compile lists of the circumstances and people he has

tried to repress; of the people he is grateful to; catalogues of life's beauties.

Morally speaking, he has too much sense of justice to despair.

"What if one day he gets the feeling that he has said what he is capable of saying?" If the compulsion to self-disclosure and the compulsion to stay silent should balance each other out within a conscience finally at rest, one possible result would be speechlessness. The strain demanded of the author is undertaken partly out of moral conviction.

Deprived

of almost all the media and mediations found in the literature of the past, this author is forced to set himself at risk directly. Admittedly, that is claiming a lot, maybe too much, for he says that "anyone who remained fundamentally truthful would never come back once he entered chaos—unless he had first transformed it." Consequently, he does not succeed in risking everything—that is, in risking his life, risking what cannot exist in literature—except in a literature which could transform life—and so his feeling of guilt remains; and with it the reproach of untruthfulness. This self-reproach was unknown to authors of the past, because they felt they had fulfilled their task once they had "told the truth"—for they believed they knew what that was—even resisting external threats to do it. In writers like Frisch, external threats are replaced by self-doubt. "In between lies only the untruthful."

I experience, O reader of today, fear and hope, even catharsis —as I try to pursue this self-investigation.

At least in his thoughts, Frisch wants to go the limit. He puts himself through mental trials—in a striking parallel to the view of the Catholic Church that mentally committed sins can be as grave as those which are committed in fact. For instance, he tests his ability to act without thought and without imagination, that is, to commit the types of crimes invented by this century. "[Flying] over a little town that looks like an architect's scale model, I discover unintentionally that I would be quite capable of dropping bombs on it. Strange . . . that our imagination is not more powerful than that."

The desire to "return to a human scale"—the scale from which flying and technology in general has freed us—is by no means just the fanciful notion of an author. The transformations and deformations Frisch alludes to have befallen every one of us, often without our wanting to recognize them; but he tries to become aware of his own share in producing them, which is his way of pointing out to the rest of us that they have occurred.

It seems to me that almost no word appears in his writings more often than "to fail." Now reflecting, now describing, diagnosing, or narrating cautiously, experimentally, he circles around this center. I believe one can detect a growing maturity in his fear of failure—which he learns to view as the response of a sensitive male to the intolerable demands of this male-run society. There is no contradiction in saying that his fear matures: even our fears can grow up. *His* fear begins with the early, overwhelming experience of self-rejection ("Only insofar as I know it has never been my life can I accept it as my failure," says a line from *Stiller*)—and moves on, in the late phase, to the question directed to the "I" of the diaries and thus to every one of us: "So, you were satisfied to be *comparatively* guiltless?" He ranges from the direct fear of inferiority—which speaks out of his first books, which he fends off with work, and which brings with it an irresistible melancholy ("after work the onset of melancholy")—to the daring venture of his second diary, to penetrate his self-deceptions without stopping for anything, and then to report his findings. A suggestive parallel to his fears can be found in those sketchy narrative fragments, all of which treat a man who is insecure or off balance.

So Frisch goes from a fascination with the absolute, which is mistaken for radicalism, to an appreciation of practical reason, which seems, if anything, almost exaggerated; and from dread of the original sin of trying to define oneself or others—"to make a graven image"—in any way but by love, to the realistic effort to relate to the world as it is, in specific yet ever-changing terms.

At the end, the contradictions he experiences very likely gall him no less than they did at the start; but they are more distinct and even—if I may say so—more substantial. The proneness to departures and unconditionality which characterizes his early fictional characters is not simply condemned or disposed of by the recognition that it gets you nowhere wishing to be someone you are not, or pretending you cannot see the facts, or working yourself up into unfulfillable passions and fleeing from reality. Instead, it is suspended in increasingly probing questions about the contingent features of such attitudes.

Dismayed

by the "impossibility of being and living morally—which intensifies in times of political terror"; deeply troubled by the contradiction

117

between his thought and his action ("For instance you have lived in a society you describe as accursed, you called for changes and so on, that is clear from the innumerable words you produced but not from your actions"), Max Frisch all his life has resisted the silent treaty with the status quo, resisted being swallowed up. Paradoxically, his refusal to believe in meaning—in the sense of an inner necessity that things be so-and-not-otherwise—leads him not to disgust, loathing, ennui, but to a sobriety which releases energy, and to recognition of a task which he can take on himself as his *mission*: setting up counterimages to combat the monstrous deformations of man in our times. "Where truthfulness is achieved, it will always make us lonely, but it is the only thing we have to fight back with."

So Frisch does succeed after all—maybe he is unaware of it—in discovering a terra incognita. It is not a country or locale, nor a "zone" of subject matter, nor an ideology, nor a breed of man, nor a social class. He begins and ends, fortunately, with something personal. But what he does manage to achieve is to let us start from a productive basis, to think things through more thoroughly. The designs he supplies go beyond himself.

One design is to live in meaningful relation to others.

This viewpoint seems to lie outside literature; but then I think that the motives for literature are to be found not in literature but in ourselves. Yet it remains to be shown whether the prose forms which Max Frisch adopts or develops—especially the hybrid form of his last diary—match with any precision the motives he has under study. A finished, rounded-off form would seem the last to interest him— or us who read him.

Fairy tales? I hardly think so; not even fairy tales in Kafka's manner. I imagine Frisch faithfully following up his leitmotifs, intensifying even further the elevated tension between the two poles of *discretion* and *indiscretion*. I think he will go on asking himself what these days is virtually the most indiscreet question of all: What do you believe? He will always see to it that the pain, the injury he speaks of, afflict us, too.

August 1975

Meetings:

For Max Frisch,

on His Seventieth Birthday

———

Dear Max Frisch:
The places where we have met have been transformed in my memory into islands against which the tide is rising. Remembrance, in our latitudes, is turning increasingly into a kind of salvage operation for fossils and antiquities. We talked about that actually, without knowing it, in Stockholm in May 1978, when we discussed your next book. In the meantime, *Der Mensch erscheint im Holozän* [*Man in the Holocene*], has been published and in the dedication you recall that conversation in which G. and I believed it behooved us to take on the role of your future readers—readers of a rather demanding sort. We have not seen each other since then. The islands are sinking, sinking; one wonders where the mainland is: *A path is a path even in the fog.** The undertow of the unreal, of the nonexistent, has already caught hold of many; the living turn into those who just wish to survive, grief is crowded out by weariness. First the heart is touched, then feeling touched goes out of date, the heartrent author finds himself stranded: *Nature needs no names. The rocks have no need to be memorized by him.*

In our first conversation (held ten years before the last-so-far), sentences like that were nowhere in sight. Nature *had* names—the Volga River, the banks of the Volga—the date was May 1968, and the boat hired to transport a group of writers who had met to honor Maxim Gorky was called the *Gogol*. We were talking. We sat opposite each other in the boat's restaurant, the banks slid slowly by, the heat

* *Man in the Holocene* (New York: Harcourt Brace Jovanovich, 1980).

119

let up, it turned to evening, then to night, the bright strip on the western bank went dark while—by now it was almost morning—a pink strip glimmered on the eastern bank, details reappeared and, last of all, the outlines of the onion-domed churches along the slope of the river embankment. "Now I have seen enough churches," you said. A boat pitching gently on a dark river, between dark land masses, under the starry sky of the northern hemisphere: an abstract situation which could have made us forget who we were, where we were. We did not forget for a moment. We were aware, if not of *being* representatives of our societies, at least of *appearing* to be.

"Suspicion," you wrote to me later: you said you had detected a look of suspicion when we were introduced. How much what we see is determined by what we expect! Suspicion is the last thing that would have occurred to me, but how could you know that? To some extent, we had to live up to stereotypes before, to some extent, we could dismantle them. If we stuck to the pattern, I had to be suspicious of you; you were obliged to point out the freedoms you enjoyed in a bourgeois society; then I was bound to respond by showing you how precarious they were; and in turn it behooved you to accuse me of an unquestioning faith in the state. This automatic system did not function quite in the normal way. Wine and vodka contributed what was in their power, but I imagine that a different "spirit" must have been at work, too. Because during that night—while the *Gogol* paused many times, the head wind dropped, heat streamed in through the open windows; while the boat sailed repeatedly into the basin of a ship elevator and steadily overcame the difference in level between Moscow and the city of Gorky (we could tell that by the way the chains of lights would sink on either side of us); without ever reaching a point where we could say: It's happening now!—we seemed to sail across boundaries which ordinarily hem us in; Gogol's ghost haunted us; after midnight we found ourselves under guard by mute companions from another dimension—although we were talkative enough ourselves—and against the regulations and without any ifs, ands, and buts, we met each other on the soil of Utopia. Afterward we thought it was the morning breeze, but who knows what blew on us, making us forget what we had said, making you feel you had to ask, for caution's sake, when we met again for a late breakfast, "So tell me the truth—are we still speaking to each other?" By the time the *Gogol* sailed into Gorky, it was nothing more than an ordinary Volga steamer. The ground which had seemed so solid underneath us acquired a steep gradient. Sometimes we found that all the good spirits had abandoned us; but we went on talking all the same.

If we ever end up back on board the *Gogol* (but that is not likely),

I could show you the spot on the upper deck where you leaned against the ship's wall and spoke the name of Ingeborg Bachmann, expressing your personal regret that she had declined to come. Several times I noticed that you try to anticipate what thoughts other people may have about you and thereby risk starting them thinking along lines which had not occurred to them before. The growing openness which people show about their private lives—doesn't it indicate, among other things, that the boundaries which bourgeois society once set between private and public are no longer intact? That a person who mediates between private and public through the act of writing suffers a serious disruption of his private world when he is denied responsibility in the public sphere?

That is the subject we ought to have talked about when we met again in the art gallery in Zurich in 1975. We did not get that far, we talked about *Montauk*.* But seven years earlier, we tried in all earnestness to define what was a "decent person"—yes, it was at that evening banquet in the city of Gorky—and the definition you suggested was: These days, a decent person is a brave person, one who remains true to himself and his friends. I am afraid that we drank a toast to that and did not return to the point, which afterward was eliminated from our possible topics of conversation. The realization that a question has been put in the wrong way and so cannot be answered leads first to conflicts and then to muteness. In 1975, after some sparse comments about *Montauk*, we walked along the Spiegelgasse in Zurich. We named—Büchner, Lenin—without commentary. We duly admired the gables of the houses. Then on to the town clerk's house. Gottfried Keller.† Bachmann's name came up again.

No more discussions of a moral nature, as I recall. Being able to feel we are decent people (whatever that may mean) is not important. That is not what counts. But we are unable, and not permitted, to stop working hard to be decent: that is our only real privilege, a permanent excitement which motivates our efforts to write, but which, increasingly, blocks them, too. It seems to me now that we East European intellectuals recognized somewhat sooner than you intellectuals of Western Europe that our morality must be practiced without safeguards, at our own risk. When we met you, we suddenly felt that we were more knowledgeable, more experienced. So that, in fact, that nighttime telephone conversation between New York and Oberlin, Ohio—between a hotel room on Fifth Avenue and the study of a

---

* Autobiographical narrative published by Frisch in 1975. (New York: Harcourt Brace Jovanovich, 1978).

† Writer and native of Zurich (1819–90).

professor on leave; between you and me—already belonged to the past before it even happened. Perhaps that is why it was so hard for you to end it. It was a throwback to the days when each one of us had to stand for his whole nation, while each of you was exempt from any share in the most serious problems of your society and represented only yourselves.

I have not told you how, the day before we talked on the telephone, I learned that the Chancellor of West Germany had resigned. The year was 1974; a young American teacher told me while he was showing me group-teaching experiments at his school. He could not think of the Chancellor's name, and for a long time I was struggling to understand the English word "spy."* Besides, I was freezing cold that night in Professor C.'s study. For fifteen or twenty minutes you kept repeating the same sentences, and I kept repeating one sentence over and over in reply: "But what did you expect?" I envied you your indignation; but mixed with the envy was another feeling, of cold. In the circle of light under the desk lamp lay a copy of *The Magic Mountain*. I had found it in the professor's library and read it greedily, but as something exotic; and I was afraid that the question of whether one must live without choices would gel into a formula in my mind. I thought about the young teacher, who merely in order to get some kind of exchange going between the black and white children in his classroom, who sat inflexibly in their separate groups, had them read aloud an ancient Eskimo legend about the birth of the sun and moon, with a white girl playing the role of the sun and a black boy the role of the moon. I thought about the fifteen-year-old girl who, when urged to tell what the phrase "East Berlin" meant to her, looked out the window for a long time and finally brought out in a hesitant voice: "The wall . . ."

A leap in time. Formulas may be useful, but one cannot live by them. I believe you saw that when you came to visit us in the Friedrichstrasse [in East Berlin] in December 1976. You came out of friendship and decency, nothing behind-the-times about that, and we were grateful. It was very cold, as I remember, and extremely dark, when the four of us walked to Checkpoint Charlie. The question was: What is left when the makeshift supports break down one after the other, and what attitude might best express our feeling of helplessness? Withdrawal does not necessarily mean giving up. But how does one get around the fact that sending no message is secretly interpreted as a new message, that is, as something other than what it appears

---

* Willy Brandt, the West German Chancellor from 1969 to 1974, resigned in the wake of a spy scandal in his government.

to be? How can we manage, in our disappointment and self-pity (we talked about morality, did we not?)? How—with all that we consume both physically and mentally—can we go on feeding the inner drudge who has become part of us and is always itching to be kept busy? And how do we deal with the fear which breaks out when we begin to fight this inner collaborator?

"Literature in Disguise" was the topic assigned to us in Stockholm in May 1978. The participants were required to take it seriously. A bottomless theme. Literature as masquerade; the writer, disguising his material and disguising himself, no longer able to tell the difference between his mask and his face, and yearning for devices that are not artifices. Feeling that as a type he is disappearing, he is compelled to emerge more as a person: an odd movement going in two directions at once. Your nervousness before the two of us delivered our talks in the auditorium of Stockholm University. "Do you also find it impossible to eat anything before you give readings of your work?" I ate salad and fish.

When does that "How" I mentioned enter our lives? The houses in Stockholm, with their clear-cut outlines, look as if they were built out of children's toy blocks when you glide past them on a skerry-coast steamer. Once again we were on a boat. The Old Town in Stockholm looked like an Italian city on a hot summer evening, you said. We had never been to Italy. In that case, you said, why stay put now? Why didn't we pick up and go to Lapland together for a couple of days to pet the reindeer? You meant it seriously, but we could not help laughing. Why didn't we go with you? Had we already been taken over completely by that preemptive decree that it was "impossible"? One simply did not travel to a place just because one felt the urge. One did not give in to whims. One needed a plausible reason for everything, to justify it even to oneself. The bar we were sitting in was filled with businessmen, and writers who had taken part in the congress. No ghost was haunting the place, no unearthly beings were in circulation. Even had we been able to drink more, we would have stayed stone sober, standing on the solid ground of facts which are backed up by nothing but themselves. A bomb is a bomb is a bomb.

This sentence—which you did not say—is the precondition behind your sentence: *The ants . . . attach no importance to our knowing about them.* You said that you were going to travel to Ticino to work. You needed encyclopedias for your work, you said. An old man (you told us), cut off from the world, trapped inside his house by a natural disaster, would use scraps of notes and encyclopedia extracts to make a record of the natural history of organic beings, while all around him a flood was rising. A sort of second creation would arise inside the head of this old man, who would not live much longer. That is what we understood you to say. A concrete incident, you said, described with fidelity to details. But with further implications? we asked. Yes, but not disparaging what existed in nature, by shrinking away from it. A strange sort of bravery behind the mask of stubbornness, with the world ending all around him . . . *A path is a path even at night.* "Let's call each other *du*," you said. You jotted down a couple of words on the inside of a cigarette pack.

December 1980

If at First
You Don't Succeed . . .*

Every time I write about Anna Seghers it seems to me that it gets harder. She and I have known each other for fifteen years. Of course, I knew her before then; that is, I had read her books, had seen her at gatherings, heard her speak, admired the aura that surrounded and still surrounds her. There is a legendary person known as "Our Anna" who, like every legend, is only partly identical with the original, and for the rest is made up out of the needs of the people creating the legend. In those early days, I did not see what sort of problems can arise for the person the legend is attached to. I marveled to hear total strangers chatting away about "*die Anna.*" In 1959, I was working on the editorial staff of the German literary magazine *Neue Deutsche Literatur* when I was told: "Go see Anna and get an interview."

It was a hot day; the awning had been lowered over her balcony. A subdued summer light filtered into the room and it must have appealed to me because I still remember it. I must have been pretty young: for, with all due reverence, I still hoped her replies to my questions would match the ones I had dreamed up for her. Now I know that I really gave her a hard time, and I know what it means when she throws back her head and cries in an imploring voice: "*No*, that's not it at all!"

That day we sat in the same place where we always sat in the years to come. When she was thinking over a reply, she would gather inside herself the same way she does now, tilt her head a little to the right, and murmur experimentally with her eyes almost shut. I won-

* In honor of Anna Seghers's seventy-fifth birthday.

125

dered that she still needed to test out her answers to simple questions like mine, the kind that other people must have asked her dozens of times already and that she must also have asked herself. Maybe, too, I still had some notion in my head that fame, and what we used to call "being at the top of your profession," made people's life and work easier for them.

At noon she announced a light summer meal of cauliflower au gratin and white wine, which I enjoyed very much.

When the staff and I read over her answers back at the office, we said reprovingly and with a touch of concern: "Anna's determined to go her own way as usual"—because of course *we* were very well up on what we took to be Marxist literary theory.

The last time I saw her—the last time so far—was when I visited her a couple of months ago. Right now it is October 1974 and the pieces people are writing to honor her seventy-fifth birthday have to be finished before her seventy-fourth, because it takes so long to get things into print these days.

Four p.m. is the usual time I arrive so as not to be there so late in the evening. You really have to stretch to reach the kitchen shelf where Anna keeps her flower vases. She brews our coffee the conventional way, because something went wrong when she tried to use the new coffee urn and she has not repeated the attempt. The table is set in the same way as always. (I have taken over her recipe for apple pie.) Anna drinks very little coffee, just a few sips now and then. We are sitting in the same chairs as always, nothing in the room has changed—except the new cushion covers and the new gas heater, which to my sorrow has put the beautiful tiled stove out of action. Admittedly the light is not the same as it was the first time, even though it is summer again. Anna Seghers has gotten thinner, but when she concentrates she still tilts her head to the right, closes her eyes, gathers inside herself, and moves her lips indignantly. "Now, listen here!" she says, as she did the first time. And she cries imploringly, "No, that's not it at all!" when her view of a person, a book, an event disagrees with mine. And we *do* disagree, although probably we keep silent about it more often than we express it. In a moment of deepest seriousness she opens her eyes wide, looking implacable—then bursts out laughing and says something in the Rhenish tones of her native Mainz.

That's the moment—or maybe it's a bit later when we have switched over to "having a good gossip," as she puts it, which is something we both love, and sometimes right in the middle of laughing she suddenly turns serious—or maybe it's later still, when she is letting me help her wash up in the kitchen, which is something she never used to do—well, *some* time that afternoon it occurred to me that one day I really ought to say just what would be missing from my life if I had never gotten to know her.

At once I recognized that such a plan was unworkable. After all, it was not a question of "influences"—even though I can reproduce the tone of her novel *Transit,** or the attitude of the female narrator in her short story "Ausflug der toten Mädchen" [The Excursion of the Dead Girls] any time I like without having to refer to the books— and even though I know well what power of suggestion lies in the use of this tone and this attitude—and even though lines and short passages from her books, essays, talks, and conversations light up in me like signal fires on certain occasions. Take the last sentences of Part One, Chapter 1 of her novel *The Seventh Cross*, for instance. No matter how often I read them, they always give me the same feeling, a sigh of relief, almost happiness: "We have arrived now. Now, what happens will happen to us." Sometimes I recognize this same feeling in the midst of events unrelated to *The Seventh Cross*, and then these lines recur to me, too, because they are linked to the feeling.

But any attempt to follow all the traces that the work and life of Anna Seghers together have left on me would be bound to fail. If I think only of the landscapes whose first impression on me was colored by the fact that I had read her descriptions of them, or knew she had seen them . . . Once, I tried to locate the vantage point from which the character Franz Marnet looks out over the plain where the Main flows into the Rhine, at the start of *The Seventh Cross*. One time in Mainz I followed the route which is indicated exactly in "The Excursion of the Dead Girls," which leads from the steamer jetty under the plane trees along the riverbank to the family home, which of course was destroyed by bombs like most of central Mainz. I managed to talk with one of the schoolteachers who had gone along on that excursion, a very old woman who remembered it clearly and said, "Yes, it was just the way Anna Seghers described it." A former classmate of Anna's told me over the telephone, "She was a bit different from the rest of us. In my room she sat down on the carpet and asked, 'Which one do you like more, your father or your mother?' I mean, I ask you: How can you answer a question like that?"

Once, I went to the town of Winkel on the Rhine, where I looked

* Anna Seghers, born in 1900, had to leave Nazi Germany in 1933 and, on her return in 1947, settled in East Berlin. The works mentioned here—the novels *Transit* (1944) and *The Seventh Cross* (1942), and the 1946 short story "The Excursion of the Dead Girls"—treat the experience of exiles, concentration-camp internees, and other victims of the Nazi regime.

in the cemetery and found the grave of Karoline von Günderrode,* whose name I had run across again and again in the essays and letters of Anna Seghers. She mentions Günderrode along with other German poets of the same generation who "rubbed their heads raw on the wall of society" and were unable to reach the perfection of the classical ideal. One day when I was passing the Café de la Paix in Paris it occurred to me (although I do not know if it is really true) that Anna Seghers used to work there sometimes, so the story goes—until the German army marched into Paris, forcing her to move on. For a few seconds I wished the kind of thing one is not supposed to wish: that the café and that part of the city had been preserved exactly as they were then. And when my plane landed in New York, strangely enough I could not help thinking of her, even though she had come to America almost thirty-five years earlier, by boat and as an immigrant; and even though there was nothing similar in our experience except the arrival itself, and the fact that I felt a glimmer of that same deep-penetrating foreignness which she must have felt.

There are moments when my view of things is transformed by hers, even *into* hers—as far as it is possible to say that. I feel the presence of her language and the fascination of her attitude: the attitude of the woman who is capable of speaking such a language, which automatically precludes its being merely parroted by others. All these things are "influences," certainly, but I am talking about something more and something different. Is Anna Seghers what you would call a "role model," then? But that could turn nasty. Too often, our generation has been asked to follow a certain model. That is exactly what she is *not* after. Groundless admiration, dependency, submission are the last things she needs. Anna Seghers's authority is great but not overpowering. She herself respects authority, by the way, and so probably is susceptible to being deceived temporarily; but no extrinsic authority can overwhelm her.

No, what I am talking about is something else. It is that rare and lucky chance when a sustained and penetrating interest in a pattern of life fundamentally different from your own enables you to know yourself better. I believe that nothing more curative can happen—in fact, everybody longs for it—than to have your emotions and your mind engaged equally, and affected equally, by this ongoing experience of another person—not an easily dented role model but a human being whose own inner contradictions give her a keen ear for the conflict of these times. When I say "curative" I am perhaps

---

* Karoline von Günderrode (1780–1806) is the subject of Christa Wolf's 1979 novel, *No Place on Earth.*

referring, too, to that "remedy" which Goethe habitually used to counteract the "great advantages" he discerned in others in contrast to himself, and which he called love.

Even so, it cannot be denied that people of different generations remain to some extent in the dark about each other. Now and then they become aware that they are standing on opposite sides of the generation gap. They do not always understand each other, they strike each other as really strange, and whether or not they say it out loud, they are hurt by the feeling of strangeness within the zone of intimacy which they so desire. They have to expose themselves to this pain, which is a necessary one, along with all the unnecessary pains we inflict on each other.

What I am talking about here is not ideas—or not *only* ideas—but art. Time flows differently for Anna Seghers than it does for me; it brings her different examples, shows her fates that are more finished and rounded off. It is not just that she has seen a different reality—she also sees reality *differently*. A pedagogical reserve is clearly apparent in many of her books.

There is no doubt that she shows the same reserve in her relations with the younger generation; but you can see through it easily, so it can be ignored. She plays down her own worries, or denies them, and she will not admit that young people have them at all. Consequently, it is all the more moving when you see her act openly and unreservedly out of concern for someone. I will never forget the time nine years ago when she made me go to the East Asia Museum, at a moment when the last thing I felt in the mood for was looking at East Asian sculpture; and although we did not talk about what was weighing on both our minds, she communicated with me largely by gestures, trying to get me to see what was really important.

She does not believe in emotional display. She grew up in the school where people learn to pull themselves together. She has no liking for extravagant emotions and excessive reactions, neither in life nor in the arts. When she sees them, the word she uses is "overdone": "I think that's overdone," she says, or, "That's way overdone." On these occasions you can even hear her say something she hardly ever says otherwise: "I don't understand that."

Moderation—who wouldn't want to have that quality? Maybe Anna herself is surprised to have arrived at her sense of measure. You could not exactly describe her ideal as "noble simplicity and tranquil grandeur"*; in fact, it would be hard to sum it up in any formula. And yet it is based on certainties, unquestionable and un-

---

* Winckelmann's phrase, the motto of the German classical ideal.

questioned. There is no other way to arrive at a measure, still less to keep it. I have seen Anna upset by the far from measured doubt which the new generation once again feel compelled to draw upon, and which is yet another stumbling block in the way of their achieving classical perfection. And yet she knows from her own case what circumstances are needed to produce a writer of the full-blown classical type, and also how desperately some generations struggle—largely in vain—to round off their times into a concise image. Moreover, Anna herself is lively, uneasy, and curious, and so she is able not only to accept but joyfully to welcome talent wherever she sees it and, when necessary, to defend it. Who knows better than she how fateful is that meeting between a generation and certain moments of history?

And now I break off my attempt to write about Anna Seghers. I must give up a scheme which I knew from the start was not feasible. Many things get in the way: one of course is the awe I still feel, another my nervousness about touching on those taboos between people which ought to remain inviolate. What one person gives to another—when it is given not by some single trait and not by isolated actions but by his whole being—is difficult to put into words. And when the reasons for gratitude are so many, they cannot all be named.

November 1974

The Shadow of a Dream:

A Sketch of

Karoline von Günderrode*

―――

1

"Yesterday I read Ossian's 'Darthula,' and it made such a pleasing impression on me. My old desire to die a hero's death seized me with great intensity. I felt it was intolerable to go on living, more intolerable still to die a peaceful and ordinary death.—Why wasn't I born a man! I have no taste for women's virtues, for women's delights. I like only what is wild, great, glorious. There is an unfortunate but irremediable disproportion in my soul, and so it will and must remain, for I am a woman but I have desires like a man's, without a man's strength. This is why I am so changeable and so out of harmony with myself." August 29, 1801.

The forebodings which cannot be denied.

Before someone can write he has to live: that is a truism and it applies to both sexes. For a long time, women lived but did not write. Then they wrote—if this is a permissible expression—*with* their lives, and *for* their lives. Today they are still at it; or they are at it again.

The emotional disharmony which the twenty-one-year-old Karoline von Günderrode† detected in herself was—although she did not know it yet—a disharmony of the times. Prey to an incurable conflict, given ability to express her insufficiency and the world's, she lived a short life which was poor in events but rich in emotional

―――

* Preface to Christa Wolf's collection of writings by and about Günderrode.

† I have retained Wolf's spelling of Günderrode's name throughout, rather than the commoner spelling with one *r*.—Trans.

131

upheavals; refused compromise; died by her own hand, mourned by a few friends, almost unknown; left behind a small body of work, much of it unpublished—poems, bits of prose, experiments in drama; was forgotten; was rediscovered a century later by lovers of her poetry who set out to salvage her memory and her writings, which narrowly escaped destruction. Not even Bettina von Arnim's* epistolary novel *Die Günderode* (1840) could preserve an inkling of her shape; barely her name. German literary historians, accustomed to the colossal, touched-up canvases of their classical authors, blithely and heedlessly dismissed those others, labeled "unfinished"—a practice which has continued to the present day, when Georg Lukács issued his influential judgment against Kleist, against the Romantics. Accused of decadence, or at the very least of being weak and unfit for life, they now are dying all over again from the German public's inability to develop a historical consciousness and to face up to the basic conflict of our history, which the young Marx expressed in his lapidary remark that the Germans shared in the restoration movements of other modern nations without having first shared in their revolutions. An inwardly divided, politically immature people, hard to activate but easy to seduce, devoted to the progress of technology instead of humanity, buried these who went early to their deaths—these undesirable witnesses to throttled longings and fears—in a mass grave of forgetfulness.

It cannot be an accident that we have started to investigate these written-off people; that, fascinated by their kinship and closeness to us (although mindful, too, of the periods and events which separate us), we have begun to oppose, challenge, and cancel the verdict against them. The "wheel of history" has turned full circle and we, our bodies and souls moving with it willy-nilly, are only now getting our breath, regaining consciousness, getting our bearings. We look around us, driven by the need we can no longer deny, to understand ourselves: our role in history, our hopes and their limits, our achievements and our failures, our possibilities and what conditions them— and if possible to know the reasons for it all. Looking into the past, we meet restless glances which are not yet pacified after so long a time; we find lines of writing which affect us, dashed off in a generous, flowing, legible female hand on green quarto stationery—green was easy on the writer's weak eyes—and we hold them in our hands, not

---

* Bettina Brentano (later von Arnim) (1785–1859), sister to Romantic writer Clemens Brentano and wife to his friend and collaborator, Achim von Arnim; wrote several books of fiction in the form of letters ostensibly exchanged between herself and notable figures of her time, including Goethe. In 1840 she published a free rendering of her correspondence with Günderrode.

without emotion: "An age of pygmies, a race of pygmies is at play now, and plays quite well in its own way."

Günderrode's generation, like all who live in transitional periods, had to create new patterns which later generations would use as models, stencils, warning slogans, in literature as in life. These people who were young in 1800 were made an example from which others might learn, or fail to learn. For them, the existing examples did not apply. Their experience hit them directly, immediately, and unforeseeably. The new bourgeois society, still undeveloped yet already withered, used them as design schemes, hastily discarded prototypes. Its finished types could not be allowed to resemble them: which is yet another reason why they had to be forgotten. They were the product of a particular hour whose swift passing veiled their lives with sadness, but also stimulated them to give in to the allure of varied and contrary forces, to lay themselves open to tensions, to play along—to play "quite well in their own way."

They were few in number. Their forerunners, the ideologists and protagonists of the French Revolution, took as their models the ancient Romans, used-up, misinterpreted attitudes: they deceived themselves so as to be able to act. The later generation shed their togas along with their sense of mission, their heroes' roles along with their self-deception. In the mirror they met their own faces, un-made-up and unasked-for. These who were young in 1800 could not arrange to be born in a later year, nor could they think the thoughts or live the lives of an older generation. They could not deny the particular features which determined them, the grueling features. The bourgeois society which in the end spread to the German side of the Rhine without need of a revolution admittedly gave rise to no starkly new economic and social order, but did bring a pervasive petit-bourgeois morality based on the suppression of everything uncompromising and original. It was an unequal struggle. A small group of intellectuals with no backup force (as happened so often in German history from the Peasants' War onward)—supporting an out-of-favor ideal with a sensibility attuned to nuances and a headstrong desire to put their newly developed skills to use—ran head-on into the narrowness of an underdeveloped class characterized by subservience instead of self-esteem, and which had absorbed nothing of the bourgeois catechism except the commandment: Get rich! This petit-bourgeois class tried to harmonize the boundless instinct for profit with the Lutheran–Calvinist virtues of industry, thrift, and discipline; the poverty of their lives blinded them to their real needs, while making them hypersensitive to those who would not or could not be made to keep silent. Thus the little group of intellectuals became strangers in their own

133

land, forerunners whom no one followed, enthusiasts who evoked no response, callers without an echo. And those among them who could not make the timely compromise became victims.

Don't think they did not know it. Günderrode, no emotionalist but philosophical in her temper, obviously recognized the link between the all-pervasive economic ideal and Protestantism, and she did not hesitate to think out the consequences of her own situation: "For our confined living conditions cut us off from nature, our even more confined ideas from the true enjoyment of life, our forms of government from all activity in the world at large. So tightly hemmed in on all sides, our only alternative is to raise our gaze heavenward or to turn it inward, brooding on ourselves. Aren't almost all the newer types of poetry defined by this posture of ours? Either outline figures struggling to rise bodiless to dissolve in infinite space or pale light-shunning earth spirits whom we conjure introspectively from our own depths; but vigorous, pithy figures are nowhere to be found. We may boast of our heights and our depths, but we altogether lack the comfortable dimension of horizontality."

And like the young men of the *Sturm und Drang* more than thirty years earlier, she looked to the example of Shakespeare. "Since I personally will not reach beyond the limits of my own time . . ." Günderrode considered giving up writing and devoting herself to the study and popularization of the Old Masters. This was not just a passing notion but reflected the self-knowledge and self-criticism of one seeking her own kind.

My comparison of the generation of 1800 to the *Sturm und Drang* generation is not far-reaching. The *Sturm und Drang* belonged to a pre-revolutionary epoch; the later group, whom we inexactly and inappropriately call by the collective name "early Romantics," were the children of the post-revolution, of the dawning restoration, which later sucked many of them into the system they once opposed. What gave the *Sturm und Drang* confidence, hope, vital stimulation, and led to illusionary attempts at action—like the "education of princes"!—brought the 1800 group nothing but a painful sobering up and disappointment. Granted, the echo of the great ideas from France—transmitted to them, as a rule, via the works of their revered elders, Kant, Fichte, Goethe, Schiller, Herder—affected them deeply, awakened their demands, formed their ideals. But the meager possibilities for political and social practice which German society allowed to the newly developing class of the intelligentsia had already been tested by the older generation, who partly gave up, partly rejected them, and in a few cases—notably Goethe's—accepted them as one of life's necessary compromises, with all the torment and pain this entailed, and at the cost of deserting any involvement with contemporary politics. "Let us not wish upon Germany the revolutions which are capable of resulting in classic works," wrote Goethe—the idol of the young of 1800—five years before the turn of the century, in his essay "Literary Sans-Culottism." A programmatic sentence which certainly exhibits a highly developed realism but not much revolutionary fervor.

This renunciation by the fifty-six-year-old Goethe, his retreat into his own work and into the symbolic content of his own life, was an option not open to the twenty-year-olds. Their experience of the French Revolution was rule by a foreign power. They, the sons and daughters of the first generation of educated German middle-class families and of impoverished noble families who had sunk into the middle class, had a choice between the crippling, oppressive practices of the German petty princes and being conquered by Napoleon; between the anachronistic feudalism of the German petty states and the forcible introduction of overdue administrative and economic reforms by the usurper who (naturally) strictly repressed the spirit of the Revolution. This choice—if it can be called a choice—was one that suffocated action at its root when it was still no more than thought. Their generation was the first to experience fundamentally that they were not needed.

"What deeds still await me, or what second thoughts that I must go on living yet awhile?" What argument could we find to contradict her? Utopia was exhausted, faith lost, every support gone. They felt they were alone in history. The hope that others—their people!—might depend on them was used up. One cannot live on self-deception. Isolated, unknown, cut off from opportunities of action, relegated to adventures of the soul, they were abandoned without protection to their doubts, their despair, their growing sense of failure. A small thing, it seems, was all it took to draw them into the abyss whose edge they trod, keeping their eyes open. And the question remains: Was it a small thing that killed them? Was what finally killed *her*— an unhappy love affair, for heaven's sake!—only the sign given them by a fate which was sealed in any case: the fate of being abandoned, undervalued, betrayed? And were they so completely mistaken in the way they interpreted the signs?

2

German life stories. German death styles.

People are bound to call it extravagance. Exaggerated sensitivity.

You could also call it stress, if you were willing to admit that anticipation counts as stress.

Anticipation—but of what?

The critical apparatus we are used to cannot grasp it. Literary,
historical, political, ideological, economic concepts do not compre-
hend it completely. The vulgar materialism of our time cannot fathom
the dry rationalism of *their* time; the insipid dogmatism, explaining
everything and understanding nothing, which the people of 1800 tried
to fight off; the ice-cold abstraction, the whole ghastly unswerving
pursuit of false objectives which were no longer questioned; the inex-
orable strengthening of destructive patterns; the ruthless utilitarian
thinking—all left their imprint on them, in the form of fear, depression, a leaning to self-destruction.

An early poem of Günderrode's, marking her debut as a philosophical poet, bears witness to the mental attitude of her generation,
which had seen the great intellectual venture of the German Enlightenment reduced to pragmatic sophistry and the image of the world
turned pale and flat:

THEN AND NOW

A rough and narrow path the earth once seemed,
And on the mountains shone the lit-up sky
While by earth's side yawned the abyss of hell
And paths led up and down to hell and heaven.

But now the whole of it is transformed utterly,
The heaven has crashed, the pit has been filled in,
And paved with reason, the road's easy on the shoes.

Faith's heights are now demolished.
And over the flat earth strides tall common sense
And measures everything in spans and feet.

The tone is not whining. No self-pity. An authentic account,
which merits our attention.

This is a new way of looking at things, it uses words differently.
It compels us to trot out the word "soul" again, to restore a word like
"longing" to its former rights, to drop our reservations. "A floating
religion" is the phrase which Bettina Brentano used when she wrote
to Günderrode. The two of them ought to found a floating religion,
she said, whose chief principle would be "that we do not allow any
education—that is, no artificially taught behavior. Everyone is to be
curious about himself and to unearth himself the way one brings up

ore out of the depths, or an underground spring. All education shall
have the aim of letting the mind out into the light." So "curiosity,"
"imagination," is the goal—and not just the kind of imagination
described by the contemptuous, derogatory phrase "fantastic notions."
What a language these young people strike up, what delightful presumption, what a rebel spirit! What a challenge to our buried ability
to experience words as the messengers of our senses and our sensuality; to create ourselves in creating sentences; and to use our
language not to block insight but as an investigative tool. And, too,
what an opportunity to understand our own situation.

"Oh, what a heavy damnation, to be unable to move the wings
we have managed to procure. People build houses where there is no
room for a guest!—Oh, age of slaves that I was born in! . . . What?
Have you locked up the mind and stuck a gag in its mouth, and have
you tied behind their backs the hands of the soul's great qualities?"
These lines from Bettina's *Conversations with Günderode* are—she
tells her brother Clemens in a letter—"aftertones of lament"; and I
wonder if it is not really envy we feel when we try to fend off such
high-flown questions by calling them "gushy." Envy of these people's
impetuosity, of the unconstrained way they attack their distress, of
how they take it for granted that of course they will refuse to submit
to the standards and rules of a lethal normality.

In any case, the fairy tale of the beautiful but unworldly Günderrode does not hold up to closer inspection. Bettina Brentano, five
years her junior and not her only close woman friend, has given the
most exact description: "She was as smooth and soft in all her features
as a blonde; she had brown hair but blue eyes, screened by long
lashes. When she laughed it was not a loud sound but instead a
gentle, subdued cooing in which pleasure and gaiety were very audibly
expressed. She did not walk, she moved, if you understand what I
mean . . . She was tall in build, her figure was too fluid to describe
by the word slender. She was friendly in a shy way and much too
lacking in self-will to make herself noticed in society."

Bettina and Karoline met in Frankfurt, where Bettina was a
daughter in the renowned and prosperous Brentano household, living
in the Sandgasse, while Karoline had lived since the age of nineteen
as a canoness in the Cronstett Evangelical Sisterhood for Ladies of
Rank, not a true convent but a quiet, secluded institution for the
unmarried daughters of impoverished noble families. The rules stip-
ulating thirty as the minimum age for entry were waived to admit
Günderrode, which gives some indication of how desperate her plight
was. She showed little interest in entertainment; the canonesses were
discouraged from attending the theater or balls. We know of one visit

that Karoline made to the theater, and shortly before her death, an anonymous correspondent claims to have seen her in silent attendance at a masked ball. The prohibition against receiving private visits from male guests was not strictly enforced. She was free to come and go as she liked locally, but had to ask permission for any long-distance trip, and it was granted her without difficulty. Occasionally she would turn down invitations from friends, saying that she was tied up by duties for the sisterhood.

She was tied up in more ways than one. Tied to her sex, to her rank, to her poverty, to her responsibility as the oldest of six children whose father had died young and whose mother—a mother Karoline knew did not really love her—was incapable of heading a family. Documents reveal conflicts between the children and the mother over inheritance claims. Karoline helped one of her sisters to run away from their mother's home. She had to tend another sister, her favorite, on her deathbed, when Karoline herself was still very young. She spent her childhood in the area around the tiny court of Hanau. Restriction, limitation, confinement. The only way out: intellectual work, education.

For the first time, a group of women began to emerge from their historyless state at the same moment. The slogans of the age—freedom, individual personality—applied to women, too, for whom convention made it virtually impossible to take any independent step. Often their boundless desire for independence clashed with their shyness. Karoline—formally dressed in the black habit of her order with its high white collar, and wearing a cross on her breast—felt timid, when she sat at table, about reciting the blessing aloud in front of the other canonesses; and yet she dreamed, along with Bettina, of taking long trips to distant places. Together, they made a map of Italy and toured it in their minds. And later, in the wintertime, they remembered these imaginary journeys as if they had really taken place. She had to invent things to remember, to install a fiction in her memory to stand in for reality: nothing shows more clearly the limitations by which she felt she was bound. She could cross them only in dream, in fantasy, in poetry.

She was also tied to her talent: when had that ever been the case for women before? Günderrode did not have the option of developing her superior abilities at schools and universities. In the studies which she pursued tenaciously and systematically, she was dependent on her own industry and craving for knowledge, but also on the advice, help, and practical support of her friends of both sexes. She knew the meaning of productive contacts, she deliberately cultivated them: "I need to communicate." Within their circles of like-minded friends, these young people formulated, debated, and tried out the new values which they could not act upon within the petrified or rapidly petrifying institutions. This is what I mean by "anticipation": the attempt to break out of isolation and to adopt fresh, more productive ways of life, born out of the spirit of a group.

Günderrode, while certainly not the center, was nevertheless one member of a loosely knit circle of young literary people and scientists who used the brief spell between two historical periods to formulate and express, with lightning speed, what they felt about life. They had to defend themselves on two fronts—against narrow feudalism and against the dreary acquisitiveness of the new age. This is what gave the elegiac, broken, and ironic tones to their statements; what made them treat themselves as objects of their own observation and description; what further heightened their sensitivity, as well as their danger and their forlornness.

Impossible as it is to classify Günderrode using literary-historical definitions—"early Romanticism," "classicism"—it is equally impossible to imagine her apart from her intellectual contact with the men who were setting the new literary trend in turn-of-the-century Jena—the Schlegels,* Tieck, Novalis, Clemens Brentano, Schelling, scholars like Karl von Savigny, Friedrich Creuzer, Christian Nees von Esenbeck; and with the women—the sisters, friends, sweethearts, wives, and, for the first time, the collaborators of the men, even though in some cases they might still keep silent about their work, as Dorothea Schlegel did about her share in the Shakespeare translation. Some of the women became famous: Caroline Schlegel-Schelling, Bettina Brentano, Sophie Mereau-Brentano, Rahel Varnhagen, and their names stand for others who were equally educated, equally restless, equally searching—as Günderrode's correspondence testifies. They were women who succeeded in mirroring their own situation: a privilege which like every privilege had to be paid for. The price was the loss of shelter and security, giving up the self-evident role of the dependent woman without the guarantee of gaining a new identity. Originality, naturalness, authenticity, intimacy were elements of their joint demand for happiness. They rejected the hierarchy's demands for coldness, formality, segregation, and etiquette. Relying almost unconditionally on ideas alone, without the support of social, economic, and political facts, they were condemned to become outsiders, not revolutionaries like the Romantics in other

* August Wilhelm Schlegel (1767–1845), German scholar, critic, poet, and disseminator of the ideas of Romanticism, and his brother Friedrich von Schlegel (1772–1829), writer, critic, and creator of philosophical ideas which inspired the early German Romantics.

European nations, which made a different, a political use of their so-called Romantic writers. In Germany they were driven into isolation, confusion, and self-doubt, which they tried to fend off with grimaces and overexcited gestures—and then were reproached for it, adding to their stress. We see them carry out feats of daring, reckless climbs, extravagant experiments. The ground burned under their feet. The philistine set his foot on that ground, occupied it piece by piece, determined from then on what counted as rational, and began to persecute them with his incomprehension, his scorn, his hatred, his envy, and his slander.

Günderrode, too, had to fight off gossip and slanderous tales all her life. Incredible is the only word for the bold way she owns up to her "masculine proclivities" in that 1801 letter we quoted at the start: a letter which, incidentally, was addressed to Gunda Brentano, sister to Clemens and Bettina. A woman who did not want to be a wife, did not want to be subject to "womanly virtues"! It is only too easy to understand her exasperation at the close of the letter: "Gunda, you will laugh at this letter; even to me it seems so disjointed and confused."

Were her inclinations to become public, she would surely be accused of being "unnatural." She withdrew into herself, brooding. When she decided to publish her poetry in 1804, she chose a masculine pen name: Tian.

After her death, people claimed that her life and her love were not based on reality. The ones who said and wrote that forgot that there *was* no reality to base anything on. She worked her way conscientiously through the roster of possibilities that were given her, escaping again and again into new roles which at least in part allowed her to show her true face. That sapped her energy, and in the end she saw herself abandoned to the most banal of all roles: that of the rejected lover. A five-year gap lies between her letter to Gunda and her death. This was the time she gave herself to work at the perfection she strove for. It was a kind of self-trial, and she knew it.

Stress? Günderrode often lay in her darkened room suffering from headaches and chest pains. "It's an ugly flaw of mine," she wrote in that same letter to Gunda Brentano, "that I can so easily fall into a state of nonfeeling, and I rejoice at everything which pulls me out of it." Psychology, which could have explained her "states" to her, did not exist yet, nor did the word for the feelings of premonition she experienced. Her sensitive antennae picked up signals which settled onto her chest and head like oppressive goblins. For the first time, people felt the uncanniness of the everyday, which in her case took the form of "nothingness" and the fear of nothingness. She fled from this fear into nonfeeling, which by a macabre law merely resulted in her becoming further estranged from herself. We know the word which she did not know: "alienation." And we know that giving something a name does not give you power over it.

"An ugly flaw of mine" is what she called it, and regarded herself as cold when her feelings broke down under the strain. She was proud despite her low self-esteem, and who knows, maybe she would have accepted the fatal judgment of the man who was the idol of them all, Goethe. It seems almost wicked to quote one more time his prejudiced remark that he regards the classical as the healthy, the Romantic as the sick. Not self-confident enough to let these young people carry on in peace, or to put himself in their shoes; no stranger, himself, to the moods he attributes to them; unable to bring himself to speak the approving word which would lift their spirits; detesting and fearing their inner conflict; uncomprehending, unappreciative, he strikes them down. Hölderlin is put through his rejection; so is Kleist.

Hölderlin. Whichever of these figures we touch, whichever thread we tug at, the rest always move along with it, the whole fabric stirs. It is hard to put into a temporal sequence, a linear narrative, all the factors which converged on Günderrode at the same moment, from many sides. The garden of the Cronstett Sisterhood abutted the garden of a family called the Gontards. True, Friedrich Hölderlin no longer lived there as the family tutor*; but he did live only "three small hours distant" in Homburg until 1801 and paid secret visits to Susette Gontard, his Diotima—whom Karoline never met, as far as we know—until Susette's death in 1802; and in 1804 he again lived in Homburg, serving as court librarian to the Landgrave. Karoline jotted down this line from Hölderlin in her study journal:

> *What we call love is our hunger: and where we*
> *see nothing, think there dwell our gods.*

She shared his clear-sighted skepticism, having shed naïve faith. As a rule, the personal and political tragedies of writers come to light slowly, with the publication of their letters and of the police records of political trials. According to Bettina Brentano in her letter-novel, she and Günderrode talked about Hölderlin, whose poetry they loved, questioned his friend Sinclair about him, and attributed the onset of his madness to a "refined constitution." They had no way of knowing that Hölderlin had been not just grazed but thrown into turmoil by

---

* From 1795 to 1798 Hölderlin was tutor in the home of a wealthy banker, J. F. Gontard, in Frankfurt, where he fell in love with Gontard's wife, Susette.

the French Revolution, and that in 1805, when Sinclair was arrested on suspicion of conspiracy in revolutionary intrigues, Hölderlin ran into the street shouting in panic: "I'm not a Jacobin, I do not want to be a Jacobin!" And then he went mad—although Sinclair would never quite believe he really was insane, as if madness were a voluntary hiding place, a self-protection to escape the clutches of something unendurable.

Günderrode's name has often been linked to Hölderlin's, not without a certain justice where the spirit of their poetry is concerned. She is more closely related to him than to the Romantics, notwithstanding her veneration for Novalis, her love and admiration for the poems of Clemens Brentano. Her kinship with Hölderlin goes to the roots; surprising parallels can be found between them. Günderrode of course knew nothing of how Hegel, Schelling, and Hölderlin had met in the mid-1790s to draft a systematic program for bridging the gulf between "ideas" and the people: for the gulf grieved the two German philosophers and the German poet who had described his people as "poor in deeds."* How ought the world to be constituted, for a moral being? They began their inquiry with this, the question of questions (Johannes Bobrowski took it up again later because it was still unsettled); proved that the state must "stop"—"because every state is bound to treat free people as mechanical clockwork"; demanded that reason replace superstition; demanded the "absolute freedom of all minds which . . . can seek neither God nor immortality outside themselves"; and arrived at the "idea which unites all": the idea of beauty, of poetry as "mankind's teacher." They had the vision of a "mythology of reason" which would make "the people rational" and "the philosophers sensual" so that "enlightened and unenlightened must join hands at last" to see the realization of a holy desire: "Eternal unity will reign among us then. Never again the scornful glance, never again the people trembling blindly before their wise men and priests. Only then will we see the *equal* development of *all* our forces, of the one individual as well as of all individuals. No energy will be oppressed anymore, universal freedom will reign then, and equality of minds!"

That is the language which goes before the loss of hope. It is the illusion of idealists who expect ideas to revolutionize circumstances. But keeping in mind the past and present history of the Germans, who would dare to smile at such propositions?

It is surprising how closely the evolution of these ideas parallels

---

* Reference to Hölderlin's poem addressed "To the Germans," whom he describes as "rich in thought" and "poor in deeds."

the steps of Günderrode's intellectual development—up to and including the moment when she turned to mythology as the source of many of her poems and philosophical tracts. If, led by the above "systematic outline," we consider the possible reasons for this turn, and look at the resultant points of comparison with Hölderlin, we may perhaps find it easier to penetrate her works, whose alien husk is unfamiliar to us.

3

Disguise, masquerade.

The French Revolution is mentioned only once in the documents which relate to Günderrode: in a letter which the Marburg law professor Friedrich Karl von Savigny wrote to her on January 8, 1804. "Come now, dear friend," he writes, "what peculiar sentiments and resolutions you have been cherishing. You have downright republican attitudes. A little hangover from the French Revolution, do you suppose? Well, you are forgiven, provided you promise to let people poke fun at you for it occasionally."

This letter wounded the twenty-three-year-old Karoline in her sorest point: in her unrequited love for Savigny—although the political language was designed to mask it. Masks were habitually worn by all the actors in the drama which was being played out here, and Karoline, as the rejected party, the third corner in the triangle, the one who had the most to hide, needed to wear hers nonstop. "Republican attitudes"? Her friend Gunda Brentano, who by now had become engaged to Savigny, complained to her fiancé about Karoline: "Dear Günderrode suddenly is taking it very hard that I partly control the relations between you and her. And since it really galls her to be dependent on anything in the world, and not to be completely unfettered and, quite simply, the primary person in any relationship—just imagine, she would like to tear herself away from you and me with might and main, and fancies that she would have achieved something very splendid."

Savigny was not so far off the mark in his reference to the French Revolution. Before the creation of the French Republic, it is unlikely that any woman would have felt in a position to crave freedom and independence. For Savigny, a serious and politically thoughtful man, the republic could only serve as the butt of a joke which at the same time was a threat. Republican sentiments were no longer in fashion. In 1803 Savigny published his treatise on the right of property [*Treatise on Possession*], in which utopian ideas of equality were broken on the

143

wheel of the civil law. A brilliant mind, a realist, an agreeable and stable man, he was generous and empathetic, too. Günderrode loved him. She met him in the early summer of 1799 on the country estate of friends. He immediately made a "deep impression" on her, she confessed to a woman friend, and she described a process that was typical of a girl with her kind of temperament: "I tried to hide it from myself and to tell myself that I felt merely sympathy for the gentle melancholy which emanates from his whole being. But soon, very soon, the growing intensity of my emotions taught me that what I felt was not sympathy but passion."

An all too familiar story. The only unusual thing was that this woman who loved in secret—believing of course that she was unworthy of the man she loved—turned to books to forget her pain. She read Jean Paul's *Siebenkäs* and liked it very much; but, especially, Herder's *Reflections on the Philosophy of the History of Mankind* made her forget her own "sorrows and joys in the weal and woe of all mankind." She clearly departed from the role of the young girl who was meant to concern herself only with her own affairs and those of people who were close to her. Nevertheless, she implored her friend to write to her about "S." "That is all I can have of him, the shadow of a dream."

It is enough to make you superstitious: she has just pronounced her own doom.

She wanted to reconcile irreconcilables: to be loved by a man and to create work which measured up to absolute standards. To be a wife and a poet. To establish and care for a family and to show the public daring productions of her own. Unattainable desires. Three men played a role in her life: Clemens Brentano, Savigny, and Friedrich Creuzer. Three variations on the same experience: that what she desired was impossible. Three times she experienced what she could least endure: she was turned into an object.

While she loved, longed, suffered, kept silent, learned, wrote; while Savigny began a successful career which would take him to the post of Prussian Minister of Justice; while Karoline's family secretly waited for him to propose to her—during this time, Clemens Brentano (who had not always been indifferent to Günderrode himself, but had withdrawn from her after an embarrassing incident about which they maintained a discreet silence) arranged a marriage between his friend Savigny and his sister Kunigunde, known as Gunda, who was Günderrode's friend. The social circle within which they all moved was a small one; many eyes saw everything, many mouths discussed it. Savigny really was looking for a woman who would make a good professor's wife, and Günderrode made him uneasy; he thought in conventional terms and could not decipher her. In a letter, he asked whether he "ought to believe the rumor that she was a flirt, or a prude, or a forceful, masculine spirit; or instead believe her blue eyes, where dwells much gentle womanliness."

Sancta simplicitas. He carefully refrained from getting to the bottom of the rumors and from investigating the incompatible claims made about her. Instead, he courted Gunda, who seems not to have inherited much of the genius of the Brentano family but who shared in the education and culture of their group, and who was kindhearted and generous enough to insist that her friend Günderrode be included as a third party in their alliance. How convenient for Savigny. Finding himself in reliable hands, he could afford to begin a jocular, ironic, and harmless correspondence with the woman who did fascinate him after all; and he retained the noncommittal manner which harmed no one—except the woman who loved him.

"Well, miss, it was not the dear Lord's will that I deliver a letter to you in Giessen."

To which she replied: "In all seriousness, I resent very much the unkind way that Heaven intrudes in my affairs."

Learning that she planned to travel to Marburg with her aunt, he pronounced, "It is absolutely essential for you to see the sights here, in fact I can hardly understand how you managed to get along without them until now."

One might think him a bit cruel, if he gave much thought to what he was saying. Günderrode bravely kept up the tone when she informed him that, to her regret, she could not make the trip after all: "Among the notable sights of Marburg which I was especially keen to see were some of its scholars, or maybe just one (I am not very good at counting)."

That was their manner. Verbal skirmishes, playing with fire. A novel about a narrowly avoided love affair, written in the style of the time; that is, in letters. But the authors of the novel were at the same time its protagonists, and that is a modern feature, which brings with it the danger—perhaps even the temptation—to overstep the boundary between literature and life. Moreover, the interior plot unfolded in a disguised form. The dark underlying theme—renunciation—could not be shown openly. It was cautiously smuggled into phrases which sound completely innocent: "Gunda claims I have a slight passion for you . . . but surely that's not so, surely not."

Surely not. If only she would not shift her mood between one clause and the next, if only she would not drop her smile and speak in a voice without disguises: "If you knew me, you would know that it cannot be. But you do not know me, perhaps it is a matter of indifference to you what I am like, what I can and cannot be. And yet I have the courage to hope—in fact, I know it for certain—that I will one day be close to you as a friend or a sister. I can picture it clearly, and my life will be much richer for it. But only when—I am sure you know when I mean." We know, too: when Savigny has married Gunda.

To be known: the urgent desire of women who do not want to live through a man but through themselves. Here we seem to see the roots of that desire. And it is still felt today, although even now it goes unfulfilled more often than not, because "individuality"—the rallying cry by which the bourgeoisie acceded to power—could never be fulfilled by mass production. The notion that the relations between man and woman could be governed by something other than dominance, subordination, jealousy, property—that is, by equality, friendship, mutual help—is a daring one. Günderrode made unprecedented proposals: to be a sister, a friend. (And she used the masculine noun for "friend," *Freund!*) She gave proof that need and distress breed fantastic ideas which can never be realized but can never be completely eliminated from the world again either.

The language Günderrode used to talk to herself—poetry—sounds different from her letters.

LOVE

Rich poverty! Blessed giving that receives!
Fainthearted courage! In freedom yet captive.
 Speechmaking mutely,
 Hiding for all to see,
 Victor by timidity.

Living death, manifold all-in-one,
Feasting in penury, docile in rebellion.
 Starving that makes full,
 In view yet insatiable,
 Life doubly life and nothing but a dream.

One of the first totally frank love poems by a woman in German literature, without mask or disguise. A poem born out of insoluble contradictions, sustained by the tension between incompatibles, and itself the evidence of this tension: combining intimacy and restraint. "Poems are a balm laid upon everything in life that is unappeasable."

He who has gone so far as to try out this remedy, and experienced its effects, cannot go back. He can only work, come what may, to develop this remarkable tool which, while it relieves one pain, produces another: oneself. But the work to become an autonomous self went against the spirit of the times, which aimed for utility, profitableness, and the conversion of all relationships into barterable goods. It was as if objects and people had been placed under an evil spell. How could those people not feel uncanny? How could they not have evil premonitions and express them in evil, uncanny fairy tales? How could they help feeling emotionally empty? ("This age seems shallow and empty to me, a yearning sorrow tugs me with violence into the past.")

"For I believe"—it is still Savigny speaking—"that a certain yielding softness and the famous chiaroscuro do not belong to your real nature at all . . . Do not be too tender and too melancholy and too yearning—be lucid and stable and yet full of warmth and the joy of living." A man who wants to form her in his own image. It is no longer 1803. In December, their exchange of letters had prepared them to admit things they had concealed from each other before. Their secret codes and role switching, pushed to an extreme, finally resulted in a clear message; two negatives produced a positive. Savigny pretended to believe that a certain thing he wanted to tell her would not interest her, "which of course is not true at all." His position secured, he then told the touching tale of the pain he sometimes felt in his right hand where "someone" slammed the door on it when he was trying to help her into a carriage. For weeks afterward, he said, he had experienced a pressure in his hand which recurred whenever the weather changed. Some famous doctors in Saxony had concluded that he must have burned his hand and said that they could not help him. Then he added in a melancholy tone: "People talk a lot about the sorrows of young Werther, but others have had their sorrows, too, and simply never described them in print."

And then he replied to her earlier offer of friendship. As the "burned child," he was afraid of the fire, he said; but he could not guarantee not to fall a bit in love with her from time to time. This was bound to break up their friendship; yet it would be "monstrously unnatural" if the two of them did not become "close, close friends."

Günderrode was beside herself with joy. "Your letter made me so happy, so truly happy, deep down." She was fonder of his hand, wounded, than if it had always stayed well and whole. The depression she had often felt when she read his letters ("it was an ugly feeling, cold as death") seems dissolved. "Now you both are part of my fate."

She degraded herself, pursued self-pitying fantasies, found it "so very good and much more than good" of Savigny and Gunda "that you can still think about Günderrode, that you do not say: Go away, find yourself a place to stay, we have no room for you."

After the exuberance came the inevitable backlash: her attempt to free herself from a relationship in which she was not the first and only. This stimulated Savigny's roguish reply that she seemed to be guilty of republican sentiments, and he went on to a well-reasoned digression about the rights of the stronger in all matters of property, including the immaterial. In other words, the two women were free to compete for the available intellectual valences of the man, and he would award the victory to whichever of them had more to offer him at any given moment. The market was open, and the right of the stronger applied universally. Values were now to be set by economics.

"How spiteful, how ironic, how abominable!"—her helpless attempt at self-defense. Günderrode lacked the kind of realism that Savigny had called for. "Such a system of political economy ought not to be brought into the feelings."

Too late! The spell had been cast, and the women, bewildered, knew no magic to counter it. So they turned their backs on realism. It was the men who determined what was realistic, the men who controlled politics, production, trade, and research. When they withdrew from their women, when they withdrew as whole people in order to devote themselves to what was really important—that is, to business or to the service of the state—the women experienced a terrible loss of reality and at the same time felt they were inferior. They became childish, or avenging furies, tried to raise their status by cultivating "beautiful souls," or depreciated themselves by turning into coy, conventional Hausfraus who felt unnecessary and kept their mouths shut. The few who talked, wrote, and sang used their talents, for the most part, to encourage their sisters to look on their fate as desirable. "Women's literature" came into being. Only a few women, who had not turned into domesticated house pets, voiced a wild and "masculine" desire for happiness:

> Were I a hunter on an open plain
> or a soldier of low degree,
> if I were any kind of man,
> heaven would stand by me.
> Instead, no gesture of mine is free.
> I must sit neat like a well-mannered child,
> I can only loose my hair secretly
> and let the wind blow it wild!

Who, apart from specialists in German literature, would guess that this stanza was written by Annette von Droste-Hülshoff, a poet who was often described as neurotic, or at least "neurasthenic"?

For as long as she was able, Günderrode kept to the rules which Savigny stipulated. She toned down her feelings and conserved her emotional and mental energies for her work, which was her second passion. "I feel like a fool to tell you, but I am writing a drama, and my whole being is wrapped up in it. I project myself so vividly into the drama, I become so much at home within it, that my own life is becoming alien to me. I have a strong leaning to that kind of abstraction, to that kind of immersion in a river of inner observations and productions. Gunda says it is foolish to let oneself be dominated to this degree by such minor artistry as mine. But I love this flaw in me, if indeed it is a flaw. Often it makes up to me for everything else."

Her tone has changed. This is the voice of clarity and stability, the voice of a woman declaring her loyalty to her work, to her talent, even if she cannot hope to achieve "excellence"; who is learning how her work connects her with the reality that is important to her; how it gives her seriousness, composure, self-understanding. She addresses the man as an adult, self-confident woman. But the last sentences of this very same letter show how easily she loses faith in herself: "I believe that my nature is uncertain, filled with fleeting apparitions that come and go in turn, and without enduring, heartfelt warmth. Yet I ask you to forgive my inherent shoddiness."

Two months later, shortly before Savigny married "dear Gunda," Karoline forgot her pride and, moved by an overwhelming passion, sent him this sonnet:

THE KISS IN THE DREAM

The breath of life a kiss breathed into me,
stilling my heart's deepest languishing.
Come, intimate dark! and wrap me with your wing
of shadow, that my lip may suck new joy.

Such life there was, plunged so deep in those dreams,
that now I live to see dreams all my days:
prepared to scorn what other bliss may blaze,
because the night alone such healing beams.

Love's dear delights are sparse on day's horizons,
day's vain parading sun wounds me with fire,
I'm eaten up alive by its harsh glow.

So, eye, hide from the light of earthly suns;
dip down in night which quiets your desire
and cures the pain like Lethe's cool flow.

The meaning of the poem is clear enough. But on the original (in the Berlin National Library on Unter den Linden), we see that she felt compelled to add this note: "S.–g.: It's true. This is the kind of thing little Günderrode dreams about, and of whom does she dream? Of someone who is very dear and whom she will always love."

If we compare the poem to the footnote, we see how much freedom and independence can be derived from art, from the compulsion to form. Günderrode quite possibly was shocked by her ability to combine thought with emotion, and to give shape to both. This ability, which is the precondition of art and its conflict, may well have led her to accuse herself of inconstancy and coldness.

As a poet she was authentic; that is, as a human being, too. "Dream" and "pain" became key words for her, but she did not go in for the staged emotions which were a convention of her time. When she said "dream," she meant that she really had dreamed; when she said "pain," she meant real suffering. She was not a crybaby.

During these same weeks, a literary review appeared in Kotzebue's periodical, *Der Freimüthige*, written by a former private tutor to a noble household in Frankfurt. Himself a failed poet, he had composed a sweetly sour piece about Günderrode's first published volume of poetry, *Gedichte und Phantasien* [*Poems and Fantasies*]. Although she had had the book published under the pen name Tian, the reviewer had discovered her true identity. "Many people mistake for original ideas what are merely reminiscences." Günderrode's friends tried to comfort her, but she adopted an air of composure and detachment. Clemens Brentano, after a prolonged estrangement, wrote her a letter enthusiastically applauding her work, although he expressed disappointment that she had not approached him about it first. She replied as follows: "You ask how I hit on the notion of getting my poems printed? I have always felt a dim inclination to do so; I rarely ask myself why, or what purpose it will serve. I was very happy when I found someone who undertook to negotiate with the book dealer for me. So, carelessly and not knowing what I was doing, I broke down the barrier which segregated my innermost soul from the world. And I have not regretted it yet, because there comes to me, ever new and vital, the longing to express my life in an enduring form, in a figure which makes me worthy to join the most excellent, to greet them and to keep them company. Indeed, I have always desired to belong to this company, it is the church toward which my spirit ever makes its pilgrimage upon this earth."

But for this naïve and reverential attitude, she would not have dared to take the dangerous step of revealing herself to the public. The "most excellent" whose company she craved were not easy to win over. Clemens Brentano, apparently overcome by genuine envy of her work, and feeling that she had rejected his love and seen through his ploys, criticized her poems to others behind her back. Goethe acquired a copy of *Gedichte und Phantasien*—along with a review, probably written by the Esenbecks—for his literary period-ical, *Jenaische Allgemeine Literaturzeitung*. He was moved enough by the book to write this notation in the margin: "These poems are really an unusual phenomenon, and the review is useful." Then he passed on the little volume to Frau von Stein, who—although Günderrode was dead by then—wrote this about it in a letter to her son: "She published extremely engaging dramatic verse and other poetry, under the name Tian. I was astonished by the depth of feeling and the wealth of thought in these beautiful verses, and so was Goethe."

The "novel" which Günderrode was writing with Savigny came to its predictable conclusion. There was no happy ending. In May 1804, Savigny married Gunda Brentano at Trages, his beautiful coun-try estate, surrounded by all their friends. Karoline attended and stayed on for a couple of days before returning to her study room at the convent. There she devoted herself to reading history, became absorbed in Schelling's philosophy of nature, and worked on a new play. The sparks still flew now and then in the letters she exchanged with Savigny. In August, she informed him that his "magical pres-ence" was "all too dangerous to those of tender disposition." A few days later she traveled to Heidelberg to visit a childhood friend who was now married to the theologian Carl Daub. On the castle balcony in Heidelberg, she met a friend of Savigny, the classical scholar Friedrich Creuzer. In the tangled love affair which followed, Savigny, by an ironic twist, became a confidant, arbiter, and adviser—some-times at the lovers' request, more often against their wishes. Gün-derrode no longer had anything to fear from him. In the drama that began now, she was no secondary figure but the protagonist. She was called on to play the role of tragic heroine. "So now I live to see dreams all my days."

One hundred and seventy years later, Sarah Kirsch, one of Gün-derrode's successors, wrote these lines:

> *I dream many dreams*
> *I dream you are dreaming*
> *that in one of your dreams*
> *you came into my kitchen*

The dreaming woman dreams about the dream another dreamer is having . . . The spiral keeps on turning.

4

The suppressed passions.

"Every day I am less able to fit myself into the world and the domestic order, Karoline. My whole being aspires to a freedom of life which I shall never find. Yet it seems to me that love ought to be free, entirely free from the confining bonds of respectability."

Lisette Nees von Esenbeck, one of Karoline's women friends, who had known her for years, wrote this to her in June 1804. Lisette had recently married the botanist Christian Nees von Esenbeck—incidentally, the first scientist to recognize Goethe's morphology of plants. One of the most intelligent women in Günderrode's circle, she knew French and English literature, could speak Slavic languages, was learning Italian and Spanish. The letters she wrote to her friend were literary reviews—although most of her advice did not fit Günderrode. Born into the von Mettingh family of Frankfurt am Main, Lisette met Karoline when Karoline entered the sisterhood. An early letter reveals that what she felt for Karoline was more than friendship. She reminds her of a scene when Karoline "went out through the back door" to send away an uninvited female visitor, and at the door "I was waiting for you again, it was all so mystical and I felt as if you were my lover." Then—as if realizing what she has said—she writes, "That is indeed strange, Karoline."

Indeed, it is strange, because it is new for women to feel intensely attracted to each other and not to resist the attraction—which does not require the agency and sanction of men, although neither does it rule out close ties and love affairs with men. These young women have something to give each other that a man could not give them, a different kind of connection, a different kind of love. It is as if they can be more themselves when they are alone together; feel less disrupted, freer to design their lives—using designs which will not resemble those of the men.

Lisette writes Karoline very briefly after her marriage to Nees, whom she "loves so unspeakably" that when she sees the places where he lived as a child she feels like "kneeling down in front of him." "I am living differently now from the way you picture me, and one day I will tell you a lot about it. It could happen that I will need my attachment to you more than ever in order to live, so let's always stay closely intertwined, whatever has bound us together must be forever. Let me always live on with you, and you, too, must live a second life in me."

Lisette was no hyperemotionalist, any more than Karoline. The grief expressed here indicates an irreplaceable loss. It is more than fear of the daily monotony of marriage to a difficult, sickly man of volatile moods; more than a nostalgic impulse to shelter in a past relationship which she called "the youth of her life": "free, unclouded and ever serene like the sky." Without doubt, the two women affirmed and supported each other. And we might regard the circles of friends which developed at this time as the first "organizations" in which women functioned as equal members; until, a few years later, they became the actual founders and centers of such circles—the salons —in the larger cities, especially Berlin. The tone, the urgency of their mutual confessions, the direction of their interests, the topics on which they exchanged views, the attitudes and life-styles they cultivated, could be interpreted as a perhaps unconscious attempt to introduce female elements into a patriarchal culture. These young women, the first women intellectuals, experienced the start of the industrial age, the idolatry of reason, and the increasing division of labor as a violation of their nature. "Utility is a lead weight on the eagle's wing of imagination," Lisette Nees wrote Karoline. "Nature!" became the battle cry of their shared longing, as it was for the writers of the *Sturm und Drang* under the influence of Rousseau. But the naiveté of the first assault was past now; and no sooner had the *Sturm und Drang* seen an end to the polished manners of the feudal class, to the aping of French etiquette at the German petty courts which had fueled their rebellion, than the new generation of rebels found themselves confronting new "perversities," this time of a bourgeois society with a different set of pretexts for defaming the truth of feeling, for oppressing the truth of thought. "Didn't the mind-forging cyclopses with the one majestic eye in their foreheads squint at the world, instead of looking at it with two eyes to see it into health?" The world was sick and did not realize it. Women, in these few years which formed a gap between two eras, suddenly dropped out of the ancient stereotypes—including the stereotypes relating to their sex—and formed a kind of pact to make it healthy. Only in the present can the signs they made be noticed again, received and interpreted.

In 1840, thirty-four years after Günderrode's death, Bettina von Arnim published her novel-in-letters, *Die Günderode*. The book had the misfortune to fall into the hands of dry-as-dust textual critics whose skills easily enabled them to reveal it as a "forgery." Bettina was accused of taking liberties with her material, of combining letters, inserting pieces of other people's correspondence, making things up. Nevertheless, the book is authentic, in a poetic sense: as the testament to a friendship between two women, but also as evidence of the life-styles and mores of a time, and as a critique of them which fearlessly attacked their roots. I refuse to judge it a coincidence that women were the ones to discuss the evils of the age in this uncompromising way. Their complete economic and social dependence, the fact that they could strive for no job or office, relieved the most intellectually liberated women of the chore of having to justify subservience in the interests of earning a living. By a strange twist of fate, total dependency allowed the growth of completely free, utopian views, a "floating religion." That those who dare to think as their feelings direct them run a grave risk is obvious. Besides, it makes sense that a book like Bettina's would gain little notice: its tone, its spirit were alien to the German reader and very likely still are. Its language is intimate, passionate, enthusiastic, extravagant, sensual, graphic, not always correct, and certainly not sober: in other words, many readers would find it high-flown, embarrassing. It overflows with emotion, especially from Bettina, who is conducting an urgent courtship: "People are good, I am sincerely fond of them, but how is it that I can't talk to anyone?—God has willed that I feel at home only with you." "Every moment I live is yours completely and I can't change the fact that my senses are focused only on you."

Being in love is what that is: intellectual and sensual love with upswings and crashes, with bliss and smashups, with surrender and jealousy. Günderrode, more mature than Bettina, less caught up emotionally, shows more reserve, fends her off gently, tries to soothe, to shape, to educate. At the same time, she observes her naïver friend, who lives unhesitantly off her inspirations, affections, and convictions, with a fascination bordering on envy and reveals to her her secret thoughts: "To know much, to learn much, only not to survive one's youth. To die young." Whereupon Bettina writes her a letter about the eternity of youth, and another about her love for the stars, which instill her with "confidence in justice," with disdain for "earthly fate," and with the courage to obey the "pure voice of conscience" and to act nobly. "But whatever is won by courage is always the truth; what makes the spirit despair is a lie. Mental timidity is eerie and frightening. Thinking your own thoughts is the highest courage."— "I don't know how much you are capable of," Günderrode replies, "but of this much I am certain: that not only my circumstances but my nature, too, impose narrower limits on my actions. For this reason it could easily be that something is possible for you that is not yet possible for me."

She discusses poetry with her friend, dictates poems to her when her own eyes are failing, goes for walks with her outside town, and reads or studies history with her. She listens seriously to Bettina's bizarre suggestions on how to improve the world: for the two talk again and again about no less a subject than how out of joint everything is. "Why shouldn't we think together about the welfare and needs of mankind?"—"Thoughts on government" occur to the anything-but-retiring Bettina. "If I were on the throne," she brags, "I would revolutionize the world, laughing the whole time."

The need of both women was "to become whole!" In the years of their friendship, Günderrode devoted herself to studying Schelling's philosophy of nature. ("At the same time I thanked fate for letting me live long enough to understand something of Schelling's divine philosophy and to intuit what I did not yet understand; and that at least I learned to appreciate all the heavenly truths of this theory, before my death.") Her own philosophical attitude was fundamentally akin to the ideas of the young Schelling. One early evidence of this is her "Apocalyptic Fragment," which builds up the mystical longing for oneness with nature, for the "wellsprings of life," for release from the "narrow confines" of the personal self, into a vision of the unity and continuity of all living things: "It is not two, not three, not thousands, it is One and All; it is not body and soul divided, so that one belongs to time and the other to eternity, it is One that belongs to itself, and is time and eternity at once, and visible and invisible, permanent in change, a life without end."

Those of her works which she shared with Bettina were the very ones in which Karoline—in the guise of various invented characters—retraced the path to the origins, to unformed chaos, to the underworld, to the mothers, to the point at which consciousness and being were not yet separate; the place of unity, prime matter, pre-creation. A wanderer who suffers from his awareness, who craves nonbeing in his mother's womb, is informed by earth spirits:

> Becoming we can command, but Being not,
> And you already are parted from your mother's womb,
> By consciousness already cut off from the dream.
> But gaze down into your own soul's foundations:
> What you seek here, it's there that you will find it.
> The universe's seeing mirror you are, that's all.
> There, too, are midnights which will one day dawn,
> There, too, are powers which awake from sleep,
> There, too, is one of nature's forging places.

Bettina took up her friend's ideas eagerly, excited by this appeal to powers which derived from the "mother's womb" instead of from the father's brain, that is, the head of Zeus, like Pallas Athena: an alternative to the sources of classicism, a turn toward archaic, partly matriarchal models. They reread mythology—not just the Greek, which had dominated the study of myth in the past, but prehistoric myth and the teachings of India, Asia, the East. Eurocentrism had been breached and, with it, the exclusive rule of the conscious mind. These letters perceive, describe, acknowledge the unconscious forces which seek expression in impulses, wishes, dreams, thus expanding the range of experience, of what is accepted as reality. "Everything we say must be true because we feel it."

For Günderrode, the truth of feeling was anything but a license for vagueness. Sometimes she reproved her friend: "Do you think, when you are staggering around a bit drunk, that that is ineffable spirit?" Over and over she admonished Bettina to study history: "That's why history seemed important to me, to renew the sluggish, vegetative life of your thoughts . . . Persevere a little, trust me that a grounding in history is suitable, in fact essential to your imagination, your ideas . . . Where will you get a grip on yourself if you have no ground to stand on?" And then, in a phrase which fully expresses her and which could have been written by Hölderlin: "Because that's the thing—holy clarity—which alone assures us of whether the spirits embrace us with love."

The two women complemented each other. They had astonishing insights. "We live now in a time of ebb tide," Günderrode wrote to Bettina, and Bettina, shocked at the way people were turned into masks, sought the causes for their sadness and loneliness: "I was thinking how swiftly thoughts come to us and how time lags behind, unable to fulfill them, and that this surge of life which finds nowhere to empty itself is the sole source of melancholy . . . If only deeds would come to outstrip our craving, so that we would not always have to beat our breasts at the sluggish way our lives go on . . . That would be true health, and then we would learn to part from what we love and would learn to build the world, and that would bring joy to the depths of our souls. That is how it *must* be, for there is much work to do in the world: to me at least it seems that nothing is as it should be."

That is how it *must* be, but the deeds do not come to outstrip craving, and the craving itself is buried again for decades.

Günderrode, intimate as she is with Bettina—she shows her the dagger she carries and the spot below her heart which a doctor indicated was the right place to stab—seems not to have taken Bettina into her confidence about what really lay closest to her heart, her love for Creuzer. Creuzer, who had a jealous dislike of the Brentano family, and especially of Bettina, managed to get Günderrode to turn away from her friend. Both women suffered acutely, particularly the younger, who installed herself at the feet of Goethe's mother on the

Hirschgraben and transferred her overflowing emotion to her and to her revered son. Bettina entered a new chapter of her life after the death of her friend Karoline, for whom she wrote the most fitting memorial. Later she married Achim von Arnim, became lady of Wiepersdorf, his country estate in Brandenburg, and the mother of seven children. She knew sobriety, and the prose of life, in full measure. Many of her early companions—her brother Clemens and Savigny—approached or joined reactionary political and clerical movements, under the impress of the Restoration. In one of her letters to the King of Prussia, she felt able to write this about herself: "Whatever the sins of which I have been guilty, yet certainly lack of truthfulness was not one of them. For everything which took root in me in the heyday of my ideals lives on in me now without hindrance."

It is not hard to imagine what Günderrode loved in her friend Bettina: the beautiful anti-type to the pared-down, petty-minded, mealymouthed social conformist; her pride, love of freedom, the radicalness of her thoughts and hopes, her incarnation of utopia.

5

To give birth to what slays me . . .

"Last night I dreamed a strange dream which I cannot forget. I felt I was lying in bed. A lion lay at my right, a she-wolf at my left, and a bear at my feet! They were all half on top of me, and sound asleep. Then I thought: If these animals woke up, they would become furious with each other and tear each other to shreds—and me, too. I grew terribly afraid and stole out from among them and ran away. The dream seems allegorical. What do you think?"

Friedrich Creuzer, to whom this letter and this question were addressed, made no comment about Günderrode's allegorical dream. Perhaps he was scared off by the ravening animals which she saw surrounding her: presumably he was not given to such wild dreams himself. Günderrode, a talented dreamer, very probably understood her dream, which describes her situation with such uncanny precision. Her incompatible desires, cravings, and passions would tear her to pieces, were they to awaken, were she to set them free.

The few women who avoided marrying conventionally for financial support and social status, and who expressed a personal passion, faced the wounding experience that their kind of love could not be returned; and the experience could be fatal. This theme runs all through the poetry of women, for a period of almost two centuries. Günderrode set the tone:

NOWHERE WITHOUT LOVE

Burning wishes can my sad heart bear
and see life's garlands blossom all around
yet pass them by with my own head uncrowned,
and not in grief give way to sore despair?

Shall I blaspheme, renounce what I want most?
Shall bravely I to Shadow's kingdom go,
pray other gods their other joys bestow,
and ask a newer bliss from some poor ghost?

So I went down, but even in Pluto's zone
where nights are born, love's fire burns the same:
there, longing shades for other shadows moan.

Lost is the one whom love ordains to lack,
though well he may descend to stygian stream:
for even in heaven's gold he'd dwell in black.

She sent this sonnet to Friedrich Creuzer in May 1805. "Am I to give up love?" The question was asked by the betrayed nymph in a story called "Daphnis and Pandrose." Savigny had recommended to Günderrode that she read it, in the same letter in which he talked about his burned hand; the same letter in which, retreating from her unconditional love, he offered her his friendship. In 1807, Bettina wrote to Savigny, the same Savigny: "Dear old boy, Shall my whole being dry up again without being enjoyed, shall it benefit no one; go back to sleep again unnoticed, as when it first awoke?" And more than a century and a half later, the question was repeated by Ingeborg Bachmann, in a poem with a meter and a message very similar to Günderrode's:

Explain to me, Love, what I cannot explain:
Should I, for the short dreadful while,
be friends with thought only, and alone
know nothing sweet, do nothing dear?
Must someone think? Isn't he missed?

This is doom. The same moment which enabled women to become persons—that is, to create their "real selves," at least in a poem—this same historic moment compelled the men to give themselves up, to partition themselves, damaged their ability to love, drove them to dismiss as "unrealistic" the claims of independent women who were

capable of love. Men were called on to be objective. Those who could
not submit to the commandment—the poets—were pushed into the
margins. ("Where then shall I go?" cried Hölderlin, lamenting the
loss of his homeland, and then retreated to a spiritual homeland: "Be
thou, song, my kindly refuge!") Women, relying on exclusive love,
unreserved devotion, experienced the horror of being turned into
lower-ranking objects. Here lie the roots of passions from which there
is no escape.

The experience of creating one's own unhappiness in the very
act of creating one's real self—the experience of "giving birth to what
slays me"—must lead either to complete desensitization or to an
intensification of feeling. The more absolute, the more significant
Günderrode became as a poet, the more unsuitable a partner she
became for a man who was tied to a "conditional life." Compelled to
love, but unqualified for the life of a middle-class woman: how to
resolve the conflict? Forcibly suppress her aptitudes? or be sentenced
to loneliness, lovelessness? No way out. Creuzer offered her an emotion that bordered on adoration, on religious veneration—but he could
not live with her in the ordinary way of earth.

He *really* could not.

Creuzer was nine years older than Günderrode. People who knew
him described him as ugly, and he felt he was, too. Despite his great
gifts, his self-confidence wavered. As the son of a bookbinder and
tax collector in Marburg, he could not have afforded to attend university without aid from benefactors. It took him a notably long time
to tell Günderrode that the wealthy Savigny had helped to finance his
studies. This financial assistance seems to have left him with an
enduring affection for Savigny and an equally enduring resentment.
When one of his professors died, Creuzer married his widow, "out of
gratitude." Sophie Leske was thirteen years older than Creuzer, a
simple woman who had brought up several children, who kept house
faithfully for both her husbands, and who, when Creuzer wanted to
leave her, went through her own tragedy, that of an aging woman
trying to hold on to her husband with all the means at her disposal:
changing moods, changing decisions, reproaches, angry scenes followed by periods of unnatural tolerance. Once, with what may have
been unintentional cunning, she gave her husband proof that he was
lost without her. Weary of their nerve-racking confrontations, she left
him for a day. He found he did not know how to pay a bill, where to
look for the household money, where the key to a drawer was kept.
It was a housewife's revenge against the man who had been allowed
to educate his mind while leaving her to deal with the practical
everyday chores. "See, that's how things stand now!" the resigned

Creuzer reported to Günderrode. "I have paid dearly for a sin against nature—which now has turned into an iron fate."

The correspondence between Creuzer and Savigny reveals that Creuzer not only made outstanding contributions to his own field of classical philology but also, when he was called to Heidelberg to help rejuvenate the stagnating university, busied himself with its most mundane affairs: staff appointments, salaries, planning schemes, professional intrigues. Karoline, barred even from dreaming of a practical occupation, devoted all her time to her love for him. Around midnight, he subtracted an hour from his short sleep to read her letters and writings. In the end, he irritably accused her of being unable to imagine how restricting he found his situation.

In October 1804, no one yet foresaw any of this. In the beginning, Creuzer was more intense and insistent than Karoline ("Surely I am meant to say no less than my heart feels?"). He visited her in Frankfurt "to lie against her heart," and was permitted to "warm himself on her chaste bosom"—whatever that may mean, whatever the metaphor may imply or not imply. She invited him to use the familiar form of address: "Call me *du*." "*Jacta est alea*"—the die is cast—the accomplished Latinist wrote to his friend and cousin Leonhard Creuzer in Marburg. "Middle way there is none—it is heaven or hell." With a grim presentiment of the future, he attached to his short note of rejoicing the words: "*Incipit tragoedia*." The tragedy has begun. The ravening beasts are starting to wake up.

It is a bourgeois tragedy. This time Karoline, resisting the compulsion to repeat the past, plays the principal role; but those who depart from the ordinary are rewarded with death. All the supporting roles are cast according to type: the lover who shrinks from the consequences; the wronged wife defending her property, her husband; the loyal woman friend and confidante who carries letters back and forth between the lovers, gives them keys to safe rendezvous, arranges meetings: she is Susanne von Heyden, half sister to Lisette Nees von Esenbeck. Then come the true and false advisers: Savigny, dubious but offering the best advice he can; Daub and Schwarz, two theologians from Heidelberg who show differing degrees of trustworthiness and of ability to look beyond their own conventional notions of morality; gossipmongers, chief among them Sophie Daub, née Blum, a childhood acquaintance of Karoline's and "an abyss of prose and conventionality." Friends, onlookers, innocent bystanders. The scenes of the action: the balcony of the castle in Heidelberg, the theater in Mainz, Karoline's room at the convent. Brief meetings at inns. Two or three times, a rendezvous at the Kettenhof near Frankfurt. It does not suit Karoline to sneak there to meet her lover. She does it anyhow. She would do anything.

Letters, more letters. Creuzer's letters to Karoline were published in 1912, and fill a volume more than three hundred pages long. Of her letters we have only nine extracts, and even these were not found until the 1930s—irony of ironies—among the papers of the Leske family, the family of Creuzer's wife. The snooping Sophie had copied out passages from the letters which her rival wrote to her husband. Karoline's friend Susanne von Heyden, on the other hand, burned all of Karoline's letters after her death: an immeasurable loss. Everything in this story happens upside down, to satisfy the upside-down moral: after the victim's death, the evidence against her is confiscated.

And yet this perverse morality played its role in the drama all along. Much of the communication between the lovers was devoted to the precautions they had to take so that they could send and receive letters without Sophie's knowledge. They talked about when, where, and whether they could write; whether the cover addresses were safe; and since the correspondents could never be completely sure that their letters would not fall into the wrong hands, they also decided to use Greek alphabetical signs and quaint aliases to conceal their identity. So Karoline became known as "Poetry" and Creuzer as "the Pious Man"—apparently he earned this title by marital abstinence —while Sophie became "the Kindly One" and the intriguer Sophie Daub was "the Enemy." It would all seem like a children's game if the stakes were not so high, and if gossip, misunderstanding, and malicious rumors had not worn down their resistance. The persistent rumors alarmed Creuzer again and again. And the more intimidated he became, and the more hopeless his prospects of marrying the woman he loved, the more exalted was the picture he painted of her. At first he had addressed her as "dear, dear girl"; then she turned into the "pure and simple handmaid of the Lord," and "angel," "the most holy virgin" (*sanctissima virgo*), the "Muse," and finally "Poetry." But Günderrode was a young woman who would gladly have given up the elevated status of an allegory in exchange for the opportunity to live and work with the man she loved. For in their ideas, knowledge, interests, and talents, the pair were a good match for each other, and they stimulated each other to productive work. Creuzer suggested Greek philosophers for Günderrode to read and shared with her his views about ancient Greek culture, which he regarded as based in the Orient, and about the derivation of all religions from a mythology common to all the races and continents. Günderrode valued his criticisms of her writings, which show clear traces of his influence;

and in turn, his later work, *Symbolik und Mythologie der alten Völker* [*The Symbolism and Mythology of Ancient Peoples*], 1810–12 could not have taken the shape it did without her influence. Their work bears witness that they were able, in their best hours, to go beyond their unendurable dependency on the outward circumstances of their lives.

Creuzer, prone to upset and self-pity, shackled to his job, shrinking from an act of "human sacrifice," wrote to Karoline—he was thirty-five at the time: "I am already an aging man. I have pledged my word to marriage and to the state. I accepted that some thoughts of mine ought to last for twenty years, and to have a solid social foundation. I am supposed to set an example of steadiness to the young, with whom I am charged in the role of mentor; I am not supposed to have any poetry myself, although at the same time I am called upon to speak of poetry to others." To judge poetry while having none themselves has been the fate of most professors in Germany; but those who came later seem to have experienced this as less of a conflict than did their unfortunate forebear.

Günderrode, meanwhile, compelled to put on disguises again, once more adopted a man's role: for she could not entirely avoid repetitions of the past. She referred to herself as "the Friend," using the masculine form of the noun, as she had done with Savigny. And when she wrote to Creuzer, she was forced to formally deny herself by speaking of herself in the third person: "The Friend was just here . . . I assure you that he is completely devoted to you. Tell me, how did you win his affection to such an extent? As for the other parts of his life, I notice increasingly that his heroic soul has completely dissolved in love's tenderness and longing. This condition is not good for one who must stand on his own and who very probably will never be united with the object of his love." She went so far as to change the title and pronouns in one of her poems from the masculine form to the feminine, so as to make it appear that it was addressed by a man to a woman instead of the other way around:

THE ONE AND ONLY

How is all my sense confined!
To one alone I bend my mind.
This one being to make mine:
here's my sole desire defined.
One joy only, my eye can see:
to feed this longing secretly;
by dreams deceived, this world to flee,

consumed by what I wish would be,
and giving birth to what slays me.

There is no more joking, teasing, irony, and self-ridicule. The tone of deep and imperative earnestness is maintained throughout, sometimes tinged with serenity or resignation, more rarely by passion and revolt—more and more often by despair: "My soul is bleak."

Their situation is hopeless. They realize it, forget it again, are forced to rediscover it; the strain is unending and unendurable. The trap closes on all three people. It is already a *fait accompli* "that two people are being sacrificed here, merely because they are unable to sacrifice the third." "It is better to die than to kill," Creuzer consoles himself. Only he is not the one who dies. Sublimating what he calls his "lustfulness," he splits himself into two people, one who exists on the surface and one inside: "I am one of the wooden figures of Silenus which themselves are poorly made, but which serve as containers for magnificent statues of gods." Karoline was expected to bring off the trick of loving not his appearance, his habits, his manners, not *him*, but only what was beautiful about him: the divine image sealed up inside him, his inner nature. "There you see the guideline for your conduct toward me: Leave me, or rather, teach me to leave you as a woman—but do not abandon my beautiful soul." Then he swore an unsolicited and unwelcome vow: he would "henceforth not allow to arise again the simpleminded notion that in order to have poetry, one must necessarily couple with it."

Creuzer was not the first man who castrated himself for the privilege of serving at court. Now that the two bodies, stripped of spirit, had been made to see reason, the two spirits, disembodied, were free to approach each other. They were supposed to form a mental fellowship in which Creuzer would play the part of adoring worshipper while Günderrode's poetry arched above them like a rainbow. This is mortifying the flesh as the basis for kitsch! Creuzer set up his lonely bed far away from poor Sophie's bedroom, and concealed Karoline's letters under innocent-looking piles of paperwork until late at night, when he took them out to read. But this was supposed to be a tragedy, not a comedy. The ending is what decides. Self-mutilation founded on simplemindedness. It should not surprise us: after all, we are almost in the Victorian Age.

Günderrode was confused. She dreamed up fantastic schemes whose extravagance stood in marked contrast to the banal obstacles that blocked her way. She thought of coming to live in Creuzer's home as the third party (the third, once again!) in a *ménage à trois*, with Sophie serving as housekeeper and maternal friend to the two lovers!

Then when Creuzer was invited to teach at the University of Moscow, she wanted to accompany him dressed as a man and pretend to be one of his students, so that she could be around him all the time. Unfortunately, the rumormongers got wind of this absurd plan. Sophie intercepted letters, and Lisette Nees wrote angrily to Karoline: "Your imagination may well take revenge against you, for trying to transfer it into the realm of domestic relations." The circle of people who still understood her, melted away. Unhappiness with no way out makes a person alone.

Suddenly—just as Sophie changed her mind again and agreed to a divorce—a few gossips and friends of Creuzer's voiced doubts as to whether Karoline was really fit for marriage, and one theologian expressed concern that she might be a "follower of the newer philosophy," meaning the philosophy of Schelling, which dispensed with belief in a personal God. So now her beliefs were to be regarded as the crucial test of a woman's fitness: admittedly a step forward, compared with the criteria of the past. Günderrode gathered her pride together and said, "Am I to apologize for what I consider one of my good points?" And once she told Creuzer that each time any conflict arose, he always seemed willing to sacrifice her, in preference to anything else.

But Creuzer, too, arouses our pity. "Oh, if only Sophie were really great or really awful—in either case, I would be saved. But this deadly goodness!" In a situation like this, when the claim to normal happiness looked out of the ordinary, a person who was merely average seemed to block it more effectively than a superman or a monster. Renunciation, resignation turned into virtues. Love turned into guilt. The answer Günderrode gave was: grief.

MY ONE COMPLAINT

Who the deepest wound of all
knows in spirit and in soul:
the pain when two must part—
He who loves what he then loses
and must leave what he still chooses:
that beloved heart.

Who sees how joy with tears is filled
and love's longing never stilled:
in twoness to be one—
in another, self to find

so boundaries vanish out of mind
and being's pain is gone.

Who thus heart and senses whole
fastens on another soul,
he is not consoled
when for joys today erased
new joys come to take their place:
they're not like the old.

This sweet life, so soon to go,
this give and take we cherish so,
word and sense and look,
both this searching and this finding,
all this thinking and this minding:
no God gives them back.

Deeply sad, exhausted, she voiced a longing for death. Creuzer, who once had seemed resolutely prepared to die, now implored her: "I will not stop until you promise me that you will stay alive as long as you can; and this is the only purpose of our union: that we will be glad to go when Nature calls us away, filled with glad confidence that we will find love even among the shades."

Günderrode—trapped in the mistake so many women make, that they are unable to separate life, love, and work—made this reply:

Your letter, which I received a short time ago, looked so strange to me this afternoon, and I could not clearly understand either its language or its looks. It is so sensible, so filled with the urge for useful activity, and so content with life. But I have already lived for many days in Orcus and had thought to wend my way there soon and painlessly, not just in my thoughts, no, but with the whole of me. I had hoped to find you there, too, but you are thinking about other things. You are just now getting really settled in life, and as you say yourself, the purpose of our union should be 'that we will be glad to go when Nature calls us away'—which I expect we would have done anyhow, even if we had never met each other. I had something very different in mind, and if this is all you intended, then you are quite mistaken about me, as I am about you, because then you are not the man I take you to be . . . The friendship that I meant to have with you was a union for life and death. Is that too serious for you? Or too irrational? Once upon a time you seemed to attach great importance to the idea of dying with me, and of pulling me down to join you if you should die before me. But now you have much weightier things to consider—that I could still prove useful in the world somehow, and then it would be a pity if you were to be the cause of my dying so young. Now you expect me to follow your example and think the same thoughts about you. That is a kind of rationality that I do not understand.

Her letter is a horribly calm confession of loyalty to a different kind of reason, which did not fit into the world, which could not be tolerated because its mere presence made nonsense of the idea of usefulness, the delusion of rational people that they must give themselves up for the sake of something "greater." "I want to apply the finest flower of my male intellect to a work which, in striving to reveal what lay at the heart of the ancient world with all its piety and sacredness, seems a not unworthy offering to lay on the altar of Poetry." So wrote the unhappy Creuzer to his beloved. She was spared nothing. A living woman, turned first into an abstraction, an allegory, and then into an idol to whom the man makes sacrificial offerings. And what does he offer? His noblest possession, his achievements.

"Only a miracle can bring you two together: death or money." This laconic remark from Karoline's loyal friend Susanne von Heyden summed up the situation perfectly. Susanne meant that the lovers could be saved only by Sophie's death, or by enough money to make Karoline independent, so that Creuzer could supply his wife an adequate income after their divorce.

More and more, their letters showed them as people who were forced to misjudge each other, against their will.

Sad soliloquies.

Karoline: "I am alone after all, it doesn't matter to anyone if I look sad or merry."

Creuzer: "Are you really alone? But you have me. See, I am yours and I look forward to the springtime when I will be permitted to enjoy your company innocently, and to love you as one loves a faithful friend."

Karoline: "You speak as if it is not necessary for me to belong to you."

Creuzer: "Ah, nothing satisfies or ever will satisfy me but the dear tangible presence from which I now am torn away."

Karoline: "I had a terrible moment recently. I felt that I had been insane for many years and had just come to my senses, and when I asked for you, I was told that you were long dead. This thought was madness, and if it had lasted more than a moment, it would have torn my brain apart. So do not talk to me about being happy in some other love."

Creuzer: *"Oh, sanctissima virgo!"*

Karoline (in Latin): "I love you unto death, sweet dear friend, I wish to live or die with you."

Creuzer, while walking along the Rhine: "I would have liked to throw myself in, so the strong wide river would carry me to you!"

Karoline: "Ours is a sad fate. Like you I envy the rivers which can merge. Death is better than a life like this."

A remarkable self-protective instinct prevented Creuzer from seeing the signs which all pointed to her death. He kept trying to pacify her, as Savigny had done in the past: "Do not give way to such storms of emotion!" He ventured to assign her the ideal "climate" which ought to reign in her soul: "Cloudless, clear, calm, and gently refreshed by a mild heat." He went so far as to demand: "You owe me peace!"

Filled with inner foreboding, we watch the professor submit to being put through his paces for two long years. In the end he had had enough. "I must endure your thinking me a very limited person. Which I know quite well that in fact I am. How could it be otherwise, growing up as I did, of German stock, in an impoverished milieu, and living on among soulless, dull bourgeois."

So his life dragged on. Had literature already pronounced this verdict? Or was it still to be spoken? Segments of time overlap. Lenz had already been dead for fifteen years. It would be thirty years more before Büchner invented that line to describe him.*

For Creuzer, there was no more rebellion, no plans, no hopes. There was still sentiment, self-pity; concern that Günderrode might have too idealized a view of him; resentment of his salaried position, compared to the life of the "freelance" author. He complained that he was forced to lead a life of complete dependency, "not a life like yours, where every day is Sunday." One can see him becoming more petty. Jealously he would accuse Günderrode of being "frivolous" in the way she treated casual acquaintances. She seemed willing to oblige all his wishes, so he managed to separate her from Bettina and from the whole Brentano family, "power-hungry and vain as they are." He was capable of writing her sentences like this: "It all stems from the fact that you have no courage." Before meeting her in Winkel am Rhein, he warned her to watch out for all the Frankfurt families there!

He made no more stops in his headlong flight. In seven carefully structured paragraphs, the pitiful man explained the logic of his behavior to the woman who apparently had complained about some-

---

* "So his life dragged on" is the last line of Georg Büchner's 1839 novella *Lenz*, about the life of the deranged writer J.M.R. Lenz, who died in 1792.

thing. When he reached point 7, he delivered the crowning blow: "Love I may permit myself, but not the full possession of a love which is forgetful of self." And finally, to pay her back for reacting as she had, the bitter and resigned assertion: "Your letter of today proves to me what I have long known: you cannot imagine what a life as restricted as mine is like."

The little bit of solid ground under her feet had given way. Reality, in larger and larger chunks, kept invading her dreams, and her nightmares. Günderrode had been through this before. "And so I live to see dreams all my days." In May 1806, she wrote to Creuzer, whom she had christened "Eusebio": "The Friend was with me only a moment ago. He was very lively, and an uncommon flush burned upon his cheek. He said that in his morning slumber he dreamed of Eusebio, of how he was wholly united with him and had walked with him through enchanting valleys and wooded hills, in blessed love and freedom. Isn't a dream like that worth more than a year of my life? If I spent only a few months as happy and as guiltless as in this dream, how gladly would I die, and with what gratitude to the gods! It would be too small a price to pay if in exchange I should lay my head on the execution block, and without turning pale like a coward I would await the fatal stroke."

Anxious messages sent over a yawning abyss. At the end of July Creuzer visited her once more in Frankfurt. Nothing is known about this meeting. He returned from the trip deeply exhausted, his strength used up. He became very ill, lost consciousness, developed a fever. In a moment of clarity he gathered his friends around him, and through Daub he sent Karoline word that their relationship was at an end.

Karoline in the meantime had gone to Winkel, where she stayed on the country estate of a merchant, Joseph Merten, waiting for news. She received a brief stay of execution when the horrified Susanne von Heyden, to whom Daub had written, passing on Creuzer's message, wrote back to ask if it was true: Creuzer's decision, she said, could mean Günderrode's death. Daub confirmed his friend's pious decision. Susanne took precautions, and sent on the fatal letter in an envelope, with disguised handwriting, to another friend of Karoline's who was with her in Winkel, asking her to prepare Karoline gradually for the blow. But Karoline, charged with foreboding and unable not to live up to the absurd conventions of tragic drama, intercepted the letter, opened it, and read her death sentence. She wrote a few lines in her room and then calmly told her friend that she was going for a walk. In the evening, when she failed to return, people found the letters in her room and began to search for her with growing alarm. Toward morning, a farmer discovered her body on a spit of land by the Rhine among a plantation of willow trees. Her upper body lay in the water. She had stabbed herself to death.

The place of her suicide was later covered by the river. Günderrode was buried in Winkel, by the cemetery wall. She wrote her epitaph herself. It was a quotation from an East Indian poet which she had found when reading Herder, and she went on to change the wording slightly. It perfectly expressed her general feeling about the world, and the frame of mind in which she went to her death:

Earth, you my mother, and you, air, who nourish me,
   Holy fire, my friend, and you, O brother, the mountain river,
And my father, ether. To you all, with reverence, I say:
   My cordial thanks. With you have I lived here below.
And I go to the other world, glad to leave you.
   Farewell, brother and friend, father and mother, farewell.

6

"It would be sad if all mistakes had to end that way!"

Said Savigny. Each of Günderrode's friends commented on her death in a way consistent with his own circumstances, the degree of his independence, and his ability to identify with her feelings.

Lisette Nees, who regarded Karoline's passion as an aberration, wrote to Susanne von Heyden: "Any defection from nature is as much a sin as a defection from morality, because morality after all is only a higher form of nature. Lina sinned against both." This reversion to the Christian tables of the law is astonishing in an enlightened woman like Lisette. But apart from that, she gives a perceptive analysis of the forces which brought about Günderrode's downfall: "She was a victim of the times who fell prey to ideas which affected her powerfully and to moral principles which had gone slack prematurely. An unhappy love was merely the form in which all this manifested itself, the trial by fire which was destined to glorify or consume her."

Susanne von Heyden notified Karoline's brother Hektor of his sister's death: "Her dagger, with which you are so familiar, stabbed the angel through the heart. She could not live without love, her whole being was eaten up with weariness of her life . . . Her heart was greater than this world, only the most heartfelt love could keep it alive, and when this died, her heart broke, too."

Bettina wrote a long letter about Günderrode's death which was worthy of her friend. She happened to be traveling on the Rhine when she heard the rumor about a "beautiful young lady" who had committed suicide in Winkel, and she was convinced that it had to be Günder-rode. Her suspicion was confirmed. "Oh, you great spirits, what monstrous power moved this innocent lamb, this timid young heart, to such an act?"

And Achim von Arnim, who had known Günderrode since 1802, wrote: "We could not give her enough to chain her here, not sing loudly enough to blow out the Furies' torches of an unhappy passion that was alien to her nature." He described as "gruesome" the dissection performed on her body by a doctor who claimed that her spinal cord revealed a predilection to suicide. This incident made a macabre parallel to the medical dissection performed on that other suicide, Heinrich von Kleist, whose "clotted bile" led the ignorant physician to conclude that his subject was given to "hypochondria." Years later, Arnim revisited the spot where Günderrode died: "Poor singer, can the Germans of our time do nothing but keep silent about what is beautiful, forget what is excellent, and desecrate what is earnest?"

This question would be memorial enough.

Whose comment is still missing? Goethe's. He made no reply when Achim von Arnim sent him the news. In 1810, he walked with Bettina in the park at Teplitz and afterward recorded these notes: "Detailed account of her relationship with Fräulein Günderrode. The character of this remarkable girl and her death." These lines might well belong to an outline for a play. Then, in 1814, Goethe went traveling along the Rhine. "I was shown the spot in a willow thicket by the Rhine where Fräulein von Günderrode took her life. Hearing the story of this calamity on the spot where it happened, from people who had been in the area and had taken part in the events, gave me the uncomfortable feeling which is always occasioned by a place of tragedy: just as one cannot go to Eger* without feeling surrounded by the spirits of Wallenstein and his companions." And with that remark, he disposes of whatever discomfort he may have felt.

And what about Creuzer?

Creuzer continued to be seriously ill for several more weeks. People spared his feelings in a way that they had never spared the dead woman's when she was alive. The news of Karoline's death hit him hard. He believed that he would never again be able to teach, and recovered very slowly.

After Karoline's death, the tragedy seemed to deteriorate into a Gothic play or a melodrama. Her mother warned Creuzer that Karoline's brother Hektor, who was studying in Heidelberg, might seek vengeance against him. "Ridiculous generosity!" Creuzer said fu-

---

* The Czech town of Cheb, where Wallenstein was murdered.

riously. "How pitiable I would be if I had need of it! and how unworthy is any fear, any passion, of the blessed peace which now surrounds her sleep!" It is hard to imagine a more extreme repression and misunderstanding than this. The man was done for, as a man. From then on, he always referred to his wife as "my Sophie." He even outlived her, married again, and lived to the age of eighty-seven. He never mentioned Karoline again.

Now he was wax in the hands of his friends. They convinced him that it was essential for him to get hold of all the material that he had written to Günderrode. So Frau von Heyden emptied out her friend's desk, whose most intimate secret was well known to her, and handed over the evidence. In return, Creuzer gave her all the letters Karoline had written to him, asking her to burn them. She conscientiously carried out his instructions.

But his friends were still busy thinking. They decided that it might be unwise to destroy immediately the letters which Creuzer had written to the "dear departed"—"because who knows, you might have to make use of them." In plain language, he might have to use them to prove his innocence of any wrongdoing. We cannot really disapprove of this calculating behavior, because it at least preserved Creuzer's letters, except for a few especially compromising bits. Creuzer's loyal and pious cousin Leonhard kept them safe. "And let me hear nothing more about them," Creuzer said.

So was the tragedy now at an end?

Not quite. The curtain rose once more. There was an epilogue, owing to the unfortunate habit that writers have of leaving pieces of paper behind them in the faithful hands of posterity. Posterity is then free to kill the dead all over again, by malice or neglect. In unfortunate cases, the agents whom the author blindly entrusted to look after his writings are the very people who destroy them. Günderrode's case is one of those.

In January 1806, she had sent her friend Creuzer her newest manuscript, entitled *Mnemosyne*, and asked him to help get it published. Creuzer wrote to her: "You won't believe how happy you have made me with your idea about the little book *Mnemosyne*, and what a rapture it is for me to see the love of the pious man and the friend glorified in this way. Will I publish it? No task could delight me more. But you are right when you say that the greatest secrecy must be observed." He mentioned the book's title and the pseudonym which its author had chosen. When Günderrode, against his advice, persisted in wanting to use the pen name Ion, he finally agreed: "Ionia is, to be sure, the birthplace of poetry. Very well, the child shall be called Ion." On the other hand, she accepted his suggestion when it came to the title. They decided to call the book *Melete*, after an ancient Muse associated with the life of the senses. Never, one might think, has an author entrusted his work to a more reliable agent.

Among Creuzer's letters are some that are as thorough, knowledgeable, and helpful as any poet could wish to receive from his friend, and any woman from her lover. He wrote to Karoline about metrics and the philosophy of Schlegel, about women poets who had written in Latin, and about the strong and weak features of her writing; and his judgments were such that a critic of today could readily agree with them. Karoline's field, Creuzer said, was not drama, and certainly not bourgeois drama, but lyric poetry, myth, and legend. He understood the value of the work she had entrusted to him, and even expressed fear of the mental superiority of the woman he loved: "Alas, I no longer have the courage to tease you like a child and make you my vassal in love (as we men like to do) when I behold such wisdom. You scare away your Eusebio. Truly, you must behave foolishly when I come, and play loving games, to give me courage. You must put away your excellence—otherwise, I cannot be gay when I am with you." We cannot know, and dare not suggest, whether Creuzer's feeling of inferiority to this woman, who was his intellectual equal, may have influenced his behavior later, without his realizing it.

But at first he did his best to get *Melete* published. On February 23 he wrote to Günderrode: "I have sold *Melete* to the firm of Zimmer and Mohr right here in town." He explained his reason for choosing this firm—which, incidentally, later published *Des Knaben Wunderhorn*, and mentioned that the fee would be a carlino a page: "The more I feel the inner value of a work, the less able I am to haggle about its outward price." Everything got off to a promising start. But the little book was never printed. After Karoline's death, Creuzer, foreseeing that he was going to "sink back more and more into the desert of ordinary life," reclaimed "Ion's" manuscript from the publishers. This is an unusual case in the history of German censorship and self-censorship, which is rich in bizarre and lunatic events. Why did Creuzer do it? Self-interest, pure and simple. "Daub marshaled arguments which . . . convinced me that it was absolutely necessary to suppress this piece." Desperation took hold of him again. Günderrode's mad dreams became reality.

Sucked into the absurd logic of it all, one cannot help thinking that it is just as well that she died before she saw that happen: it might have driven her mad. For unlike us, she was not acquainted with the history and literature of the next one hundred and seventy years, which accustomed us to the evil transformations which the ruling moral code can cause in those who submit to it.

And what happened to her book? It disappeared for a long time. Fifty years after Günderrode's death, when the first collection of what purported to be her "complete works" was published, *Melete* was not mentioned. Nor did Creuzer's name appear in the book. Apparently, the attempts to wipe out all connection between the two of them had been successful. It was left to chance to resurrect her book. Incredibly, a single copy, composed partly of printed sheets and partly of manuscript, had ended up in Castle Neuburg near Heidelberg, where it was preserved. Not until 1896 was the public informed of its existence and given some sample selections. The first unabridged edition of *Melete* was published in 1906 by Dr. Leopold Hirschberg, who printed four hundred copies. The same Dr. Hirschberg edited the beautiful complete edition of Günderrode's works, which was published in 1920.

Creuzer had recognized the truth about this book: its remaining texts are a ceaselessly repeated declaration of love for him, her "guardian angel," "one and only," "Eusebio." It gives him immortality: an offer which was too much for him. We who know the history of the little volume cannot read the dedication without feeling moved:

> *For you, in hours of quiet gravity,*
> *in holy solitude, with watchful mind,*
> *the many flowers into a wreath I twined*
> *which now and in the past have bloomed for me . . .*

And yet: who can stigmatize him as "unworthy"? Who can blame him for wanting to live—when Karoline herself showed him the fate of someone who was not able to make the compromises that living demanded? Peace and quiet were all he wanted, and the peace of the grave was not the kind he had in mind. Günderrode understood clearly what had happened to Creuzer: "You became a stranger in your own home, when you found a home in my heart."

7

"The earth never became my home."

We, her descendants, cannot be expected to rescind that verdict. Her demand for wholeness, unity, depth, and truthfulness of feeling is too alien to our time, as it was to hers; too uncanny is the absoluteness of her need to harmonize life and writing.

It is no easy thing to assimilate her works, especially because we are not used to their mythological wrapping. Without doubt, she did not reach maturity as a writer. In her dramas and playlets, which address the grandest themes (*Mahomet*, for instance) and which she set great store by, she presents pallid characters, often in contrived plots, merely as vehicles to express her ideas, her feelings about the world. Her achievements in poetry and in lyric philosophical prose are extraordinary. Hers is a language of great beauty. Her views, though meaningful, often are not suitably conveyed by the forms available to her. The same is true, in a metaphorical sense, of her life.

Equally strong in intelligence and in the depth of her feeling, she can neither find satisfaction in cool reflection nor dissolve in emotional enthusiasm. She uses writing to bridge the abyss between the poles of her character. She can be herself only when she writes or loves. These two things, writing and loving, are the most authentic expressions of her nature. Her letters form part of her opus, and we can read her poems properly only if we first know her life. She may survive as a figure who had to confront unconditionally the experience of fruitlessness and alienation.

The crack in her times goes through her, too. She splits into several people, one of them a man. "But for this reason I fancy that I am seeing myself lying in the coffin, and my two selves stare at each other in wonderment." She invokes a dream: "A time must come when every being will be in harmony with himself and others." And she sees very clearly how things are going to be, for a long time to come: "Life is taken out of our hands, it is lived for us: part of us lives it as a deputy for the other, larger part which remains half asleep and is consumed with longing in the brief moments when it becomes wide awake."

The diagnosis is apt, and we can hardly say her reaction is exaggerated. She is among the first to find an image and an expression for the process of alienation, when she depicts the inner struggle between nature and "proud reason": "Barbarian! do not rejoice at your victory, it is a civil war that you have waged, the conquered were your own nature's children, you killed yourself in your victories, you died in your battles. The peace bought with such sacrifices was too costly for me, and I could no longer bear the thought of destroying part of myself so as better to preserve another part."

So she herself explains why she cannot go on living: because it was life she craved, not death. What she abandoned was not life but non-life. She had gambled, with herself as the stake; but another game was going on whose rules she did not know or wish to learn. Can we picture Günderrode as an aging canoness whose poems were bound to dissolve into sentiment and abstraction, cut off as she was from the sources of experience and emotion?

But what else would she have had left?

Writing is kin to utopia. That is, it has a painful yet joyous yen for the absolute. Most people cannot stand to hear others express dissatisfaction with the diminished life which they are forced to put up with themselves. Günderrode is quite familiar with those who belong to "the world" and are unable or not permitted to escape from it. "I was never one of them," she makes one of her characters say; significantly it is a man. "I just had a sort of agreement with it: it gave me those of its goods which were indispensable to me, and I gave it what I could. This agreement has ended."

Hers was one attempt to allow art to fit without loss of integrity into a society whose standard of value became quantity at any price; and it failed. The thoroughgoing division of labor has borne its fruit. The producers of material goods and the producers of mental goods have become strangers confronting each other from opposite banks, prevented from joining forces to produce conditions in which they can live. All are laid open to a destruction which is not always clearly evident. The literature of the Germans as a battlefield: that is one way to look at it. It is not complaining to say that writers are predestined to sacrifice and to self-sacrifice.

October 1978

Speaking of Büchner*

I thank the German Academy of Language and Poetry of the city of Darmstadt for awarding me this year's Georg Büchner Prize. On an occasion like this, the dissatisfaction a writer feels about her own work rises to fever pitch and her doubts about her chosen way of life intensify. I will skip over my ongoing struggles with this subject, my account of them being vain and maybe futile, too. I will also omit the pages I wrote about how hard it is for me to talk here today. With Büchner's example confronting me, I feel more troubled than ever by the hidden links between writing and life, between responsibility and guilt, which produce the person who lives by writing and writes while living, and which threaten to tear that person apart by the same process. Today, I believe that these links must be not only endured but accepted. In moments of weakness, it may seem desirable to be innocent and without responsibility; but it is escapist. In the concrete conditions in which we live, write, grow up, learn to see, get involved, fail, rebel again, and crave new experiences, no space is provided for a state of irresponsible innocence. We cannot get away from the here and now, and our masks are torn off as we go along. When the masks come off, "Do the faces come off with them?"†

To read Büchner again is to see your own situation more clearly. "I accustomed my eye to the sight of blood, but I'm no guillotine!" The laborious, often dislocated, plodding, violent, depraved march

* On being awarded the Georg Büchner Prize of the German Academy of Language and Poetry, Darmstadt, West Germany, October 16, 1980.

†* Quotations from Büchner's three plays, *Leonce und Lena* [*Leonce and Lena*], *Dantons Tod* [*Danton's Death*], and *Woyzeck*, and from his novella *Lenz*.

of the Germans through history might suitably be paved with the words of their poets. I'd like to give a speech that was made up of lines from Büchner, which would sound as if it had been written today. But we cannot make up now for what we failed to achieve in his lifetime.

Büchner could never have gotten himself into the embarrassing scrape of having to issue a public thank you. How justified we are to look to him and to his work, the work of this very young man— revolutionary, poet, and scientist—who accepted every risk in order to pluck a livable alternative from the dark conditions of his time. A young man whose feverishly sober dialogues, whose clairvoyant, terse lines of prose must have been wrung out from the press of hellish pain. "The pain began to restore him to consciousness. He told his tale rapidly, but like a prisoner on the rack."

The consciousness that comes out of the pain of madness is no longer the same consciousness he had before. And the tortured language to which it is confined to express itself is alien to the man. Lenz goes mad when he loses his agreement with common sense. We who have sobered up right through to the bones stand dejectedly, face to face with the dream products of a type of thinking which still refers to itself as "reason" but which treats things as means to an end and which long ago abandoned the Enlightenment's quest for emancipation and independent maturity, in exchange for the delusion of naked expediency with which we entered the industrial age. The metaphor of the sorcerer's apprentice, which today is a harmless fairy tale, was initially a stern warning. Once the drive for profit had fused with technological progress, the slogan "Everything is permitted" could be used to cover up every act of violence. Then bourgeois literature, galled enough to fight back, drew the portrait of the aged, blind Faust, who, in a grotesque act of self-deception, interprets the sound of the shovels which are digging his grave as a part of his happy vision of the future. That is a metaphor which sends a shudder through us, more than it could through any previous generation. We are contemporaries of that civilization which treasures money and flawless technology above all else, and which is insane and benighted enough to devote these treasures to products which will bring about its own destruction. We are contemporaries, too, of the new Faust, the "father of the atomic bomb," a man with a humanist education who, when he is blinded by the light of a bomb that is brighter than a thousand suns, remembers lines from a sacred East Indian epic: "I am death, the thief of everything, the shaker of worlds."

What abuse will we see befall literature the next time? What more can happen before words fail us altogether? Into what snarls and what deaths will literature follow us, as the faithful attendant at mankind's funeral? No longer assisting our lives but only our deaths? Confined as we are by a past which for the most part we do not understand, banished into a present which is virtually stripped of alternatives, and full of evil premonitions of the future—how are we to speak? A new cycle of historical conflicts is preparing itself. Will it have time to evolve, in this age when there are means enough to kill each of us many times over? If we imagine a literature whose language and forms express the intellectual and behavioral models of the West, and whose structures have been developed to portray contradictions and to build upon a productive bond among people at a time when we can no longer count on the existence of such a bond —must that literature not be the accomplice of the whole process of alienation? No matter how much it may struggle, twist, and turn? Isn't it true that the only choice literature has left is between crude and refined techniques of deception? In an age when the word is technologically reproducible, isn't it, too, turning against us, who produced it? And isn't all that can be said about our time being said in plastic, concrete, and steel? Isn't what is said monstrous, grim, self-betraying, and mighty, with a might which language cannot attain? So, is the language of literature going to fail us?

"Noble is man!" Goethe said. And Büchner said, "We were created wrong." A fifty-year gap separates Goethe's statement from Büchner's. Büchner saw that the hallmark of the new age was paradox. His century, which resolutely refused to regard itself as paradoxical, quite logically punished him—by ignoring him. Early in life, he experienced that loss of meaning and certitude with which we are so familiar now, and which brings with it a disgust with language. A whole host of words has been taken from us—words which we believed we could rely on, like "liberty," "equality," "fraternity," "humanism," "justice"—and turned over to news journalists, now that these words no longer correspond to any reality and no longer command belief. By the logic of language, their opposite numbers have also lost their meaning, because words such as "terrible," "disastrous," "hideous," "threatening," and "barbarous" do not adequately describe our realities either. In their place—in place of all the well-informed and know-it-all words, all the judgmental, air-of-triumph, or giving-up words—comes the plain quiet word: *wrong.*

"The state of the world is wrong," we say, testing the phrase. And we hear that it rings true. We have found a sentence that we can stand by. It isn't beautiful, it's only accurate. And so it soothes our ears, which have been ravaged by shouts of the grand words. It also soothes our consciences, which are troubled by too many words which proved false, or were falsely used. Could this phrase become the first in a new, accurate language which we would hear with our ears but not yet speak with our tongues? Perhaps a train of other accurate phrases might emerge out of this one, phrases which are not just the negative of the old phrases but express a different sense of values tailored to our times. (Although we must not forget for a moment that naming things is not the same as putting them right, or repairing or changing them.) But with such new phrases we could say something to each other again, and tell each other stories without having to feel ashamed.

Those who would search for this language, however, must be able to tolerate the almost complete loss of their self-esteem, of their self-confidence, because all the patterns in which we are used to speaking, narrating, thinking, and writing poetry would no longer be available. Such people would no doubt learn what it really means to lose your grip.

We are not the first to go through this. What gets fractured, at the fracture points between different eras, is: courage, backbone, hope, direct contact—all things that you need to be able to speak. Fear jumps in to fill the gaps. In poetry, the precursors are almost always premonitors, too: they sense the fear which later will overtake many.

"Dance, Rosetta, dance, so that time keeps step with the beat of your dainty feet."

"My feet would rather go out of time."

There is a rhythm which pounds into your sleep, into your dreams. It can nail you down, it can drive you crazy.

My feet would rather go out of time.

Dance, Rosetta.

Rosetta dances. Sings: "Ah, dear pain." Goes away, because Leonce cannot love her but only the corpse of her love. "Tears, Rosetta?" "Diamonds, I expect, they are cutting into my eyes." Leonce, alone: "It's a funny thing about love." Meanwhile, his "brother" Danton, on the next stage over, announces: "I will retreat into the citadel of reason. I will burst out with the cannon of truth and mow down my enemies."

But where are the women, while the man holes up in the citadel of reason? Where are Rosetta, Marie, Marion, Lena, Julie, Lucile? Outside the citadel, of course. Unprotected in the foreground. No edifice of thought will shelter them. They have been made to believe that rational thinking is something you can do only if you are dug into the trenches! And they have neither the education nor any real inclination to do so. From a vantage point below and outside the citadel, they observe the strained mental activity of the male, which he directs increasingly toward safeguarding his fortress with exact measurements, calculations, and ingenious number and design systems. This activity thrives in the iciest abstraction, and its ultimate truth is a formula. How could Rosetta suspect that it is the fear of contact which causes the man to retreat from reality's abundance? That his fragility, and his fear of recognizing it, is what drives him to take refuge in his insane systems? That wounded and torn, and robbed of his wholeness by the ruthless division of labor, he is hounding himself, driving at reckless speeds, just to avoid having to make the "descent into hell" that is self-knowledge—even though, Kant says, reason cannot exist without self-knowledge? And how could Rosetta guess that a man who does not know himself cannot know a woman either?

And so their ways divide. Rosetta keeps silent. Loves. Suffers. In the person of Marie in *Woyzeck*, she is murdered. As Julie in *Danton's Death*, she follows her husband into death. As Lucile in the same play, she goes mad. Sacrifices herself. In the role of Lena from *Leonce and Lena*, she laments: "So, am I like the poor helpless well which must reflect in its silent depth any image which leans down over it?" One of Büchner's women, the prostitute Marion from *Danton's Death*, listens to her own nature. That is how far Büchner pushes his realism.

People did not know how to read him. They refused to recognize that the progress which was just beginning to unfold on a grand scale had in it the stuff of a new mythology. That progress could produce craving, but not love. And that its most powerful engine was the fear people felt of their own inner emptiness.

Büchner recognized very quickly, and with horror, I think, that the pleasure people took in the new age was rooted partly in a desire for destruction. But he did not see its full-blown grimace, the paradox that yokes creation to destruction. He did not know words like "megadeath," the multiple deaths that the new weapons hold in store for each living person. He gave his fictional characters a love of death. But it would not have entered his head that people would refer to a flawless but murderous technological solution as "sweet," or would write the names of women on missile hulls. His character Leonce feels confined in a room lined with distorting mirrors; but Büchner could not guess what later Leonces would resort to, just in order not to go without any mirror. For Leonce and his more powerful and industrious successors fall prey to a deadly fear as soon as they have no mirror—no eyes or body of a woman, no theater, no corporate mergers, no powerful organization, no nation, no earth, no cosmos—to reflect their own image back to them, magnified to larger than life-size.

"Oh, if we could just once see the top of our own heads!" If any man ever wanted to do the impossible, to make visible the blind spot in our civilization, it must have been Büchner. He surrounded that blind spot with a ring of his characters and drove them to the limits of what could be said in words. Once, he tried using a scream: when Lucile loses her reason over Camille's death in *Danton's Death*. But "that doesn't help, everything is still the way it was before," she says. A dramaturgy of screams is an absurdity to a theater based on more or less soluble contradictions. You cannot bring an adequate representation of reality onto the stage. That was another fact that Büchner collided with. So, in his drama of the As-if—which he attached loosely to traditional dramatic structure so that the audience could still just barely imagine that they understood what they were seeing—he created a space in which to put sentences which have to be spoken tonelessly, one breath before a scream: "My feet would rather go out of time."

It is Rosetta's fate to live invisible to herself and to Leonce, speechless, stripped of reality, in a space that is denied, sound-proofed, manipulated away, and which the rest of her world cannot see no matter how hard they try. Her character is definable by what she is *not*.

She lets her own history be taken away from her. Lets her soul be taken away. Her reason. Her humanity. Her responsibility for herself. Lets herself be married. Serves her husband. Gives him heirs. Is forced to believe that the pleasure he enjoys is denied to her forever. She hides her unhappiness. Dances. Hears him reproach her: "I want to sleep, but you have to dance."

Rosetta lets her rights be taken away. Lets herself be forbidden to speak. Forbidden to grieve. To feel joy. To feel love. To work. To know art. She lets herself be raped. Be prostituted. Locked up. Driven crazy. In the role of Rose, she lets herself be worked to death, exploited; "twice over," as the play says. Lets herself be forced to bear children. To abort children. Lets her sex be analyzed away. Gets caught in the net of impotence. Becomes a nag. A whore. A vamp. A cricket. In the role of Nora, she leaves the Doll's House.

At last—her name is Rosa now—she begins to fight. Then she is murdered, thrown into the canal. In persecution, her rights equal those of the man, who is oppressed and persecuted, too. Dance, Rosetta. She dances. Now her name is Marlene: "I'm supposed to laugh? Fine, then I'll laugh./I'm supposed to dance? Okay, I'll dance./ I'm supposed to captivate you? Absolutely. At your service."

It's a funny thing about love. Rosetta, under her many names, would rather be destroyed than admit what is happening to her: that when Leonce the thinker says "I, the autonomous self," he is never referring to her, to a real woman. That he classes her among the objects. That is, that he . . .

There she stops. She does not struggle through to the final insight. Prefers to deny herself. Suppresses her talent. Under her many names, some of which are no doubt familiar to you, she supports the genius of the man who thinks, writes, paints. "You love me, Leonce?" "Sure, why not?" Sometimes she can become peculiar, even harsh, jealous, bitter. She cries out, she screams at him. Gets hysterical. Starts drinking. Commits suicide.

During the wars, she replaces the man, proves her worth on his machinery of production and destruction. Her ultimate admission is that now she has become like him. She sets out to prove it to him. Progress, for her, is that she works like a man. And it *is* progress. She stands beside him, tending the machine, day and night. Sits next to him in the lecture hall and in the board room (although she is in the minority there, of course). She writes, paints, composes poetry like him—*almost* like him. Here one sees the first fine cracks in her performance. People attribute them to her oversensitivity and make allowances; or they don't make allowances. To some extent, she sticks to the mental and visual framework which the man evolved, and to the forms in which he couched his attitudes, and his melancholy, too. So she walks out of the "blind spot" and gets discovered. She is found worthy of being put into print. Worthy of being critiqued. Becomes a "talent," a name. Is found worthy of praise—in the right circumstances.

Will people believe her when she talks about her ambivalent feelings? It took her a long time to understand herself. To understand why she still goes on feeling so strange. Why she goes on feeling that the praise and blame she reaps don't apply to her but still apply to that other woman, somewhere off to the side of her, to that false image she pretends to be. Why she feels that she herself has barely been mentioned yet.

Once she enters the citadel of reason, she, too, succumbs to its paradoxical laws, so she finds herself—paradoxically—forced to abet the misunderstanding of who she really is. For the sake of being free, she has put on new chains. To achieve self-realization, she is driven into new kinds of self-denial. Her intentions were good. She staked her hopes on the scientific age. She trusted in its rationality, only to fall prey to the irrationalism where it fled for refuge and which it made impregnable with expert scientific testimony. Time has never kept step with the beat of her feet, she has to confess now. But in an oddly persistent and sometimes uncanny way, she is ready to take herself seriously. And now she meets resistance. In the past, whenever things got serious, she was looked after, spared this seriousness. People did not trouble her about the construction of weapons and super-weapons systems which could make old-fashioned individual death obsolete and which have already reduced each one of us to radiation, ashes, and dust seven, eight, twenty times over, in the fantasies of nuclear planning staffs. She—the woman Rosetta under her many names—is allowed no further initiation into the secret meaning of the military, economic, and political strategies which encircle the globe. She sees the man, the upholder of the balance of terror, sitting exhausted in front of the TV set —the planner of economic monstrosities heading for a heart attack— the worldwide distributor of hunger reaching for the bottle. They are working themselves to death—and not only themselves.

Dance, Rosetta, dance.

She does raise her voice at last: admittedly it may be too late. She asks: "Gentlemen. Friends. Colleagues. Comrades. Don't you think that the ground has gotten rather thin, even for light feet?"

She is not allowed to talk that way. Now she has really become ungrateful. She is really dancing to her own tune. She drops out of the net of her helplessness—as if this is a joy ride that she is free to skip if she wants to—even though the meshes of that net were as finely knit as the stuff dreams are made of: the nightmares of thought alienated from self.

Now the fear sets in.

Her fear *and* his. For now they share the terrible secret, the taboo of taboos. Leonce, under his many names, cannot love; he can love only what is dead. ("Beautiful corpse, you rest so sweetly on the black pall of night that you make nature hate life and fall in love with death.") So, does Rosetta, under her many names, have no other option but to be driven back into her dead space, or to become like Leonce? Doesn't every step she takes toward freedom increase his fear, his defensiveness? So, is *she* supposed to hole up now in the citadel of reason, and from it fire "the cannon of truth"? Is she supposed to regard the man as her enemy whom she must "mow down"? And: Is there no way for them to work together, to bring each other to their senses? Are the two of them, both wedded to the same paradox, incapable of taking a single step toward each other that isn't wrong? And is this unprecedented moment in history already a failure?

Once again, the old beat is heard—loud, very loud, especially

at night. My feet would rather go out of time. Then fantasies stir
beneath the threshold of consciousness, where perpetual threat sets
off perpetual alarm, and a ceaseless hunt goes on for alternatives that
can be lived with. The troubled consciences of the men or women
who feel compelled to write help to feed the fantasies. But can one
write on this paper-thin ground? No longer "for hope's sake" but only
"for the emergency case"?

"Nothing pleases me anymore" begins the last poem of Ingeborg
Bachmann.

> *Should I*
> *deck out a metaphor*
> *with an almond blossom?*
> *. . .*
> *Should I*
> *take a thought captive, lead it*
> *into the lit-up cell of a sentence?*
> *Feed eye and ear*
> *with word-tidbits,*
> *Grade A?*

The poem ends:

> *(Yup, I should. Let the others do it.)*
> *My portion is meant for loss.*

That is language beyond faith, but it's still language, all the
same. A metaphor is used to break with metaphors. The lines which
renounce the grade-A tidbits are grade-A themselves. The poem to
give up art with paradoxically is forced to be a work of art. All the
products of our age (or almost all) carry the seed of self-destruction
inside them. Or at least the seed is inside the anti-product which
they give rise to. Art cannot cancel itself as art, nor can literature
cancel itself as literature. A woman does not eliminate herself by a
complete act of self-expression. Her desire to eliminate herself remains, bearing witness. Her portion will not be lost.

We all know only too well that books can be burned. But a
literature which despairs of itself, and is sick of itself, must endure
—canceling out both despair and self-disgust. It must endure, unless
it fails to come into being in the first place because its authors have
gone away: into another country, another profession, another name,
into an illness, into madness, into death—all of those being metaphors

for silence, insofar as the affected person is a writer. To be silenced. To choose silence. To be forced into silence. At last, to be allowed to be silent.

But—before this "But," you have to picture a long pause whose color (if it had a color) would be black—the three languages which Büchner held together in his own person, at the cost of excessive strain to his body and mind, the languages of politics, science, and literature, have been separated beyond repair since his day. It is, strangely, the language of literature which seems to come closest to the reality of man today, and which knows him best, regardless of what statistics, numerical descriptions, standardized tables, and performance charts may say to the contrary. The reason for this, perhaps, is that the moral courage of the author—the courage for self-knowledge—always enters into literature. Contracts are written into literature which over the centuries have woven the fabric we call "civilization," however laborious the process, and however fragile and frequently broken the contracts may be. Our surprise at this old-fashioned word "civilization" may make us realize the threat that exists to what the word stands for. And yet this word—unlike the terms used in politics and science—has a halo, an aura, similar to that of other words which just happen to occur to me: "peace," "moon," "town," "meadow," "life," "death." Do we really want to discard them? Replace them with words like "nuclear stalemate," "earth satellite," "settlement area," "grassland cultivation," "matter in its motion modality," "exitus"?

Scientists have devised a specialized language to safeguard their inventions from their own emotions. Pseudo-logical linguistic constructions support the fixed idea of politicians that the way to save mankind lies in the ability to annihilate it many times over.

Literature has to be peace research.

Writing has not become easier since we learned that our two countries—both of which once bore the name "Germany" and forfeited it through the name of "Auschwitz"—that the land on both sides of the Elbe River would be among the first to suffer extinction in the event of a "nuclear confrontation." I expect that maps already exist which record the phases of our extinction. Cassandra, I think, must have loved Troy more than herself when she dared to prophesy to her countrymen the ruinous end of their city. I wonder, have our two countries not been loved enough by their people? And do they consequently desire to destroy themselves and others, like a person who has not been loved and thus is incapable of love himself? I ask this only to vehemently deny it. As evidence to the contrary—absurd as

185

it may seem—I take literature. I know that literature does not give a people enough of a homeland on its own. Yet—because any proposal, however farfetched, deserves a hearing—I propose that literature should be allowed to draw its own map, to counteract those maps of death. The villages, landscapes, and human affairs which literature describes with precision, accuracy, and bias—describes painfully, critically, devotedly, fearfully, and joyfully, ironically, rebelliously, and lovingly—should be removed from the death map and counted as saved. And finally, just for once, the literature of the Germans should not remain ineffectual. Whatever grief work and joy work literature in the two Germanys has achieved over the last three decades, whatever "worldly truth" it has confronted, should be entered in the books now, should be credited to both nations. Finally, just once, literature should be taken at its word, and should be applied to help ensure that the things of this earth endure.

"That's lucid madness," you say. Fine. So in psychiatric terms I lack insight into my illness, and I give way to this lucid madness, in order not to succumb to the dark side of reason. Maybe a member of the General Staff will really find it harder to wipe out a city which has been tenderly and exactly described in a book than a city which no one has read about, which no one cared about enough to feel the need to portray it as the city of her childhood, the place of her humiliation or of her first love.

Now you are smiling at my naïveté, at my irrationality. Büchner describes the mad Lenz this way: "He seemed completely rational. He conversed with people. He did everything just as other people did. But there was a ghastly emptiness inside him. He no longer felt any fear, any desire. He experienced his life as a burden which could not be avoided."

People speak, albeit softly, even in that country beyond faith. A conversation about trees, about Water, Earth, Sky, Man, strikes me as more realistic than the sheer insanity of speculations about the end of the world. Once we had thoroughly investigated the truth contained in the word "wrong," no doubt we would happen on some other words which we could say, too, not boastfully but warily. We would know that none of them, not even the most sincere, is the last word. We would hope that none is the *last* word.

This skin, too, will be stripped away and turn to rags.

Summer 1980

Your Next Life

Begins Today: A Letter

about Bettine[*]

*There is a lot of work to be done in the world. To me at least, it
seems that nothing is how it ought to be.*
—BETTINA VON ARNIM

Dear D.:

Instead of the letter which you are expecting, I want to write to you
about Bettine. Maybe this will help us both. I will escape the normal
rules for writing an afterword to a book. You will learn something
about an ancestor with whom you are not yet acquainted. We will
both be able to continue working on the basic themes of our dialogue-
in-letters, as we rediscover the same themes in Bettina von Arnim's
letter-novel *Die Günderode*; and the historical distance between her
time and ours will give us the advantage of perspective. In fact, Bettine
herself made use of this kind of historical gap. The letters on which
she based her book in 1839 were actually written back in 1804 and
1806, which for her was not merely a different era but amounted to
a different lifetime. Bettine was not yet twenty when she met Karoline
von Günderrode (whose family wrote their name with a double *r*, by
the way, although we have only reverted to this spelling since the
1960s). The two met at the home of Bettine's grandmother, the famous
writer Sophie La Roche. Bettine immediately attached herself to Günderrode, who was five years older; visited her daily in her room at
the convent in Frankfurt am Main, read aloud to her, jotted down her
poems, made long trips with her on paper, and shared everything

---

* The variable spelling of Bettine's name, which was sometimes written with an *a* at the
end and sometimes with an *e*, has been retained by Christa Wolf.

with her, because otherwise she felt alone and estranged in the midst of her large family and in the fashionable world to which the wealthy Brentanos belonged, and was driven to make all sorts of wry faces. "Dear Arnim," her brother Clemens wrote to Achim von Arnim in 1802, informing his friend about his sister: "This girl is very unhappy, she is very ingenious and does not know it; she is thoroughly abused by her family, and endures it by quietly eating away at herself."

But Bettine, a plucky person behind all her masquerades, promised herself that she would never consider herself unhappy and, if the ideal form of life proved unavailable, would accept the life she was offered and make it her own as far as possible. In this respect she differed from Günderrode, who not only felt subject to the bourgeois code of life, as a woman, but made herself subject to the bourgeois code of art, as a poet; who was under compulsion both from sensitive moral feelings and from a sensitive artistic conscience; and who was driven to the point where the things she needed in order to live her life became incompatible. A woman and an artist of her kind does not take her life because the man on whom she has staked everything abandons her. The question one must ask is: Why did she stake everything on him?

It was that same man, the classical scholar Friedrich Creuzer, who some while before Günderrode's suicide persuaded her to stop seeing Bettine. But first she appears to have returned Bettine's letters, as Bettine requested. In these letters you can read that Bettine was able to defend herself against the reproaches of her family, who were concerned about how the twenty-year-old girl would find a husband when she refused to adapt to domestic virtues and instead was learning Hebrew from "an old black Jew." "A man is repelled by that sort of thing," her oldest brother wrote her—"dear good angel-Franz," who acted as head of the household because both their parents had died young. "I wrote him that . . . there was no longer time enough left for me to change; and that the time with the Jew was just something I had worked into my daily schedule to protect myself from being eaten up by the moths of domesticity; and I had noticed that people who are happy in their domestic life always spend their Sundays counting the roof tiles on their neighbor's roof, which I find so terribly tedious that I prefer not to marry."

Bettine's dread of philistine life stayed with her all her days. But she had an equally strong fear of being useless ("better dead than unneeded"). In 1811 she married Achim von Arnim, the friend of her beloved brother Clemens, and at his side she began to live a radically different life in Berlin, Prussia's capital, which was at that time occupied by Napoleon, and put herself through the school of self-denial with scarcely a word of complaint. Twenty years of marriage, seven pregnancies, seven births, the care and education of seven children, exhausting moves from one place to another, financial worries, household annoyances of every sort; and not least, a relationship with her husband which was not "simple" or untroubled—the natures and needs of the pair were too different for harmony—but which she sincerely did all she could to live up to. Arnim was a patriot who, disappointed by developments in Prussia, withdrew in resignation to Wiepersdorf, his country estate, where he was plagued with problems of management. But Bettine never stopped seeing the poet in him, and persistently urged him to bring out that part of himself, to become what, in her inner vision of him, he "really" was. The evidence of her first life meanwhile rested, unheeded and forgotten, in some drawer: the letters from her friend Günderrode, along with the letters from Goethe's mother, from Goethe himself, from Beethoven; the wooing, often effusive letters from her brother Clemens; and the rather pedagogical letters from her brother-in-law Savigny, whom she met again in Berlin when he entered government service in Prussia. Locked and barricaded in a drawer or a cabinet lay the spirit of her youth, preserved intact, waiting to revive in the work of a fifty-year-old woman: a rebirth which can never astonish us enough.

Her book, this book of letters which I am recommending to you, bridges a span of thirty-five years in Bettine's life. No one who knew Bettine as an ecstatic child, as a wild young girl, would have thought her capable of metamorphosing into a housewife and mother who subordinated all her exuberant fantasies and wishes to the demands of her large family. Thus it is remarkable that she should have been the one, in the circle of the Romantics, who resurfaced in the 1830s with her Romantic principles intact, and who—no easy achievement in the stultifying atmosphere of Prussia in the period between the downfall of Napoleon in 1815 and the March revolution of 1848—earned the title of herald of the revolution for later generations. Who readopted the positive, provocatively naïve attitudes of her childhood and early youth, because only a child can get away with saying what everyone knows: "The Emperor has no clothes." Who—and this is one reason why I recommend her to you—did not accept the false alternatives which were imposed on all their lives; who did not consent to be an ineffective outsider on the one hand, or a well-adjusted philistine on the other. Those alternatives had exhausted her generation, the descendants of intellectual revolutionaries. Clemens Brentano had described the choices this way at the turn of the century: "In today's world, one can only choose between two things. One can either become a human being or a bourgeois, and all one sees is what ought to be avoided, but not what ought to be embraced. The bourgeois have occupied the whole of temporal existence and the human beings have nothing but themselves."

That is the radical voice of the early Jena school of Romanticism, whose spirit Bettine preserved faithfully. Her letters to Günderrode (who was not one of the Romantics but was linked to them by friendships and intellectual exchange) are a remarkable reflection of Bettine's seemingly playful involvement with the Romantic motifs of longing for another, better life—at a time when practical reality had taken a totally different turn.

She knew the aura that surrounded her, and she knew the fear of having the aura stripped away, of being freed from her magic spell and turned into one of those terrifying human automatons who made their debut in literature during her lifetime. To Goethe, the greatest of her imaginary lovers, she confessed her insights, her fears, and her suspicions about herself. On June 29, 1807, she wrote to him— when Günderrode had been dead for a year:

> These magic charms, the power to cast spells are my white dress . . . but, sir, I cannot deny the presentiment that the white dress will be stripped from me, too, and that I will go around in the common garb of everyday life, and that this world, in which my senses are alive, is going to perish; that what I ought to shield and protect, I will betray; that where I ought to patiently submit, I will take revenge; and when childlike wisdom artlessly beckons, I will act defiant and claim I know it all. But the saddest thing is that I will label with the curse of sin what is not sin, just as they all do. And I will be justly punished for it.

Everything that she tried to keep from happening to her—everything that she succeeded by her spells in warding off—actually did happen, before her very eyes, to the friends of her youth, both famous and unknown, as hope—animator of souls—drained away from them. Some died young, like Novalis; others committed suicide, like Kleist and Günderrode; while others wandered throughout Europe searching for someplace where they felt at home, like August Wilhelm Schlegel; became political reactionaries, at least for a time, like Friedrich Schlegel; or drowned in Catholic mysticism like Clemens Brentano.

Bettine saw friendships break down under pressure from reactionary political forces, she experienced painful separations and estrangements—from Günderrode, from Clemens, from Savigny, from

Goethe; saw how their need to earn a living forced the men to adapt. Joseph Görres, for instance, who moved by a series of steps from being a revolutionary to joining the clerical reaction, said in 1822: "Of the whole generation who saw the [French] Revolution . . . who went through all the honor and disgrace, not one [would] behold the promised land of freedom and peace."

The land of Utopia, the supposed abode of liberty, equality, and fraternity, yielded to the reality of the Holy Alliance and the Carlsbad Decrees within the German petty principalities, especially in Prussia.* It was smashed by reactionary politics on the public scene, and by Biedermeier tastes in private life. It drowned in persecution, censorship, and spies; was lost in a social order which clung tenaciously to the idea that middle-class production methods could be combined with a monarchical regime, and which refused to acknowledge its own internal contradictions. And finally, it was carried abroad by its most radical literary adherents—Heine, Börne, Büchner—when they were forced to emigrate, and was preserved only in their melancholy, painfully questioning, ironic, lonely, and rebellious songs, plays, and essays. Social conditions in Germany, which the young Karl Marx described as "below the plane of history," isolated those who had the qualities to serve as spokesmen of a historical movement. Meanwhile, Bettina von Arnim, who had withdrawn into marriage and spent her days with her children "like a cat with her kittens"; who kept silent, wrote letters, and drew sketches—was perceptively described by Joseph Görres (the same Görres who fell prey to reactionary Catholicism in later life) in the 1820s, when he saw one of Bettina's drawings: "It's not classical, and not Romantic either. It's Bettinical, her own charming genre somewhere in between."

The unclassifiable Bettinical, which did not fit into any frame or into any of the movements with which she came in contact in the course of her long lifetime; the fact that she lived "in the order of her own nature" is what has made Bettine's work survive. At the same time, it made her a unique case, easily underrated by posterity. She cannot readily be used to demonstrate any thesis. Later generations clung to the magical image of the young Bettine, projecting their own

* The Holy Alliance (1815) was an agreement between the rulers of Russia, Austria, and Prussia, later joined by others, confirming the political system that was restored after the fall of Napoleon. This was followed in the German states by the Carlsbad Decrees of 1819, which enacted further repressive measures, such as government censorship and surveillance, and strict controls on university life. After the revolution of July 1830, the persecution of democratic thinking was stepped up yet again.

unfulfillable longings and wishes onto this impish, untamable, seemingly ageless being; this youthful enthusiast; this ingenious, somewhat shocking, immature child, a second Mignon: androgynous, enigmatic, dusky, fey. Bettine, fully aware of the temptation to immerse herself, and if possible to transform herself, into this artistically manufactured figure, brought off the difficult trick of destroying her own myth, the deceptively finished image of herself as she was in her youth, and allowed herself to be caught up in an "ordinary," everyday life. Who would be surprised to learn that she was often overwhelmed by feelings of misery? "I have spent the twelve years of my marriage on the rack, physically and spiritually, and my claims to consideration are not being met," she wrote from Wiepersdorf to her sister Gunda von Savigny in Berlin, at New Year's, 1823. "What I always endured patiently because I felt I was strong enough I now endure with impatience because I am weak enough. What I see ahead is the end of everything."

The importance of such isolated remarks must not be exaggerated. All the same, it is impossible to exaggerate the degree to which Bettine was ensnared in everyday drudgery and cut off from the dreams of her youth. This picture of her as a woman groaning under the burden of self-denial and monotony did not last. But to show how complete her desperation could be, I will quote you a few more lines from the same letter:

> One loses the ability to write here where all day long, all year long, one's whole life long, nothing happens which would make a person bother to stir a leg or an arm. I know of no task which saps the mind more than doing and experiencing nothing. In every thought one struggles to escape one's situation. One flies up and soars far above the present, exerting one's strength, only to fall all the deeper and more dangerously back to earth, feeling as if one has smashed every bone. So it is with me. I keep candles lit all night, I wake up every hour, I compare what I think to what I dream, and only too often I am forced to realize that both alike drag me down into the emptiness of my daily surroundings. Nothing so weakens the mind as not to be called on to perform those operations which uniquely correspond to its nature . . . Oh, how my demands on life have lowered. And the less I demand, the more life makes me agree to give up, and will grant me nothing except to turn into a rogue or a scoundrel.

The embers glowing under the ashes. The same fear of the one sin, giving up her true self, that she had expressed sixteen years earlier in her letter to Goethe. But hard-pressed as she may often have been by the "earthly guest," it did not succeed in driving out the "heavenly guest" from her completely, in the twenty years of her marriage. In her letters to Arnim, the affectionate tones became less frequent, and the irritated, self-defensive tones more so, when his extremely sober and spartan habits challenged her unselfish devotion as a mother and wife. Even so, her pain at Arnim's early death in 1831 was deep and genuine. Bettine was forty-six and did not marry again. Never, as far as I can tell, did she express any regrets or changes of heart about her marriage, once it was over. Her character was noble, like Arnim's. Although she could be capricious and cranky, she was not self-pitying, hostile, and bitter. In the first letters she wrote to friends on the day that Arnim died, we can see her burning the earthly dross from her husband's image and resurrecting him as a new and saintlike person whom she could venerate. But besides this emotional Bettine, there was another Bettine inside her, a levelheaded person who never lost sight of life's day-to-day demands. She administered her husband's estate for her children. She arranged for the publication of the first collected edition of Arnim's works, and contributed substantially to preparing it. And to everyone's surprise, and the displeasure of her family in Frankfurt, she became a productive author after her husband's death, publishing six books in seventeen years and leaving behind an unpublished manuscript, letters enough to fill volumes, and scores of notes and outlines. Bettine began her third life.

"I am very happy. Is there anything more blissful, than from the simple spent years of the past, as from the fire's center, to burst into newly awakened flames? . . . Last night I could not sleep because a thought rooted in my childhood was putting forth so many blossoms." She wrote this to Prince Pückler* in 1835. Is it important to know to whom she expressed her feelings, and who disappointed her by rejecting them? Is it important that she sometimes used the wrong approach? With a sure instinct, she took what she needed to stoke up her desire to create. The incubation period was over, the virus which had lain dormant for so long awoke and incited its host to feverish activity. Frau von Arnim began to be active—of all things—in the most petrified decade of the nineteenth century. She made her home in the heart of the Prussian capital, at 21 Unter den Linden, turning it into a meeting place for independent spirits. With complete disdain for mail censorship, surveillance, and government spies, she welcomed visits from travelers and admirers,

---

* Prince Hermann Pückler (1785–1871), German writer.

and received so many letters each day that she could hardly cope with them all. She tended people sick with cholera, as well as the poor in the "custodial land" outside the Hamburger Gate. And she wrote.

In 1839 she produced her second letter-novel, the book on Günderrode. (The first was *Goethe's Correspondence with a Child*.) That same year represented the nadir of the political trough through which Germany was passing: the exact midpoint between the revolutions of 1830 and 1848. But people at the time could not know that an upswing lay ahead. There was no talk of any "springtime of nationalist liberation." Twilight reigned, a mood of gloom and doom. The liberal Berlin journalist Adolf Glassbrenner commented that every Prussian seemingly was born into the world equipped with an "inner gendarme." Yet in that setting, hard as it is to imagine, the students of Berlin actually held a torch parade in Bettine's honor, right after her Günderrode book was published in 1840. It seems certain that they had read no more of it than the dedication—it was dedicated to them—and had interpreted it exactly as it was meant: politically. "You who first sprouted again like golden flowers on the trodden-down field!" An effusive speech, no doubt, but above all a daring message. For it dared to mention the banned students' associations (there is a reference to "the student anthems"), expressed confidence that "the times will change," and wished the young men that "a gentle star may shine protectively upon you." Such language is understood by those who know that in December 1836 the Prussian High Court in Berlin had sentenced first to death, and then to thirty years' fortress confinement, forty-one students from Greifswald who were members of student associations; that in 1832 Prussia's response to the participation of student associations in the "Hambacher Fest"* was to saddle them with another tyrannical law "for the maintenance of public peace and lawful order"; that the peace of the graveyard ruled in the states of the German Bund, and especially in Prussia, after a few isolated democratic-republican protest actions were defeated in the 1830s; that the senseless assault on the Frankfurt guardhouse in April 1833 was followed by the relentless persecution of the participants, mostly students; that the *Hessische Landbote* was confiscated in 1834, its revolutionary co-author Friedrich Weidig arrested, and Georg Büchner forced into flight and emigration; that the writings of "Young

* A democratic protest demonstration held at Castle Hambach in May 1832. Protesters called for democratic freedoms, for German unity in a federated German republic, and for an alliance of democratic forces in various nations such as Poland, France, Italy, and Greece. The German Bund, a loose federation of German states, replied with more reactionary policies.

Germany" were banned throughout the confederation.* A well-organized government and security operation stifled every free impulse in German society. And as always when political discussion is suppressed in public, the differing parties and opinions waged their struggle in the form of literature instead. In the 1830s (although you will find it hard to believe), Goethe and the unpublished works he left behind at his death were an explosive topic. And Bettine's first book, *Goethe's Correspondence with a Child*, was in all innocence addressed to this now controversial figure. The *Correspondence*, published in 1835 under the magic seal of the motto "This book is for the good people, not for the bad," went virtually unscathed by the debate and created a sensation. Its author became famous overnight and was regarded by her contemporaries as a prodigy or an apparition. For the second time—the first was in her adolescence—people treated her as a figure outside history.

"Our political parties evidently have gotten mixed up over this mysterious child," wrote a Young Germany newspaper. "Those who ought to be for her are against her, and those who ought to be against her are for her"—a sign (as we have cause to know) that the political parties are at the end of their tether. Bettine, called "the sibyl of the Romantic era in literature," was dubbed, by the followers of Young Germany, an "inspired, romantic, mystical, prophetic, impish will-o'-the-wisp." The ardent democrat Ludwig Börne termed her an "avenging fury" and, from his vantage point in Paris, reinterpreted her volume of homage to Goethe so as to turn it into an attack on Goethe instead; and the historian Leopold Ranke stated: "The woman has the instinct of a pythia." If all the contradictory traits which were attributed to her could be joined into a single person, they would produce a kind of monster. It seems to me that this tells us less about Bettine's character, temperament, and aspect than it does about the need of people in her time for a figure who stood outside and above history, who alone might appear capable of introducing some ferment into the stagnant swamp of German society, especially in Prussia.

Prussia was a state where every chair was occupied, every post filled: from the Minister of Culture to the board of Supreme Censors, from the Privy Councilor to the secret government deputy at the university, from the Minister of the Interior to the Postmaster General (whose name at that time was Nagler, by the way, and who showed

---

* The *Hessische Landbote* [*Hessian Courier*] was a revolutionary pamphlet published by Georg Büchner in 1834. In 1835 and 1836 Büchner had to flee to Strassburg and then to Switzerland to escape persecution. "Young Germany," c. 1830–50, was a literary movement with radical political leanings which included a number of authors viewed as "enemies of the state," such as Karl Gutzkow and Heinrich Heine.

such a commendable interest in the letters of authors under surveillance that he often insisted on reading them personally). The spectrum of intellectual workers ranged from the official state poet to the popular leader locked up in the dreaded town jail, the "tin box"; and all the roles in the opposition seemed to have been handed out, too. With the benefit of hindsight, we could say that only one role remained to be filled: a woman in a high-ranking position, barred from holding any official post and not a member of any existing faction, but a critical thinker, educated and fearless, committed and empathetic, clairvoyant and a skilled dreamer. This sounds like the description of a chimera, and it fits Bettine.

Do you feel the proper amazement at how subtly outward circumstances can coordinate with a person's innermost needs? Bettine deserves credit for having accepted the role assigned to her and filled the gap, apparently without asking what the consequences might be. One cannot help but feel a secret satisfaction at the skill with which she used the advantage which sometimes is hidden in the disadvantage of being a woman in a male-run society—provided that the woman can tolerate being considered slightly crazy. Bettine began early to practice this skill, as you will see by reading her letters to Günderrode. She often referred to herself as a "simpleton." In serious times, it can be a protection not to be taken absolutely seriously. Writer Karl Gutzkow's deep sigh when he read Bettine's *King's Book* testifies to this: "Sad indeed that only a woman is permitted to say what any man would have been locked up for saying." Who would lock up a sibyl, an imp, a pythia?

But was there ever really any danger of her being locked up? Actually, we are still on the subject of how she dedicated her Günderrode book to the students, remember? But before we go back to the book, we need to forge ahead into Bettine's later life, to look at this question of whether she was really in danger of imprisonment. I will quote to you a passage from a surveillance report written in 1847:

Social questions were discussed even at tea parties. The political leaning at these tea parties is socialist, in that members of the gathering prefer to talk and debate how the substance and form of life could be improved. The female sex especially long for liberation from the bonds of tradition, fashion, convention. Among all the women of this type in Berlin who enjoy a public reputation, Bettina von Arnim is indisputably the chief and most prominent. It is generally known, even to the court, that her soirées have the character I just described. She is left in peace because she is held in universally high regard here, and no fault can rightly be found in her.

This report was written by one of those trustworthy confidential agents who worked for the Central Information Bureau in Mainz, which Prince Metternich himself had urged should be established, not least because of the unruly student population ("The struggle of eternal justice against the principle of revolution is imminent and unavoidable"). The Central Information Bureau was one of the very few institutions which transcended the borders between the individual German states. By the end of the 1830s, the Bureau's confidential agents reported, the spirit which now reigned at German universities was very different from what it had been in the previous decades: students engaged only in drinking bouts. But even though the Mainz Bureau, and other spy organizations, no longer felt that the student population posed a threat, they continued to show a marked hostility toward the intelligentsia. Wittgenstein, the Prussian Minister of State, merely said out loud what others were thinking when he declared that "bookworms and hairsplitting scribblers" were a blot on human society, and that he would gladly contribute to fighting them. And a leading post in the "central committee," which processed instructions and reports from the Mainz central bureau, was held by an unspeakably vile privy councilor named Tschoppe, who died in a severe state of mental illness. Tschoppe loved dramatic effects. One morning when the banned author Karl Gutzkow came to ask that the ban on all his writings be lifted, Tschoppe—who was still shaving—greeted him by saying, "You were at the theater yesterday!" He enjoyed posing as a powerful man who knew everything. Triumphantly he showed the dismayed writer a list of all those who, the evening before, had claimed free passes at the Royal Theater in Berlin.

The Prussian capital teemed with political anecdotes and witticisms. Frau von Arnim no doubt was familiar with most of them, for people thronged to her democratic salon. Of course, she was only too aware that the decision by the police and censors to let her carry on her activities in peace, owing to the wide respect in which she was held, could not be relied on. Moreover, she had not been *given* this right but had won it, and expanded it, by her own bold and sometimes reckless efforts. People were not certain how to interpret her. Was she naïve? Or only pretending to be naïve? Was she cunning? Or did her habit of acting as she saw fit simply not match any of the categories available to people bred to self-censorship and subservience?

When Bettine dedicated her *King's Book* (1845) to the King—

"This Book Belongs to the King" was simultaneously the title and the dedication—one high-ranking censorship bureau was determined to believe that this was a subtle ploy on the part of the now famous author to escape the ban which ought to have been placed on the work. "Born of the vineyard country, baptized by sunshine!" So the flattered King addressed the startled Bettine in his letter of reply, although in fact he had only leafed through her book. Not so his Minister of the Interior, who gave it a thorough reading and afterward felt compelled to address a letter to the monarch, Friedrich Wilhelm IV. He tucked its central idea into an involved bureaucratic argument which is worth quoting here:

> If the book were not written in a tone of prophetic ecstasy aimed at a small readership but instead in the form of simple logic and prudent reflection which would make it accessible to the public at large; and if the author (whose identity is well known if not expressly named) did not by her quixotic nature render doubtful the practical accuracy and applicability of the doctrines the book contains, it would, according to the prescriptions of law, have to be declared among the writings which are hazardous to society, owing to the irreligion which it expresses and defends, and owing to the utter radicalism which it preaches.

The man was in the right job.

Besides, time verified what he had said. Two rather shorter works were written as a follow-up to Bettine's book, and their authors translated her "prophetic ecstasy" into the plain political German of the time. One work, ironic in tone and printed anonymously in Bern four years before *The Communist Manifesto*, called Communism a "specter" and linked it to the author of the *King's Book*. ("So now the devil stands before us unmasked, in all his hideousness, and the name of this darkly threatening specter is: Communism.") The second work, which condensed the "putative meaning and content" of the *King's Book* into a fifty-six-page pamphlet, was published in Hamburg, whereupon the King promptly confiscated it on political grounds and it was banned by the supreme censorship tribunal. ("Nineteen pages are dangerous, but with twenty you're in the clear," people mocked: books of twenty pages or more, with the author's name on them—Bettine had always refused to have her name on the title page—were not subject to censorship.) This was a lesson for Bettine. In times when a lack of public political forums forces literature to fill the gap and become the conscience of society—which was the case now, for Berlin's three daily newspapers were subject to censorship, so that Bettine did not even read them—literature will be prey to increasingly severe sanctions, the more intelligibly it communicates to the public. Bettine wrote in 1844: "What else is one to publish in Prussia today but religious pamphlets, reading primers, and fairy tales!"

But when she dedicated her book to the King, was that really a deliberate hoax? Clearly, Bettine was safeguarded not only by her popularity but by her illusions as well. When Friedrich Wilhelm IV ascended the throne in June 1840, many advocates of democracy hoped to see him support their cause. Bettine believed that he had the will and energy to bring about fundamental changes. "No, the disgrace of mental enslavement does not emanate from him!" Her devotion to the idea of a populist monarchy had an element of fantasy in it. "We must save the King!" But only six months after the coronation, in December 1840, Varnhagen von Ense recorded this about her: "She is beside herself about the state of affairs that is developing here, she distrusts all the King's intimates and favorites, she wants a constitution, freedom of the press, air and light." But in her *King's Book* she suggested to the King in all seriousness—or was she less serious than she seemed?—that he might bypass his courtiers and ministers, that "circle of heraldic beasts," and with the aid of the people he might "throw the old machinery of the state onto the scrap-heap," replace intellectual slavery with "freedom of thought," and rule jointly with the popular leaders who so far had been persecuted.

Was that naïve? shrewd? deluded? In any case, the surest way to lose one's illusions was (and still is) to try them out. Nine years later, in Volume II of her *King's Book* (called *Conversations with Demons*, 1852), she wrote this sardonic description of a utopian state: "I do not mean any state where the censors can cross out my views, I mean a different state altogether, located beyond the Himalayas, which is the reflected image of the state I could be thinking of. But if the censors should try to erase that one, too, well then, that is not the one I have in mind either. I do not have in mind anything which could be crossed out."

In the interval between the first and second volumes of the *King's Book* lay the period before the March revolution of 1848 and the failure of that revolution. In the interval, too, lay Bettine's persistent clashes with the censors, which forced her to found her own publishing house, the Arnim Verlag, and the new troubles which it brought her. In the same period, increasingly grave accusations piled up against her, including the charge that she was a Communist. (Gutzkow: "If the most ardent, intense love of humanity is Communism, then we may logically expect that Communism will attract many followers.")

In 1843, by the way, Bettine reportedly met with Karl Marx and his fiancée, Jenny von Westphalen, in Bad Kreuznach and, to Jenny's annoyance, took long, solitary walks with the young doctor of philosophy.

Once—this event, too, fell in the interval between the two volumes of the *King's Book*—Bettine broke off work on one of her books because she could not have gotten it printed. The Prussian Minister of the Interior, in a typically ministerial confusion of cause and effect, accused her, in 1844, of having made the weavers of Silesia "rebellious." "Merely wishing to help the poor is now described as preaching revolution," a friend wrote to her in warning. Then Bettine stopped writing her *Book of the Poor*, a sort of first attempt at a sociological study of the living conditions of the Fourth Estate, using many examples from the huts of the Silesian weavers. She must have realized that this incident marked a clearly defined boundary which she could not cross with impunity—the point at which social conflicts, and the impossibility of resolving the conflicts under the present regime, were most sharply in evidence. The energy to revolutionize society had not been developed, the times were not ripe for anything more than an ineffectual willingness for self-sacrifice. What alternative was left? To write to the King again, saying that instead of the cathedral in Berlin, he ought rather to build a thousand peasant huts in Silesia. The fate of the Silesians (she said) is more tragic than Sophocles'.

—Don't you agree that this is a significant aesthetic statement, even if, as often happens in the history of German literature, aesthetic statements take the place of the action which the case really demanded? The statement is significant, because Bettine regards the rules of tragedy, which derived from the conflicts of the ruling elite and from a "high" art form, as applicable to the situation of the "lower" classes. But, as you will see, the roots of this attitude go back to the letters she exchanged with Günderrode.

"Bettina allows her humanity to lead her astray. She always believes that the oppressed are in the right," remarked Gunda von Savigny, Bettine's sister, in a tone of mild reproof. Undoubtedly, her view of the matter was correct. It made Gunda—the wife of the Prussian Minister for Legislative Review—uncomfortable to see where her sister's radical humanism could lead; namely, to a disregard for any official authority which Bettine did not consider morally justified. In 1847, when a Berlin magistrate forcibly accused her of tax evasion in opening her publishing firm, because she had neglected to obtain Prussian citizenship first, she responded with a withering counterattack. She was sentenced first to three months' imprisonment, and then, after a review, to two months—the maximum penalty for persons of rank. Influential people, chiefly her brother-in-law Savigny, managed to stop the sentence from being carried out. But Bettine realized that a technical mistake on her part had been used as a pretext to show her what was in store for her if she did not watch her step. A witness reported what Bettine said about the matter later, at a social gathering, that the charges against her had been trumped up by government ministers who wanted to get her out of Berlin because "His Romantic Majesty's female court jester was causing them noticeable inconvenience."

So, you see, at least once she really was in danger of being locked up. But, as a rule, material threats drive a person even further beyond the mental limits which seemingly are set by his background and mode of life, if he is the sort of person who does not depend on the approval of the establishment; that is, who cannot be bribed and who is radicalized in his views and principles. This is what happened with Bettine. Her court hearing enabled her to pass an impartial sentence on the structure of her society, and to determine what developments would be necessary in the future. As evidence of what I am claiming, I will quote to you several paragraphs from the letter of defense which she wrote to the Berlin magistrate who heard her case:

> As for your last remark, that there was no reason to extend Prussian citizenship to me as a mark of esteem, I do admit this, especially because I value the right of citizenship more highly than noble rank . . . By the same token, I value even more highly the class of the proletariat . . . The treasure of the poor consists in the inherent wealth of nature; the merit of the bourgeois lies in using and exploiting this wealth, which by means of his professional skills, and for his own advantage, he bestows upon that class of humans whose arrogance, pampered nature, and poorly educated minds devour everything, precisely because they have no productive energy of their own. —Thus, the reason why I attribute the highest value to the proletarian is that he is exempt from the baseness of profiting from the condition of society: for the proletarian gives everything and in return he consumes no more than he needs in order to revive his energy, so that others may profit . . . And if I . . . therefore prefer the crown of citizen to a medal of honor, yet rather than that crown I would prefer to have the approval of the people, whose renunciations are heroic and whose sacrifices are the least self-seeking.

Now back to literature, back to the year 1839, when Bettine wrote her Günderrode book. I would like to convince you not only that this comparatively quiet year brought Bettine experiences which prepared her for the directly political conflicts of the 1840s but also that her very preoccupation with the ideas and feelings she had known at the start of the century gave her a deeper insight into contemporary patterns. Her actions and writings in midlife show that she remained loyal to basic themes of her youth, and continued to develop them, before broaching them in the Günderrode book. At the same time, this book in many respects reflects the emotional upheavals she went through in 1839 and 1840: the drama of her last romance, and her passionate defense of the unjustly punished brothers Grimm.

While Bettine assembled key pieces of her correspondence with Günderrode and elaborated them into a novel in letter form, a second letter-novel was born in that same year, made up of her current correspondence with a young student, Julius Döring from Wolmirstedt near Magdeburg, who began to write to her at the beginning of 1839 to express his admiration of her Goethe book. It disturbed Döring that she had dedicated the book to Prince Pückler, and he called on her to dedicate her next book to the students. She responded enthusiastically to his suggestion: "It is time for the young men to bloom from my mind with joy, for I am a tree that bears young-man blossoms. The buds are just about to open, and how should I not live on into the future, since it is being born from the marrow of my mind?" And she wrote to another young male admirer, with whom she shared a more intellectual and less erotic fascination: "I am nothing, but such an air blows around me that I believe the young people must snort it like mettlesome horses into their wide-open nostrils!"

It is apparent that she intended, with her Günderrode book, to pass on the legacy of her own youth to her grandchildren's generation. Emotionally stirred, she yielded to visions from her early life which at times approached the intensity of supernatural visitations. She kept Döring informed about the progress of her work, and in November 1839 she wrote to him from Wiepersdorf:

> I am so buried in work that I can no longer make room for sleep. At 1 a.m. I go to bed where, too excited by the work to sleep, I often read a play or some other material. And scarcely is the room heated again than I am at my desk, and work continuously without getting up from it, sparing barely four minutes for a midday meal, so that I can build you all a monument wherein refined minds can perceive everything which I have not said to you and to others, or which you all have misunderstood. In four weeks I hope to have reached the point that I can begin printing [the book] in Berlin.

She was mistaken about that. The printing did not begin until the spring of 1840, mainly because amid the most intensive work on the manuscript, she pushed it aside and began her great confrontation with her brother-in-law Savigny on behalf of the Grimms. So in January 1840 we find her saying—still referring to the Günderrode book—in another letter to Döring:

> I have worked very hard up to now and, strangely enough, during this work I have needed more sleep than usual . . . but on the other hand, the past has become so vivid to me that I could not say like Thomas, "Let me put my fingers in your wound so that I may believe it is really you."—Günderrode stands before me, and she often calls me away from my place when the light burns in the evening. [She stands] there in the corner where the tall green pines have stood since Christmas, reaching to the ceiling in front of my sofa, and then I wrap myself in my coat because I cannot resist going to meet her in my thoughts, and then sleep overcomes me . . . just as if Günderrode were sleeping, and so now I must sleep, too, because I have come close to her again through my awakened memory. —But in the daytime I feel so close to everything in the past that I am absolutely convinced of the enduring presence of everything which we have truly experienced.

The deeper meaning of this vision, which she describes in a biblical metaphor and links to the calling-up of spirits, is the desire to win love; and the same secret impulse lies behind her work. "Whoever reads this book of mine and does not love me has never had youth in his heart." I will say it: she compensated for giving up the possibility of consummating her real-life love by transferring her desire into other areas over which she could exercise control. She must have found a peculiar gratification in connecting her last love to her first by a thousand well-considered threads. This woman, now in her fifties, offered an overflowing erotic devotion to an average young man who believed he had to be a poet. ("Sensuality in the brain," old Count Pückler had woundingly labeled it.) She poeticized Döring, turning him into her lover, and revealed to him her emotional secrets ("I have not felt a breath of life in poetry since the sun set for me back then, when Goethe rejected me"). Soaring to biblical language, she dedicated this young man to poetry, to become the new Goethe ("And I will give you that, Be thou a poet!"). She played the role of a priestess out of whom "the spirit" speaks, and pined for a repetition, in midlife, of that "painfully sweet" surrender, that traumatizing scene which she claimed to have experienced with Goethe, when she lay down on the ground in front of him and would not "be still until he placed his foot on my breast so that I could feel the weight of him."

Blissful with self-induced illusion, she revealed the intellectual-sexual proclivities which had marked her at the age of twenty-two, practiced a fetishistic cult with the plaster cast of a young man's foot on her bed, and, inspired by this current source of stimulation, became receptive to the "spirit's breath" of her early life. Not some speculative act of will or thought-out policy but this compelling inspiration was what moved her to open herself up to visionary memories of the life she had shared with the friend of her youth, Günderrode. "For long years I was cut off from any such power as had called up my love in earlier years . . . Ah, I was far too alone."

She experienced feelings of rejuvenation, a pedagogical eroticism that continued to glow even after the brief rush of intense emotion for Döring had yielded to sobriety: "But I do not trust you, you are no genuine somnambulist, and reality is firmly imprisoned in your heart. You press your thumb into reality's eye, it dares not budge, then you slide home the bolt and mock it for being your prisoner." Why am I quoting that to you? Must we intrude into Bettine's late adventures of the heart? Must we summon again the painfully insecure tone of the questions in a letter she wrote in the middle of the year, a letter in which she sounds as if she were waking up from a dream: "I will not give you up— You don't mean to vanish from right under my nose, do you? —You cannot be merely a figment of my imagination: you really are live, aren't you? —Everything has stolen away from me. —How strange, if you, too, should prove an illusion." On the other hand, I think it is a good idea for us to listen to these most personal sounds, because I feel sure that these same sounds went into forming the Günderrode book as we know it today. Because—with the illogic of emotional events—when Bettine relived her separation from her first love, Karoline, that made it easier for her to renounce her last love, and love in general. Because she could not and would not disassociate the person she was in 1839 from the feelings and fantasies she had known in 1805; and because it is the book's connection to her life which gives it its luster and attraction, its rich treatment of time. For it is not all of a piece but is built up of layers atop or intersecting each other, of intercalations whose edges are not smoothed over but left rough. It contains inaccurate transitions, discrepancies, cracks. And that very fact reveals the indissoluble contradiction and secret sorrow of her life.

But first—I hope that you are not getting impatient—we have not yet looked at the case of the brothers Jakob and Wilhelm Grimm, which occupied so much of Bettine's attention in the year 1839 that, as I said, she set aside her Günderrode manuscript and postponed the printing in order to tackle it. On November 1, 1839, she wrote to Döring from Bärwalde-Wiepersdorf: "I have just written an epistle to Savigny on behalf of the Grimms—and said all manner of things. It is eight pages long. I would be so interested to have you read it—in fact, it would certainly be useful to you your whole life long—for you to see how far one can and should express the truth openly."

The case of the Göttingen Seven—seven professors among whom were the two Grimm brothers—is brought up frequently, although few people know its fascinating details. I must describe it to you, at least in its general outlines, because Bettine followed it closely and cared deeply about it. In October 1839, she had visited Jakob and Wilhelm Grimm in Kassel, where they had taken refuge after their banishment. Some time earlier, she had read Jakob's little treatise *On My Dismissal*. Savigny, of all people, had given her a copy, because he himself felt convinced by the sincerity of Jakob's statement: "If things are as he describes them, then indeed I must concede that he is right," he allegedly said to her. "Why didn't you tell the King, the Crown Prince, the people what you thought?" Bettine asked her brother-in-law, in her eight-page letter to him, which later became famous.

I would like to see Jakob's treatise put into the curriculum of our secondary schools, as a thrilling example of how strength of character and loyalty to convictions have the power to shape a person's writing style. "The lightning which struck my quiet home is stirring hearts in every walk of life," it begins. And I must keep a grip on myself, so as not to start quoting long passages from the treatise, and from Bettine's epistle, for my fierce pleasure and yours. —Here, briefly, are the details of how the conflict unfolded between the University of Göttingen and its overlord, the newly crowned sovereign, King Ernst August of Hanover: In the summer of 1837, the King, on his own authority, abruptly revoked the comparatively progressive constitution of 1833 and released all his civil servants—who included the university professors at Göttingen—from their oaths of allegiance to basic constitutional law. After waiting patiently for some time, several members of the university lodged a "most humble complaint," dated November 18, 1837, stating that they could not in good conscience stand by silently while the nation's constitution, which was in their opinion still valid, was destroyed "solely on the grounds [that the King] had the power to do so." Instead, they said, they had to consider themselves "permanently bound by their oath." Moreover (they asked him almost ingenuously), how could the King take seriously any future vow of fidelity and fealty he might ask them to make if it came from men who a short time earlier had sacrilegiously violated their oaths?

In a powerful passage, Jakob Grimm explained without anger or heated emotion why, in the end, only seven professors signed their names to this petition: Dahlmann, Albrecht, J. and W. Grimm, Gervinus, Ewald, Weber. Jakob told of the many ways in which the others, with the same or similar views, withheld or retracted their support; and how many, as a last resort, anchored their cowardice to the most specious but most convincing "argument" of all: that by abandoning the legal constitution without a struggle they were saving the university. "People's characters began to shed their leaves like the trees of autumn in an overnight frost," Jakob remarked tersely. Business as usual. Jakob Grimm then described, "leniently" but "freely and without constraint," how this conflict of loyalties swelled to incredible proportions, intruding into the personal and civic life of all, owing to the stubbornness of authority, which did not wish to examine objections but to coerce confessions of guilt and enforce submission; and how—because there was no way that a royal university trustee board could debate a case whose salient feature was the King's violation of the law—they were driven to inflict absurd accusations and punishments. "The truth is the only thing that lasts," Jakob Grimm asserted, and the disarming fact is that he believed it. Just as Bettine believed it. It is not hard to imagine her enthusiasm for the dignified, courageous language of this man who thought as she did. "Men still exist who show conscience, even when confronted by force."

Jakob's treatise is a model from the first line to the last. The seven professors were dismissed from their posts, and several were banished from the state of Hanover. ("I never invite the attention of power, until it compels me to carry away my hearthfire and light it in a new place"—Jakob Grimm.) Was it for insubordination that they were banished? No, not in this age of absolute monarchy, post-Enlightenment-style. The university tribunal which immediately summoned the seven to try their case addressed only one issue: How could news of the "most humble complaint" have leaked out so quickly to an English newspaper—a matter about which none of the seven knew anything? "In the feeling that other causes were lacking [Grimm wrote], they attempted to interpret the rapid publication of that statement [the professors' "complaint"] as something culpable . . . Are we to blame if a correspondent from an English or French newspaper, someone we have never met, heard of our intention and reported it? . . . And even if we really had to confess that we were directly responsible for its immediate publication, would that act merit banishment, or indeed any kind of punishment, if all we did was to convey a statement to the authorities?"

Indeed, not what they wrote to the King, but the fact that they might have mentioned him to a third party was the cited reason for banishing the Grimms. Bettine, trembling with outrage, reproached Savigny for not following his initial urge to do all he could to assist the brothers, two of the finest scholars in Germany, to immediately obtain material support for their work from the Berlin Academy; and for instead hurting them even more by trying to "excuse" them to the authorities on the grounds that they had been led astray by others. "When I had to leave a home that is full of innocence, where God's blessing spreads serenity and peace, I thought of you, and how truly miserable it is that you, who in the prime of your life enjoyed their noble companionship, should now be separated from them." It is glorious to see how she tells off Savigny, by now the Prussian Minister of Justice as well as the guardian of her children, and at last gives free rein to the anger which she has held in for so long. She reminds him of the role he played in her own youth, when he "shielded her freedom of thought"—a freedom to which she has stayed loyal, unlike Savigny himself. She appeals to the scholar in him to show solidarity with two outstanding members of his profession. "But no, you will leave me in the lurch and not help me. For ever since you cut off your long hair, your strength has gone from you, and I say to you not what was said to Samson: The Philistines will rule over you, but rather: You will dwell among the Philistines, as one of themselves!"

Incidentally, when the Crown Prince succeeded to the Prussian throne one year later (1840), the Grimms were in fact called to work at the Berlin Academy. But in the meantime Bettine's efforts to defend their rights gave her a deep insight into the way that kings, politicians, and their administrations thought and operated. All of a sudden she realized the whole perverted separation between the morality of government and the morality of everyday life (an observation which would bear fruit in her later books).

> One sees that false politics do not create mental discernment. Look how Metternich said to the deputies from Hanover: We admit that morally you are in the right, only our policy is such that we must oppose you. —And Prussia is based on this kind of attitude, which makes the state no more enduring than a mayfly . . . I know that you would not talk this way to the King. For to tell a monarch about the mistakes in his government, or to show him a higher point of view, would violate the policy of respect which bids you treat sovereigns like automatons.

207

Indeed, you do not trust yourselves to think, and you hide from the truth as if from a creditor whom you cannot pay. You tell sovereigns only the things they expect to hear, so that they can reply without waking up.

Do you want to know the link between these political views and Bettine's book on Günderrode—not just chronologically but thematically? If so, then read what Bettine claims an older friend told her when she was young, about those who serve princes: "The more they are weighed down by the demands which their times place on them, the more they believe they must shelter behind philistinism, and seek support in old, worm-eaten, burdensome prejudices, and create advisory bodies of every kind, both secret and public, which neither secretly nor publicly are anything but wrong—because genuine truth is so incredibly simple that, for that very reason, it never comes to the fore." I would be surprised if, when an older Bettine was reviewing Günderrode's papers, sentences like these did not remind her of the case of Savigny and the brothers Grimm.

But Bettine's political views are not what I am asking you to explore; or at least not the only thing. When I think how I recommended the publication of a new edition of Bettina von Arnim's *Correspondence with Günderrode* and wonder how I am to justify it, apart from the tired formula that we need to "preserve the Tradition"; when I reread her writings, more dubious than confident that today's readers, accustomed to thinking soberly and objectively, will be able to tolerate the dithyrambic language, the often effusive tone, the intemperance; when I consider whether readers will be able to get beyond feeling disconcerted by the relationship between the two women, and locate the contemporary features in their dialogue—then I think of you, your unappeasable curiosity about history and your earnest efforts, through liberated language, to rub off the layers of unlived life which segregate your mind, your consciousness, your feelings, and your body from each other. And I think about the connection between the layers of our history which were left unfinished, the productive beginnings which were mowed down by an "iron" tread, or merely by the crush of busy feet, and our own alienation. We should change our lives. But we are not.

I see how irredeemably naïve this remark is, and how disputable. And yet, as the letters of Bettine and Günderrode prove, men and women have never spoken such sentences without facing dispute from others. Nevertheless, I feel bound to confess that something in me contracts with envy and grief when I read and picture the innocent way (that is not to say the casual and carefree way) that two young

German women were able to treat each other. For poetry, the truly human, flourishes only in the innocent; and they had poetry. We have poems, but poetry as a form of human intercourse is barred to us. No doubt, people of a different culture miss that quality in us. And we would seem to have gotten over the loss, except that many of us appear to suffer from a sort of phantom pain which makes us visibly eager to escape into phrases, activities, and actions remote from our emotions. I cannot help thinking: Am I perhaps recommending this book as a way to keep the phantom pain alive? But no, our ancestors cannot relieve us of anything. They can only add something to us.

The most striking thing about this book is the easiest thing to overlook, because it is not explicitly formulated: the statement made by the book's structure; namely, its refusal to abide by any aesthetic canon. I cannot help smiling at the cunning of our [German] language, which makes "literature" and "aesthetics"—both of them authorities to which we submit secretly—into words of feminine gender, although women's share in these fields is slight, and (as you yourself know by painful experience) a woman who takes on the task of creating her own individuality cannot move within their magnificent systems of rules without feelings of constraint. For one achievement of this aesthetics, which was developed and established by classicism during the lifetime of the Romantics, was the method of separating the "work" from its creator and allowing it to soar away into another sphere, the sphere of art, once it was freed from the life circumstances out of which it first arose. The letters which Bettine and Karoline exchanged do not lay claim to being "art," and gathered into a book, their very formlessness gave a suitable form in which to transmit experiences without having to de-form them. Of the then existing literary genres, not one—not the epistolary novel à la *Werther*, and certainly not the bourgeois novel—would have adequately allowed this. But when, toward the middle of the nineteenth century, Bettine remembered the forms proposed by the Romantics (which had since been forgotten), she did not simply reproduce literally the letters which she and Karoline had exchanged. The form that she felt compelled to adopt was a hybrid, a form which had the flexibility to follow the motions which the two women experienced with and through each other, and to show the person whole, incommensurable and contradictory; whereas the closed form of the novel would have been forced to reduce, to judge, to classify, and to regulate. This tells you something about the resistance to the domination of a certain canon of form: a canon to which they both submitted all the same, as a standard for their work. Günderrode, especially, tried to meet that standard, because to be a "significant" poet meant to serve the canon. But was it equally ap-

plicable to a woman poet? Bettine invited her friend to enter her
School for Insignificance, offered her relief from day-in day-out aus-
terity, from the immoderate demands which taxed Günderrode's
strength. We should not be deceived by the lighthearted tone of
Bettine's offer. After all, we know what it means and always has
meant to refuse the one-sided training of the abilities which make a
person "significant" in the world. Almost hesitantly, Günderrode accepted the role of Bettine's disciple in insignificance: "The same way
that you regarded yourself as my pupil when I wanted to mold you
into a powerful mind. Now that I am headed backward, you must
become my teacher."

Backward? The word is startling. It betrays her, and no doubt
sprang unconsciously from a feeling of relaxation after too much
tension. Günderrode's choice of this term reveals her idea of what it
meant to move "forward." But Bettine, despite her convent education,
felt less compelled to submit to the norm and was quite unself-
conscious about expressing her pleasure: "I am so happy that I am
insignificant. That means I don't have to dish up clever thoughts
anymore. When I write to you, all I have to do is tell a story." After
all, she says, she has no "head for philosophy."

What does she mean? That she is not capable of thought? On
the contrary, no matter how people badgered her on that account,
Bettine insisted on using her head. No, what she means is that she
believes that the way "philosophers" think is wrong; that is, unnatural.
"But a philosopher seems to me no philosopher if he lies on the bosom
[of nature] and is intimately devoted to her with all his strength. —
Instead, I think that he is bent on plunder. Whatever he can swindle
out of her he messes up in his secret factory, and there he has all he
can do to keep it all running, as here a wheel jams, there a weight;
one machine meshes with the next." The soulless, mechanistic approach which derived from the rise of industrial machinery and was
then transferred into social relations and applied to man was a horror
to Bettine. And she was flooded with premonitory insights into the
possible pitfalls of our dependency on human reason: insights for
which science had not yet invented any system or even a name. Just
read the description she sent to Günderrode, of the philosopher who
cobbles together "his whole edifice of thought," not "to understand
himself," but merely "to display the hocus-pocus of his Superlative
Machine." But the only one to be "imprisoned" by this machine, she
says, is the "futile man" who is "out of touch with his own feelings."
Today's psychologists would say the "frustrated" man, although the
new nomenclature does not improve much on the old.

The views which Bettine and Günderrode exchanged on this

subject—whether to think in the way prescribed by philosophers, which Günderrode tentatively recommended to Bettine because Günderrode herself was susceptible to "rational" intellectual structures —make up the inner plot of their "novel," as exciting and worth telling as any plot there is. Must or can a person leave himself out of the account in philosophy, history, and art? Are thinking and writing to be used as a *means* to create oneself; or as an *end*, an object one manufactures—a work, a system—which ultimately turns against its producer? Bettine, who was often scolded for laziness and whom Günderrode assigned to study history ("Where will you get a grip on yourself if you have no ground to stand on?"), complained that her "teacher" had driven her into a "desert of history." "Meanwhile, I am all fired up about the present, I would like to apply myself to that, without first laying myself down on the anvil of the past and there letting myself be hammered flat." But she voluntarily studied the twelve emperors of Rome in order to compare them with Napoleon in his threatening rise to power and in order to rediscover in every tyrant "the same monster of mediocrity." And don't you agree that that is an astonishing insight, given that she did not have access to the data on dictators which our century so abundantly provides?

"I feel moved to accept your feelings and your actions as valid, without raising any objection," Bettine says, gently winning Günderrode over to side with her counterproposal, her woman's philosophy, her "floating religion," which, if it had only had a slight chance of being realized, would not have been driven to the brink of self-annihilation by the male culture of aggression. The two women philosophized in unison about a religion of *joie de vivre*, of sensory pleasure and humane attitudes, and developed "thoughts about government," ideas of how they would "revolutionize the world while they laughed out loud." And along with that, they formed a bond of love—one of the very few examples in our literature (perhaps the only one?) of an alternative to male bonding, and to the teacher-pupil relationships which are so prevalent.

> I cannot write poetry like you, Günderrode, but I can talk with nature when I am alone with her . . . And when I come back . . . we put our beds side by side and chat away together all night long . . . and we two philosophers engage in . . . great profound speculations which make the old world creak on its rusty hinges, if it does not positively turn upside down as a result. —Do you know what? You are Plato, and you are exiled to the fortress there, and I am your dearest friend and pupil Dion. We love each other tenderly and would be willing to die for each other if necessary, and even if it only *might* be necessary:

211

for there is nothing I would rather do than risk my life for you . . .
Yes, that's what I will call you in future: Plato!—and I want to give
you a pet name, I will call you Swan, which is what Socrates called
you, and you call me Dion . . . Good night, my Swan, go to sleep
there on the altar of Eros.

Thinking together, out of love and for love's sake. Using love,
using longing as a means of knowledge; not having to leave oneself
out of the account in order to think and know; making each other's
"temples burn" with "ardent zeal for the future." Giving each other
names, playing roles which did not tally with everyday reality and
which nevertheless allowed them to step outside themselves, to go
beyond themselves. Playing with language, inventing new words and
calling them out to each other: "spirit's-eye," "day-nature," "web-of-
art," "reality's sensing-nerves." —You will discover all this, and
much more, for yourself. You, and many others, I believe, will understand this language, as if you had dreamed of it. You will understand that this book describes an experiment which two women agreed
to carry out, supporting each other, strengthening each other, learning
from each other. A utopian experiment, certainly. It ended with them.
But why have we let the word "utopia" deteriorate into a term of
abuse?

I know why. Who has more cause than we to shut the door on
irrationalism in all its forms? But, reading Bettine's book, you find
a form of thinking which tries to unite in one person a heightened
rationality with an intensified ability to feel; which fears the one-
sidedness of instrumental, objective thinking (a *different* kind of irrationalism!)—and we are the first people who are really able to judge
how justified that fear is; which sets up a personal way of approaching
nature—including human nature—that differs from the soulless, mechanistic attitudes of "spirit-killing philosophy." An alternative, yes.
An alternative which was conceived and proposed at the very moment
when the society switched irreversibly onto the track of the exploitation
of nature, the twisting of ends into means, and the oppression of every
"feminine" element in the new civilization. The melancholy note in
Bettine's questions shows that she felt all this; Günderrode's suicide
proves her despair.

Naturally, Bettine knew Goethe's *Faust*, or as much of it as had
been printed at the time—including the vain struggle of Faust the
scientist to force the Earth Spirit to serve him. How differently Bettine
addresses nature.

I have very often had this feeling as if nature were lamenting in a melancholy voice, begging me for something, so that it tore my heart not to understand what she was asking for . . . Then I stood still for a while, the roaring seemed just like a sigh to me, which sounded as if it came from a child; and I spoke to her as if she were a child. "Sweetheart!—what's wrong?" and when I had said that, a shudder came over me and I felt ashamed, as if I had addressed someone who is far above me, and then I suddenly lay down and hid my face in the grass . . . and then, lying on the earth with my face hidden, I felt tender.

What a different scene from Faust's confrontation with the Earth Spirit! Not a declaration of war to the death, not the unconditional subjugation of nature, not the hybris of the "Faustian" man who, casting aside Faust's doubts, gains knowledge by putting nature on the rack, forcing confessions out of it with screws and irons. Hers is a different kind of progress. A different kind of magic from the diabolic sort for which Faust sells his soul, and which destroys him, a man become a stranger to himself. How different an adversary was created by God the Father when he made Mephisto to incite man to ambivalent creation than was bred by Mother Nature when she made her army of witches, nymphs, and sprites—those beings who now, in the Faustian age, were repressed, accursed, and labeled taboo, and whose ranks Bettine, their latter-day descendant, joined trembling with emotion. What a counterdesign we find at the roots of this culture going astray! What boldness in the dialogue of the two women!

Here on this globe, where people slide apart as if it were covered with a sheet of ice; where they have not the power to hold on to each other for the space of a breath and yet are forever dizzy with passion. If love were real, it would show itself not as a ghost in the form of passions but would be our native element, and then of course there would be no need to talk about restraining oneself. Look! Am I not right in not asking to be loved?—since a person can do nothing to oblige himself, not to mention someone else. I do not love, but everything I do is to oblige others . . . My ideal is this *irony in love*, which smiles at not achieving its end, but does not "lament" at its forlornness.

I know of no more apt explanation of what is called "romantic irony," which, psychologically speaking, consists in bravely concealing a wound. The theme of love denied permeates Bettine's entire life, taking the form of a painful knowledge, of paradox, of contradiction, of an "innermost secret." The passage I just quoted to you

213

is from her last letter-novel, *Ilius Pamphilius und die Ambrosia* (1848), which became a vehicle for her experiences with Julius Döring. And remarkably, this "painful knowledge" of hers was linked, from the outset, to a conviction that she was as much barred from writing poetry as from loving. When Günderrode sent Bettine her *Apocalyptic Fragment*, Bettine wrote back: "The fire of jealousy rages inside me when you do not stay down on the ground, where I am . . . I cannot write any fragments, I can only write to you . . . Nor can I change the fact that my senses are focused exclusively on you . . . That is how it is for someone who is consumed by fire and yet cannot endure that any water should put it out . . . I know how it will be for me my whole life long, I know it well." And then she went on to struggle nonstop—how could she help it?—to repeal this sentence.

An obscure but meaningful link exists between these evidences of a forcible renunciation of love and Bettine's refusal to write poetry. She resisted Clemens's importunings. Irresponsible as the young Bettine may have seemed, she observed herself closely, and self-knowledge forbade her to exploit her talents as a poet. She expressed it with astonishing clarity to Günderrode: "It would be sacrilege for me to write poetry, because I drink wine and feel the god while I am intoxicated, because the mind's urge to make divinities passes through me, making me tremble . . . I myself will not create love, no more than I will create a poem, that is what I feel. And also there is a secret contradiction in me: I do not want to be disturbed, in the inner workshop of my spirit, by having my love returned."

Not being disturbed also means: not being destroyed. Unconditional surrender makes a person defenseless. Thus, being unable may be equivalent to not wanting to. The two women, each in her own way, are rigorous thinkers who think things out to the end even if they must oppose their own interests, and this kind of courage is where they understand and touch each other most intimately, sometimes without words. You will find much that is unspoken, deliberately held back, carried along on the river of the spoken.

Bettine sensed that the aesthetic structures she knew must in some way be linked to the hierarchical structures of society, whatever the form in which these were mediated. An insoluble paradox of literature is that it is dependent on the very rules which it must continually overstep in order to become literature. Bettine tried to get around this trap. She surrendered herself neither to love nor to art. Günderrode did not have this strategy at her command. Her letters are tuned to a more earnest note. She could only surrender herself completely, or refuse herself completely. She wanted to be both a lover and a poet. So she placed herself within a system of laws based on the masculine concepts of "artwork" and "genius," which demanded of her what she could not achieve: to separate her work from herself as a person; to create art at life's expense; to create in herself the detachment and coolness which produces "the work" but which kills the direct relationship with other people because it turns them into objects. I wonder, and I ask you: Couldn't the frequently (and sometimes hypocritically) lamented scarcity of women artistic "geniuses" relate not only to women's social condition but also to their unfitness to adapt to an image of the genius which is modeled on a man?

Didn't Günderrode herself intuit something of the sort? It is evident that in her poetry, too, she saw herself captive between irreconcilables. She never forgot that, in poetry, "nothing is more essential than that its germ spring directly from the inner self." At the same time, she complained of the strictness of convention, which made it so hard for the laws of nature to operate successfully. "If only the playing field where energies now exercise by traditional rules were to be deregulated, to make it easier for nature to change its laws . . . I have controlled myself, too, and learned to obey."

Couldn't it be that the thing in her which she had to suppress in order "to obey" one day rebelled against her, self-destructively? That she exhausted herself in the struggle to attain those "simple forms" which "at the same time assist creation, in a feeling of inner harmony," and which, as she said, characterized only the "supreme master in poetry"? No doubt of it, she toiled over the aesthetics of the masterpieces which she could not hope to produce herself. (Have you ever heard the term "mistresspieces"?) She renounced those masterworks for the truth's sake, but felt inferior as she did it.

> I myself often could not help but recognize the poverty of the images in which I couched my poetic moods. I sometimes thought that lusher forms, more beautiful vestures lay close by, ready for use, and that more significant subject matter was easily available to me; only it did not originate as a primary mood in the soul, and so I have always rejected it and have stuck to what deviated least from my real feelings. This was also why I dared to have [my poems] printed. They had that value for me, the sacred value of graven truth. I regard all the little fragments as poetry, in that sense.

We are indeed witnessing the attempt at a new aesthetics, and the fragments of it merit our collecting them. We will hear Georg Büchner say very similar things. The experience of being unable to actualize herself, either in love or in art, led to Günderrode's death.

She envied Bettine her greater degree of inner freedom. "I myself often do not know which wind to steer by, and let myself be driven by all. Have patience with me, since you know me, and keep in mind that it is not one voice alone that I have to oppose but a general voice which, like the Lernaean serpent, continually produces new heads."

I will close with this image. The "general voice" which imposed on Günderrode a standard that was not her own is what killed her. You know the lines in which she said goodbye to the world: "Earth, my mother, and you, air, who nourish me . . ." Those same lines would have fit into Bettine's book, into her dialogue with Bettine, in which the underlying tone of earnestness is made all the more apparent by the gay and playful arabesques in which the two women bravely engage. You know what happened to Bettine later in her life. You know she could not stop proposing a different way of being in the world, a way that would not kill. This book is a beautiful document, a moving voice from a time that is long gone.

You know how the general voice speaks to us today, and what it is speaking about.

December 1979

On Schiller[*]

Schiller? I thought when I learned that I had been awarded this
year's Schiller Memorial Prize. How did I first meet Schiller? How
did Schiller introduce himself to me? That lean, overly industrious
man who was ill for a long period and whom I could never help
picturing as too tall for the rooms of the Schiller House on the Es-
planade in Weimar; whose Ferdinand from the play *Kabale und Liebe*
[*Intrigue and Love*], likewise a very tall man, ran around with giant
steps on the stage of my hometown, shouting so everyone could hear,
when I was thirteen or fourteen. *Kabale und Liebe* was the first real
play I ever saw, after the fairy tales that were put on at Christmas
and the operetta *Frau Luna*. The stage scenery was wobbly, I giggled.
Just this minute, it occurred to me to wonder: Did I ever afterward
picture the poet as looking like that actor? Of course we learned
"The Song of the Bell" by heart, and the ballads—and also the
parodies of them with which generations of schoolchildren used to
stave off the deadly boredom of their German lessons. We must have
been taught to regard Schiller as *the* representative German poet,
because I remember my outrage and incredulity when, after the war,
a new German teacher in a different city told us that *Don Carlos*—
the first Schiller text that we were asked to study—had been eliminated from the repertoire of the German National Theater during the
final years of the Third Reich, and that it had also been banned from
the curriculum of German schools. "Sire, give me my freedom of
thought."[†]

* On being awarded the Friedrich Schiller Memorial Prize of the State of Baden-Würt-
temberg in Stuttgart on November 13, 1983.
† The Marquis of Posa's line in Act III of the play.

This teacher considered my essay on *Don Carlos* "stilted," and she was right. I had tried to bring off the trick of criticizing *her* by way of Schiller. Other people had made similar experiments in the past, people who like me were unwilling or unable to speak openly —among them Friedrich Schiller himself. I did not know those writers then, I did not know that indirect criticism can be voiced in a polished, trenchant, and subtle style, but equally may produce a style that is long-winded, obscure, and stilted. Then, during a long illness, I learned many of Goethe's poems by heart. I learned only a few of Schiller's, one of which was the "Ode to Joy." Five or six years later, when I was living in Leipzig/Gohlis, as Schiller had, I saw the little house where he reputedly composed the Ode, summoning all his capacity for friendship and joy. I learned "The Ideal and Life" and scanned these lines:

> *Man anxiously must choose between these two:*
> *the senses' joy, or else his peace of mind.*

Such antinomies suited me just fine. I also had a taste for high-flown appeals like the one to "Artists":

> *Man's dignity is given into your hand—*
> *Hold on to it!*
> *With you it sinks! Will rise again, with you!*

Such were the haughty moments the poet could purvey. I had not yet learned to ask why this particular German poet was so addicted to issuing stern injunctions from the realm of ideas. I fear that many generations of German readers based their image of a poet on this kind of mental gymnastics in which ideas were condemned never to bear political fruit, and which, because it lacked any real social foundation, appeared hazardous at the same time that it looked beautiful and well crafted. For years I felt no affinity with Schiller.

At the University of Jena, we read Thomas Mann's short story "*Schwere Stunde*" ["A Weary Hour"] as part of an elocution exercise. The tale strangely fascinated me, not so much because it was about Schiller but—as I admitted to myself even at the time—because of Mann's open yet secret identification with this author from the past. "Was not talent itself pain?" I believe that this question, with all the rhetoric in which it was couched, was new to me. But I disagreed: wasn't this an attempt to segregate and elevate the writer of Schiller's type to a status above the "ordinary"? "Greatness! Extraordinariness!

World conquest and an immortal name! What was all the happiness of the eternally unknown compared with this goal?" How could anyone ask such an undemocratic question? I did not think it was right to despise the happiness of the eternally unknown. No, I do not believe that this soaring language could kindle my sympathy.

From the windows of the university hall where we were sitting, we could look out across the street at the botanical garden, formerly the garden of the house where Schiller allegedly went through his "weary hour," struggling with the brittle material of *Wallenstein.* Yes, I could admire this exceptional man—but could I feel affection for him? Thomas Mann, when he delivered his great speech "On Schiller" in both the Germanys in 1955 (the year of Mann's death), dedicated it to Schiller "affectionately." Who else could say that now? I thought, still mulling over the thank-you speech I would have to make here.

I will not elaborate on my various encounters with Schiller. It is time to say that the place where this prize was to be awarded, the city of Stuttgart, suggested another name to me, which lit up like a signal fire and took its place beside Schiller's, indeed supplanted him. The person I thought of is the one I would most have liked to invite to this occasion. I would have been only too pleased to introduce to you this good friend of many years, a citizen of Stuttgart who, along with Schiller, Hölderlin, and a few other writers, formed my picture of what Swabians are like: and what a flattering portrait of the Swabian they give! My friend would have been extremely pleased to come with me, first taking me to his parents' home on the Annastrasse in Untertürkheim, where now—I thought—I will go by myself; and where I already have gone by the time I give my speech. "Where you already *will* have gone," he would have said, correcting my grammar. For he shared with his more famous compatriots a pleasure in the meticulous use of language. He would not omit one pluperfect or one future perfect, nor would he let me get away without it. He believed that great obscenities often begin with little imprecisions.

Okay, I thought, my friend cannot travel with me because he was buried four years ago in a small village near Potsdam. But it would seem quite unnatural to me to go to Stuttgart for an occasion like this without him. So I will at least talk about him when I get there. And what about Schiller? Don't worry, I told myself: those two dead men will get along just fine. I must try to ask the dead poet the kinds of questions which my friend from Stuttgart thought were matters of life and death. I do not mean that metaphorically but literally. At the time that my friend read the German classical authors, including Schiller, he was in prison, and was talking to his fellow inmates about the reasons for their defeat. The date was 1934, 1935, 1936. I do not know if they were aware that they had inherited certain half-begun patterns, the same which the dramatist Schiller had struggled to give shape to in the past. As a playwright, Schiller had searched in vain for a protagonist, a national hero worthy of depiction on the stage; had searched for an appropriate subject, which, for the same reasons, it seemed could almost never be German; had searched for a way to avoid artificial solutions in the structure of his plays but was forced to resort to artificial solutions because the common people, who might have represented his point of view against the power games of the great and famous—who could have portrayed a *natural* chorus, for instance—played no visible role in the German petty states during Schiller's lifetime, and by their absence spoiled the aim of the man who had it in him to become the great dramatist of the German nation. That much I know, it would never have occurred to my friend from Stuttgart that if he and Schiller had been contemporaries, a man like Schiller might have grabbed eagerly at a man like him, to make him the protagonist of his plays—in much the same way that he himself reached back to Joss Fritz, a hero of the Peasants' Revolt, as a model for his own behavior. These problems in finding one's own identity make me think about the cracks in time which gape throughout German history: all too often, heroes were cut off from their own present.

Once, admittedly—in his very first play, *Die Räuber* [*The Robbers*]—Schiller did roundly declare: "History's abode is Germany." And once, the common people did appear on the stage—I would say they were Swabians—in the guise of a band of robbers. Schiller, then a very young poet, hatched them out in the night hours while his comrades were sleeping, in the big dormitory at his school, the Karlsschule, where white lilies, planted by Schiller himself, bloomed outside the barred windows. This entire arrangement, with all that pertains to it, already makes too flagrant a point of itself for me to push it as a symbol. There he sits, the army-doctor-in-training, always short of sleep, always overworked, writing lines like this one: "Put me in command of an army of fellows like me and Germany will become a republic compared to which Rome and Sparta will be convents of nuns." Two words stand out in this burst of temper from the robber chief Karl Moor: "Germany" and "republic." In the oppressive society in which the young Schiller grew up, there was no "Germany," only the duchy of Württemberg. There was no "republic," only Duke Karl Eugen, who appointed himself "father" of the students he forced to attend his military prep school. There were the regulations, the studying, the drilling, the punishments; the separation from family, from nature, from girls; there were the pacts and oaths of friendship among the so-called young men. There were the books. But the nation?

Freedom? A republic? All longing, all utopia. Yet all—already—literature.

Unlike the young Schiller, my friend from Stuttgart was no lover of idealistic blueprints. If he could be here, he would analyze the conditions which existed in Germany a decade before the French Revolution, which were bound to give rise to the notion of a German republic: a phantom which produced a phantom pain. He would be shrewd, amused, and amusing, precise but not pedantic, cogent but not dogmatic, fraternal and "chummy" with his compatriot Schiller, and would shove under Schiller's feet a solid economic, political, and ideological base for his irreverent dreams and his daring plot about a noble robber, so that the poet would not have to dangle in the air so uncomfortably. But, as I said, my friend and Schiller never met. Only one and a quarter centuries after *The Robbers* were revolutionaries born in Germany who, had they become punctually active on a large enough scale, would have given a different direction to German history in our century. *Could* have given—the construction of compound tenses in our grammar does begin to make sense to me as I look at the TV screen and see the modern gangs who camp out in the Swabian woods, whom probably we do not call "robber bands" simply because there are too many of them—and who, I might add, are forced to go into the woods today, because the rebellious peasants whom Luther called robbers and murderers lost their fight here in Swabia, as they did everywhere in Germany. Whichever thread we tug at, the whole fabric stirs.

The Swabian city of Schwäbisch-Gmünd does figure in Schiller's biography; his family lived there for only a few months when Friedrich was very small. He grew up in nearby Lorch, and I imagine that his latter-day successor could today be roaming among the crowds that fill the palace and market squares and the streets of our cities. Today's young Schiller would stage his first improvisational plays using lay people as actors, who on his signal might lie down in a row on the street as if they were being mowed down by a shock wave. Or he would pass out texts to his fellow players which express the fundamental problems of people now, as Schiller expressed the problems of his generation. "The accursed inequality in the world!" says the robber Karl Moor in the first version of the play, which Schiller had to tidy up for its premiere performance in Mannheim.

It is remarkable that he did not direct his anger against fathers. Probably his own two strict fathers, his biological father and Duke Karl Eugen, who usurped the role, weighed too heavily on the young man's chest and he simply could not manage to portray an evil father. The father he created in *The Robbers* was weak, vacillating, easily duped, a ball tossed back and forth by his sons. Schiller's characterization of the sons was made by cutting a whole man in two, right down the middle, so that half fell in one direction and half in the other: one good and the other evil, the enemy brothers. Karl: "Why are there despots? Why should thousands upon thousands of people bend to the whims of one belly, and be dependent on its belches?" In such lines the Germans begin to spell out the words: "equality," "freedom"—but it is not the people, it is a do-it-yourselfer who is reciting the alphabet. "The law has not yet produced a great man, but freedom leaps over the palisade of custom and breeds colossi and extremities." A self-propelled genius, the good robber captain, whom we could also picture in a melodrama. But then Schiller the realist showed his stuff. Much as it might pain him to do so, in the middle of the play he changed this noble robber into a bandit chief, whose actions were determined by the gang with whom he collaborated. Karl Moor could not be saved; he could not survive, any more than his scoundrelly, cunningly self-controlled brother Franz, who was maddened by his position as the second-best son and obsessed with the idea of being master: "I want to wipe out everything around me that hems me in, that stops me from being master." The dramatic scheme served as a touchstone, revealing that the self-help technique of the *Sturm und Drang* was an inadequate alternative to despotism. The young Schiller made this fact evident: he let all his characters die. Nothing worked anymore. A major playwright.

But Schiller's public applauded the aims and speeches of Karl Moor and overlooked his deeds: especially the public which consisted of Schiller's fellow pupils from Karl Eugen's military nursery-cum-slave plantation, who had generously tolerated having their night's rest disturbed by the murmuring, knocking, and stomping of the young poet, and who, released from the forced march they had all made together, had arrived at a clearing in the woods where they could listen, excited and enthusiastic, to the product of those sleepless nights. The names of Schiller's fellow pupils have been preserved, and to my unspeakable satisfaction, one of them was called Schlotterbeck. The son of a mason: that, too, was possible at Karl Eugen's model school. What could stop me from imagining that that young man was the direct ancestor of my friend—even though Schlotterbeck is a very common name in Swabia? My friend was also called Friedrich Schlotterbeck, Frieder for short. He was the son of a metalworker from Württemberg. The first Schlotterbeck, the mason's son, reputedly was a capable painter and engraver; my Schlotterbeck became a carpenter and writer. I am sure of one thing: If my friend had been alive when *The Robbers* was first performed, he would have sneaked off to the city with the other students, lured by the prospect of listening to forbidden literature. But my Friedrich Schlotterbeck actually faced very different dangers for the sake of forbidden reading. He believed deeply in the effectiveness of words, and risked his life for leaflets on which was printed the truth about Hitler. He was tried for high treason and sentenced first to three years in prison and then to almost seven years in a concentration camp. During the trial, he would have preferred to have defended himself by quoting unabridged passages from Goethe's *Faust*.

"The best must leap into the crack of time"—that adage was assigned to him at his school graduation ceremony. It may have flashed into his mind dozens, perhaps hundreds of times, in the most desperate situations; he clung to it, in both senses of that verb. "Learn first to know the depth of the abyss, before you jump in," the robber Karl Moor admonishes a new candidate for his gang. "Here you are stepping outside the circle of humanity, so to speak. Either you must be a higher man or you will be a devil."

Always these false alternatives, which derive directly from the unevolved social conditions in Germany. Frieder Schlotterbeck had no choice. There was no way for him to measure the abyss before jumping in, and he had to do that to *avoid* being thrown outside the circle of humanity. The choice between "higher man" and "devil" was foreign to him, as a worker and a Communist. But he *was* the heir of his Swabian ancestors. Several times in his life he confronted terrible alternatives. For instance: whether to betray his convictions, his class, and the purpose of his life, or to elude the clutches of the Gestapo himself but, by doing so, risk the lives of those close to him. The unsettled conflicts, the half-fought struggles and half-resolved oppositions of German history, were what drove him to this point: a "simple" man, a man of the common people, of those classes who finally, in the drama that was played out at their expense, chose not to become notable for their absence. No weak father inhibited my Schlotterbeck. A decisive, class-conscious worker brought him onto the path. By the way, Schlotterbeck delivered the memorial address for him at a trade-union celebration in the Singers' Auditorium here in Stuttgart-Untertürkheim in 1969. He said of him on that occasion: "He was convinced that there are no small people, but only people who are made small; that no one is simple, but that every person is unique and unmistakable."

—No enemy brother tried to get rid of my Schlotterbeck. His younger brother Hermann, faithful to the family tradition, worked in the German resistance, as he did; and because the older brother was able to escape to Switzerland, the younger was murdered in his place.

"All those who were named Schlotterbeck, that is, who were born with that name, and several of their most intimate friends, had to die." Father, mother, brother, fiancée. The German language, well versed in monstrous events, fails when it comes to this. Frieder Schlotterbeck addressed the dead with words he could have read in Schiller: "The dead here died for the dignity of man, for his right to personality, to a little bit of freedom."

In these words, German classicism seems at last to have arrived at its goal. Here we have the proof of its effectiveness: the common people died for the values which the classical writers had set up. A delayed, macabre meeting between spirit and impotence. People who could not have known a man like Schiller found that they needed him. Man's dignity was given into *their* hands. There were no award celebrations. Those who had to defend man's dignity were persecuted outcasts. I have reread again and again the description which Frieder Schlotterbeck gave in his autobiography of his illegal errands in Leipzig in 1933. There his footsteps may have crossed the long-vanished path of the poet who, in this same city, dreamed up what may perhaps prove an immortal line: "Joy, lovely spark of the divine."* No thought of that in Frieder's account. "Shivering with cold, I stamp my feet on the slushy snow. Where can I spend the night tonight?"

Now I am beginning to make up a story; I am designing a utopia that aims backward, into the past. If, in Karl Moor's time, there had been something besides a robber gang to occupy his urge for freedom; if there had been the slightest chance of turning the student pranks and ruffianism of men like Roller, Spiegelberg, Schweizer, Schusterle, and Razmann into a student *movement*—then Karl Moor would not have become a robber in the Bohemian woods—i.e., the Swabian woods—but, for instance, the leader of a bourgeois-republican political party. Still in danger of course, risking life and limb, by no means safe; but at least not an outsider whom his perverse superman's ideology turned into a monster: "There I stand, on the brink of a hideous life, and only now, with wailing and gnashing of teeth, I learn that two people like me would be enough to bring down the whole edifice of the moral world." What remains? Sacrifice—so frequently the outcome of German tragic plays. The woman Amalie is sacrificed; then the foundered hero sacrifices himself, caught in the fatal mistake of believing that this is the way to "appease the violated laws" and to "heal again the order I abused." He surrenders to a poor odd-job

* First line of the "Ode to Joy."

man who has "eleven live children" to support, so that the man can turn him in to the authorities for the reward which has been set on Moor's head. There we have another fine solution to the social problem! Another way to establish a pact among the oppressed and enslaved! Another form of solidarity! If that isn't an end to a German play . . .

So it goes; one is sometimes tempted to think it will go on that way forever. Again and again we meet the crack in time. Again and again, the inspired or rebellious young people, or simply alert and reflective young people, split in half (if they are middle-class) into the good and the evil brother or, in recent times, into the good and the evil sister, too. Again and again, the Establishment forces them to shift the direction of their striving for unconditional freedom, bars their way into a world whose order they feel is immoral. "Do you realize that they are ferreting us out?" Roller is driven to ask his fellow students, shortly before he becomes a robber. Again and again, in the absence of a strong revolutionary movement, we see rejection, exclusion, the escape into a sect, a group, a gang. The break with a traditional morality which, there is no denying, maintains a double standard. The break with the fathers, who are beginning to horrify the young. Again and again, the noble terrorist. Ghastly deeds, atrocities, and the punishment for them. In Stuttgart you have Stammheim, the stone evidence of a lack of alternatives.*

If you took all the places which Friedrich Schlotterbeck names in his memoirs, you could construct a map of the prisons, jails, and concentration camps around Stuttgart: Welzheim, Bad Cannstatt, Rudersberg, Ludwigsburg, and of course Hohenasperg Fortress, where during Schiller's youth the radical poet C.F.D. Schubart was confined and where, shortly before Schiller left his homeland of Württemberg as a fugitive using a false name, a sad and farcical meeting took place between the two. Schubart had been carried off to prison by the Duke, and the same Duke had driven Schiller into exile by forbidding him to publish his work. The "unnatural copulation of subordinates with genius" came to an end.

Schiller's play—like all literature, produced during "cracks in time"—did away with long and carefully repressed taboos. But it also contained a trace of that prophetic knowledge of the future without which no play would survive. Just consider the following brief dialogue between two doomed men, who must give each other courage by exaggeration and boasting:

---

* The Stammheim Prison in Stuttgart housed the members of the Baader–Meinhof terrorist gang, also called the Red Army Faction, while awaiting and during their trial in the 1970s.

KARL MOOR: You're sure there is enough powder?
SCHWEIZER: Powder enough to blast the earth to the moon!

This is no realistic, pragmatic exchange about the potential of a materially existing weapon; and if that is how people hear it now, then it may be time for us to think about new plays. Plays whose dramatic structure can no longer hinge (so I believe) on the idea "It's either you or me"—on the victory of one of the enemy brothers and the death of the other. Instead, the new drama ought to concentrate on the forces which are beginning to sprout up from the ground under the fighters' boots, which usually get trampled by them.

In Schiller's first drama, poor Amalie, tugged back and forth between the men, cannot get beyond viewing one of the brothers Moor as the Devil himself, and the other as her god. Thus unintentionally she reveals the quality which she herself lacks: her own independent center.

My friend Frieder Schlotterbeck, who was your fellow country-man, met with hatred and hostility and destructive frenzy. He experienced things which I dare not describe or even hint at, yet he never experienced the temptation to demonize his enemies. He never viewed Hitler and his vassals as the Devil and his diabolic crew. Nor did he follow the practice of some members of his own movement by creating false idols. For his fellow Communists, too, were seared by the history of the Germans, their movement was a product of that history, and its members have occasionally fallen prey to irrational actions: one of which was to throw Frieder Schlotterbeck back in jail, this time falsely denounced by his own comrades. To the end of his life he continued to try to analyze even this experience, and never let himself be carried away to the point of demonizing historical events. Today I know whence he derived this freedom, which we younger ones often found incredible. He no longer felt any fear, not even of the surprising things he might realize about himself—for he knew himself. And not only that: there was not a trace in him of the things that he was fighting. German Fascism had no part in this man. He was not suppressing anything in himself which would force him to give birth to it in devil form. He was humane through and through, a historical being completely exorcised of demons. Capable of conflict and of peace. Today, he would very likely have joined with this new force which we call the peace movement.

Today, more than ever, the "crack in time" gapes wide for all to see. And as I have tried to indicate, it is no accident that this rift runs all through Germany's past. Must "the best" now "leap into" the abyss once again? Or ought they to try—cautiously, discreetly, taking small steps—to lead their countrymen back from the abyss? Starting by withdrawing them from the drug "demonization of the enemy"— because you no doubt have noticed that this speech of mine aims to promote that withdrawal, in a small way—while taking care that the strenuous and unsettling weaning process does not become *too* strenuous and *too* unsettling? And that the fascination with the abyss is not allowed to drown out the tiresome effort of addressing our many unsolved problems, in a sober and rational way?

Because: if this next war, for which so many prudent, careful, far-reaching and determined preparations have been made is prevented, we have been promised no paradises to take its place. Even without war, our prospects for the future are not dazzling. No rapid changes. So does that mean that the best we can wish for is the maintenance of the status quo?

Franz Moor regards it as a proven fact that the "circular swamp of human destiny" cannot be changed, and uses this deterministic view to justify his own shallow egotism. "The man who thinks against his own interests is a fool." But if thinking exclusively in terms of one's own advantage would destroy not just the enemy but oneself, then such thinking has become obsolete: The only attitude which is really advantageous is one which aims for the advantage of all. And it seems to me that the people who act advantageously, that is, realistically, are those who—caught between two enemy poles which are strained to the breaking point—demonstrate in a frank and open way their desire to live (but what a miracle openness is these days!), and thereby create their ability to live. Their behavior is advantageous to the other side, too, to those who today still ignore, mock, suspect, persecute, or lock them up. It is also for the benefit of those others, it is with the intention of saving them, that they try out new forms of coexistence, which, transitory and swiftly destroyed as they may be, seem the only things capable of changing the status quo, and of pumping something like hope into the iron logic, the entrenched structures of the dilemma called "history." I would like to get involved with the dramaturgy which they suggest. A life which is not reducible to mere survival, which would include writing and talking. So that Franz Moor's fearful pronouncement would not become a true prophecy: "There was something and will be nothing. Isn't that tantamount to saying: There was nothing and will be nothing, and about nothing no word will be exchanged?"

November 1983

For Hans Mayer,

on His Eightieth Birthday[*]

————

Honored Hans Mayer, Ladies and Gentlemen:

A week ago today I dreamed that a big party was being held in a house which I did not recognize. Many people I know had come— most wore masks, by the way—but I was sitting in a small office above the banquet hall and editing this speech, which I had to deliver before the end of the party. Again and again, someone would look in on me with a worried and urgent expression, until finally I was awakened by a loud voice which said, "I can't finish." It took me a while to recognize this voice as my own. And then I had the idea of taking the hint seriously. Why couldn't I simply come to you and say, "Professor, I can't finish," and why shouldn't you reply in your generous way, "You need an extension? Granted!" My relief did not last long. It occurred to me that the date of a birthday cannot be postponed. And unfortunately, ever since I was a child, I accustomed my teachers to my being on time—and myself, too. For instance, I delivered my first university paper in your class on time. It was in late autumn 1951, and the subject was Romain Rolland's novel *Jean Christophe*. You won't remember, it was in your beginning course on Great Novels of World Literature. I would rather have attended your upper-level seminar, but you had to refuse—with thorough politeness—to admit this transfer student who had arrived from Jena. Not until I read your memoirs did I understand fully why that was so. You suspected, I think, that this new student of yours had been infected with the theories of your enemies from Professor Scholz's circle. Well, you

* Speech delivered in March 1987 at the West Berlin Academy of Arts.

228

were right. Only later did I come to feel that your views on the German *Sturm und Drang*, and those I was taught in Jena by Professor Scholz's collaborator Edith Braemer, were not so very far apart, after all. In any case, I had to write this paper on Rolland, sitting on an extremely uncomfortable bench in two empty rooms in the Leipzig district of Gohlis and scribbling on a small "club table" of a species which is now virtually extinct. The walls were hung with gloomy oil paintings which belonged to the main tenant, and I could not help feeling afraid that the child I would shortly bring into the world might be damaged by catching sight of such paintings so early in life. This may partly explain why I no longer have very clear memories of my four semesters in Leipzig, or at least not of my university work. I was occupied with other things—not, I admit, with the tribulations of a student who, despite having a child, had to take her intermediate examinations on time—there it is again, that phrase "on time"!—but rather with what you later called "religious discussions." These kept me busy, indeed. Questions of true belief and pure doctrine; the endless conflicts about deviations and deviant people, among whom one did not wish to number oneself but whom one ended up joining on occasion; renewed attempts to find the "correct standpoint"; much effort vainly spent, much feeling of strangeness and doubt, glossed over with self-torture and rigorism. No: the Leipzig of the early 1950s was no place for me. That became clear to me again when, with emotion, I reread that concise remark of yours: "My place was Lecture Room 40 in Leipzig . . . Moments of my life when I was completely by myself: the view from the podium of what was formerly Lecture Room 40 at Leipzig University." Well, I could describe to you how things looked from the opposite direction, from a seat in the seventh or eighth row on your right, where I normally sat, facing the podium. I also remember how you became angry one time, when you announced that you were canceling your next lecture because you had to travel outside the country and we applauded happily like schoolchildren instead of showing regret. Just an anecdote. We did not inquire very eagerly into the life history which lay behind our professor's easily wounded feelings.

I have begun to rummage around in old boxes; naturally, I will never finish my speech this way. I have not found what I was looking for. On the other hand, I did find my transcript, so I can document that in the three semesters in question—because in the fourth, intervening semester I was on leave, "due to illness" is what my records say, but since when is the birth of a child an illness? and what is the meaning of this official stamp that says: "Study fees collected owing to fee waiver"?!—the main lectures that you delivered were the following: "German Literature in the Period of Imperialism." "The Literature of a Democratic Germany." "German Literature since 1830"—accompanied by a discussion group on Goethe—a name I hesitate to mention here, where will it lead? In one of your books with the insidious title *Goethe: Versuch über den Erfolg* [*Goethe: A Venture at Success*], you scrupulously trace the chain of fiascos and failures which occasionally, in a certain type of person, add up to success in the end. But let everyone read that for himself, I want to talk about the Young People's Goethe Festival in Weimar in 1949. I have searched in vain for the program of that event, which you attended just after moving from Frankfurt am Main to the Soviet occupation zone, and where you delivered your first speech, a commemorative address: "Reflections of Goethe in Contemporary Life." And I must have attended, too, invited to give a paper on the topic: "Goethe's View of Personality and Society." I have found that paper of mine, by the way; it is pretty voluminous. But it was in August that I was in Weimar—so was it definitely March 22 when you spoke there? It really was hot when I was there: warm nights, two young men who, like me, had won prizes in the essay competition accompanied me to my lodgings late in the evening after we saw a production of *Faust* with Lothar Müthel as Mephisto. One young man was too tall for me, the other was too short, neither suited me, but certain it is that I heard Otto Grotewohl speak, too: "You must rise or sink, suffer or triumph, be the anvil or the hammer!" That made sense to me. And when you wrote: "I became addicted to Goethe," I could have replied—with the respect due from one of my mere twenty years—"Me, too." I must have sat in the auditorium listening to you—is it possible that you repeated your speech again in August? —I believe I can still hear the actor you mention and his interpretation of Goethe's "use of symbol." I could have recited every word by heart along with him: "Neglect not to practice / the energies of goodness." That belonged to the basic supply of literature-to-live-by, the literature of good resolutions, which I hastily stored up after the war as a sort of self-rescue operation. "We bid you hope!" That above all, and after all, what else. Yes, you are right: The people who came to hear you in the National Theater in Weimar were the generation born in 1929 and 1930, and it was not chance but the necessity of that "moment in history"—to borrow one of your favorite expressions—which had brought you and us together out of God knows how many different directions, to meet at that place, on that occasion. We began to feel how urgently we needed teachers like you. You had just accepted this special teaching assignment, which went far beyond the mere transmission of knowledge. "Is it not true, O Mother, that he whom

the gods love they lead to where there is need of him?" Elpenor's*
remark, which Goethe coined for himself in Weimar, you took as a
reference to your life in Leipzig. You did not discover this message
in Goethe until late in life, but it probably described equally well the
feelings you had when you gave that early lecture. Somewhere between
being needed and not being needed any more lies what clinches the
decision of whether to stay or to go. That's something I understand
much better now than I did in 1963. Even then, I accepted your
decision with regret. I can also still feel, along with you, the longing
which you describe as one motive—perhaps the main motive—for
your wide-ranging rapprochement with Communists and the Communist movement: the longing "to belong to a community, to work
for something together with others, to live with a purpose in view."
This longing was not confined to just one generation. What we were
after was something fundamentally opposed to National Socialism: to
link ourselves to the republican-democratic-socialist tradition in German history which was completely unknown to us in the younger
generation; which had been buried and finally beaten into the ground;
and to continue the progressive-bourgeois and the populist-socialist
tradition in German literature. All of us who met together in the
Weimar National Theater in 1949 to honor Goethe were, I think,
concerned to find a valid alternative. The "unruly principle of hope."

Anyone able and willing to look at all sides of all the conflicts
that were determined at that "moment in history" could have predicted
to us that things were going to get rough. If I even began to enumerate
them I would never finish, I literally cannot "finish" with them. You,
Hans Mayer, experienced them at their harshest: as a "test-model
German"—one who had not chosen that role, I may say—you nevertheless exposed yourself at once, irrevocably and without insisting on
your right of appeal, to the whole battery of tests that a writer in either
of the Germanys could be put through, to try out his tensile strength.
What is it that Elpenor's mother says: "He who is noble seeks out
danger, and it seeks him, so they are bound to meet." I don't know
how you see all this today. But it seems to me that now, as in the
past, it is worth making any effort, and even overstraining oneself,
to help overcome the "unhappy mentality" of the Germans, and especially of German intellectuals: to prevent, reduce, delay, or at least
to keep us aware of the "gap that is opening again between political
and intellectual 'Germanness' " (as you defined this "unhappy mentality" in your most recent book). In the university lectures you gave
in Leipzig—because I have to confess that I also managed to trace

---

* Character in a drama fragment by Goethe written in 1783.

some lecture notes—you were already applying your special skills to explore the tricky points in the personal biographies of poets, because writers' most personal impulses meet (and often collide with) the conditions of their society. Beginning with innocent-looking questions like: Why, in the first decades of this century, did Heinrich Mann write literary essays only about French authors, while Thomas Mann wrote only about German authors? Why did Goethe go to Italy in 1786?—you evolved a panorama of conflicts between writers and their times. You showed how each writer's decisions, even the decisions of Johann Wolfgang von Goethe, revealed that he was "fed up with the here and now." And so even back then, at a time when this was by no means obvious, you avoided attributing Goethe's flight to Italy merely to his personal characteristics, to the famous "disappointments" he suffered at the court in Weimar or to the "disagreement" with a lady, and instead you investigated the profound life crisis of a political man who, confronted by the miserable conditions of his day, felt that he was "driven back to writing" and to—what a horrible thought!—"a creativity without society."

One takes in information, even if later one cannot expressly recall the details. Today I feel surprised that, in my student days in Leipzig, I did not wonder where my professor had derived his convincing way of treating literature, which I expect I carelessly thought of as the *only* convincing way. Not until much later, when I read the books you wrote after you left Leipzig, did I learn to know you better, and discovered in your writings words which I would not have expected you to use. One such word, which always turned up at critical moments in your personal biography, was "awakening." You experienced one of your first "awakenings" through your early reading of Georg Lukács, who, when you were twenty-one, demonstrated to you "where I stood, or could stand, at this moment in history. Gone was my lethargic acceptance of the status quo, which I now found more and more intolerable, even though, or because, it lacked nothing—except any meaning. I discovered history and Marxist thought." However numerous and extensive the modifications which you naturally had to make by the time you reached the age of eighty, you never went back on this discovery, nor did you find an alternative. Another teacher, Carl J. Burckhardt,* whom you met when you emigrated to Switzerland, taught you "not to use the works of writers as an index to the material of history, but to take them seriously as creations in their own right." So there you had the basic components in the range of skills you deployed later, as a literary analyst. But above all, from

* Swiss writer, historian, and politician (1891–1974).

232

then on, you accepted the fate of being a writer with a leaning to drama. By the way, "Why didn't I become a playwright?" you asked. Allow me to hazard a guess: because the roles which the theater would have offered you would in a certain way not have satisfied your ego, which needed the roles supplied by the poets: still deeper hiding places, still more dependable masks, still more secret possible identities. I don't know whether you are aware how often words like "secret" and "secretly" appear in your memoirs. I have seen you tuck the weightiest confessions into parenthetical or dependent clauses, or other "sequestered spots" in those volumes—where those who choose may find them; that is, those who read with exactness, and with sympathy and empathy, too.

The alternative way of life which left-wing intellectuals hoped for—and no doubt desired too impatiently—cannot be realized in this century, but instead their life will be spent in the never abandoned search for it, and the work to bring it about. Awareness of this may lend a new color to our "unhappy mentality." At any rate, it forbids us to make ourselves at home there. Thirty-seven years after the Goethe festival in Weimar, twenty-three years after you left Leipzig, we sat together in a lecture hall once more. You know what I am referring to. Once again you were lecturing, this time on the theme of Karl Kraus.* The auditorium belonged to the East German Academy of Arts, it was November 1986. A new "moment in history" which, if I am not mistaken, appears to hold the germs of hope—hope in a very changed form—along with immense and intensified "risks." It did not seem exaggerated to me to count your presence (your very existence) among the hopeful signs. And once again we are looking for a viable alternative, especially for today's young—a demand which, we will see, cannot be fulfilled by ensuring our mere survival, urgent as that need may be. Instead, mere survival cannot be guaranteed, in the long run, without working on the question of why and what for—that is, without the development of a fundamentally alternative way of thinking. If I read you correctly, you are holding out to us, with one hand, the dictum "The Enlightenment has failed!" while with the other hand, so to speak, you work ceaselessly to challenge and cancel that dictum. But the verdict that the Enlightenment has failed to produce results can be canceled only by groping our way to the roots of this lack of results: the fact that the Enlightenment, this imposing mental structure, was built by a small group of European intellectual males who used themselves as the standard by which to measure what it meant to be "human."

* Austrian critic.

Do you remember our supper in Tübingen in the spring of 1976, when you recommended that I order the trout ("Here you don't have to be afraid to eat poached trout"—is that still true?) and you gave me a copy of your most recent book, *Aussenseiter* [*Outsiders*]. Then, for the first time, I understood the importance writing has in your life: it is born out of an extreme receptivity to the problematic aspects of being human, a receptivity which is primarily artistic rather than scholarly. Learning through suffering, not being able to choose one's theme but being chosen by it.

"The monster as the test case of humanity." I was struck by that line, it sheds light on the substratum of our civilization, on what was driven into hiding by the rationalism of the Enlightenment. Intently I followed the twists and turns you gave this theme in your chapters "Judith and Delilah," "Sodom," and "Shylock." No, it isn't "auto-biographical," I agree with you there, but it *is* perhaps one piece of a great confession. (That many women today are in a monstrous condition—that owing to the offer of liberation within completely male-run societies, women risk being unable to find and redefine their identity and instead may lose it for good—and that this dilemma cannot be embraced within the fictional characters of Judith and Delilah is, I suspect, a fact of which you are aware. Admittedly, you did not have at your disposal very many fictional characters who would have expressed it all completely.)

The more important this most radical of your books became to me, the more I regretted that my own most recent book, which was published a short time later, did not appeal to you. The truth you demanded from me then was not my truth, I could not produce what you expected. It was not that we misunderstood each other, it was that we had different viewpoints based on different decisions. The flaws in my book could not be attributed to "dishonesty." The conflict which you felt was missing from my subject (along with other things)—namely, the distortion of the Communist movement during the Stalinist period, and the results of that for all the members of the movement—while centrally important to me, too, could occupy only a marginal place in my confrontation with German Fascism. Also, I had to give a different slant to the problems of East Germany, which I still hoped to help change, than you did, now that it was impossible for you to take any action. I saw no alternative to the decision I made, and so, as an author and as a person, too, I have always proceeded very cautiously whenever I saw even modest signs of creative changes taking place in social practice here. (Cautiously but not uncritically or insincerely, I may say.) It was always crucially important to me

—and still is, as I have observed in these months of rekindled hope—whether or not I could still detect these signs of life.

There is also such a thing as an authentic silence, a silence which can be eloquent. After reading your memoirs, I believe that you are thoroughly familiar with this principle and silently enforce it. Not everything is sayable at all times, and not everything must or ought to be said. The same applies to this speech of mine, which I cannot finish, as you, too, must now admit.

Because I still have to jump back to Leipzig again. Leipzig remains the point of reference between you and me; there is nothing that we can do about that. And I cannot get around mentioning a scene which, once again, was played out in your lecture room and which is not without a certain comic aspect. Back at the start of 1953(!), I had gotten it into my head to write my state examination paper—to write it on time, of course, what else?—about the prose literature of the GDR. You gruffly responded: "Red-painted gazebos!"—and then you went on to say the same thing publicly, too, for one finds the identical description of GDR literature in your memoirs. Ignoring my dissent and my indignation—because I could, after all, have quoted a few titles to you, by names like Seghers, Claudius, Strittmatter—you assigned me the theme: "The Problem of Realism in Hans Fallada"—not such a bad idea, as it turned out. Well, I had read my Lukács, too, so I knew all about realism, and with gradually diminishing indignation I made the long trek each day to the German Library, where I sat reading the tall pile of Fallada's novels, trying slowly to read it shorter. But soon (from the very start, I fear) it became clear to me what I could prove in my thesis: that Fallada's petit-bourgeois ideology had greatly detracted from the realism of his books. You accepted my findings—which I can only say was amazing, now that I have unearthed my paper again and skimmed through it. No, it does not give evidence of any "awakening." But with a newly earned diploma I could at last devote myself to the literary scene in the GDR, which irresistibly fascinated me. (Soon, by the way, I, too, wrote protesting the red-painted gazebos.) And so our ways parted, and once again it was not by accident. You found a new literary home in Gruppe 47,* and I experienced a sort of phantom pain when I saw the warmth with which you wrote about the gatherings you all had. The groups and the friendship circles where we met had no name. They went unnoticed in the West, just as our literature did, for a long time. The abstention from politics which formed part of the

* A postwar West German literary group.

regimen of Gruppe 47 was something we could never imagine. On the other hand, perhaps we placed politics too much in the center, so that it acquired the power to bind and to loose. The departure of comrades, which in many (although not in all) cases testifies to a growing inability to integrate people into our society, is a very painful experience.

No, I have not finished. But I am coming to an end. Again, we are sitting in an auditorium together. The situation is reversed now: I am addressing a speech to you, instead of the other way around. If someone had predicted to me, at some point in the past, that I would publicly congratulate you, Hans Mayer, on the occasion of your eightieth birthday (or just before it), in the West Berlin Academy of Arts, I would have called him a dreamer. But that is the way you wanted it. Actually, I would have preferred to avoid this difficult arrangement, which for me has been not only dreamlike but troubling. Yet once again I have been on time, I have not asked for an extension. And have I done you justice, too? I wanted to. I hope that this is a festive moment for you, a moment of "fulfillment"—in the way that you have described other moments of your life as happy and fulfilled. I wish that you may enjoy it, and go on feeling it for a long time.

Thank you.

March 1987

In Praise of Thomas Brasch[*]

—

Ladies and Gentlemen:
When I was assigned the tricky job of finding a recipient for this year's Kleist Prize, I set out in search of "the Kleistian." The Kleistian element in and about a contemporary author. I also wanted to try to live up to the tradition which this prize has set since the 1920s. Its standards are exacting, and moreover it impels you to follow a certain line. I felt relieved when Thomas Brasch came to mind: he seemed to me to fulfill both conditions. Now, after reading or rereading all his work, I am sure of it. Meanwhile, secondary reasons for choosing his name have occurred to me. They involve the intensive development of literature in the GDR; the contradictions, the strangeness, the curiosity, the envy between the generations; the tendency of older people to feel guilty toward the younger; the hazy processes of attraction and repulsion between woman and man. I do not want to elaborate on all that, do not want to probe into how many of these obscure motives influenced my decision. Quite definitely, one thing I had in mind was a scene which took place eleven years ago in our apartment in Berlin. Thomas Brasch told us that he intended to leave East Germany. He was not the first person to sit there and tell us this, but he was the first whom I was unable to dissuade from going. In that sense, his leaving was a turning point for me, too, although he is unaware of it. I suddenly faced a new question: Why stay? And I had to answer it not just verbally but through work, because only

* On the presentation of the Kleist Prize for Literature in October 1987 in Frankfurt-am-Main.

237

productivity can generate that inner freedom which erases doubt about one's choice of a place to live and work. If I am not mistaken, Thomas Brasch is one of those people who cannot stop wrestling with their experiences even after they have left this country, and who remain capable of recognizing new developments and drawing new conclusions.

What is the first thing that comes to my mind when I think of the name Kleist? The crack in time, which runs right through the man. The longer I spent reading Brasch's writings, the more clearly I could feel him resist any insistent attempts to interpret him; a shyness about self-exposure; a warning not to intrude. I wish to respect this appeal. It is the same feeling I have about Kleist: that his works derive from two opposing needs which are almost equal in power: to make himself invisible, but also to lay himself completely bare. And the crack in time? It has left its traces on those texts which are self-revealing:

> Really, how many of us are left by now?
> The one standing there at the crossroad,
> wasn't he one of us?
> Now he wears rimless spectacles.
> We would almost not have known him.
>
> Really, how many of us are left by now?
> Wasn't that the one with the Jimi Hendrix record?
> They say he's an engineer now.
> Now he wears a suit and tie.
> We're all keyed up. He is well fed.
>
> Really, who are we by now?
> Let's get a move on. What are we after?
> What's the name of this hole
> in which, one after the other, we
> disappear?

That is a quotation from the cycle *Papiertiger* [*Paper Tigers*], written in the midseventies and clear to everyone of his generation, to everyone he refers to as "we." Brasch was their spokesman. I do not wish to "explain" this poem to a West German public, and perhaps it really isn't necessary. But there is an expectation that we have about literature from the other Germany, which, although it is well-meaning, can result not only in our misinterpreting texts but in our actually dissolving them, as if placing them against a different background blurs their sharp outlines, making them invisible. Thomas

Brasch never catered to that expectation, and very soon after he arrived here, he began to struggle against being swallowed up. Possibly he did so at the cost of being ignored, because of his oddness. Poets of the Kleistian type want to be needed, and against their will have seen themselves hurled into an eccentric orbit by the literary history of the past two hundred years.

> *I do not want to lose what I have but*
> *I do not want to stay where I am but*
> *I do not want to leave the ones I love but*
> *I no longer want to see the ones I know but*
> *I do not want to die where I am living but*
> *I do not want to go to where I'll die:*
> *I will stay where I have never been*

A remnant of utopia never wholly consumed, a longing for the land the Germans did not know how to create for themselves, where one could live like a human being, a land to deal with on human terms. But if it is not to be, then face the fact head-on: the crack that runs through the country, the open wound that is not understood so long as one denies it, or just laments it; that is incurable unless one traces it back to its origins, to its first, fine causes. Brasch's Till Eulenspiegel vision. Brasch's angry-sad description of the Peasants' Revolt in "Hahnenkopf" ["Cock's Head"], of the army of peasants outside the city of Weinsberg:

> *In the morning they stormed*
> *The city's gates.*
> *Drove the princes along*
> *A street of pikes.*
> *In the evening they quarreled.*
> *At night they separated*
> *Going in three directions:*
> *Against the army of the princes in the south.*
> *Across the border.*
> *Back to their villages.*
> *Coming from three directions*
> *The army of the princes*
> *Beat two weeks later*
> *What was left of the peasants' army*
> *And captured*
> *Those who had fled*
> *And beheaded*

Those who
Had hidden
In the barns . . .

And the princes brought order and harsher laws, obedience and subservience; and the Prince of Homburg* broke those laws and was condemned to die, for reasons of state. But Natalie, who loved him, pleaded with the Prince Elector to spare his life, and forced incompatibles to meet in two lines of verse:

The laws of war, I know well they must rule.
But the tender feelings should rule too.

Utopia again, its case past pleading except by the mouths of women. The demand for a fatherland "which needs not this harsh stricture, cold and waste." Which abandons its sacred but unnatural order for a disorder more affectionate to human beings. "A dream, what else?"

One hundred and seventy years later, Brasch treats the same theme:

HAMLET AGAINST SHAKESPEARE

The other word behind the word.
The other death behind the murder.
The incompatible, put in a poem:
Order. And the crack that breaks it.

The fictional character presents his inventor with a bill which has gone unpaid for far too long. The Brasch texts which I have quoted, except for the last one, are taken from the volume *Kargo: 32. Versuch auf einem unter-gehenden Schiff aus der eigenen Haut zu kommen* [*Cargo: Thirty-second Attempt to Escape One's Own Skin on a Sinking Ship*]. Members of the cargo cult reportedly believed that men with white skins were spirits of the dead who could not rest, who were no longer alive and not yet dead. The "sinking ship" of the title is the continent of Europe. Brasch does not suffer from Eurocentrism.

He was born in England, of Communist parents—his mother was Jewish—who had emigrated from Germany and lived in exile in Britain. Their son grew up in East Germany, where at age ten he was sent to a military boarding school—just like Kleist, a remarkable

---

* In Kleist's play of that name.

coincidence—that was later dissolved. "A ruling class which works to preserve and consolidate the state it governs gets rid of its children by entrusting their education to a bureaucracy commissioned and paid by itself." That is Brasch commenting on Robert Musil's *Young Törless*. In the boarding school (he goes on), the son is reduced and promoted to a worn-out Oedipus who will either become a tool of the officers in the next war and be broken in the process or will write a description of the land that has fathered him. While wishing to avoid inapt or cheap conclusions, I cannot consider it an accident that Brasch delivered such a harsh and precise commentary about this particular subject. Like the young Kleist, the young Brasch became devoted to a philosophy, and like Kleist, he suffered a cognitive shock which disillusioned him. But there was a crucial difference: Kleist, caught in the endless mirror-play of subjective idealism, despaired of the possibility of knowledge per se, whereas Brasch became more radical, more uncompromising, and more anarchic in his desire to change things through a Marxist philosophy. "That one must walk on a razor's edge to move a little way forward probably sounds to you like a sentimental thought." The word "sentimental" is one that a writer of his kind can't stand, by the way, precisely because his cocky attitude is doubly, triply steeped in feeling. I do not want to talk about sentiment here, but about a certain kind of radicality which has been forced on young German poets since Hölderlin, and which we find in Lenz, Kleist, and in Büchner, of course, and again in our century. Brasch criticized the socialist state from a left-wing vantage point, and experimented with "childlike as well as populist forms of resistance"—forms which the state, at least then, did not tolerate. Brasch was sentenced to prison, an experience about which he has said very little.* The following poem seems to explain why:

> *Silence is the sister of madness.*
> *Between the stool and the door are five steps and*
> *the pulse is between the temples.*
> *The poses:*
> *resistance/the test of toughness/self-pity/lament/laughter*
> *are used up: lead articles in one's own official party paper.*

After prison, he worked in an office. A clear and significant theme runs through his writings of that time. "The Sons Die before

---

* Brasch was sentenced to prison in East Germany for protesting the Soviet suppression of Czechoslovakia in 1968, and his works were banned from publication.

the Fathers."* Pain is concealed by insolent or mocking or cynical remarks. The mythological hero of the Hercules type is finished. A poet like Brasch must follow complicated aesthetic pathways to arrive at characters of a different sort: highly dubious types with whom it becomes possible for him to identify, completely or partly, and always at some risk to himself. He shows no fear of "down-and-outers": on the contrary, he is attracted by them. Lovely Rita. Sindbad. Rotter. Lackner. Then, in West Germany, the robber-murderer Gladow. Lisa the actress. Sakko and Oi, who are unemployed. A remarkable ensemble, unusual in the literatures of both the Germanys. Not one "character" in the traditional sense who is justified by a life which expresses an inviolable "inner core." The scenarios are hard to unravel. The film *Domino*, for instance, is described as "a play with pictures, about the rupture of imagination." But Kleist—aside from the fact that he made no films—could have described every one of his plays in the same terms. The character Lisa, dropping her role as actress in a slow-motion shot, declares: "The old stuff doesn't work and the new doesn't work either. And there you all sit."

I have already mentioned some poets to whom Brasch feels a kinship. Kafka is another who belongs in that group. So does Chekhov, who seems not to fit in with the rest but whom Brasch has translated. (In fact, Brasch is drawn to Russian literature in general, and to early Soviet literature: Mayakovsky is a fruit of his years in East Germany which he does not let wither on the vine.) To these figures one must add Georg Heym, the subject of Brasch's play *Lieber Georg* [*Dear Georg*]. "Because this play treats a prewar situation and the main character is a poet—that is, Georg Heym—who is radically affected by this prewar situation—that is, the crack which runs through the society runs through him, too—and the character of Georg Heym also gave me the opportunity to be extremely autobiographical, and to write a play according to a new scenario, new for me." The next-to-last scene is captioned "Outside the Play, 1979" and is a reflection on the nation's recent resolution to limit arms:

> My hand with the chalk in it moves swiftly
> over the stones and now I know that I am
> writing a play about a poet amid the deafening
> silence of a prewar between invisible laws of
> economics, weighed down by an antiquated aesthetics . . .
> What I must do is to bring about, in the most rapid
> manner possible, the downfall of the poet who is the

* Title of a prose text by Brasch published in 1977.

*subject of this play, in a theater which does not
exist or which does not exist yet—I think, and my
hand writes the title of the last scene.*

This title is "In the ice at last." "An early death. That's something,
too. Then we don't need to learn a profession." "Lurid and tasteless"
is how one reviewer described Brasch's characteristic sound. And
rightly so. Creativity, which Brasch regards as a fundamental value,
is something he no longer finds except in artists and criminals.

In the same way, Kleist was unable to serve to Goethe—however
much he pined to win Goethe's favor—a dish of inoffensive classical
contradictions, of conflicts neatly divided into good and evil, healthy
and sick, respectable and criminal. "Contradiction," in fact, is too
cozy a word for the permanent friction which writers of the modern
era are forced to experience. It is banal to point out that aggressive
postures are usually a screen for deep wounds. Issues never were
settled humanely in German history, and because of this, young
Germans have always been forced to rebel against their fathers and
mothers. The statement "The daughters die before the fathers" is as
true as that the sons die. It is lovely Rita who says so, and right after
that she says: "Pathos." Brasch and his characters share a horror of
pathos. "You mustn't drape a garland around every word. I don't want
to see emotional gymnastics here." Brasch detests high-flown thoughts
and feelings, and the literary turns which go along with them.

His protagonists speak from the fringes, because that is where
they live. "My characters are definitely people who stay on the fringe,
from inability or because the middle is too confined for them. On the
edge they are always in more danger . . . of being gobbled up, of
course. On the other hand, they belong to something, and at the same
time they are next to the wide-open spaces." From the fringes, I move
toward that central point in Brasch which I wish to call "Kleistian,"
more than all else. He stands between two systems of value, both of
which confront him with false alternatives. In radical natures, that is
bound to lead to paradoxical choices. Kleist traveled from Paris to
the French coast, intending to die fighting against England, in the
service of his archenemy Napoleon. Brasch, with the clear-sightedness
which was all he had left, forsook the country which by commitment,
by agreement, by collaboration, by effort, by friction, by contradiction, or by resistance had made him creative. He left the GDR when
his need "to make something public" could not be satisfied; when his
plays, "objects of daily use," remained lying in a drawer where they
could "teach nothing" to their author; when he was at last forced to
ask himself: Do I build little barbs into things, so that I can go on

wearing the crown of thorns of being banned? Brasch, shaped by the values of this nation, whose central idea has been and still is work —work as a social category; as a means of uniting the individual with society; as collective labor which has the purpose of changing the relationships among individuals and among groups, and which might prove able to create new needs. In the West, Brasch met the power of money, compulsive consumerism, and he met the marketplace. He met the "decay of the order known as the state, and its raging struggle for survival between the old which is dead but powerful and the new which is essential but nowhere in sight." Quickly he turned into the stranger with the evil eye. The exotic plant. The man who impolitely and ungratefully rejected the categories tailor-made to fit his case; who did not want to be called a "dissident," or a "writer in exile," or even an "East German writer living in the West." Who at once began to defend himself again: "For me, all these categories are no more than clumsy attempts to make a writer more easily consumable, by reducing him to a single point." In amazement, he observed "the almost complete absence of any social base to the experience of most art producers of my generation, in this country." That must have to do with the type of wealth here, he suggested . . . He has decided the question of whether he wants to produce artistic insight, or serve the marketplace. He has not set aside the tools of probing social critique which he acquired in the GDR. He is finding that once again his work "is (in a different way) not needed, used or applied to any debate."

"Kleistian"? I want to guard against reducing Brasch, in my turn, to a single point. A line which says a lot about the area of tension in his work: "The material of yesterday, and the form of tomorrow." While he was still in East Germany he wrote a play called *Rotter*, which he describes as a "fairy tale from Germany." It's a play about someone who is no longer of use to any society, a "handicapped Woyzeck." Kleist, too, wrote fairy tales: what else would you call his play *Das Käthchen von Heilbronn*, which compares to *Rotter* like the positive to the negative pole of an evil nightmare? The dream play, *Der Prinz von Homburg* [*The Prince of Homburg*] and *Penthesilea*— all Kleist's plays are fairy tales, beautiful and bad fairy tales for grownups, with utopia glowing at their core. In Brasch we find the "blueprint for a world which would be worth living and striving for." This blueprint is not very visible in the actions of the characters (they, in fact, are incapable of action), and certainly not in the finales, but rather in how the plays are structured. Brasch experiments with new forms and scenarios, finding them far more revolutionary than any content they are able to convey. He uses them to counteract the

bourgeois art consumer's demand for enjoyment. The public—forced
to repress or explain, with heroic or banal illusions, the compromises
it has made after the bogged-down revolutions, and the restorations
to which it has fled for safety after the uncomprehended disasters—
finds its wishes ignored in Brasch's plays. Wielding the sharpness of
his form like a scalpel, he tries to scratch the hide of post-bourgeois
society, with its withered relationships and pseudo-values, and sated
with frustrated, perverse desires.

Brasch explicitly mentions Kleist twice, both times in connection
with death. In *Lieber Georg*, a character tells about a double-murderer
named Brunke who shot two sisters and then failed to kill himself as
they had agreed. In the courtroom, Brunke testified that he had thought
of the poet Kleist.* Heym's response is: "Kleist? Don't make me
laugh. There are copies everywhere."

Kleist is mentioned a second time in an interview about Brasch's
play *Lovely Rita*. Brasch says that in Kleist's character Penthesilea
—who is one of his models for Rita—the power of thought is so acute
that she thinks herself to death. Rita, on the other hand, "comes to
a fatal end by surviving."

Thus a female character serves a male author as someone to
identify with—just as Kleist identified with Penthesilea. Rita belongs
to a "historyless generation" and so, Brasch says, she cannot "identify
with what was . . . nor with what appears to be coming to be," and
from the gap between her exalted demands and her trivial reality,
she "criminally extracts the time which comes closest to her own
notion of happiness or value."

A peculiar observation about the female element in art follows
this. It is not a coincidence, Brasch claims, that "art" is a female
noun [in German]. "The ability to think the unthinkable has something
very feminine about it. Women tend much more to think monstrous
things . . . Art done by men is the work of men who take the privilege
of reacting like women; that is, of playing something out in imagination."

Kleist could not have said this, however much it applied to him,
because he felt too threatened by the "feminine" in himself. He had
to express his deepest wound as a man, through a female character,
the militant Penthesilea. And a Prussian officer was the character
through whom he expressed his deepest "womanly" longing, for a
rational order where feelings would be recognized as valuable, too.
It is as if he tore himself in two, crosswise (if it is possible to picture
that). But Brasch is not forced to tear himself apart; he can dull the

* Kleist died in a suicide pact.

pain of normality by exaggerating it. Faced with the choice of two evils, he chooses one of the evils without ceasing to view it as an evil, explains his choice in terms that are as ruthless to himself as to others and extorts from his situation the opportunity to work. To stay in the game perhaps represents a new morality and could even set a trend. To regard the work process—and Brasch, if possible, would prefer a collective process—as more important than the end product. To show how thoughts are manufactured in the process of talking. German history has not developed, for its male avant-garde, radical forms of existence which do not end in asocialism, in death or suicide, in isolation or acts of violence, in hatred, loathing, and self-loathing, or in total ineffectualness. I will say nothing about its female avant-garde, for whom no provision of any kind was made. What if, today, "thinking monstrous things," "reacting like women," and "playing something out in imagination" meant seeing all the possibilities, and even the slightest chance of being needed, of being used . . . At this point, Brasch might ask me if I do not see that the "results-oriented society has already slopped over onto what once were the virgin continents." And haven't I heard the news that in the near future six multinational corporations will have divided up between them all the media and all the branches of the entertainment industry in the Western world? Yes, I have heard that news.

But I cannot help reading with a flicker of joy, like a signal beacon that I recognize, what Brasch said recently to an interviewer in East Germany: "Possibly yes, maybe my work will be needed now in the GDR. That would be more than a hope for me, it would be productive. That is, I could learn something. And people who can't learn any more can die."

October 1987

ON WAR

AND PEACE

AND POLITICS

—

Talking German

―――

1

*So now it's been said, and in plain German . . . because we all
know what it means to talk German with someone and we'd rather
keep the peace.*
—JOHANNES BOBROWSKI, *Levin's Mill**

People are talking German in Germany again. German for Germans,
German for foreigners, good German language courses for everyone.
It didn't just happen overnight; it happened a short time ago in two
West German state parliaments. It seems high time that we listen
more carefully to what is being said.

So there they are again, standing "man to man, shoulder to
shoulder," "foursquare behind the German soldier of the past and
present," paying their respects at the graves of the major war criminals, and resolved "to make clear to the Russians that we will never
be forced to sign a surrender." Rejecting war as a political instrument,
naturally, "but we can't change the fact that wars exist." They call
themselves "the national fist," Germany's "watchdog," and in these
capacities call for "the restoration of our unified settlement area" and
"an end to the one-sided trials attempting to come to terms with the
past."

―――

* The German idiom "to talk German" is equivalent to "to speak in plain English" about
German racism. Christa Wolf plays throughout on the double meaning, turning the idiom into
a pun.

Unattractive words. Unattractive formulations of unattractive desires. Or at least slips of the tongue, indecent sounds in the well-
perfumed democratic salon. There are other ways to say all that, after
all . . . Officials of the NPD* do not mince words when they tell the
intimidated bosses of the other parties where to get off. These others
feel quite insulted, so they turn away, while the NPD serenely goes
on talking German. For instance, if you translate the verb "to hu-
manize" into plain German, it sounds like this: Of course, we don't
want to "downplay anything from the Nazi time," and "certainly not
the terrible problem of the treatment of the Jews." Here the plain-
speaking German tongue suddenly resists the plainspoken German
term "mass murder." And the normally far from squeamish *Deutsche
National- und Soldatenzeitung* [German Nationalist and Soldiers'
Newspaper] strikes a similar note when it maintains: "Not until the
coming of enlightened modern times was an attempt made to comply
with the precept of reason and human dignity, by humanizing the
procedure for execution. The painless gallows was invented: the elec-
tric chair—and the gas chamber."

That little dash is a trick we must all try to master. The signs
are that we are going to run into it again—into the dash and the
clever Nazis who blithely and unobtrusively laid it across the yawning
gap in this abyss of a German sentence.

There are real specialists at work here. A former propaganda
officer of the Nazi Federation of German Technology, and a former
spokesman for the Nazi Party in Silesia, drafted the model speeches
used by NPD members in the state parliamentary elections in Hesse
and Bavaria. On occasions like this, people cannot simply be allowed
to blurt out any old thing that their German hearts move them to say.
One still has to keep a tight rein on them; catalogues are handed out
which list answers to the currently most asked questions, and the
mouths of all NPD members are expected to voice unanimous indignation at the "completely unjustified hue-and-cry about Nazis." The
achievements of NPD party spokesmen, bound as they are by linguistic
prescriptions, are thus all the more remarkable if you consider that
—as they assure us—they have all the "human resources" they need
to get their point across. They address "that part of the population
who still have a national instinct in their attitudes and sentiments,"
who are still—or again—"inspired by German virtues"; that is: "selfless devotion unto death, hard work, and doing one's duty." In Hesse

* National-Democratic Party of Germany, a neo-Nazi party established in West Germany
in 1964.

224,548 voters, and 390,286 in Bavaria, voted for selfless devotion unto death. Are they the only ones?

The day after the state parliamentary election in Bavaria, the value of German stocks fell on the New York Stock Exchange. The already heavily taxed spirits of the "legitimate right" in the West German parliament fell by the same degree. These oafish outsiders with their coarse way of talking appeared to have spoiled West Germany's foreign credit rating. So something would have to be done about them, after all. "Keep smiling," every businessman tells himself, when the fight between his employees and the bailiff in the back room starts to be heard out on the sales floor. "It's nothing," Undersecretary von Hase said: he knew nothing about any "revival of Nazism in the Federal Republic." And Herr Hess himself, a member of the NPD's management federation and a member of the Nazi Party since 1930, agreed that von Hase had "never been Nazi in his ideology" —the evidence for this being that he had "always felt that Richard Wagner's kettledrum was the musical forerunner of National Socialist propaganda," so that since 1950 (!) he had "always said: 'We play woodwinds, oboe, clarinet and strings, but not tuba and kettledrum and tambourines.' "

That reassures us. And presumably only woodwinds were used —if not an oboe, then a chair leg at least—to beat that journalist out of the hall when he attended an NPD rally recently. He sorely needed to have someone talk German to him.

All that is just the beginning, say the leading party officials.

Unfortunately, we can believe them.

2

The combined strength of our allies is enough to wipe the empire of the Soviet Union off the map.
—FRANZ JOSEF STRAUSS, *1956*

As if the problem were the NPD.

It is not always pleasant to be proved right. These days I often think about a letter I received from Hanover a year ago, when, after spending some time in the Federal Republic, I expressed concern that Fascism might be developing there again. "But no one listens to those madmen!" the letter said.

And there is some truth to that. Because if people had been listening, for many years past—if they had not gotten used simply to ignoring one unbelievable remark after another from politicians—we would have no reason to be quite as surprised and dismayed as we are now.

Not to mention what was said by former West German Minister Seebohm of the CDU:* "We pay tribute to every symbol of our people—I say expressly to *every* symbol—for which Germans have sacrificed their lives for their fatherland." A notorious former Nazi, a blot on the now defunct Cabinet. But people were not listening.

Or perhaps Franz Josef Strauss, an inexhaustible well of candor back in his wild-and-woolly years, before the *Spiegel* affair put him in involuntary quarantine. "Our plan: diplomatic-political steps first, then economic-technological, finally military." So he said in 1961, although it is not clear if that was before or after August 13.† People were not listening.

People were not listening, or not really reading, the macabre accord between this unambiguous sentence and a pithy proclamation from poet Wilhelm Pleyer—the same Pleyer who in 1945 called on those Germans who had disappointed expectations by staying alive, to die for the Führer. ("The great trial which sets the pattern of our days, culminates in the unconditional risk of our lives." Quoted from the *Völkischer Beobachter*, March 18, 1945.) Twenty years later, he ended his book *Europas unbekannte Mitte* [*The Unknown Heart of Europe*] with this observation: "This much is clear: regardless of whether the global political situation proves ready in the near future or looks 'hopeless,' Germans must be prepared—for every possibility. The first step in this preparedness is education, the next is patience, but at the end comes the victory of truth and justice, the return of Germans to the Sudetenland." Any further questions?

The Americans have invented a word that sums up the process which Strauss and Pleyer were both describing: "escalation." Now, apparently, everything hinges on the interpreters: can they manage to squeeze in, between the sentence of a present-day government minister and the almost identical sentence of a long-time Nazi, the hair-thin gap on which we pride ourselves—between what is "still" democratic, and what was "once" Fascist?

There is no more denying that the recent elections in West

* The conservative Christian Democratic Union Party.

† Strauss was a conservative, anti-Soviet West German politician (1915–88) who served as Minister of Defense from 1956 to 1962 and who during his term of office promoted German rearmament. In 1962, the weekly magazine *Der Spiegel* was charged with treason for allegedly revealing state secrets in an article about West German military policy and its capabilities. Strauss and other Cabinet members had to resign and a new government was formed. August 13, 1961, is the date on which the Berlin Wall went up overnight.

Germany reminded foreign journalists of certain past events and that
the memory "made their flesh creep." Feuchtwanger's novel *Success**
reads like a contemporary work or at least a subdued, more harmless-
sounding prediction of the hard-to-picture world of modern-day West
Germany. Would the friend who wrote me that letter understand me
today if I ask: Isn't it better to regard as possible what everyone thinks
is impossible? Better to listen when the language of neurotics is being
spoken again at rallies and in state parliaments anywhere in Germany?
Better to take coalitions of politicians seriously—of anti-Communists,
for instance; of nationalists, for instance?

Better to remember that what begins as a bad farce can end as
a tragedy?

Just think what Strauss said once—back in his blunt, Bavarian
period, when he still had the opportunity to stop the German Socialist
Party from carrying out a couple of modest efforts to socialize the
country: "A woman can't be a little bit pregnant. Either she is completely pregnant or not at all."

So, how democratic can a federal republic be—if it is also a
little bit Fascist?

3

*I believe that we must first make one thing clear to the public:
there is no such thing as an entrepreneur. Entrepreneurs do not
form any kind of a cohesive social group, they do not constitute
a social class.*

—DR. ERNST SCHNEIDER,
president of the West German Chamber of Commerce and Industry

These people are magicians and illusionists. Compared to them, a
professional who can make a white elephant disappear off the stage
in full view of the audience looks like a rank amateur. Hosts of amazing
creatures of every possible species vanish up their wide sleeves in
the twinkling of an eye. The entrepreneur, for instance: he does not
exist. Still less does the *class* of entrepreneurs exist. Least of all does
the working class exist (if a further degree of nonexistence is possible).
The reason for this is that we are living not in a capitalist society but
in a "pluralist" one, where policy is determined not by special-interest
groups but by political parties (which are completely independent!).
And the line formed by the Oder and Neisse Rivers is not a real

* The first part (1930) of a trilogy about the Nazi period.

border, nor is our neighbor state to the east a real nation, it is a so-called German Democratic Republic.

No recognition, no recognition, no recognition.

The denial eats its way into everything; it becomes a way of thinking. You are forced into using language that is hazardous to your health. If the words were bridges, no one would want to walk across them. The number of facts that no one talks about keeps growing. The number of taboo subjects keeps rising. A language of the initiate becomes necessary. A language for the prophets, a language for the accomplices. And a language for the public, aimed at saying as little as possible, using as many blurred and vague terms as you can. To avoid being taken at your word.

Material prosperity—as long as it lasts and is free of crisis—shields you from reality. If some slow-witted individual asks about the reality, the white elephant, he is shown the white limousine or the washing machine, instead. "Persil stays Persil no matter what!" and "Now we're somebody again!"—ad slogans devised personally by ex-Chancellor Erhard.* But "security" is a good solution only as long as the security lasts. A "free-market economy in recession" is no longer such a good deal. But how come, people start asking: how did that happen?

And that has always signaled the moment for people to let out those great big feelings that they have been struggling to hold in. "Do you see the moon over Soho?" Oh yes, they see it, the modern Mack the Knifes, and they are still singing its praises. One can't help feeling touched when one hears the entrepreneurs talking about love at their conferences instead of about the rate of profit. A love that would make them happier than all this filthy lucre: namely, the love of their "employees," which, sad to say, is not flowing toward them in the desired measure. Or they talk about blood and tears. After all, what are their businesses built on? "Our businesses, mine included, are built only with toil and sweat, they are built with blood and tears" —with "the heart's blood of the entrepreneur," to be precise. Only one man cannot refrain from reminding his colleagues of the simple hard facts of everyday life: every one of them ought "to get onto good terms with the press, radio, and television, with every local newspaper editor and every small shopkeeper," he advises: otherwise, "things could turn nasty." What, did someone have it in mind to accuse them

* Ludwig Erhard (1897–1977), economics minister and from 1963 to 1966 Chancellor of West Germany, advocated a market economy and was the chief architect of the West German "economic miracle."

of "swindling" or "bribery"? A lot of "love" will be needed to cover up an ugly word like that . . .

Reality is coming closer, getting more uncomfortable. The normal democratic techniques of self-delusion, drugs and narcotics, are starting to lose their effectiveness. And that has always signaled the moment for an even stronger tobacco: for "national defense." A drug for the disappointed. Although it does dampen one's spirits to see how they don't even bother to try to come up with a new wrinkle.

The magicians on their dimly lit stage pretend to be shocked, when really they have only been caught in the act. When they can no longer ignore the commotion in the theater, they start to insult the galleries. Their performance has been irreproachable as always, solid German goods. But those clodhoppers kicking up a fuss out there—how can they be so crude, so lacking in political instinct, when they have had twenty years to train themselves to appreciate these feats of magic?

Maybe one magician or another even toys with the notion of showing the audience a chunk of that white elephant, reality—which has been standing in the wings the whole time—just to scare them off. But by now it seems too late for that, too.

4

What interests me now is only the conscience of the nice average housewife, which can be quieted by a brand of detergent. And I do not find it hard to picture Mr. Clean working in a "clean-up squad" [purging political undesirables] . . . The Whitest White which is cherished by the nice little average housewife, and by her husband Mr. Clean, is the perfect Nothingness where there is no longer anything left to put in order.
      —HEINRICH BÖLL, *"Letter to a Young Non-Catholic"*

The magic spells, the abracadabra of the ads for the Washing Miracle, have started to lose their magic power. What can you do with people, fully occupied up to now in producing "the most radiant white of their lives" again each day, who suddenly notice that they are bored to death with it, and who now prefer to play around a bit with bats and clubs?

When the entrepreneurs surrender to love, and the politicians to their hobby—black magic—writers must start talking about politics and profit. Heinrich Böll, for instance, talks about them in a bitter, sarcastic, deeply troubled language, with clear undertones of sorrow and despair: "Mr. Clean and his nice little average housewife are the last, the very last beacon warning us that no more glimpses into conscience will be granted to this conscienceless society . . ." Böll does not rule out the possibility that even this last signal of all may be ignored, trampled; that the ruling class may achieve its goal again this time, and in the future, too, as it did in its successful promotion of rearmament: "by terror, by money, by propaganda, by bringing the opposition and the newspapers into line almost completely, and by the systematic denunciation of all adversaries." Nor does he rule out the possibility that the majority of people may no longer be capable of seeing through the slogan "We are all sitting in one train," so that, as a result, we who sit in the train are no more than "cattle for slaughter"—as Christian Geissler entitled a television play he wrote some years ago.

We look with hope at photos like the one of the rally in Frankfurt am Main opposing the government's plans to declare a state of emergency. Hans Magnus Enzensberger said at the rally: "Those who are huddling in the bunker there, violating the constitution in the very hour of their political demise, are afraid of every single one of us; and they are right to feel afraid. And because these political bunker-corpses are afraid, because they themselves are the emergency they are babbling about, they are cooking up legal paragraphs which are designed to perpetuate the emergency. 'In case of war,' von Hassel [the West German Defense Minister] said, 'the only thing able to function is what was already functioning in peacetime.' But since it does not want to function in peacetime, the easiest thing will be to do away with peace altogether."

With hope we see a managing director of IG Metal standing next to Enzensberger; we read his clear analysis of the causes which led to the bunker maneuvers of the entire Cabinet in Bonn; we hear his appeal to unite against the danger that is looming. We breathe a sigh of relief, hearing a language that tells it like it is, that can be used as a tool with which to debate, to analyze, to convince, to resist. A language which was not invented to cloud the issue but to reveal it. Which calls gray the brightest white the nice housewife recommends, and which calls a society that has "closed ranks" a dictatorship of monopolies. And which shows how one is related to the other.

Our language. The accurate, serviceable language of reason. It carries the hope and the responsibility that we, too, may talk German. That people may hear our words, may read our proposals and statements. That these words, founded on reality, on the moral and material strength of the other Germany, may this time dismantle the eerie mechanism of that fatal old model which has just undergone yet another refurbishment. That we may stop the train before the last warning signal, after all.

It must be said repeatedly, patiently, clearly, and convincingly that these *are* our last warnings. And that although many people in West Germany, even the troubled ones, still hesitate to pay the cost of saying no now while there is still time, this cost will one day seem nothing compared to the cost of silence: because that will cost us our lives.

Our hope is that German will be spoken in Germany. Keeping the peace.

December 1966

On That Date

—

Communists? If she knew any, it was Sell, the shoemaker from the village of G——. She used to assign him, or rather his horse-drawn cart, to perform heavy chores, like any other such vehicle. Then he would slam his visored cap down on the table in the office of the town hall and shout: "Always me! Isn't that obvious? Been taking bribes from the big farmers, Fräulein?" Then she would slam her clean, impartial list down next to his greasy cap and yell, too, and shoemaker Sell would take to his heels, slamming the door behind him. But the mayor, whose term in office was limited because the higher-ups would not accept, in the long run, the fine distinction he drew between being a Nazi Party member and being a Nazi—the mayor taught her the meaning of justice. Justice, namely, was not equal treatment for all, but privileges for whoever happened to be in power at the time: earlier, that meant for the big farmer Otto Müller; today it was for the shoe-maker Wilhelm Sell. "A list is a list," she said, "and a horse is a horse." The mayor replied: "You may be able to speak English, Fräulein, but otherwise you still have an awful lot to learn."

Then there was the other one, a dead Communist, the beer-wagon driver whose son had informed on him. "Listening to foreign radio," Krüger the book dealer said. "Spreading subversive propa-ganda. That means off with his head, when he was a Communist on top of it." So, evidently there were still Communists running around loose. That amazed her very much, and she took a closer look at all beer-wagon drivers after that. One of them—the one who had been reported by his son—drove his beer wagon through her sleep, and she asked him why these Communists could not stop listening to foreign radio even though it was forbidden—and unnecessary, too: what was it that they were determined to find out at any cost? She believed she had to protect the son from the father, but the father permitted himself a certain look (that was the only thing about him that she saw clearly: what did Communists look like, anyway?), which, when she saw it, drove the idea of defending the son out of her head again. She suffered from an overly vivid imagination, and so she could not help picturing over and over how the good son had made his up-right decision. How he set out to look for the agency which accepted information of that sort: what was that agency called, by the way? The name came to her. But where was it located, in her town? People were right to accuse her of not knowing practical facts. Now the honest son was hunting for the room specifically appointed to record de-nunciations of fathers. And mothers, too? What did the sign on the door say? Now the son entered. Clicked his heels; his right arm shot into the air; he gave the Heil Hitler greeting and stated: "I hereby denounce my father, the beer-wagon driver." After that, she felt compelled to imagine how the father found out what had happened: "But it was your own son who dutifully informed us. Do you want to accuse your son of lying?" Then she had to picture how the father maybe was dead now, and the son was supposed to wake up every morning and live his life. And she felt, without expressly stating it even in her thoughts, that she was not especially eager to run into this extremely dutiful son. Although this was not impossible, because there were more beer-wagon drivers' sons running around the streets of the town than there were beer-wagon drivers.

Then she broke off the chain of imaginings and tried—unsuc-cessfully—to forget the beer-wagon driver.

On the date in question, the day itself must have had no special characteristics. Next door, the widow Gideon was chasing her son Heiner around the table: that thief who had eaten her bread. She resorted to the carpet beater. "Ow!" cried Heiner. "You old sow!" His father was off in the war. At her own table, separated from the other two by a thin door, the girl eats the two slices of heavy black rye bread which the farmer's wife whom her family boards with slipped to her on the weekend. She does not starve yet she is never full. In the big mirror of the washing commode there is a face, behind it the head of a bed and a faded carpet; and she cannot quite think what all those facts have to do with each other.

She runs down the four steps, through the gateway, along Fritz Reuter Street into the town, to the school by the church pond where each morning the English teacher, a native Englishwoman, uses the same smile to apologize for having to search the heads of grownup schoolgirls for lice; and if there is anything that the girl feels curious about, it is how long the supply of this smile will last. "I've already had typhoid fever, anyway," she can state serenely, just to try out whether certain people are still startled by certain words. This is the third day that Hildegard Pietsch has been absent. Does one of the young ladies happen to know . . . ? One of them knows. "It's an abortion, Miss Heymann. What is the English word for that?"

"Schiller's *Don Carlo* was banned back in the Nazi period," says the German teacher: " 'Sire, give me my freedom of thought!' " Why, one must fight like a demon to make her take that back—of course, Schiller was not banned here, that's a downright lie. Then suddenly the girl tells herself that she couldn't care less whether Schiller was banned or not, and lapses into silence. The only thing is, she would like to know why her German teacher was crying in the street yesterday. During recess, her teacher explains with embarrassment that it had to do with potatoes; once again she could not get any potatoes, and her mother was sick . . . On the girl's essay on "People Who Are Building the New Order," her teacher has written the comment "Stilted style"—but she doesn't care, because how could one *not* write in a stilted style about a subject like that? Ruth has gotten an A, her essay is judged "Convincing." So are you convinced? The girl shrugs. Are you going to bring forget-me-nots to International Workers' Day on May 1 or not? Well, of course, who do you all think I am?

One really ought to be able to do something to stop this feeling that one doesn't care about anything, these ridiculous forget-me-nots included. But there is nothing she can do. Ruth has found another letter under her seat, her boyfriend is coming into the boys' class which is taught in this same room in the afternoon. She is going to marry him, and her mother, who is going to die soon of cancer, has agreed to it, she says. The girl never finds a letter under her own seat. Now she has to arrange not to care about that, too.

Elisabeth faints in the middle of math class. It's true, in the past few weeks her eyes have looked bigger in her little face than eyes have the right to look. She is carted off to the water faucet, and her wrist held under the jet. "That helps," she says in a weak voice. "I was hot, that's all." Of course, it can never be hot in an unheated school in April, but Elisabeth is a refugee from Königsberg and has four younger brothers and sisters at home. Someone asks the unsuitable question whether anybody happens to have anything to eat with them, and Elisabeth denies vehemently that she is hungry. During the break, her mother brings her a slice of bread procured with the new bread-ration cards, and she eats it on the sly. Ilsemarie gets one of her coughing fits ("Of course, you caught it from her," the lung specialist will tell the girl two weeks later. "She tested positive and she's highly infectious"). The girl leans over the same Latin book as Ilsemarie. "We're supposed to be in a brand-new age," the Latin teacher says, "but the old texts are still with us, and I would just like to know if you can translate a simple sentence like this: *Tempora mutantur*, 'The times are changing' as we Latins say, 'and we are changing with them.' "

"What do you think?" the girl asked her German teacher when she visited her in the old parsonage, where her teacher came to meet her with bare feet. "The times are changing," the teacher said, "we are changing. Christ stays the same. Who do you think gave me the strength never to salute that flag, never, not one single time? Do you know Goethe's play *Iphigenia in Tauris?* You don't, really? Here, take it, read it." On the bed in her room at the widow Gideon's, she reads: "Pure humanity atones for all the ills of humankind." Yeah, sure. She does not want to be impolite.

The skinny lady in black, in the restaurant with the big arched windows half nailed shut, carefully pokes the eyes out of four greenish boiled potatoes with the tip of a knife each noon. Then she crushes them, skin and all, in the standard Gravy No. 2 and eats them up. She never says a word, because she cannot eat boiled potatoes with their skins left on, right out in public, and at the same time chat with her table companions as if nothing were amiss. Outside, Ruth passes by with her boyfriend; he has curly black hair, whereas she is a blonde. Their fingers are intertwined; they see no one else. You can follow them as long as you like—you have always wanted to know what "love" is.

You stare everyone boldly in the face; it's a game you play every day because there is no danger that you will suddenly recognize a face. Then one of the faces stops after all and begins to address you happily, but that face is Anneliese, don't you recognize her? Time winds back inside you, in fast motion: a different city, different streets, a schoolyard—yes, of course, it's Anneliese. You pretend to be genuinely scared that the train Anneliese escaped on was the very last to get out, the one that the lead tanks shot at until it caught fire. She ran into Sieglinde recently: don't you remember, the district party leader? Yes, of course. District party leader Sieglinde had once made a terrible scene because the theater group bored tiny peepholes in an expensive stage curtain: "German girls don't do things like that." So now the district leader has washed her hands of it all; the big wheels from the county board just left her high and dry, after packing their cars full of boxes of food. She doesn't want to hear a word about it anymore. If only you didn't feel so completely indifferent to everything that the district leader has now put behind her.

"The idea may have had its good points," Anneliese says, "but the way it was carried out!" You say goodbye quickly, after giving Anneliese a phony address so that you can go on lying undisturbed on the widow Gideon's bed, reading Diedrich Speckmann's *Herzensheiligen* [*Holy to the Heart*]: "Wilt thou, O heart, arrive at a worthy goal, then must thou dangle peacefully from thine own pole." "He seems to me the greatest who swears allegiance to no flag."

Now and then you try going over to the window, which reaches all the way down to the floor, to look at the street below, at this teeming mass of people who have nothing to do with you, whom you cannot go over and join. This undertow that pulls you to the window is a weird thing. Then you hold on tight to the bed, or you flee into the kitchen, where Heiner at least is sitting at the table, watching how every evening you cook some oatmeal into a watery soup.

The date was April 21, 1946, and the truth is that I did not read my first Marxist text until two and a half years later. It was a beautiful autumn day; I ate by the pound the tart little apples that my grandmother handed in to me at the window. At night I jotted down the title in my journal—incorrectly as you will see: *Feuerbach und die ausgehende klas-sische Philosophie* [*Feuerbach and the Waning of Classical Philosophy*].

Today I have to admit that if this had not been the beginning, then something else would have been—but, anyhow, this is what it was. "And so, in the course of development, everything which once was real becomes unreal . . ." If I had learned anything, it was this: how what once was real gradually becomes unreal, consumed by an incurable illness to which you yourself could easily succumb, along with the rest. What people called "time" drove past like a hermetically sealed train with no sign of a destination.

What came after that day is a long story which I share with many of my generation and which perhaps I will one day be able to tell. But, whatever happened later, this was the beginning, and I have often thought back to it, without wishing to recapture it—in the same way that today I look at the old pencil marks I made in the margin of that text by Friedrich Engels, and cannot help feeling moved. "The dying reality is replaced by a new reality which is capable of life." That was the process which was destined to fill up my life. Did I guess it, on that first evening? Not a bit.

I will try to be precise. I ran outside. It was a cool autumn night; the air was thin and clear. We were living on a mountain. The stars overhead and the lights of the town below seemed to reflect each other. I walked up Thomas Müntzer Street to the Blood Chute, a furrow where, after the massacre of May 15, 1525, the blood of the rebel peasants is said to have flowed down to the valley. I found the beauty of the night repulsive. The symmetrical crescent moon, this refined deception, disgusted me. The crooked church tower, the romantic symbol of the town, ought to have given up being so stubborn and finally tumbled to the ground. Everything ought to have taken its cue from us—from us, whose time of indifference had now come to an end.

January 1971

Reply to a Reader[*]

————

At the start of September I got a letter from Freiburg im Breisgau [West Germany]. A "young person," as he calls himself, a father of three who works with mentally handicapped children and is studying medicine, wrote and asked me several questions.

The first was: "Do I still have reason for hope?" The second was: "Are there still ways out of our danger?" The third was: "Have you found a source of strength that will hold up in the future we face?" And the letter ends with an exclamation: "Please, let us put everything we have into seeing that there is peace between our countries. Really everything, and then some!"

"Dear Mr. D.," I wrote him at the start of October, "what can I write to you? I have had your letter for two weeks and can't stop thinking about it. Its tone is so urgent that I cannot respond with evasions, and so personal that it demands my reply be personal, too. Although I cannot and will not swear to reveal all my resources like an insolvent debtor hauled up before the law, I *will* swear to reveal some of them. One of my first reactions to your letter was a feeling of defensiveness, which I could sum up in the phrase 'Why me?' How come *I'm* supposed to know 'ways out of our danger'? Why should *I* specifically be obliged—much less entitled—to express an opinion and have someone else treat it as more important than all the other opinions expressed in recent months?

"I do not know whether my feeling of defensiveness also reflects a desire to run away from the problem, but I don't think so. What it

* Originally broadcast over Southwest German Radio on December 31, 1981.

264

reflects, I think, is more something I have learned in my life—after all, that is what you are asking me to tell you about, what I have *learned*: that a great many people in this century and in our society, including me at times, have given in to a powerful craving for authority figures and are still doing so now." I will break off the text of my letter today, more than two months after I wrote it, to explain what giving in to a craving for authority means. It means taking *your* thinking, *your* action, and *your* responsibility for both, and turning them over to an "authority figure." I am sure that this is not what my correspondent wanted, and I imagine he understood my explanation that I did not want to participate either actively or passively in such a transfer.

"But here we are already discussing the problems," I continued my letter. "And if we can look on it as just that, as a discussion, a mutual reflection which does not have to lead to conclusive answers, then maybe it is possible for me to go into your questions.

"Whenever I watch myself, whether it is daytime or nighttime, I catch myself in an ongoing interior monologue which scarcely stops for a moment: Can Europe, can *we* be saved? When I consider in a tough and rational way all the information available to me about the weapons on both sides, and especially the mental attitudes which underlie the weapons, then my answer is: 'No, we can't be saved,' or 'Probably not.' "

Ought I to be broadcasting statements like this over the radio? Once again, I put my letter aside. In April this past year I experienced one of those alterations of consciousness which are rare in people's lives and which they never forget. A television news commentator reported that a conference of experts held in London had concluded that Europe would not survive for more than another three or four years, if present political policies continue. At that point, I spent a minute experiencing the annihilation which supposedly is due three or four years from now. The effect this minute had on me was not purely negative—paralyzing: besides, isn't paralysis meaningless now, anyhow?—it also released anger in me, and freedom. If they dare to include the destruction of Europe in their military calculations, then we—we who already figure as fatalities in the statistics of nuclear planning staffs—are surely entitled to take a few liberties: even our subordination to logic—that logic whose ultimate manifestation is the nuclear missile—has turned into absurdity, and this means that there is no such thing as being too radical when we question the causes of so radical a threat. Given the "position"—militarily speaking—in which we find ourselves: shouldn't we think, propose, and try what "can't possibly work"? Since the "ground of facts" on which we are constantly being asked to stand is potentially contaminated, is it so farfetched for us to look around for some other ground? When even those antonyms which seemed to define history—"attack" and "defense"—stop being opposite and both pile into the single crater word "annihilation"—shouldn't we try to talk in words that still have meanings?

That is what I think today. My letter to Mr. D. continued: "A civilization capable of plotting its own destruction and of providing itself with the necessary tools, with the terrible sacrifices this entails, seems to me sick. It is no accident that our civilization produced these missiles and bombs. They are the logical outcome of thousands of years of expansionist behavior. They are the embodiment of the syndrome of alienation in the industrial societies, which have subsumed all other values with their cry of 'greater quantity! greater speed! greater precision! greater results!' and which have simply swallowed up many values that were built to a human scale and not to the mammoth scale of giant instruments. They have forced the great masses of people into an unreal, an object existence and most especially have impressed the sciences into serving this end. They have elevated the facts which the sciences provide to the level of the only valid truth; that is, what is not measurable, weighable, countable, verifiable, virtually does not exist. It does not count—just as for the past three thousand years women have not counted and do not count, wherever the designing, planning, and manufacture of the 'real' and the important goes on. Half the people living in a society have *by their very nature* no share in the products by which it recognizes itself for what it is." And consequently—it occurs to me—they have no share in those experiments in thought and production which help or prevent its destruction.

In fact, not one woman has participated in the research for our age's weapons, in developing their technology, in planning their deployment, in the power to command them. If the men have tied their fate to the objects they manufacture, come what may; if the men are determined to confuse ends with means, allow technical processes to take precedence over themselves, submit to a strict division of labor, be structured into rigid hierarchies and trained to "factual" thought and behavior divorced from emotion; if the men are forced to lose themselves—then how much *more* lost must the women be who stand even lower in this pyramid of achievement? Unless they revolt? But where can they find, where can *we* still find a place which at the moment it secures our livelihood does not at the same time injure and undermine the basis for biological life on this earth?

Do I seem to be rambling from one subject to another? Can it be an accident that all the contradictions of our death-addicted society are observable within this one area of its weapons systems?

"Dear Mr. D.," I wrote, continuing my letter, "no small number of voices, moved by suffering, conflict, contradiction, have described how these things work. To say they were ignored is an understatement. Unfortunately, we have seen confirmed what artists have been saying ever since Hölderlin, Goethe, and Büchner, and again, with special emphasis, in our own century; what they have been misunderstood and derided for, had their books banned and burned for, and been exiled, locked up, and tortured for: for saying that we ourselves produce what kills us; that the absurd is true, the fantastic is realistic, and the formal, logical thinking of the 'healthy human mind' is insane. The forecasts of the arts are proving correct, while the predictions of a science obsessed with progress are now turning against their makers. The needs—frequently 'perverted'—which the sciences nurtured and awakened, and now service—have gotten out of control and are driving them. Where to, hardly anyone dares ask.

"How fatal the gaps in our thinking and feeling appear now, how fatal seems the absence of all those things which we were not and are not allowed to see, hear, smell, taste, feel, and say. I wonder about that censorship and self-censorship whose chief aim is always to keep us from seeing ourselves as we are. It suppresses the need for self-knowledge, producing a sense of profound helplessness instead, and since without knowing ourselves we cannot love ourselves, it produces a general inability to love. How do censorship, self-censorship, all the other limits imposed on our vital needs, relate to the violence of our civilization? To the mistaken belief that more and ghastlier weapons mean more security? To our fear of the 'enemy,' that myth which we generate ourselves? In short, to the danger that we may, by an act of violence, wipe out an opposing system—a system whose contradictions serve to veil and cover up the contradictions of our own, as ours serve to cover up theirs—instead of resolving them through constructive change?

"I am asking, dear Mr. D., I am asking. If the ghosts awaken . . .

"To live in a reality which is completely or partly false and which we have falsified ourselves means, too, that we are never far from drunkenness and delusion; but drunk and deluded people seem immune to the arguments of reason. Why is this so? Presumably because the emptiness which drives people to escape into drunkenness and delusion, to drug themselves this way, creates a panicked fear of confronting themselves and of undertaking the protracted, strenuous work of self-education and self-knowledge which might lead them, eventually, to stop needing to transfer their own fears and weaknesses to the image of an enemy. This ability to experience oneself, even to experience oneself as 'strong,' when one has given up *demonstrating* strength by the use of weapons, is, I think, what is meant by 'maturity'; and it is hard to come by in our society. It is easier for us just to defame people who do not agree with us, by accusing them of being 'unrealistic.' " Here I put down my letter, start thinking, hunting for protests I could lodge.

An alarming conclusion arises irrefutably from my work of the past few years. I am haunted by the thought that our society—which could achieve what it calls "progress" only by violence, by internal suppression, by the annihilation and plunder of foreign societies, and which has limited its definition of reality to the pursuit of material interests, and become instrumental, and is concerned only with getting results—that a society like this was *bound* to end up where it is today.

And almost more troubling still is the sentence which keeps forming in my mind: Hitler has caught up with us. He almost, though not quite, achieved the destruction of Europe; but the destruction may be completed now, as a result of the constellation of power he left behind him at the end of the Second World War. I am finding it hard to push aside this thought so as to get back to my letter. "Dear Mr. D." What is there left for me to say?

"Dear Mr. D., around 1800, Hölderlin began one of his elegies with the line 'Come out into the open air, friend!' This is a utopian invitation, which he modifies a few lines later by coupling it with a clear-sighted view of reality: 'It is dark today, the lanes and avenues are sleeping and almost/it seems to me we live in the Age of Lead.' He could have found no apter metaphor. In another place we read that a steel sky is closing over our heads.

"I ask myself, and I ask you: Ought literature—which began, in Homer's great epic, with descriptions of battles and weapons, with the cult of the heroes and the glorification of godlike army commanders—ought literature to participate in the expulsion of utopia? Can literature, by linking itself to the sumptuous description of the shield which Achilles bore, strike up a hymn to the neutron bomb? Wouldn't it *have* to do so—if the neutron bomb and our other weapons really were what their inventors and potential users claim: the true peacemakers?

"*No.* We have not been abandoned by all good spirits. You, dear Mr. D.," I wrote, "work with handicapped children, whom you cannot turn into productive members of society, and in this work you must experience feelings similar to those I have when I write—when I go ahead and do it despite its seeming futility—'for hope's sake,' as Johannes Bobrowski said. *Is* your experience similar? When danger threatens, our reflections, searching, and sense of community with others step up their intensity. We do not permit ourselves monkey business like despondency, feelings that the end of the world has come. We know in all clarity—like a man who has found out that he is incurably ill—that we want to live and that we must learn to think and also to feel in a changed way.

> *For what we want is not vast but is true to life,*
> *and seems at the same time suitable and joyful, too.*

"Hölderlin. Suitable and joyful? What exactly is he referring to? What he has in mind in fact seems like asking an awful lot: 'to taste and behold what's most beautiful, the land's abundance.' And yet *we* cannot settle for less than that, either. We ourselves must create all that is ignored and denied by our society—friendliness, dignity, trust, spontaneity, grace, fragrance, pleasing sound, poetry: life in its natural state. The first things to go when our peace-less peace threatens to turn into prewar. The truly human things. The things that are able to move us to defend this peace.

"What can we Germans do but be especially *peaceful*—with all that the word implies in terms of understanding and knowing history; in terms of self-criticism combined with enlightened self-esteem; in terms of attentiveness to the needs and vulnerable spots—often produced by Germans in the first place—of neighboring peoples; in long-term sympathy for the manifestations and aims of other cultures; and in a feeling response to people anywhere in the world who are starving to death, or at risk of annihilation?

"You see, dear Mr. D., I cannot manage to think in very small segments of time. Only when my thoughts can break through the black wall which lies in front of us and get out 'into the open air' do I feel at all free of my obsessive idea that we are past saving. I hardly dare hope that one day our more fortunate descendants may look back at us and feel that something else Hölderlin said is true of us: 'We have done our part the best we could.' "

My letter is almost finished. How shall I end it? Dear Mr. D., I see clearly how disputable are these reflections of mine which, I do not deny, revolve around our helplessness, and our need for a miracle if we are to turn Nothing into Something, to turn impotence into effective action. But isn't this miracle exactly what the peace movement in West Germany is achieving? And doesn't it prove that the fear of annihilation can overcome the fear of the authorities, and that young people are fighting the verdict of "no future" which hangs over their heads, with their vision of a violence-free society? A few days

ago at the Berlin Congress for the Advancement of Peace—a conference of writers and scientists from both the Germanys and several
other nations of Europe which some months ago I would not have
believed could happen in this city and in this spirit, or be attended
by the people of these nations—the peace scientist Robert Jungk said
much the same thing. Aren't these things a sign that in some places
people actually are undertaking what "can't possibly work"?

Isn't it worth noting that for the first time the peoples who are
supposed to be called up to fight each other *do not* hate each other?
Does this simply deepen the tragedy of the future—or does it, on the
contrary, bid us hope?

"Thank you," I ended my letter, "dear Mr. D., I thank you for
your letter and send you my regards."

December 1981

A Conversation with

Grace Paley*

―

GRACE PALEY: We're going to have something like a conversation, although I mostly want to hear what Christa has to say. A lot of people hear what I have to say often enough, so no more of that. For me, the problem I've had in preparing for this conversation or question-and-answer or dialogue or whatever has been that there is really so much to talk about with you, Christa. One would wish that one's first conversations with you would take place walking around the city. I want to ask you first what it is that you don't know about yourself or about the world that you want to know about and that has created such enormous pressure and energy in your books and makes you tell the story in a different way almost every time. What is the journey that you take? For instance, there is a physical, geographical journey taken in *Christa T.* and *A Model Childhood* (or *Patterns of Childhood* when it comes out again in English). But in *No Place on Earth* and the books that will be coming out—the Cassandra book—there is a historical journey that is taken. Do you think that's worth talking about?

CHRISTA WOLF: When we met in Berlin, Grace and I, she asked me less difficult questions than this one. I think I'm less certain with each book about how much I really know. I think my first two books showed more opinions, convictions, than the latter books. With each successive book, more and more questions came up in my mind. I wasn't as sure of what it was that I wanted to express. I want to

* On May 26, 1983, Grace Paley and Christa Wolf conversed at Greenwich House in New York City. Christa Wolf's remarks were translated by Christine Friedlander.

271

mention a concrete example. In my first book, *Patterns of Childhood*, for instance, I wanted to show what it meant for a person to have grown up under Fascism without resisting it, without opposing it. I also wanted to pose the question, which in our age is important in many places in the world, of what it means to live under a dictatorship. In my second book, *No Place on Earth*, I wanted to find out where the roots of alienation exist, which, in our age, almost seem to bring the world to destruction—self-destruction. In this new book, *Cassandra*, that same question is posed in a sharper light and brought back into a more recent mode, or area, of history. What I want to explore in my books more and more are the roots of the self-destruction that we find so much now. And I want to explore it in myself, too, because it is such a prevalent question for everyone.

PALEY: I believe that when we think about writing (this is related; it won't sound like it is related, but it is) we have to think about the reader. We were talking earlier (we did happen to talk a little bit earlier; we walked and talked a little) and I didn't ask quite this question, but I wondered really what it was about society that you were trying to understand in a storytelling way, which is different from a sociological or economic way—as an artist. You answered that you were really trying to understand yourself, and I guessed that, because I live in a very individualistic society, which thinks about itself all the time, I was a little unnerved by that answer. So I said: Well, the books don't really read like that to me. Do you know what I mean?

WOLF: Yes.

PALEY: But then I worried a great deal as we walked slowly on Tenth Street, and I thought it wasn't exactly so. If I could press you a bit on that.

WOLF: Yes, I think I have to explain this a little bit further. One has to know the background of the whole development of writing in my society to explain that this is not just a narcissistic occupation, my writing. I'm a person who is very strongly rooted in the society in which I live, and what I usually write about are the conflicts between individuals and the societies in which they live—and the society is always shown as a very strong factor in the individual's life. I should explain that for us writers who started to write after the end of the war, after the end of Fascism, we first had the impression that we should not write about individuals as much as about the role of the society and the developments in the society. But gradually we began to understand that in literature and in prose the individual has to play a big role and one has to go into the individual's role. During the 1950s, there were many books in our literature that we would now regard as dogmatic and following a certain scheme, and if you opened the first page you would more or less know what was going to follow. Gradually we have learned to write differently. You have to describe individuals more and go deeper into their problems.

PALEY: There is not a writer who doesn't after a while understand the power of form. One of the very interesting things about your writing is its relationship to form. You take very unusual formal steps, really, but in the most natural way, and in a way which seems to come from the material, from the subject matter. I read someplace (it may have been in the copy of the *New German Critique*, or maybe in the other copy, I'm not sure) in a discussion with you about Wolf Biermann being asked to leave Germany in 1976, that you were very offended by that experience. You were stopped by that experience and by the repression that followed.

WOLF: Yes.

PALEY: The book that came after that, *No Place on Earth*, was very different from its predecessors. Could you tell us a bit about what happened and about the form that freed you all of a sudden.

WOLF: It is true that I was in a lot of conflict before the book *No Place on Earth*, and I think that book shows a resolution of this conflict. Most of my books mirror a conflict that is going on in myself or has been going on in myself. Actually, I don't think about form very much. I make many starts; I write things over and over and sometimes, if I seem to have hit the right tone for the subject matter, then I go on in this tone, in this form. For me it always seems very simple and very evident that I'm writing in this particular form. People always ask me, "Why do you write in such a complicated manner?" I really never understand how they can say that.

PALEY: One wants always to be as simple as one can be, and yet as complex as is necessary.

WOLF: Yes, that's right.

PALEY: And this gets us into trouble, too, sometimes. A question was asked of you this afternoon that I thought was worth asking again: To what degree is there an inner censor in you? When the question was asked I thought: Every society is full of the projections of inner censors, which begin when we are about three years old. I wondered what you could say about this.

WOLF: While I'm writing I'm sometimes aware of some inner resistance that maybe you would call an inner censor. This inner resistance can refer to all kinds of things, not only conflicts with society, but maybe some sexual questions. I've noticed for myself that I cannot break down this inner resistance unless I'm completely ready to do it. But I can see that each one of my books overcomes a bit more of the taboos that I myself experience. I often am reminded of a sentence of Ingeborg Bachmann; basically, "How terrible it would be to have a society without any taboos!" Yet I'm of the opinion that the role of literature is to widen the limits of taboos, to push them always a little bit further. I think the worst taboos are the ones that the writer is not aware of at all. As long as one is aware of the taboos, one can deal with them. But it's terrible if a writer does not feel that there are taboos. It is interesting to me that whenever I go to a different country, I always notice right away the very different kinds of taboos that exist there. But, so far, I've never yet been in a country where there are no taboos at all.

PALEY: To go back to what we were speaking about earlier, our American individualism, a lot of our readers and writers are really under the impression that they live and write in total and absolute freedom. So much of our literature is already so heavy with pressure from our society. People don't know it, don't want to know it. We were also moving one step beyond that question to the question of how much the writer means in Eastern countries, and how little the writer means in our own country (except in cases that we'll talk about shortly). We really can say some pretty terrible, rotten things and nobody will care too much.

WOLF: Maybe we can't say all the things that you can say here, but, on the other hand, people listen to us much more. Not only the readers, but the politicians as well. Maybe in some cases this is not exactly an advantage because literature has to take on all kinds of tasks that maybe should not always belong to literature. Maybe these should be the tasks and themes of sociology or psychology; but now it is literature that has to do the work.

PALEY: For my part, I like that. I like it and I think that where you have a readership for women writers especially, that task has been taken on in many ways and has been welcomed. It makes the literature richer. But it also makes the writer happy.

WOLF: Not always.

PALEY: Regarding your new Cassandra books that are coming out, I have to say that I've read about them and talked about them with my German friends. The story itself has taken you way, way back into human history. You have here a woman, a seer, who has been given the gifts of prophecy and wisdom by Apollo and is also meant to be laughed at. Could you tell us a bit about that book?

WOLF: When I started the book I knew as much about, or as little about, the story of Cassandra as probably most of you know. But I became interested in Cassandra, who was a priestess and seer, a prophet, who predicted the fall of Troy. Everybody laughed about it.

She wasn't only laughed at; she was also locked up in the tower and her profession as a prophet was taken away from her. It's no coincidence that I've been working and thinking about this story for the past three years, since I'm constantly thinking about the dangers that are threatening us in Europe. I was able to go to Greece and work there and imagine what it must have been like in Cassandra's time. I suddenly had another real shock when I realized that in the past two thousand years women really have not been able to exert any public influence. I tell this story in the first person singular. It became like a voice to me out of the past and at the same time like a voice from the future, because it is so long ago that one really doesn't know the exact details. One cannot really reconstruct the details. So, for me this book, which of all my books goes the furthest back into the past, is the most utopian of my books. I happened to give a series of lectures last year in Frankfurt, where there are always poetics seminars in the spring and fall, and spoke about the beginnings of this book—how I came to it—and the book's development. In the meantime, I'd completed it. So, *Cassandra* is not just a finished product for me; it's like a piece of weaving, like a piece of tapestry. It shows me a whole development, something in process.

PALEY: This book, I understand, has just come out in West Germany. When it's published here it will appear as one volume, *Cassandra*, with the lectures.

WOLF: In the GDR it will also appear in one volume.

PALEY: A lot of us here are very interested in all your books. But for us women who see the intentions toward this world of war, which we all think of as man-made, we think the book will have a tremendous effect, both in Germany and here. But I want to ask you something. A number of women in the U.S. are organizing a peace camp on the lines of the Greenham Commons Peace Camp in England, the difference being that the Greenham peace camp is receiving the missiles and we, that is, our country, is sending the missiles. Are there women's organizations or women's groups doing any of this work in the GDR?

WOLF: I'd like to say first of all that in the last two or three years it has become more and more obvious for us in the GDR that there is a really serious nuclear threat. We feel this more and more now. And just in the last two or three years there have been various groups which have been working quite actively for peace; among them, one has to mention the Protestant Church. (In the GDR, it is the Protestant Church, and not the Catholic Church, that is involved.) It has a lot of appeal for young people. One of its slogans is (and one cannot really translate it into English): "Disarm Yourself. Be Upset. Be

Offended." There are special peace days when the churches are big forums of discussion. There have also been two joint events for writers from West Germany and East Germany. The writer Stephan Heym organized a meeting for West and East German writers, which took place last year in East Germany, and this year, 1983, in April in West Germany. It was actually the first time in many, many years that there had been such open discussion between these two groups. It shows that the danger of war has brought us together. Of course, the fact that we sat together and discussed these questions also shows us that there are differences of opinion. The basic conflict that came up was whether, in order to avoid war, you have to be well armed and have a strong defense, or you have to disarm, which is my opinion. Another question was whether it matters to count missiles and warheads when humanity can destroy itself maybe twelve times over. There were differences of opinion about this. Also, there had been a group of women who wrote a letter to the government of the GDR saying that they, as women, did not want to do any service—military service—and there have been a number of students who organize a minute of silence to express their opposition to war. I think it's very important and very meaningful that Germans, who so often have started wars, show very strongly that they want peace.

PALEY: I just remembered that statement by the women of the GDR. It appeared in the *END Bulletin* which comes out of England. The question was whether they would be conscripted or not; the women chose not to be. They said, "We choose not to be equal with men in this respect. We want to stand equal with those men who refuse to fight."

WOLF: I want to ask you a question. My husband and I have the impression, and have quite often discussed this, that certain things are not recognized as much here as they are in Europe. Olaf Palme suggested that the whole of Europe be made a nuclear-free zone and the GDR said it would accept that; so did the Soviet Union. However, it seems to us that this has not been really acknowledged in this country. Another example is that the Soviet Union said it would never start a nuclear war, that it declared itself against a first strike. It seems to me that *this* has not been recognized, really, in this country.

PALEY: Well, it has been known; it is one of our shames. Most of the people in this room are pretty ashamed that our country won't take a no-first-strike position. In fact, the U.S. is adamant about refusing to take it.

WOLF: I don't even want to talk about this particular question. The Soviet Union has no interest in having a continent devastated by nuclear arms at its doorstep, so this really presents a chance for peace.

PALEY: Yes, I agree with you on that. The question that comes up sometimes is of unilateral disarmament, that one of these countries had better start first, that the arms race really consists of two countries arming themselves, both us and the Soviet Union. Since we have enough nuclear missiles to murder them twenty times over and they have enough to murder us twenty times over, we could start disarming any time, and that would be true for the Soviet Union, too. But both countries have held each other in some mystifying terror.

WOLF: We ask ourselves all the time in Europe and in Germany: What can we, as writers, do to prevent a war? In Germany and in Europe, there have been very strong movements among writers against the war—before the First World War and before the Second World War, and yet both these wars took place. So we constantly discuss and ask: What can we do as writers? I think that one of the basic things that happens when a war is being prepared, as it is now, is that the enemy is depicted as the devil. When I'm here, I feel a certain obligation to counteract the picture of the socialist countries shown here. I'm glad that my being here and my books being published here might contribute a little bit to correcting this picture. When I'm at home, I express myself quite critically, sometimes about my own society, but when I'm here, I feel that the most important task for me is to counteract this mystification of the enemy—or the future enemy—and to do as much as possible to correct it.

PALEY: I understand that. I've been living in New England and Russians were invited by Bridges for Peace to come up there. That's one of the things people are trying to do. We have to maintain this network of people who can speak to each other, as we here can speak to you and you to us. Also, PEN, which has sponsored us, which has brought us together here, has, in one of its international meetings, passed a resolution . . .

KAREN KENNERLY (PEN): Well, there are two resolutions, actually. One came from the GDR and the other came from Holland. Both resolved that writers should exercise their authority to prevent war. It sounds simple, but . . .

PALEY: It sounds simple, but it took many years of many people going to those meetings to arrive at a statement like that. So PEN is one of the networks. The other network, of course, is our women's network, which has carried forward these great demonstrations in England and Italy and elsewhere, and which will encamp at Seneca Falls this summer. There are other things. When you begin to talk of what to do, I always think of what *can* be done. Well, you wrote this marvelous book, which will probably be very important and influential in this respect. But what can *we* do? And you have to do something, you have to take an action. I've been trying to remind people about war-tax resistance and that they shouldn't pay the telephone tax, which is a war tax. We can do that. And we should think about other taxes as well. We've been picketing for peace, but we continue to pay for war. So people should think about that very seriously. It's a nice white-collar action.

WOLF: I spoke to somebody in Ohio the other day who was very disturbed by all the questions that face us. We were talking about what he might do, and he said that maybe it would be a good idea if people would send their children for a time to a family in the Soviet Union, and the Soviet Union would send a lot of children here, to the U.S. I doubt that a country that has thousands of its children in this "enemy" country would declare war against it. We have to start being very creative and think of the most impossible things first, because we're trying all the possible things right now. Maybe we have to bank on the things that seem impossible because they may be the ones that work. For instance, in the schools, it would be good if at least once a week somebody would come from the "other system" to tell children what it's like to live in his country; that way, the children would hear different viewpoints once in a while.

PALEY: I just looked at this clock here. We would like to continue this conversation, but we would also like the audience to take part in it now. If any of you would like to address questions to either of us, please go ahead.

Q.: In relation to that last idea, would the East German authorities be receptive to such an idea of people coming here to speak?

WOLF: I said before that some of these ideas seem impossible, and maybe they are. Maybe they would not work right away. But just to pose the question, to bring up the question, would mean something. People might start talking about it. It could work out in the end.

Q.: You spoke about the drive to self-destruction. Do you think this is something that is personal or societal, or do you see that as an artificial distinction?

WOLF: I think that I'm not quite clear myself yet about the answer to this question, but I've thought about it a lot. I believe that our culture goes back to the ancient Greeks and to several other societies whose roots lie in this Greek civilization. There is one thing that these various cultures have in common: they are built on a very hierarchical system that has excluded women from power and influence. They developed an increasing competition for material gains, producing societies that became more and more void and empty. I think this is one of the causes of this drive toward self-destruction.

Q.: You were talking about the different taboos which you encountered in different countries. Could you talk about the taboos that you perceive here, in this country, which are very different from the ones in your own country?

WOLF: This is the second time I've been in the U.S., and this second time I've been here for only ten days. I want to be truthful, but I also want to be polite. It seems to me that the pressure to conform in this country is more subtle, but at the same time extremely powerful, while in my country you can feel the pressure. There is a very definite feeling that you should conform to society in the GDR, but at the same time it has a somewhat liberating effect. People feel freer to be themselves and to express themselves and to resist.

Q.: I think what I'm about to say relates to the last answer. I'm going to allude to a point of personal trivia. One can understand a representative of Farrar, Straus and Giroux saying that there are only three books of Christa Wolf published in this country, but the publishing house with which I'm associated has also published a book by Christa Wolf, which contains a series of essays that discuss many of the thoughts discussed here tonight. I would like to suggest that when you meet at other publishing houses, ask them why when Farrar, Straus and Giroux publishes a book, it gets reviewed in *The New York Times*, but when International Publishers publishes a book *The New York Times* will not review it.

PALEY: The name of that book is *The Reader and the Writer*. I have to say that I feel for you, Mr. International Publisher. It is certainly true that there are a lot of books that don't get reviewed, but it is serious. It's a terrible thing. It's one way our society tells us what to read and what not to read. That's really what publishing pressure is all about.

Q.: I have two questions. One is about the Cassandra books, in which you develop a very different, basic line of evolution for men and women in history, where men wind up with power and women with none. My question is whether you believe it would be meaningful at this point in time to establish an international women's peace politics based on this historical difference. That's the big question. The other question is: What American, English, or French women writers do you think are important to you?

WOLF: In *Cassandra*, I am really trying to present a new interpretation of the Cassandra story and of the story of the war of Troy. I want to show that for me, in the end, the heroes are really like devils, and the victims are really the most important, much more worthy of being

279

written about than the heroes. I would also like to say that, in principle, I would welcome an institution where women could get together
and deal with problems of war and peace. At the same time, I have
some reservations because, as you may have noticed at times, if women
get together and express their feelings and opinions very forcefully,
men feel attacked. At this point in history, it's so important that men
and women talk to each other and work together. That is the only
solution in our situation. To your second question about women writers
whom I admire and who have had much influence on me, I would
first of all mention Anna Seghers, not just because of the fact that
she is a woman writer, but because she is Anna Seghers. There are
many other women: Virginia Woolf, Simone de Beauvoir, Margaret
Atwood, Ingeborg Bachmann. I'm going back to women writers who
have written in earlier times, but at this point in literature I'm particularly interested in what women are writing now because it seems
to me that they address themselves more clearly and more consciously
to the taboos that are being faced today.

Q.: Why is it that Christa Wolf's books are not advertised by the publishers?

AUDIENCE: That's not true. Christa Wolf's books have all been advertised by the publishers in various places, including *The New York
Times*, which reviews the books.

Q.: I don't want you to misunderstand my question, so first I want to
make it very clear that I am very critical of my country, the United
States, and I would not hesitate to say that the U.S. is a devil, to use
your figure of speech. Now I'll get to my question: You said that you
would like to correct the idea that socialist countries can be characterized in that same crude way. Now, in my opinion, the U.S. is
a devil and the Soviet Union is a devil, a different kind of devil, but
a devil all the same. As far as I can see, there's really no difference
between these two devils except one: As a citizen of the U.S., if I
don't like living under the dictatorship of the devil, I can leave and
go elsewhere. As a citizen of the Soviet Union or the GDR, I don't
have that choice. I can either commit suicide or stay. How can we
actually claim that it's possible to correct the idea that the Soviet
Union is a devil. Do you believe that?

WOLF: I cannot think the way you do because I actually don't think
that the U.S. is a devil; nor do I think that the Soviet Union is a
devil. I think that in any country there are things that can be criticized
and, when I'm there, I can say that I don't agree with this or I don't
agree with that. But I think it is very wrong to build up this myth of
a devil—anywhere—because I don't believe that either country is a

devil. It's very important for people to get to know each other. You have to start to analyze the people in the context of their particular country's development. If you think of the people who live in those countries, you can't think of them anymore as devils.

Q.: A stereotype exists that people born after the war do not incorporate the Nazi experience, and its meaning, into their lives. I was wondering if you think this is true. I was also wondering if you think that by incorporating the meaning to Germany of the Nazi experience, it can be of some help in the whole nuclear pacifist movement.

WOLF: I don't believe that the Nazi experience has not been incorporated into the experience of the young people who were born after the war. I know that, on the contrary, young people are dealing very much with the whole Nazi past. After my book, *Patterns of Childhood*, came out, I received many letters from young people who told me about the experiences of their families during the war under Fascism, experiences their families never talked much about. I know it from my daughters and their friends, who very much make a connection between Fascism and the mass destruction that took place in the Hitler years—and its causes—and the things that are going on in the world today, including the danger of nuclear war.

Q.: You spoke earlier about conformity and the individual, and conformity in society. Would you say that was the major problem in *Christa T.* and, if so, would that work against reading that novel as a *Bildungsroman?*

WOLF: Yes, I think you're right and maybe I wasn't even conscious of it while I was writing the book. The problem that I was dealing with was how an individual can assert himself or herself in a society in which there is a strong pressure from outside to conform. I would not regard this book as a *Bildungsroman*. I think that's much too conventional a form.

Q.: As an artist myself, I have to deal with the taboos and to face the reality of our society. In our society, for instance, racism has become a weapon to divide the people. This is a taboo that I, as an artist, have to work with, and still have not overcome. People look at me and say, "Ah, you write about black people." They don't understand that the essence of speaking, of writing poetry about our black and brown sisters is being able to develop a consciousness, a social awareness about them, their lives. These are taboos we really have to work with.

WOLF: I think it's important, what you've expressed, that we, as artists and writers, see the taboos in our own societies, the conflicts in our societies, and help to solve them in our own way, so the society becomes conscious of these conflicts and does not project them onto another society and blame another society for what are really its own conflicts.

PALEY: We have to finish now. Thank you, Christa and Christine. You both worked so hard.

THE END OF

THE GERMAN

DEMOCRATIC

REPUBLIC

(1989 – 1990)

—

Thoughts about

September 1, 1939*

I found it hard to write my speech for this occasion, for several reasons. I have already recorded my memories of the first days of the Second World War and do not want to repeat myself. On the other hand, the events which are taking place right now, on this anniversary, show violent upheavals in the floes of time. Older layers of history are coming to the surface and are still able to produce powerful effects. Unforeseen links have emerged between our wartime past, which is still close to us, and what is happening in the present; and more such links are becoming evident. On an evening like this, I can talk about September 1, 1939, as more than a simple date in history. However, I am not sure that I am in a position yet to express the ongoing agitation I feel about the most recent occurrences in our history.

Just think how our impressions change in the light of later events. I remember very, very dimly when the *Landsberger General-Anzeiger* reported the nonaggression pact with the Soviet Union which Germany had signed how I, then a child of ten, wondered in a hazy and unformulated way whether this meant that a book my parents had in their bookcase—a volume with a frightening cover, called *The Betrayal of Socialism*—was no longer valid. I don't know how my parents themselves felt about the news. Not until the late 1950s did I learn, from German Communists who had emigrated or been imprisoned in concentration camps, about the tortured conflicts into which they were plunged by the Hitler–Stalin Pact. And it was just some twenty-five years ago that a Lithuanian writer told me, on the shores of the town

* Speech delivered at the Academy of Arts, West Berlin.

of Gagra in Soviet Georgia, of that supplementary agreement which had turned Poland and the Baltic States into objects of barter between the two great powers: an agreement which, paradoxically, is now a problem to those very forces in the U.S.S.R. which are starting to face up to long-suppressed truths of Soviet history.

I could trace similar links between current happenings and a whole series of historical events which I witnessed as a child and as a young girl, at a time when I was deeply interested, although mis-guided and immature. Take the start of the war, Germany's attack on Poland, for example. That day left an imprint on me sharp as a woodcut: the soldiers of the German Wehrmacht, in precise ranks, their gaze fixed straight ahead, their rifles between their knees so that the barrels deliberately pointed in a straight line, being transported past our house, headed east. "As of 5:45 a.m. this morning, our troops have been returning fire." (Even the time given in the German news bulletins was false, as we now know.) With that hysterical voice sounding in my ear—at the time we took it for the voice of history —I stood outside and threw little packs of cigarettes at the passing vehicles. German people were not drunk on war, their mood was subdued, and that was true in my own home, too. My father had almost died when he was eighteen, in the heavy barrage outside Verdun. Now he had been drafted again. For several days he had been on guard duty in a small village at the border between Germany and Poland, while a Polish guard stood watch on the other side. Each time the two met by the tollgate, they looked silently at each other before turning and marching back. At approximately 4:30 a.m. on September 1, 1939, my father was ordered to raise the barrier. The Polish border patrol was no longer there, and my father's unit advanced into Polish territory without meeting any resistance. As a precaution, one especially nervous soldier tossed a hand grenade into a small Polish customhouse, where it ricocheted off the window bars and then exploded a few yards ahead of the troops. Fragments hit the man who had thrown the grenade, who thus became one of the first to be wounded in the war. My father just told me this story for the first time only two days ago—an ailing man, ninety-two years old.

On the "home front," meanwhile, the media, especially Reich Radio, tried to pump up the tepid atmosphere with musical fanfares accompanied by special news announcements. People developed a craving for these trumpet calls, which produced a mild continuous fever, a sense of elation and a jubilant confidence of victory which washed away the justified fear of war that most felt. It dulled their sense of reality, which had already been weakened anyway. And it wiped out the imaginary and the real slights and humiliations dealt to their national pride since World War I, a pride which, being so unstable, was both exaggerated and easily wounded—and chained their fate irrevocably, for better or worse, to that of an insane criminal.

I know from personal experience how hard it is to end this kind of disastrous identification; but to do so was among the most urgent tasks we Germans faced after the collapse of our national identity, at the end of the war. Today, Germans in both the Germanys are finding out the extent to which we succeeded in offering the postwar generations, our children and grandchildren, identities that they feel able to accept. Our success depends partly on our developing and promoting awareness of the problems implicit in our own postwar history—a history which now spans forty years. As far as I can tell, the generation of war criminals and collaborators in West Germany has been largely spared from grief, remorse, and shame, or has even been expressly exonerated—so as to be redeployed in the Cold War. Incidentally, I must add that one important reason why East Germans of my generation became active was that we saw in the West a mass denial of Germany's crimes, and a refusal by Germans to identify with the criminals. Even so, I would not have believed possible that, fifty years after the German attack on Poland, legally approved political parties could emerge in West Germany which are able to rally sizable numbers of voters behind slogans that are unspeakable (if not yet unspoken): "Silesia: Ours, Now and Always," "The German Reich Back to its 1937 Borders"—and which can brand as "traitors" members of the national "Free Germany" committee. This is fatal, dangerous; for one thing, some right-wingers in the Federal Republic believe they must move closer to the extremist right in their debate and policies. What is really going on there? Has an unholy alliance suddenly been forged between unteachable grandfathers and untaught grandsons? Are we trying hard enough to find out what is driving these grandsons into retaliatory, nationalistic organizations—which is another way of saying that they do not identify with the publicly stated aims of the Federal Republic of West Germany?

I will let this question stand and turn to the burning issues in our own country. These, too, have to do with success or failure in finding an identity. There is no need for me to go into detail about what I felt last year when I talked with an East German skinhead who carried a photograph of his grandfather in Nazi storm-trooper uniform and who quoted his grandfather, and his grandfather's Führer, to support his hodgepodge of ideas about All-Germany and Pan-Germany, anti-Semitism and revenge. Certainly this is a marginal phenomenon in the GDR, and the numbers involved are small; yet it is a warning signal which ought to be more generally perceived and analyzed, and not just in the court records.

In the years before and after the founding of the GDR, we in our part of Germany confronted German Fascism uncompromisingly and thoroughly. This anti-Fascist phase of our postwar development allowed people who were young then to identify gradually with the GDR, over a period of time, and with those revolutionary traditions in German history which are the foundation of the GDR, but which were denied or fought against in West Germany under Adenauer. It was important to us to develop a different, an alternative Germany. Today many of us see that at first we were in danger of just substituting one doctrine of salvation for another. Because it is much harder, and much more tiresome, too, to work out new structures of feeling and thinking than simply to change the contents of an old faith for a new one (although this was not "simple," either). Many of us stopped at the point of finding a new faith, and became frozen in this posture of belief. They are the parents, teachers, and bosses from whom so many young people today are turning away. They cannot talk with each other—no more than *their* parents could talk in concrete terms about their own share in the ideology and actions of National Socialism. I know these things from the many letters I have received on the subject. At a certain point, which of course cannot be defined exactly in terms of years, the little group of East German anti-Fascists who were governing our country and who claimed to have overcome the effects of National Socialism extended this claim to cover our whole nation and its people. I believe that this public claim conflicted with what people were actually experiencing in their families and in their every-day lives, and that the conflict created feelings of emptiness and confusion in the young people who were growing up in the GDR, and made them feel they were being left to deal with important problems on their own. Literature tried to fill these vague, empty spaces by depicting concrete reality and by evoking the contradictions in this country's past which affected our present. Often, writers had to fight official policy to do this. As East German citizens and as writers, we had to deal increasingly with the conflicts which grew out of unresolved problems in the history of the German Communist Party, and out of our unavoidable adoption of Stalinist structures and attitudes here, in this first socialist state on German soil. Writers, including me, repeatedly called for changes in the direction of democratic socialism, through the medium of literature, which for the time being seemed our only avenue. We saw no other alternative, if we were to avoid breaking the commitment we had made—and which in part had made us—despite the often lacerating conflicts we experienced. Now, over-night, the reforms which Mikhail Gorbachev introduced in the Soviet Union have increased the number of East Germans who are hoping for reform of our country, too—even though the change would nec-essarily take a completely different shape here than in the U.S.S.R., Hungary, or Poland, because none of those countries faces complex-ities identical to those of the GDR, which are conditioned by our history and geographical position.

Am I still talking about the topic I am supposed to discuss here? I'm talking about the connecting lines which stretch from recent German history into the present. I am talking about the long-term effects of German Fascism and of the war into which it plunged Europe: effects which still persist and no doubt will continue to exist for a long time yet. And thus it seems essential to me to include a mention of those pictures which have appeared on West German television recently, showing us crowds of young East Germans waving their brand-new West German passports, racing across the border into Austria and Hungary. I believe that someone who is still living in the GDR needs to say publicly—and I will be the one to do it—that their leaving hurts me, that we miss all those who have left the country, and that I regret it deeply that conditions in the GDR did not allow the young people to identify with this nation—not even in a conflict-ridden way, not even as an opposition group. Contradiction must not only be tolerated in the GDR in the future but made pro-ductive, used as a learning tool to investigate and solve problems which are still denied on a public level. I think that this process is essential and that we must begin by using a different, a concrete language in the media of the GDR. I believe that there are enough people in the GDR, both old and young, who are capable of the truth and who are only waiting for a public discussion to open up, to bring in their ideas about a German socialist state and to help make the ideas a reality. Only in this way can we create a GDR which is stable and enduring. I consider this desirable, not least because a stable GDR is important to the reform process in the Soviet Union, on which every one of us is so dependent: dependent, above all, for our as-surance that the day we are remembering today turns out to be the last day when one country attacked another country in Europe and started a war. This is something that should be kept in mind by people who try to inflame emotions and to create a mild continuous fever, so as to disrupt the dialogue of reason which is critically necessary within our countries and between them.

August 31, 1989

Challenge to Dialogue:

A Conversation with

Gerhard Rein

———

GERHARD REIN: How have the pictures, the events of the past few weeks affected Christa Wolf?

CHRISTA WOLF: It's been going on for many weeks now, of course. In that time, feelings have changed—or should I say "developed," the way so many things in our country are developing very rapidly. My basic feeling, and I think the basic feeling of many people, was shock. Grief. Also a kind of bewilderment. And of course there were many questions. More questions arose the more you saw these pictures on TV of the very young people who seem to leave the country so easily and laugh as they go. Talking with people in the German Democratic Republic, I have heard them ask over and over: Do we really know our young people? Why is it so easy for them to leave? Why are many of them so silent; why is it so hard for them to articulate what disturbed them in the GDR; and what is it that they are now searching for somewhere else? Questions have come up which go much deeper than superficial astonishment, or shock. And questions of that kind will, I hope, bring about the deeper changes which are necessary here, and which will be necessary in the future.

REIN: How would you describe East German society right now, in the light of those TV pictures?

WOLF: Something extraordinary happened. In the past four or five weeks, we were all dominated by these pictures; we couldn't sleep; we felt desperate. Then came a sudden change. One sign of it was that people all at once said to each other: "We won't let ourselves be driven to total despair. We're here, we're going to stay here, and we want to express what we still hope to have from this country." Since then, those pictures are still terrible, but they no longer make us despair. Meanwhile, I have experienced something I never experienced in the GDR before. A mass discussion is taking place in which almost everyone is talking with almost everyone else, wherever they happen to meet. I could tell you about a reading I gave in a small town in Mecklenburg. A completely open, very mature and high-level conversation evolved about all the things that are bothering us so much. I could mention many other things that I have seen and heard lately. If you are looking for a general description: this is a society in motion.

REIN: Another question about the people who have left the country. You spoke about "loss" and "grief" and "pain." Is there also something like a feeling of coolness toward those who have left, because possibly they wouldn't take on any risk?

WOLF: It's true, I have heard people express views like that. There definitely are a lot of people who say: "They had everything they needed over here. How come it's so easy for them to leave, and maybe provoke a clamp-down that could make things tougher on the rest of us?" But I believe for the most part people are wondering why the young people left. I've heard older East Germans ask: "What did we do wrong to make the young ones turn away from us like this?" You know, a lot of tragedies are happening in the GDR right now. Parents are losing their children, sisters their brothers, friends are losing friends. That tears people up. It's definitely a crisis—but in a positive sense, too. A crisis doesn't always have to be unproductive—perhaps most of the time it isn't. Just the opposite. Properly understood, a crisis propels a person forward, drives him from the inside, by the power of strong emotion.

REIN: In Chinese, the word for "crisis" and for "opportunity" is the same word.

WOLF: "Opportunity." I'd like to use that word to describe the condition of the GDR. Obviously, I can only speak for myself. But I know from a great many people, I know from all the artists and art institutions, including the theater, the artists' unions, the Academy of Arts, that this great opportunity does exist, that the changes which are needed have the support of large segments of our society. In the past I hardly dared hope that there were still so many people in the GDR who can say: "Yes, I would like to live in this nation, and I would like to help make it a place where I and my children really want to live."

REIN: But what you are describing is contradicted by government leaders, the heads of the Socialist Unity Party, who are hardly sending out positive signals. Or have you seen some?

WOLF: No, I don't know of any, either. I would rather not have to explain right now why that is so. I could mention a couple of points that we should not completely ignore. We were just about to celebrate the fortieth anniversary of the founding of the GDR, with people from all over the world looking on. I don't know if you see this the same way, but reports issued in the West were already tantamount to "drum-beating." I have the impression myself that some circles in the Federal Republic have taken advantage of the wave of refugees from East Germany to cover up their own problems—and, of course, partly to make election propaganda. That's something that should not be completely forgotten. But I would like to add right off that I think the causes for the crisis are in the GDR. There were reasons why people in the GDR wanted, as much as possible, to present it as a nation where peace and order reigned. I would accept their reasons in a pinch. But the means that were used seem dubious to me. My business is to act as a mediator. I would like to ask the people who are thinking about going out to demonstrate in the streets again, to consider whom they would benefit by doing that—whether by chanting slogans, they really are helping those they support, or whether they are giving their opponents an excuse to take a hard line. On the other hand, I am quite sure, I am absolutely certain that the New Forum and other groups which have established themselves, or which are starting to form, are very definitely against violence, and that they definitely want to encourage socialist forms and structures in the GDR, so as to change the society in a way that will allow many more citizens to identify with it. So I would like to appeal to all those in a position to make decisions, to accept the readiness for dialogue which everyone is showing; to see this as an opportunity, and not to use the fact that there are rowdy fringe groups as an excuse for a general confrontation. I am very concerned. That would be a disastrous path; I believe it would undercut the future for all of us. We cannot pursue the path of confrontation. I know that it is very difficult at the moment and that people hardly listen when someone appeals to them to act rationally, and yet I see this as precisely my task. I don't feel competent to tell anyone what she or he ought to do or not do—but this is my opinion. I would much rather be saying it over the radio in the GDR [instead of here in West Germany], but I consider it so important to express my concern that I just have to do it here.

REIN: When you hear that reform groups—groups which support alternative policies and perhaps view themselves as the political opposition in the GDR—are classified as enemies of the state, or as "socially irrelevant"—don't those judgments impede what you support so strongly: that people would talk, instead of having a confrontation?

WOLF: Those are fatal mistakes of judgment; I'm convinced of that. At the moment they probably are purposeful mistakes, and I would like to warn people against them. I am quite certain that the alternative groups are not "enemies of the state," and of course I am equally certain that the debate they are trying to set in motion is not irrelevant, that it relates to a need of our whole society. That's just it, in fact. People who weren't talking to each other a few weeks ago because they were afraid of contact—who thought they couldn't talk with someone else because he or she had a different opinion—these people are talking to each other now. The talking is going on across all our institutions, and of course it penetrates deep into the Socialist Unity Party, too. Many party members are very troubled and want to try to preserve the GDR, just as everyone else does. But it can't hinge on giving in to those who suddenly are dragging the formula of German Reunification out of mothballs. I consider that dangerous nonsense. It's hypocritical, too, because those who are now talking about re-unification do not themselves believe that it is possible and necessary or even good. But they cling to this trump card, and I know that the East German reform groups we spoke of plan to oppose this formula by creating a GDR which cannot be swallowed like a light snack.

REIN: Judging by your description, we might conclude that you are perhaps a member of one of these opposition groups.

WOLF: I am talking with these groups; I have no fear of being in contact with them. I talk to them, I know their goals, I know their agendas if they have any. My opinions about them vary. But the things I say about them are based on personal contact.

REIN: Of course, I don't have as many conversations with Communists as you may have in the GDR. But what I notice is that the Party— from the top people through the "middle rank" down to the rank-and-file—that the Party is fixated on the Western media, so that news of what happens in their own country comes in second, third, or fourth place. How can this fixation be relaxed, so that the positive signals coming out of the opposition groups, and from other sources, are seen as supportive and not as expressions of hostility?

WOLF: You're right. Certain media in the West, and the people [in East Germany] who are fixated on them, are working together now, as they always do in cases like these. It really would be ridiculous if I were to appeal to the Western media to give up this role. One can't ask that of them. So we have to ask the others not to just stare in a single direction as if they were hypnotized, but actually to talk with the people they see news reports about every day, to ask them what they want, and to think together with them about what we could do at this moment. Because people's demands are clearly immoderate sometimes; notions arise which can't be turned into reality, not yet anyhow. But a dialogue would enable people to agree which those are.

I can say positively that the people from the citizens' action groups are ready to take part in this dialogue and that it is fatal to criminalize them; we should give free rein to these productive forces. You know—so much imagination, and so much fun is coming out of this, so many ideas are being generated—I have never experienced anything like it. Why should all that go to waste, or be suppressed again? It is a resource that any nation ought to be grateful for.

REIN: The groups keep saying, "We are powerless"—and in the last few days they have been saying it louder than ever.

WOLF: That's absolutely true. Yes.

REIN: But tomorrow is Monday again, and on Monday there are always the peace prayers in Leipzig. Of course, there is another kind of power. Are you afraid that violence may again diminish and destroy a source of hope?

WOLF: Yes. I am afraid of that, and it's the main reason why I have come here today and am talking to you about it. I do have that fear. And I don't believe I can influence any military commander like the one who wrote in a popular newspaper in Leipzig that, if necessary, military force would be used to maintain peace and order. That's why I am appealing to the others, to those who want to demonstrate in the streets, to be levelheaded, peaceful, and patient.

REIN: But not to wait.

WOLF: No, not to wait. The waiting is over, and it's impossible to wait anymore. This thing can't be stopped any longer; it will continue.

REIN: What might the next steps be, then? Do I understand you correctly that the Socialist Unity Party must put its authority behind the reforms, too?

WOLF: I don't like to use the word "reforms," because most people who use it don't have any specific ideas in mind—and I couldn't say, either, what reforms are necessary in the economic realm. What I understand is that the broad-based grass-roots dialogue which has begun must take place at the public level. This means—this is the first step, in my opinion—that the media must be open to it. I consider it a good sign that the theaters are starting to do this, that they are placing their halls at people's disposal, saying: "Okay, folks, after the performance we'll talk." But that's always a small group. The media have to do it. And if the media start speaking a different language, a language of reason and moderation, then certainly a great section of the population who are waiting for this language will listen. They will listen to arguments, which then can and must be countered by other arguments. But it must be arguments that are put forward, not ridicule. It can't be a sentence like that one that hurt a lot of people badly, including me: "We will not weep a single tear for those who are leaving." That is terrible. It's absolutely terrible to say that, while forty thousand young people are leaving the country. Or: "Absolutely no changes are needed in the GDR." Or other sentences I could repeat. But it's not a question of individual sentences. It's a question of the media believing that they can treat people the way they are doing now—the way they have been doing for a long time. I believe that a change in this area would be the first step in showing people that they are being taken seriously.

REIN: But, Mrs. Wolf, you know better than I that in the GDR the media are viewed as a propaganda arm of the Socialist Unity Party and that the media people view themselves that way. What you suggest would be seen as a weakening, as the surrender of part of their power.

WOLF: Yes. But there we are, back at the crucial point. Actually, I have always interpreted "power" as something else. Perhaps we may succeed, after all, in making clear that this would not be a loss of power but a means of gaining it, gaining a better kind—not power maybe, but strength, gaining strength. And as a party—particularly as a Communist, a socialist party—we really can gain strength only from where the strength is; that is, from the people. I see the dubious expression on your face, and I share your doubts. But I don't want to spread despair. I want to try to show where the opportunities lie, and what a mistake we are making if we waste those opportunities now.

REIN: One must say, too, that the last congress of the East German Writers' Union started something which led to a couple of reforms in book publishing.

WOLF: That's true.

REIN: And you could make more progress along that road. But the mass media in the GDR are still very, very inflexible. Those young people who left East Germany are a product of the national education system. Is that another area where concrete changes are needed?

WOLF: Actually, I would prefer not to run through the whole catalogue now, because there are a lot of other things that need changing. But I do believe that those in the "education system" definitely need to do some thinking about the young people who have left. I can't say very much yet, myself, about the psychological and social implications when a generation—or part of a generation—are so unable to form bonds, when they can identify so little with—I won't say the nation, but with certain institutions, or rather with certain objectives. Or perhaps with their parents. What happened there? Did a bonding ever take place, a dialogue? If not, why not?

295

REIN: I have the impression that many of the Western media are celebrating the defeat of Stalinism as a victory of their own system. *Is* this a defeat of Stalinism, Mrs. Wolf? Do you still believe—along with others who are now becoming active in the GDR again—that the utopian ideal, the goals of socialism, can be achieved, that there should one day be a successful attempt at socialism on German soil?

WOLF: Actually, I do have the impression that in the West many of the media *are* now expressing that attitude of victory, saying: "We have been right all along." I think they can use this as a mantle to hide their own problems. That isn't useful, either to them or to us. As to your question about Stalinism: I do indeed hope that this is a defeat for Stalinism, and I still hope that what you call "utopia" is not being defeated along with it. Provisionally, I would call this a concrete chance to develop structures in the GDR which could move on a productive path toward a socialist society. I am expressing myself cautiously, and vaguely. After all, we are not in the same position as Hungary or Poland. I think that the same path, the same structures that are being developed there, would not be right for us. We must consider our own geographical situation. We must consider that the border between the two Germanys is still the border between two systems. And I believe we must also consider that if the GDR develops more of an alternative to the Federal Republic, it could attract people back, its own citizens, and it could become a productive partner in Europe. A partner to the Federal Republic, too, incidentally. Things will get very difficult. I believe things will get very difficult. But if dialogue really takes place among the different groups in the GDR, if confrontation can be prevented, then I have hope.

REIN: One can't compare this situation with Poland's. But in Poland people have the example of the round-table discussions among the country's different social groups. Do you want something similar in your country, but adapted to circumstances in the GDR?

WOLF: Oh, when you call up that image . . . I'd love to see a great big Round Table, where representatives of the most diverse social groups would sit down together on equal terms and talk about the GDR and its future.

REIN: But you wouldn't include the national council of the National Front?

WOLF: The parties in the National Front would have to be present, of course. Perhaps to think about their own identity, but that point would have to be left up to them. In any case, all the groups, both institutionalized and non-institutionalized, which can assume responsibility in the GDR, would have to meet at the table and begin a responsible dialogue. A beginning like that could reduce everyone's fears. I consider it dangerous that our fear of each other is growing; and I would almost implore people to stop. Our leaders are afraid of those who are expressing their views now though they do not hold any formal authority, but they claim a responsible role—to which I believe they are really entitled. We should not have to be afraid of being branded criminals, or dismissed as irrelevant. I believe there has been such a rapid development of reason and political maturity in the GDR in these past weeks that a rational dialogue is now possible.

REIN: Does what we have been experiencing in recent days, weeks, and months still have to do with Hitler, with September 1, 1939? Are all these things effects of the past history of East and West Germany, of history which has not really been worked through yet?

WOLF: If you want to delve more deeply into the social psychology of it, then I would say yes. What I mean by that is, first, that the division of Germany, the creation of the Federal Republic and the GDR, is a result of the Second World War. And in addition to that, the relationship between the older and younger generations in the two Germanys is quite different from their relationship, and their social norms, in other countries. The Nazi period, and the general tendency not to talk about it, plays a big role in the relationship between the generations in both our nations. It's remarkable, my parents' generation has hardly talked to us about that time. People of my own generation have talked very little to our children about our childhood in the Nazi time, about the breakup in 1945, and about our attempt to—today we would call it to "find a place for ourselves"—in a new society based on new social principles. And then came the second collapse, brought on by the revelations about Stalin. Most people in my generation evidently have found it very difficult to overcome this double shock, and [as a result] are not very open to questions from younger people. Now the younger people have children of their own, and it is uncanny to see how these unresolved issues—that's a very unemotional term for what I have in mind—persist through the generations, and the kinds of effects they produce. No doubt we could discover what those effects are, if we were to thoroughly question the young people who are leaving East Germany.

REIN: I'll tell you about an experience of mine. At the Academy of Arts in West Berlin, you gave a talk about the fiftieth anniversary of Germany's attack on Poland, and I suggested to my editorial department, and to another group, that we broadcast your talk in its entirety, because I thought it was important. And this was done. Then the next day my colleagues, both women and men, phoned me to say that your criticism of the Federal Republic had tactical motives behind it. I've often heard similar things said. As long as GDR citizens criticize their own country, we applaud. But if at the same time they dare to criticize the political climate in the Federal Republic—we're not really prepared to accept it.

WOLF: Yes, that is odd. Many people who work in the Western media—and nonmedia people, too—apparently are unaware that they assume the right to express themselves however they please about the GDR, critically or noncritically, as a matter of course and often without thinking what they are saying. I don't dispute their right to do that. At least I don't dispute their right to judge the GDR. But people who have decided to stay in the GDR, however critical their attitude may be, evidently do not have a similar right to say anything critical about the Federal Republic. There is a powerful arrogance at work which I believe people have come to take for granted and do not think about, and many GDR citizens have also taken it for granted for a long time. Now that has changed.

REIN: I've read the pamphlets, papers, and proclamations of the various opposition groups, and some of them—though not all—are convinced that there must be an alternative to the Western system. Why is that so, really? All over the world, there is a flight to capitalism. There's nothing special about these twenty-year-old East Germans wanting to do the same thing, is there?

WOLF: That's true. All over the world there is a flight toward the better life which the industrialized capitalist countries can offer people, at least at the moment. I can understand that. People with a poor standard of living are attracted to places where they will be better off materially. Only I doubt that the capitalist system will be able, in the long run, to solve the problems which confront all mankind, unless it, too, goes through some very drastic changes. It seems to me that it might be in the interests of the Federal Republic, too, if there were a German alternative to the structures which have developed there —and which I'm not trying to criticize. In the area of culture, for instance, it could be important to both the Germanys if certain traditions were preserved. Revolutionary traditions, for example, which have never been taken seriously in the Federal Republic and which are evident in writers and artists who have long been accepted residents of the GDR. More needs to be said about that. I believe that foundations and structures exist in the GDR which are worth preserving, and that what we have to do is to reveal the productive possibilities in these structures, and to make them work.

October 8, 1989

"We Don't Know How"

—

Two weeks ago, in a small town in Mecklenburg where I had just given a reading, the audience very quickly transformed the discussion of literature into a discussion of politics. A physician called on everyone to say what he or she thought openly and clearly, not letting themselves be intimidated, and to do nothing that violated their conscience. In the stillness which followed his words, one woman said in a low, sad voice: "We don't know how." Encouraged to go on, she talked about the political and moral development of her generation in this country: of the people who today have just turned forty. She told how as a child she was obliged to conform, not to go her own way but, especially in school, to be careful to express the opinions that were expected of her, so as to guarantee herself the problem-free career which her parents felt was so important. A permanent schizophrenia had made her empty as a person, she said; so now she could not suddenly begin to "speak openly" or "say what she really thought." She did not even know herself exactly what she thought.

It was disturbing, if not surprising, testimony. Disturbing, among other reasons, because the managers of public education, who have been largely responsible for this state of affairs, have denied it for many years, have made it strictly taboo to discuss such matters in public, and have stifled the evidence with resounding reports of their success. Disturbing, too, because anyone who, despite these obstacles, has pointed out the fundamental distortions in our aims and methods of educating young people has been accused of being a political enemy; and perhaps that is still going on now. Books, plays, and films critical of education have met with persecution. The media

299

have kept silent or, even worse, have covered up the central problem—the fact that our children have been taught in school to be untruthful, that their characters have been injured, that they have been led by the nose, incapacitated, humiliated—with bogus words and pictures which call attention to nonexistent problems and then claim to solve them in the twinkling of an eye. I take off my hat to teachers who, in full knowledge of the situation and often feeling on the brink of despair, have tried to create a space for their pupils to think and develop freely. The organizations which claim to have been developed for young people have worked to gain their political loyalty rather than to enable them to practice independent, democratic conduct, and so have let them down for the most part. Youngsters subjected to these miserable conditions inevitably came to regard them as unchangeable. Almost all the adults left the children to endure such experiences on their own; and it was these experiences, I believe, which have driven many young people away. We have watched the results on TV news broadcasts from the West: hordes of young people leaving our country, most of them looking glad to go. Well-educated technicians, secretaries, nurses, doctors, salesclerks, scientists, engineers, waiters, streetcar conductors. "What more do they *want*? After all, they had everything they needed here," I've heard older people ask—people who had no proper childhood themselves.

Yes, they had everything they needed—except the opportunity to sharpen their critical faculties by confronting other points of view; not merely to demonstrate their intelligence by mastering the factual curriculum but to *apply* their intelligence, together with others, by engaging in meaningful social activity; to conduct experiments, including some that would fail; to experience in a productive way the pleasure of contradiction, of their own insolence, bizarreness, deviations, and whatever else the vitality of youth might lead them to; that is, to get to know themselves. To practice walking upright. By the way, whatever happened to those students from the Carl-von-Ossietzky School in the Pankow district of Berlin who did exactly that and were expelled as a result—an incident which made a mockery of the very name of their school. When will those students be allowed to continue their schooling, assuming that they want to? And on another subject, when will those who ordered violent measures to be taken against young, nonviolent demonstrators and bystanders be made to pay for their actions? And when will the violent incidents at police headquarters and garages be investigated, publicized, and punished?

We are told that violent incidents of this kind happen elsewhere in the world, not just here. I know that; I have observed it myself. But we are not living somewhere else, we are living right here, in this part of Germany which became a nation only forty years ago, which calls itself a "democratic republic" and claims to be "socialist" in its deliberate attempt to create an alternative to that other Germany which does not choose to be socialist, which for a whole chain of reasons is wealthier than we are, and which represents a permanent temptation, especially for our young people, unless there are other values here which compensate the individual for the lower standard of material prosperity. For me, it was a relief to hear people answer the slogan "We want out!" with their own chorus of voices chanting "We're staying here!" I think it was in Leipzig that that happened for the first time, and the chorus is growing. Back then, someone said to me: "We have to save the GDR."

"What did we do wrong?" a woman of around sixty asked at the literary reading I mentioned at the start. She talked about how her own life was interwoven with the development of this nation: how devoted she is to the goals to which she committed herself in her youth. I understood her very well. Naturally, she does not want to cancel out forty years of her life. Naturally, we do not want to—and cannot—wipe out forty years of our history. But we are faced with a difficult task: to review the basic assumptions and the unfolding of this history stage by stage, document by document, to evaluate its results and see how it meets the demands of the present day. A mass of dogmas which hardly anyone believes in anymore will be discarded in the process: among others, the dogma that history has "winners."

The two hundred people who met to talk about "literature" agreed late that evening that this catchphrase about "winners" was one thing that made it hard for the different generations in our country to understand each other. The small group of anti-Fascists who governed us transferred their feeling of victory over Fascism to the people as a whole, for practical reasons, at some moment which cannot be pinpointed exactly. The "winners of history" stopped confronting their real past, the past of the collaborators, of the seduced, of the faithful believers during the Nazi period. As a rule, they told their children little or nothing about their own childhood and youth. Their deep-seated bad conscience made them unfit to resist Stalinist structures and attitudes which for a long time served as the standard for "Party solidarity" and "loyalty to the Party line." These parents produced children who were completely "children of the GDR": insecure, in-capacitated, often wounded in their self-esteem, with little practice in standing up for themselves in case of conflict, and in resisting intolerable demands, who in turn were unable to give *their* children enough support, to give them backbone; unable to pass on values and guidelines apart from the drive to get good grades. I know that there are as many exceptions to this pattern as there are families. But all I am trying to do here, filled with anger and grief, is to introduce the theme of the young people, and I know that the young people themselves will take up this theme and talk about things from their own perspective. Perhaps now we will listen to them at last, and admit that torch processions and mass gymnastic exercises are signs of an intellectual vacuum and enlarge that vacuum, rather than creating ties which can grow only if everyone takes active responsibility for society in cooperation with everyone else.

We have an enormous amount of catching up to do, in many areas, but it seems to me that in recent weeks we have been learning faster, and not least from the young people: from their earnestness, their steadfastness, their humor, their inventiveness, their imagination, their readiness to become involved. I hope that many samples of the popular literary creativity which is manifesting itself so freely now in proclamations, slogans, and leaflets will be collected and preserved. I am impressed by the political maturity which has been shown in discussions and debates which I have taken part in or heard about. In the past, people said that in Mecklenburg everything arrives a hundred years later than everywhere else. But judging, once again, by the people I met at my reading, I have to say they are wrong. No way! Everywhere I see evidence of a great untapped reservoir of experience and readiness to act.

On the evening of the reading, when we were talking with the young woman I mentioned earlier, we also referred to a metaphor that Chekhov once used. He said that he had to "squeeze the slave out of himself drop by drop." During these weeks, it seems to me that many of us are squeezing the slave out of ourselves by the gallon. But let us not deceive ourselves: the marks of dependency will have a more lasting effect on people than will economic imbalances, for example. In the past, it was primarily left to art to observe and describe things like slavery, and often it has been attacked for doing so. How wonderful if now journalists, sociologists, historians, psychologists, social scientists, and philosophers, too, will do their public duty.

October 21, 1989

To Live or Be Lived:

A Conversation with

Alfried Nehring

———

ALFRIED NEHRING: "Self-experiment" is the first story of yours to be filmed by East German television. As far as I know, this is also the first time you have worked with television filmmakers anywhere in the world. In the sixties, you worked several times as a scriptwriter for films for the DEFA.* Then you turned away from the artistic possibilities of film, partly on theoretical grounds. The art world consequently is taking great interest in the film *Self-experiment*. Recent developments in this country have heightened our expectations even more. Everyone is talking about you, not only because of the large number of readers you have both nationally and internationally but also because of your worldwide reputation as a writer.

This makes it an advantageous moment to promote the film, although at the same time it makes the critical response less predictable. So I ask you to describe how you came to write the story "Self-experiment"—a long time ago—and to tell us about your situation as a writer back then.

CHRISTA WOLF: If I remember rightly, "Self-experiment" was the last in a series of stories I wrote in 1972. Two others in the series also have what you might call a fantastic or futuristic character. I'm speaking about *"Kleiner Ausflug nach H."* and *"Neue Lebensansichten eines Katers"* ["A Little Outing to H." and "The New Life and Opinions of a Tomcat"]. I gave them a satiric undertone. At least that's the case with "Self-experiment." It was a time when I did not hope or anticipate that they could be published in the GDR. I wrote them

* Deutsche Film AG, the official East German film company.

303

intending to store them for the future. Then they *were* published after all, in a collection entitled *Unter den Linden*.

"Self-experiment" was written at the special request of Edith Anderson, an American writer who had been living in the GDR for a long time and whose work was published over here, too. She introduced a new theme into our literature when she suggested that five female and five male writers should write a reply to the question: What if I were a person of the opposite sex? Irmtraud Morgner, Sarah Kirsch, and Günter de Bruyn took part, among others. The book was turned down by Aufbau Verlag. If I remember correctly, it was on the grounds that there was no demand for material on sexual emancipation. Then the Hinstorff Verlag published the book. It was pretty well received. Since then, this has been an established theme in the GDR, although, strictly speaking, a literary topic can't be established or "treated." We have seen, especially in recent weeks, that this topic is far from "exhausted." The volume we did was sort of a trial run.

NEHRING: The volume was called *Sex Change*.

WOLF: It was published under the title *A Bolt out of the Blue*, which was the name of Sarah Kirsch's contribution. "Sex Change" was Günter de Bruyn's story.

NEHRING: When you treated the subject of "changing sex," you did not write about an exchange of experiences between the sexes. You described how, in the society of that time, and maybe in today's society too, the liberation of women exposed them to the risk that they might simply be engulfed by the male norms of behavior which govern the world. They might adapt, as a precondition for obtaining equal opportunity.

WOLF: When Edith Anderson asked me if I would contribute to the volume, I decided to write about a woman scientist. My past interest in problems of biology proved helpful to me. Very quickly I realized that this woman scientist would perform an experiment on herself, or let someone experiment on her. I had a vision that this would be another, an especially dangerous variant on the centuries-old oppression of the feminine element in people; that is, in men, too. I was interested in the suppression of woman in the history of human civilization. My central idea was that a woman is forced to become like a man to succeed and achieve recognition in a man's world, and thus—in the perverse phrase that we use—to "realize herself." I wanted to show what a perverted role we as women are forced to play in our civilization.

NEHRING: This sharpening focus on the situation of women is, in my opinion, only one aspect of the impact the story has today. In a television discussion I heard a young woman who had left the GDR say that she "does not want to be lived but to live." This line—which had appeared in your story back in 1972—I think is resonant in many ways. It applies to many people in our country at this moment. They have become active; they are saying openly that they will no longer accept obsolete structures, power structures. The message of the film—ultimately it's the same as the message of the story "Self-experiment"—seems very contemporary to me, very fresh, and speaks to each individual personally: "Now we are ready for my experiment: to try to love. It leads to fantastic inventions, by the way: to the invention of someone one is capable of loving." Many people have liberated themselves—partly with the help of literature, and of the ethical integrity and political courage of artists—and are moving toward designing new lives for themselves. Some of that may come across in the film, and that is what is arousing special interest.

WOLF: Yes, maybe that's so. In the last few weeks—actually, it has only been two weeks that we have been trying out new ways of relating to each other in this country, new ways of criticizing our society, and that the society as a whole has really begun moving on a mass scale—it has sometimes occurred to me that although people are publicly demanding all sorts of things, their demands hardly ever apply specifically to women. Over in the West I've often been told that this is how it is here. It's because people in the GDR—including women, of course—have had other problems to think about—and maybe that's still the reason. Right now, the spotlight is on political, economic, and spiritual, or moral issues. It could be that the film will confirm our concentration on these basics. At a later time, when we are closer to realizing the basic social needs, the specific problems of women may perhaps become more prominent. We'll have to wait and see.

NEHRING: Perhaps, if the film is shown abroad, people's interest may focus more on the problems which the story addressed originally.

WOLF: Maybe. I have just seen the unedited version of the film. It struck me—and I was perfectly happy about this—that it is highly critical of science. Not of science as such, but of the social bureaucracy which administers it, of science as an institution dominated by male thinking. It seems to me that the film brings that out more clearly than the story did.

NEHRING: I believe that that is because of the specific properties of film, its use of image. It may be more difficult to describe "the Institute," its initiation rites and its myth, and the cruelty of experiments too, than to show it through concrete events. Besides, in 1972 the story still had strong science-fiction elements, whereas today institutes of the type shown in the film have become a reality in every sense. In making the film, we made no effort to create a science-fiction world, but simply an "artificial world" which is hidden from public view but which the viewer can accept as existing in our time.

WOLF: Yes, for me, too, it was interesting to see how developments in science had caught up with the futuristic, the science-fiction element in my story.

NEHRING: We have talked about the background of your story. Maybe it's important to explain how the film came about, too, because it makes clear the pragmatic motivations behind television art in our country and the strong expectations that people attach to it. Two years or so ago—it was the end of August 1987, I recall—I was assigned to ask you to do a reading of your novel *Accident* on television. For once, internationally known writers were being asked to express their views on TV as a way of "improving the climate" just before the Tenth Writers' Congress was held in the GDR. At the time, I suggested to you that we might film "Self-experiment," although I did not know whether I could really get the approval of East German television. I deliberately did not ask for the rights to *The Quest for Christa T.* or *Cassandra*, which are better known and perhaps have a wider dimension. Instead, I focused on a story with a more everyday theme which did not directly violate any GDR taboos. It was an interesting subject for a filmmaker, from an experimental point of view, and the director Peter Vogel, cameraman Günter Haubold, and scriptwriter Eberhard Görner became fascinated by it. Actually, it was only as we worked on it, as we collaborated with you, that the contemporary meaning of the story became evident. Also, Johanna Schall's attitude toward playing the lead role contributed a lot to the project's development. She immediately focused on what to her seemed an even more important issue than the liberation of women: the need to fight inhumane developments in our society. She regarded it as her character's most significant insight that, "without knowing it, I have been a spy behind enemy lines, and have found out what you intended to keep secret: that the enterprises in which you lose yourselves don't make you happy, and that we have a right to resist, if you try to make us participate in them, too." I believe we have to keep that insight in mind. The decision to show the film on television now is evidence of a compromise, but also reflects the subjective attitude of artists, which in turn has emerged out of social processes.

WOLF: You know as well as I do that for years scores of writers have been discouraged from contributing to East German television, not to say barred from it.

NEHRING: On the contrary, you *do* have to say they were barred from it. That was a disaster for our country, and for many of our best writers.

WOLF: So when you came to me with this proposal you must have noticed that I was hesitant and suspicious. I didn't know whether I really wanted any of my work to be broadcast by East German television. We—the film team and I—had to get to know each other first. With time, of course, a lot of my reservations disappeared. In other countries, nobody believed us when we felt obliged to mention now and then that it was impossible for writers to appear on our television in any form. I really am not just talking about myself. Actually, it didn't hurt me very much—the pain I felt came from another source and went farther back; I used the time for other projects which I regarded as my real work. But of course a whole dimension was lost, the possibility of influencing the public. Whole groups in our society, the ones who read less and who watch television more, were absolutely lost to us writers. To achieve that separation was the purpose behind the policy. We recognized that that was its purpose. We were treated as enemies by our country's television. It is a medium to which we had no access.

NEHRING: I can't deny that, although many of my co-workers in television were deeply pained by it. I have a more general question about the effects of literature. In the acceptance speech you made when you were awarded the Büchner Prize in 1980, you said: "The three languages which Büchner held together in his own person, at the cost of excessive strain to his body and mind—the languages of politics, science, and literature—have been separated beyond repair since his day, it is, strangely, the language of literature which seems to come closest to the reality of man today."

We are seeing literature, and people who work in literature, restoring the unity between the three languages at this very moment. You are a major figure in this development, because your language links democratic politics to ethical science, anchoring both on human need. Do you anticipate that the new political developments will strengthen this underlying agreement?

WOLF: That is an interesting question. It's too soon to answer it, and perhaps different writers will give different answers. What is happening now is that I and many of my friends can't avoid responding to demands which are of a directly political nature. When we are asked to appear somewhere, or to write about something, it is always some sort of pamphlet, article, journalistic material. We cannot and do not wish to avoid this opportunity and these demands. In other words, for weeks I haven't written anything "literary," because I simply don't get around to it. I don't know how long this phase will last. Actually, I would like to keep it as brief as possible. Because, of course, in two or three years people will start asking us: Where are the books you have written, the films you've made? We can't describe this new course of events right away, but we can take it as a vantage point, a sort of lookout tower. We can use it as a point from which to look back at what lies behind us. That is very, very important. I believe it will very much determine the tone in which we are going to write about the past. It really does make a difference whether you write with a sense of deep resignation or despair because you feel that nothing will change, or if you describe the identical events from the perspective of a time when things are moving. And what you write will be political, of course, but politics shouldn't be in the forefront of it. Soviet writers have taught me that. For three years or so, they have been swallowed up by *glasnost*. They say: "In the past, our books were needed to help people with things that the press did not deal with. Now suddenly the press is doing it all." And they say: "Now it's time for us to think about what the role of literature really is." The only question is whether one can still do it, once one gets the chance. We have a horde of writers who actually are journalists, who had no choice. They retreated into literature because it provided a refuge, because in literature they could still say something that could not be said in the newspapers or on television. A process of sifting out lies ahead of us; I see that very clearly.

NEHRING: I am looking forward to that very much, because of course my job in television is to oversee film adaptations of literature, of prose fiction. Our version of "Self-experiment" has some bearing on the theory and practice of filming literature. In 1968, in your essay "Reading and Writing," you stated: "Prose should strive to be unfilmable. It should give up the dangerous trade of circulating medallions, and of assembling prefabricated parts." "Medallions" and "prefabricated parts" refer to the kind of "objectivity" which we find in the images and events of a film; that is, unalterable, and posing as authentic. Whereas prose fiction conveys the author's personal experiences, but does not suggest that they are objective. Is your position on this still the same, or do you see film as having new things to offer?

WOLF: At the time, I phrased my views as sharply and distinctly as possible, so as to get quite clear in my own mind where the differences lie. You said yourself that I have worked on film, too. I realized that that is not my real métier. I stated what I look for in prose fiction: the subjective factor. Of course, more needs to be said about that. Film artists have told me that film can be subjective, too, that the camera can be used subjectively, and that film does not inevitably have to produce medallions and prefabricated parts. I accept that. I was concerned about the fact that film images can manipulate people more powerfully. I know, of course, how manipulative words can be. But visual images have the effect of suggesting, more strongly than any written description, that they are depicting or showing the objective truth. So the observer is less able to resist them. He has no counterargument and no counterweight. Whereas written prose always allows the author to be visible, in the role of the speaker, writer, or thinker of the text, so that there is an ongoing confrontation between the reader and the writer. At least this is the effect good literature has on *me*. This means that the reader is not helpless, that he brings himself along into the work, and that he himself decides what part of it he can accept, what he finds suitable. I want to add that I personally like to see good films, and that naturally I know and accept that film art has developed a great deal of subjectivity.

NEHRING: Your essay collection is called *The Author's Dimension.* I believe that this dimension of the writer is desperately needed in the development of film art, and in television film, too. Film is at a point where it relies totally on images, where outward events primarily determine the action. As a result, the audience is not prepared to absorb language in films, or thoughts which are formulated in words. I am not pleading for film to be made by writers, but for film to come closer to prose literature. Coming close to literature—that means the language you use in a film can help you to see it better.

That is why I would like to go back to something else you said. In your interview with Hans Kaufmann, you define the writer's dimension as "subjective authenticity." The film *Self-experiment* also has a structure in which the main character processes her experiences by looking back at them. Is that a way to get more of the writer's dimension into the film—via the commentary, the reflection, the abundance of thoughts which the character expresses directly, in words?

WOLF: Yes, definitely. That is a structure I use very often. By the way, I never notice it until afterward, until after a subject matter has taken on its definitive form. Before that, I make many attempts to write the story purely as a story, as I did with "Self-experiment." After a while I can't stand that, the triteness. There is a long process which apparently I can't help going through, even though really I suppose I ought to be able to realize it beforehand. The structure that comes out in the end is always a structure of memory, a reflection on past experiences. The first time that happened was in *The Quest for Christa T.* It was the same in *Patterns of Childhood*; and actually it was already there in *Divided Heaven*, in which the main character also thinks about events after the fact. That level is important to me, indispensable.

One reason I felt defensive when you approached me with your proposal to film "Self-experiment" is that I was afraid that if this level was removed, it would turn into a completely banal, superficial story. No doubt you remember that when we worked on the script—on which I collaborated to some extent—I rarely intervened except to put this level back in, because otherwise the most important element would be lost.

The question is, is the audience, or many in the audience, ready to accept that they are not watching a slam-bang action sequence but a young woman who has had a deep-lying, difficult experience which has upset her whole existence and that she is making this experience conscious in a retrospective way—and that is how the film is being narrated.

NEHRING: When your story was first published, people responded to it in a variety of ways. I think, too, that the characters, even the main character, don't require the reader to identify with them completely. Meanwhile, in the fifteen years since the story came out, women have gained self-confidence and made progress in demanding self-fulfillment, not only in this country but throughout the world. Perhaps political structures have evolved the least in that direction . . .

WOLF: May I interject something? I'm not certain that my observation is correct. From the early to middle seventies, when I went to readings or other group functions, and especially in factories, I had the same impression as you. Women really did seem to show more self-confidence. I thought that women would be the first in our society to become mature and independent. That has not proved true, in very many cases. Why is a question I ask myself. Probably our whole literature will have to ask it, if my observation turns out to be correct. I have the impression that almost the whole next generation of women had this self-confidence driven out of them. I don't mean that they stopped developing, but our schools went a long way toward driving self-confidence out of people, not only out of women but also out of young men, adolescents, and children. I don't want to generalize, and the mass movements that are taking place right now are being carried out in a very shrewd, politically mature, and disciplined way. That shows me that people are rapidly developing self-confidence again, within a period of a few weeks or months. I see that it was kept alive in small groups, including groups of women, and reemerged there. Speaking overall, self-confidence is not a very marked trait in women in this country. It has not developed as it needs to, to meet the demands of the nineties. But I think that will come quickly.

NEHRING: Isn't there a certain deficit of emotion visible everywhere, not only in women but in men, too? In the film, that idea is expressed through one of the secondary characters, a young woman named Anna, who says—after she meets Johanna, now transformed into Johann— that "men are getting lazier all the time, too lazy for love, anyway. One day they'll even get too lazy to be the boss, and then they'll pawn off on us their sheer love of convenience, pretending that they are granting us equal rights."

The film is actually a love story, a story of unrequited love in which one partner proves incapable of feeling love.

WOLF: Yes, that is the central problem. The transformation of the woman into a man, and all the rest, just serves as a means to open up and extend the range of this problem. For a long time—you can tell this from my books as well—I have been preoccupied with the question: How do people really develop this emotional deficiency, especially men? Many studies have been done which show how a young male child is intensively trained to suppress his feelings, and how, in his later development as a boy, a youth, and a grown man, society demands that he show self-denial to the point of self-hatred.

These self-denying men—especially men in leading positions— are now being asked: Why did you go along with all that? They don't know how to reply, because they have undergone a profound process of depersonalization. They don't understand this process. I believe that literature will help to expose it. It's bound to be very painful. And I'm not leaving women out of all this. That was one of the worst things that developed in our society: these rigid power structures made it necessary for people to withdraw from the social apparatus, to avoid being deformed by it. The result was that a great many people who had it in them to be creative and active in every field ended up being honorable and nothing more. They failed to have any effect, or stayed in lower-ranking positions, while those who rose to the highest po- sitions were the ones who—how should I put this?—tolerated this process of being radically deformed. I am not trying to assign blame: blame cannot be assigned to individuals when developments take place on such a mass scale. I also understand that these people aren't capable now of explaining or commenting on this process. That will take a long time; it involves the pattern imposed by Stalinism, the "patterns of childhood." The professor in the story and the film *Self- experiment*, the one chosen by Johanna to be her partner in love, is not capable of feeling or responding to her emotions. Her recognition of this fact is the real revolution in her life, and in the film—and so many women experience the same great pain.

NEHRING: I believe that in literature written by women the idea of liberating women as the key to liberating both sexes is not very strongly developed. Few women write great love stories of the sort which we find in the world literature of the past. If anyone writes a new *Romeo and Juliet*, it really ought to be a woman.

WOLF: Talking about Romeo and Juliet, what kind of social obstacles do you think would come between them today? Probably it isn't an accident that there are no great love stories today, or that we can't think of any at the moment. It must be because they rarely happen. To say that they're "rare" doesn't mean that one can't and mustn't write them. But evidently our main experience is that women who are capable of love have not found an appropriate partner—that is a stupid word—that is, someone they can love and who would love them in return. I don't know if things are developing in such a way that women, too, are becoming increasingly narcissistic—because, of course, narcissism is one of the basic qualities of men who aren't capable of sharing love. Maybe the number of people who can live together as real couples is steadily declining. That may be one feature of the modern world.

NEHRING: Love as something that stands up to conditions of extreme tension: maybe that's the point where the question of equality or liberation no longer applies, because that is the moment when partnership is fulfilled—or love as a way of mastering life together. Today there are so many big conflicts which have to be mastered. Maybe that creates an opportunity for love, too.

WOLF: I also believe that. What Brecht said, that love or partnership or marriage—I don't know exactly how he phrased it—has to include a "third" element. I have believed that my whole life, and I have found it to be true in my own experience. It seems to me that from the start, marriages and romances in my generation had that "third" element, which was our common hope, our ideal of utopia, of making this country a socialist society in our own lifetime. That kept us in suspense for many years of our life together. It never got boring; we always had this "third" thing—even when it chiefly involved disappointments, and criticism which was risky, which one had to come to an agreement about. But there was always a connection to all that, a tie which also created a tie between the spouses, or the lovers. I have the impression that young people who are committing themselves totally to the new social process that is emerging with great speed and intensity here in the past few weeks—young people who are committed to the point of self-surrender—that exactly the same thing has been happening to them, maybe without their realizing it. Suddenly families and marriages are being reshaped, and this tie to an outside element is becoming a factor again. In between these two generations, I think, came other generations which did not have that, and which suffered a lot as a result. Now they will suffer twice as much, when they look back and realize what they missed.

NEHRING: I'd like to come back to the science-fiction theme in the film. Science fiction is a popular genre; there are a lot of science-fiction films around. People are very concerned to find a new ethic —or even an old ethic—which is applicable to the progress of science as we move toward the year 2000. At the end of *Self-experiment*, the lead character sums up her position when she tells the professor: "You've done a model job preparing your drug. Our experiment was a piece of barbarous nonsense. It's too late for apologies. But I have to tell you: I didn't have any choice either, about whether to play along with this game or not."

Have we—as human beings endowed with reason and with stored-up experience—really no choice about whether to disconnect ourselves from what clearly are misguided and life-threatening developments in science and technology or to bring them to a halt?

WOLF: That's one of the fundamental questions. People fairly often describe me as anti-scientific because I ask that question in a very radical way and with an undertone of despair—but I do that intentionally. For example, I did it in *Accident*, and in "Self-experiment," too. I believe that we had that choice and that now the moment has come when the choice has almost been taken out of our hands. This is less true in a country like ours, where science has not had, and will not have, the enormous resources available to it in the U.S.A. or in West Germany, for instance, and in other highly developed capitalist nations. In those countries, scientific research has quite simply turned into an institution, the kind that is highly self-contained, barely accountable to the public and also barely understood by the public; and once it gets going, it runs automatically without stopping. You read and hear almost every week about advances in gene technology. That is a field which definitely has entered the plots of our films, and I ask myself whether it is possible now to stop these scientists who see no limit to what they can do. Let's hope that the laws to limit them won't come too late. The film describes what they are doing as "barbarous" because it shows no respect. Respect for nature, for creation, for life, is very difficult to communicate unless it is passed on to people from childhood, so that it becomes part of their flesh and blood, and is experienced as a taboo and as a job for mankind. There are limits beyond which a human being should not

313

go, not even if he lacks a belief in a higher authority which forbids
him to do it. I don't know what means still exist to bring this ethic
into the institution of science.

NEHRING: The film leaves us with hope. Johanna is a survivor. She
broke off the experiment she was performing on herself—along with
the professor—when the effects of his experiments began to punish
him through the next generation, through his own daughter. We are
told that there may be an antidote which will change her back. What
antidotes are there? Is art, is culture a channel through which antidotes
can be made effective? Do they lie in the development of democracy,
of a new thinking, in what Anna Seghers called "the strength of the
weak"?

WOLF: Right now we are experiencing an explosion of democracy
here—not in the social structures, not yet, but in the meeting halls
and on the streets. Everything which troubles people, all the questions
and suggestions they have, is being expressed out in the open. No
one knows yet what all this will lead to. We'll see. But I believe that
the only antidote to the arbitrary will and elitist development of institutional science—to its benevolent as well as to its very dangerous
institutions—is what I have to call "total" democratic supervision.
Supervision by nonscientists; that is, by people equipped with nothing
but their education, their concern, and their common sense, who still
have some actual ability, in whatever form, to influence what goes
on in scientific institutions. If gradually, all over the world, however
belatedly, we are progressing toward disarmament, including disarmament in the areas of ideas and ideology, then of course we in the
socialist countries have an advantage: we are not dependent on main-
taining total secrecy for reasons of competition and profit. It could
turn out that these undemocratic structures in the capitalist countries
will prove far more dangerous to mankind in the end. I don't know
yet of any antidote by which one could prevent a corporation armed
with giant research divisions and huge financial resources from developing horrible instruments or techniques in secret. No remedy
exists to cure that, because democratic supervision does not extend
to such places.

NEHRING: It is a subject of heated debate at the moment whether
socialism is a legitimate policy, whether it offers hope as an alternative
to other systems. The question needs to be thought through again
from this angle, too.

WOLF: I have always chosen socialism and I still do, although, of
course, socialism as an alternative needs to be redefined, and it will
take time to do that. The population of our country includes a fairly
large number who are not only intelligent but well educated—we are

seeing the evidence of that right now—and who, to the surprise of many, are ready to recommit themselves. It may even be possible to evolve a new alternative. I mean that in quite a modest sense. But I really don't see what would stop that from happening, once the very harsh and destructive structures which exist now have been altered.

What really would stand in the way of the people exercising supervision over all areas of society, including science? Supervision not in the sense of being suspicious of scientists but in the sense of working, cooperating with them. This could also have a highly liberating effect on the scientists, just as journalists and literary people are freer now, and at the same time they would get more support because they are participating in the democratic process of reaching independent adulthood, after a long period of being unable to speak out. For a long time now, every advance we have tried to make has been shunted aside. Artists have suffered many tragedies as a result. I'm referring, among other things, to the wave of people who left this country in the past decade. Theirs were not easy departures, or easy fates. There weren't many of us left here. Now we see ourselves surrounded by a great popular movement. That is very liberating. If this movement continues, if it does not content itself with fulfilling a few very important but primarily material desires—then in fact I do see cause for hope.

NEHRING: Thank you very much for this talk. It has touched on many questions which go far beyond the subject of *Self-experiment* and its possible effects but which are vital to our self-discovery, self-understanding, and self-assertion. The film may itself stir the audience and start them thinking along these lines.

WOLF: Yes, this is the ideal moment for it.

October 30, 1989

The Language

of the Turning Point*

Every revolutionary movement liberates language, too. What before was so hard to express suddenly trips off our tongues. We are amazed to hear what we have been thinking, evidently for a long time, and now we shout it out to each other: "Democracy—Now or Never!" What we mean is rule by the people. We remember the earlier initiatives in our history which broke down or were bloodily suppressed, and we do not want to sleep away once again the opportunity offered by this crisis, which has awakened all our productive energies. But neither do we wish to spoil it by rashness, or by turning around our enemy-images to face in the opposite direction.

The word "turning point" is one I have problems with. It makes me picture a sailboat when the wind turns. The captain calls out a warning and the crew duck down while the boom sweeps across the deck. Is this an accurate picture of what is happening? Does it apply to us, in this situation which every day moves on to something new?

I would like to speak in terms of a "revolutionary revival." Revolutions start at the bottom. "Bottom" and "top" are changing places in our system of values, and this change is turning socialist society upside down. Great social movements are under way. Never has so much talking been done in our country as in the past few weeks; never have we talked so much with each other, never with so much passion, with so much anger and sorrow, and with so much hope. We want to put each day to good use. We don't sleep, or sleep

* Speech delivered in Alexander Square, East Berlin.

316

only a little. We are making friends with people we never met, and having painful quarrels with others. We call this "dialogue." We asked for it, but by now we have become almost deaf to the word, although we have not yet learned what it means. We stare suspiciously at many of the hands which people suddenly hold out to us, at many faces which used to be stiff and unsmiling. "Suspicion is good; keeping watch is even better." So we twist around old slogans, slogans which once oppressed and hurt us, and "return to sender." We are afraid of being used. We are afraid, too, of rejecting a proposal that is meant sincerely. The whole country is ambivalent. We know that we must practice the art of not letting the ambivalence degenerate into confrontation. These weeks, these opportunities are a gift that we will be given only once—a gift that we have given to ourselves.

Puzzled, we watch those resourceful individuals, popularly known as "weathervanes," who, according to the dictionary definition, "adapt rapidly and easily to a given situation, handle themselves well, and understand how to use it to advantage." These people are the main obstacles to the credibility of the new politics. We have not yet reached the point where we can regard them with humor—although in other cases we are already managing to see the funny side. On banners I read, "If you can't get off the running board, then get off the tram." And demonstrators call out to the police: "Change your uniform and join our army!"—a generous offer, by the way. We also think about being thrifty: "Good laws save money on enforcement." We are even ready to make basic sacrifices. "Hey, people, turn the tube off and join the parade!" Language is shedding the officialese and journalese which swaddled it, and is remembering the words for feelings. One of them is "dream." We are dreaming wide-awake.

Picture this: Socialism arrives and no one goes away! Instead, we see pictures of those who are still leaving the country, and we ask: What can we do? We hear the answering echo: *"Do something!"* And that is what is beginning to happen, as demands turn into rights and obligations. Investigation commissions, constitutional law, administrative reform. So much to do, on top of our regular work. Not to mention reading the newspapers!

We have no more time now for parades to show our allegiance, for government-staged rallies. No, this is a "demo," legal, nonviolent. If it stays that way right to the end, we will have learned something more about what we are capable of, and stand up for that in the future.

I have a suggestion for how to celebrate May 1:

Government leaders are paraded past the people for inspection. Unbelievable transformations. The "East German people" go out

317

onto the streets—so as to see that they *are* a people. For me this is the most important sentence of the past few weeks—a cry uttered by a thousand throats: *"We—are—the—people!"*

A simple statement of fact. Let's not forget it.

November 4, 1989

"It Hurts to Know"

———

After my last article in the *Wochenpost* [*The Weekly Post*], I received one hundred and seventy letters, which I would like to see published as a historical document. They serve me as a fund of information, which I will carefully preserve, among other reasons as evidence of our mental and emotional attitudes during this period. First, the letters show the turmoil we all feel. They also prove that anyone who challenges our education system touches on a very sore point in people's lives. The pain makes them react violently to the abrupt revolution of values in our country and makes them particularly defensive about real or imagined attacks. Many things which people wrote to me about, and blamed me for saying, have by now been said dozens of times, in a variety of public settings. However, this does not make me feel less concerned about the issues, but more so.

The people who read my article showed the same divided reactions as people all over the country who are splitting into groups with opposing viewpoints. "You said what is in my heart," some wrote. Or: "Your article isn't worth reading." It would be too simple to categorize the first group as victims of oppression in the old society, and the second group as the ones who did the oppressing and who led the others by the nose. However, the old oppressors have of course not just vanished overnight. Often, the same kind of split runs through a single person, and a single letter: "Have we been learning and teaching the wrong thing? Haven't we promoted and tried to teach collaborative government—collaborative thinking—collaborative work? Unfortunately, walls barred our way to realizing those goals."

Former pupils report their experiences: "When I think about my

319

own schooldays, I feel rage and anger, even hatred wells up in me
—the memory of humiliations and of my own helplessness." "My
high-school years were the worst years of my life. I lived those four
years in nonstop fear of saying the wrong thing, and in the anxious
effort to guess what my teachers wanted me to say." "I'm turning
thirty, and I and my whole generation have heard nothing since we
were children but to be quiet about what we really think. I am sorry
to think that we spent our youth doing nothing but raising our hands
whenever we were expected to."

Other readers resist my portrayal of them as dependent children
and report that they retained their ability for critical thought and are
raising their children in the same spirit. Their letters make me happy,
even if some of them have misunderstood me: I do not at all mean
to generalize about a whole generation on the basis of individual
examples.

Teachers are the most affected by these issues. They fall into
two groups, which appear to have been living in two different countries
and two different realities and to have been teaching in two different
school systems. Some interpreted my article as a global attack on all
teachers: "Mrs. Wolf has made teachers in our country fair game,
and anyone who sides with Mrs. Wolf has leave to insult and revile
teachers and to hold them responsible for all our country's problems."
Others feel that my article depicted their problems accurately. "To
be honest, I would not have written it myself, because I am still afraid
of reprisals." Many feel called on to defend their behavior: "There
are thousands of good teachers in our country who are friends and
helpers to their students, and often continue to be so for years afterward." I would not dispute that. Others admit to pangs of conscience.
One teacher who has served his profession for thirty-five years writes:
"I have worked in the way that was prescribed to me, and under a
permanent taboo, to avoid attracting the notice of the principal or the
district school superintendent. And yet all the time I claimed to be
serving the cause of 'socialism.' " A woman teacher says: "I knew
that the courage to state their opinions openly would only bring my
students trouble later on. I, too, have been forced to live a two-faced
existence, and I have suffered great emotional damage as a result."
Other teachers defend what they have taught and how they taught it,
although sometimes they unwittingly testify against themselves: "Wolf
seems to suggest that it would have been better to have handed our
students maps of Germany with the borders we had in 1937—as has
been done in Bavaria."

The bitterest letters are those in which teachers grapple with
how their own critical faculties were suppressed by our school system:

"It is unimaginable what we had to put up with," writes a former teacher. Teachers had been "thinking about things and communicating their feelings" for a long time but received no response—no reply to a letter sent to the Ministry of Education, for example; and "outspoken teachers" had been muzzled and silenced by the district school superintendent. One teacher describes the teaching profession as a "modern form of serfdom." Another writes that he has to stand by "while we teachers are attacked, and state administrators and our own colleagues leave us to fend for ourselves." Many teachers describe their years of "desperately walking a fine line, just barely getting away with speaking up while at the same time staying loyal to the students and avoiding any behavior that would make our colleagues and superiors denounce us as enemies of the state." Some describe how they were forced to leave teaching because their bodies told them to, through "terrible stomach pains," for example, that "something wasn't working."

Many feel deeply hurt by my article. They accuse me of being "hard-hearted," "a demagogue," "one-eyed" or "wearing blinders," or even raise the old charge that I am "on the other side of the barricade." Of course, their letters express the normal differences of opinion, and justifiably insist on the truth of varying experiences. But, beyond all this, they show a defensiveness which crosses over into denial of reality, and into insults and threats: "The working class holds the political power. Wolf and her confederates should not forget that." Signed with sixteen signatures.

All that has a familiar ring. Familiar, too, are the abusive attacks on "this nation's writers," on my "hack scribbling," on "artists who now present themselves as the Grailkeepers of freedom: So where have they been up to now?" The policy of splitting off "the intelligentsia" from "the people"—a policy which has been pursued more or less deliberately for decades—is still proving effective: not with many people, but with some. This same attitude, and the vague or specific measures or restrictions which lead up to or result from it, is what has driven so many artists to leave our country. Without wishing to overemphasize the problem, I would like to warn against our continuing that fatal tradition in German history—of assigning to opposite camps the makers of material products and of intellectual/spiritual products. That split has never aided the cause of revolutionary reform.

Another thing I see is that certain information has been kept from the public: for example, the fact that some people, including me, have been barred from publishing political articles in GDR newspapers and magazines, and from expressing our views on radio and television, ever since we protested the expatriation of Wolf Biermann in 1976. "The name Christa Wolf seems to be in fashion just now," writes one angry reader. Another voices her belief that I served as a "functionary of the East German Writers' Union" who personally "collaborated in everything." The honorarium received by writers and artists has been an ongoing theme of recrimination for years. I recognize the symptoms of the same anti-intellectual movement which is found in the Soviet Union, although there it is far more powerful and rabid than here, as my Soviet colleagues have told me. I consider it appropriate to tell East German readers about these anti-intellectual trends while (I hope) there is still time.

We are only just starting over in this country, and I wish so much that we could avoid unnecessary harshness and tragedy now, in this new beginning. We cannot help inflicting pain on ourselves and others when we rip off the scabs that have formed over decades-old wounds. It may be euphoric to watch the *outer* walls fall down— but many readers write me that, inside, they "don't feel really able to be happy yet." I feel the same way. The moments of happiness are rare; anger and grief still predominate. I have the impression that many people are wondering if there is any need for this feeling of numbness—which they partly have imposed on themselves—now that the reasons for borders, secrecy, restrictions, and prohibitions, which went unquestioned only yesterday, have vanished overnight. Many people are racking their consciences, while those who were actually responsible for the events of the past "simply disappear in the dark," one indignant reader writes. Naturally, it makes people very insecure when they are expected to tear down their inner walls and open up to their fellow men, of whom they have always been suspicious until now. I understand the feelings of aggressiveness which arise, and which we then turn against others.

"Madness!" It's no accident that this was the word we heard spoken most often over radio and TV last weekend when, for the first time in twenty-eight years, masses of our people were allowed to pass unobstructed across the border into West Germany. We should not lose sight of the fact that there are people who need clearly defined, even rigid structures. Madness involves the removal of borders. Many people now are asking themselves: Was I normal before? Am I normal now? A male teacher writes: "I sometimes had the feeling of being crazy when I saw everything in a way that was so different, so disturbingly different, from many other people." And a woman teacher: "What we observed and expressed very quietly and in secrecy twenty years ago, within a small circle of our colleagues, is now being loudly proclaimed by prominent people, as if it were the most normal thing in the world."

It *is* the most normal thing in the world—now. The result of revolutionary movements has always been to introduce a new normality, and when this happens, there always are groups—and not just the members of the former regime—who feel that the world is no longer comprehensible, and who suffer from the sense that the changes have come too late for them to adjust. Then there are those who rejoice when at last they discover their true selves. "I feel alive, it's exciting to live here now."

I will refrain from offering any advice. I just hope that we are generous and farsighted enough to take with us as many of our fellow citizens as possible as we travel this new road. I believe that people are capable of change; I know that I am. And besides, isn't there such a thing as productive pain? As one letter-writer expresses it: "It hurts to know that I am allowed to say 'I' as if it were natural."

November 14, 1989

Momentary Interruption[*]

I am sure you will believe me when I say that academic honors are not what I have on my mind these days. Nine months ago, when you kindly and cordially insisted that I accept an honorary doctorate, I was living in a different age, and so was everyone else in my country. The enormity of what we have experienced in the past four months threatens now to cut us off from observers outside our borders, however well-intentioned they may be, and even from West Germans. I have grown wary of predicting the future. But it could be that this process of estrangement will continue to grow below the surface, beneath the outer layer of brotherliness and rapprochement. This could happen if, in the rapid annexation of the GDR by the German Federal Republic—an Anschluss which is being described as a "unification" or even a "reunification"—East Germany's history is publicly suppressed, once our nation ceases to exist, and is driven back inside the people who made, experienced, and endured it. This could happen if East Germans self-sacrificially devote themselves to trying to fit in, while West Germans act out feelings of superiority and victory. Oughtn't we rather to concentrate on a mutual exchange of information—not just about politics, economics, finance, science, and the destruction of the environment, but about our inner state and feelings, too?

So, although I owe you my thanks and render them gladly, please allow me not to clothe them in a celebration speech, but rather to

---

[*] On receiving an honorary doctorate from the University of Hildesheim.

express some groping, hesitant thoughts which at least suggest the problems we in the GDR are confronting today.

November 4, 1989, in Alexander Square in East Berlin was the moment when artists, intellectuals, and other groups in our society came together and achieved the greatest possible unanimity. That moment was by no means just a fortunate accident, as amazed Western reporters interpreted it. It was the end product and climax of a long process in which literary and theater people, peace groups, and other groups had been coming together under the aegis of the Church, to meet and share talk from which each learned the urges, thoughts, and language of the others, and drew encouragement for action. For years we addressed certain tasks in what we intended as our opposition literature: to name the conflicts which for a long time were expressed nowhere else, and thus to generate or strengthen a critical attitude in readers; to encourage them to resist lies, hypocrisy, and surrender of self; to keep alive our language and the other traditions of German literature and history from which attempts were made to cut us off; and, last but not least, to defend moral values which in the dominant ideology were cynically earmarked for sacrifice. Later generations, who perhaps will live in less troubled circumstances, will decide which of our efforts were superficial, inconsequential, or timid, and conserve what has enduring value as literature. In any case, these efforts were needed, as were the people who made them, and for a time we appeared justified in our belief that the fall of the old regime, achieved by the masses, would lead to the revolutionary revival of our country.

We seem to have been mistaken. Our uprising appears to have come years too late. The damage to many people and to the country runs too deep. The unbridled abuse of power has discredited and undermined the values in whose name the abuse occurred. In a period of a few weeks, we have seen our chances to make a new start at an alternative society vanish before our eyes, and seen the very existence of our nation vanish with them. A defeat does not become less painful because you are able to explain the reasons for it; nor less disturbing, if it is a repetition of the past. Is this left-wing nostalgia? In recent weeks I have been reading with very sober eyes the writings of Hölderlin, Büchner, Tucholsky. And I have checked over the names of allies who have fought for the same things for years: Heinrich Böll, Erich Fried, Peter Weiss, Günter Grass, Walter Jens . . . not a few of them Jews, not a few of them in exile. A "unification," founded on radical democratic thinking, which I would have no fear of joining.

The people out on our streets now are no longer the same ones who achieved the revolution of a few weeks ago—not as far as I can tell. The lightning disintegration of almost all our social institutions is leaving the field open to embittered advocates of partisan economic and political interests, before our society has had time to develop new mechanisms and safeguards to integrate all its different elements, or to develop an immunity against the economic slogans of Western nations. Many East Germans are disoriented and are sinking into depression. Others fly into fits of hatred and revenge to evade their understandable feelings of rage and disappointment, fear, humiliation, and unacknowledged shame and self-contempt. And what will happen to that group which is very vocal right now which hopes to see its situation improve rapidly once it lets itself be swiftly and unconditionally annexed by that other Germany which is great, wealthy, powerful, and fully functional? What political direction will they take, if they find their expectations disappointed again? This perhaps is a question for farseeing politicians in both the Germanys to consider, even in the middle of an election campaign. We have not been granted any pause for thought. While still in a state of extreme emotional upset, we must make decisions about a future which we have not been allowed to think over. Does all this mean that what we began in autumn of 1989 has already failed? I hesitate to say that, I refuse to give in to that suggestion. I want to remember the conditions which we decided were no longer acceptable. I want to remember the almost unbelievable levelheadedness of the masses of people who changed those conditions, essentially without the use of violence to this very day. I want to remember the spirit of generosity toward all which fundamentally transformed people's attitudes, especially the young people's, and nowhere as evidently as in Berlin. But I especially want us to look at the thousands of people—there are only thousands, not millions—who regard the freedom they have earned by their own efforts as a chance to take responsible action. In hordes of citizens' groups, in residential districts, town councils, and committees, they are uncovering the evils of the past, breaking up the structures which caused those evils, working tenaciously on useful projects, and designing concrete blueprints for specific sectors of society. They are grass-roots democracy in action. Incidentally, we writers can learn invaluable lessons by associating with groups like these.

But, in the midst of all the turmoil, what has happened to art? The post it occupied so long is now vacant. Too much was laid on its shoulders; and it is a relief to be free of that long-term strain. At the same time I see sources of friction. Literature is no longer forced to do the work of the press. Many books which met with opposition only a few months ago are now passé, because radical social criticism is coming directly from the public. The theaters are half empty. Even productions which a short while ago were besieged by audiences who used them to shore up their own protest actions seem deserted now. Sometimes people's feelings of inadequacy lead to a hostile attitude toward art and artists, of a kind which in the past had to be fostered artificially by state and Party machines bent on a deliberate policy of creating scapegoats. We have not yet shed the patterns which German history has spawned in this century. I think it is a mistake for artists to give way to moaning and self-pity. We need to ask ourselves if we have really been released from our public responsibility, and if not, then what should our future role be—assuming that it will be more marginal than in the past?

I wonder: what will become of East Germany's forty years of history? A history that is not a phantom, after all, although when it is gone, it will leave a phantom pain. Who will continue to express openly the grief, shame, and remorse which I read in many people's letters and see in their eyes—once everyone is busy trying to improve our material conditions? Who will still oppose the negative effects of an economic system whose blessings most people understandably desire? There is another possibility, too, although I hardly dare to mention it so soon. We may see a need for utopian thinking slowly grow back, evolving out of everyday experience rather than out of theory.

In short, literature will be called on to perform the same task it must perform in all times and places: to investigate the blind spots in our past, and to accompany us into our changing future. Any attempt on our part to deny who we are would destroy our creativity at its roots. My plea to you is to give us your sympathetic but critical attention. That is something that we should be able to agree on, so that we may gradually get rid of the old estrangements and let no new ones emerge to take their place.

I thank you for the opportunity to talk with you about this.

January 31, 1990

Postscript to an Autumn

These texts, now that they have been gathered into a book, are for the most part already obsolete. They are about "current events"— the "course of history." But what is that? Whatever it is, it is no longer the peaceful, wary gait of young people holding their candles protectively beside the Church of Gethsemane on October 7 and 8, 1989, while police moved in to threaten, obstruct, and disperse them. It is no longer the brave, resolute motion of the one hundred thousand citizens of Leipzig on October 9; nor the liberated, sovereign, almost arrogant stride of the Berliners on November 4. It's true, those who took part in these walks made history. But German history doesn't go like that, I had almost forgotten.

Erich Fried* said to me at our last meeting: We must save the world. He wanted to meet with Gorbachev and advise him—to tell him, for example, that if Marxism is to succeed politically, it must ally itself with the insights of psychoanalysis. I laughed heartily at that, whereas he meant it seriously. Then suddenly I, too, was in a position to take secret hopes seriously again—maybe too seriously —although by that time Erich Fried was dead. There wasn't a minute to spare to ponder and reflect. No space which might have let me keep an eye on what I was doing (although I was doing it myself). These essays bear witness to the fact.

I put them into a folder, over a four- or five-month period—a folder marked "Personal Writings." "Personal"? I ask myself today. Well, yes. I mean, no one else decided what should go into them.

---

* German writer, poet, 1921–88.

Yet in many cases they were things that others expected me to write. They are only signs, signals of the sort that people just managed to make as they were pulled into the raging torrent which a few weeks ago was our life. I cannot bring myself to try to describe it. I will have to settle for a subjective chronicle of recent events.

I used my speech at the Academy of Arts in West Berlin—my contribution to round-table talks on the fiftieth anniversary of Germany's attack on Poland—to describe the growing conflicts in the GDR which I could not then have made public in my own country. The letters and phone calls I received convinced me that many East Germans were deeply troubled and were waiting for someone to come out with the facts. Today it is hard to remember that in February of last year it was unthinkable for anyone to publicize through the East German News Agency a text from the East German PEN Center advocating the release of Václav Havel: a text which (I hope) preserved the integrity of our PEN Center. Today it is scarcely possible to believe that as recently as September 14, 1989, members of the East German Writers' Union in Berlin carried on a tough, hours-long debate about whether we should or should not support a proposed resolution—a resolution which those of us who drew it up felt was really too wishy-washy—because we planned to submit it both to the Politburo and to the East German News Agency. Some officials in our own union regarded this as politically provocative behavior.

Throughout September, our concern grew about a possible violent confrontation between the unteachable state authorities and groups who had been meeting for a long time and who now began to form an opposition and to demonstrate on the streets. The New Forum emerged and was immediately branded as criminal. But its popularity signaled that many people had run out of patience. The fortieth anniversary of the GDR arrived with great fanfare, and people came from around the world to help us celebrate. Security measures in Berlin were even tighter and more conspicuous than was normal on such occasions. One could see the tension growing.

On the night of October 7, as I returned home after a meeting with other women writers, it happened that I did not take the route that led along the Schönhauser Allee past the Church of Gethsemane, and so I did not run into the police barricades which cordoned off the area. At home, I was greeted with the news that there had been street fighting downtown. Was this the outbreak of police violence which we had been fearing, which would stifle any movement by the opposition?

But on October 8 people were standing outside the Gethsemane Church holding candles again. We saw them as we drove past on our

way to the Attorney General's office in the Littenstrasse, and to police
headquarters in the Keibelstrasse, to try to discover the whereabouts
of our daughter, who had been arrested during the night, along with
many other demonstrators. A friend brought us the first eyewitness
report. It was Sunday; we stood outside the doors, which were shut
tight. By the way, one realizes that it is tasteless to think of Kafka
while waiting in front of those high iron doors from which nothing
comes out except perhaps a distorted voice over the intercom, asking:
"What do you want?" We walked past the column of parked police
vehicles—vans with martial-looking red-and-white-striped shields
mounted on the front—in which young policemen and watch commanders, weary from night duty, were dozing or sleeping with their
heads propped against the steering wheel: images which reminded
me of a very distant scene at the beginning of the Second World War.
One police station was manned but claimed no responsibility. They
knew nothing about any "incoming customers" (they said); but if there
had been arrests, they had been lawful. Only the uniformed boy in
the little guardhouse at the corner of the huge complex told us anything: all the prisoners had already been moved out again, he said
softly.

Meanwhile, my daughter had been released, but all we could
get out of her over the telephone were headline captions: police van,
police station, police garage. So the phrase "Things look bad" had
not yet sunk in completely by the time I had to leave for West Berlin
to keep my appointment for an interview with Gerhard Rein. Several
friends from the New Forum had urged me to make their views known
to the public [during my broadcast with Gerhard Rein], to protest
their criminalization [by the East German government], and above
all, to warn people against any use of violence in Leipzig, where a
crowd would be demonstrating again the next day, after the peace
prayer in the Church of St. Nicholas. "Stay cool" should be the
guideline for both sides. I felt under a lot of pressure. It was risky
to try to intervene in the situation which had developed; but I thought
a bloodbath was possible and I wanted to use any opportunity, however
slight, to serve as a mediator. Gerhard Rein, who had been familiar
with the GDR's problems for a long time, made a sympathetic partner
in our dialogue, which went on the air that same evening and then
was rebroadcast repeatedly over West German radio next day. The
telephone calls and letters stepped up.

On the critical day, October 9, I had to fly to Moscow. Today,
rereading the text of my talk with Gerhard Rein, I see that it expresses
hopes which were almost unthinkable at that time and yet, remarkably,
were fulfilled exactly as we described them: the dialogue that took

place among all the groups in our society, the round-table discussions, the media freedom. But along with that came glaring mistakes and misjudgments—for example, my expectation that the new self-confidence which East Germans developed in the process of resistance would enable them in the future to withstand the intimidating *amour propre* displayed by many West Germans. I prematurely judged everyone to be like the many I knew or met in those tumultuous weeks. I also overestimated the breadth of the conscious resistance movement. It would be worth a special investigation to find out just what reduced or stripped away East German self-esteem, pride, and dignity in the time before and after the so-called turning point. "We are the People": a brief moment in time when the people seemed sure of their identity, the sovereigns and agents of their own history. "We are *One* People!"—is that really an improvement on the first version?

It is beyond my powers to fashion the texts of this volume so that the subtexts show through, or to describe the conditions which gave rise to these essays. You will find no euphoria in them, for I experienced no euphoria. Relief, yes. I did experience an unforgettable moment of relief, late on the evening of October 9 in my hotel room in Moscow, when I asked over the telephone what was happening in Leipzig and steeled myself to hear the worst. Then came the answer: one hundred thousand demonstrators had gone out onto the streets, and there had been no violence. A moment of pure happiness. Followed by other unforgettable moments, in the departure lounge at Sheremetevo airport six days later. The members of an East German madrigal choir from Halle, who had been working with a film company far from home, had heard rumors about terrible things happening in Leipzig, and I was able to pass on the news that the demonstrations had gone off smoothly. In their joy, the singers, who were grouped together among the hundreds of travelers waiting in the airport lounge, sang in concentrated and (I felt) moving tones: "O valleys far, O hilltops high." Very German, of course. But a large group of West German travelers who applauded them were clearly surprised and had no idea why these young East Germans felt they had no choice but to burst into song.

After that, I, too, was caught by the fast-forward button. Sucked into the maelstrom of rallies, consultations, resolutions, meetings, proclamations, demonstrations in which we were called on to uncover and pin down the evils of the old system, while at the same time discovering and developing qualities in ourselves and others which could help us build something new. Naturally, we were taxed beyond our abilities. We also fell into the trap of fear, both justified fear and the kind that is artificially induced. Already, it is hard for me to

331

remember how I felt in those weeks, when daily we expected violent confrontations to break out, and when people of every political stamp kept warning us what all this was bound to lead to, in terms of domestic and foreign policy. It is beyond me to describe this in detail, although it would be a useful exercise; but I grew used to being a character in a kind of political thriller, carrying on the most risky telephone conversations without even feeling very surprised by it anymore. The word "normality" had fundamentally changed its meaning.

For example, November 4, when Berliners held their great demonstration in Alexander Square. The artists who planned it intended it to be an ordinary demonstration for artistic freedom and for freedom of the press which would be legally announced and politely approved by the authorities. A "security partnership" would guarantee peaceful behavior on both sides. (This was the first time this term was used.) But the event took off on its own, came apart at the seams. No one knew if it would be possible to control it. Frightened people were called on to stand up for themselves, and their claims could not be ignored. My name was on the list of speakers. I was supposed to talk about "The Language of the Turning Point." So, before the meeting, I had begun to collect phrases and slogans from the public notices posted in the streets. Incidentally, the term "weathervane"* was not my invention. And I applied myself to helping to keep the demonstrations peaceful. Government security forces, who were still obeying orders, had disowned any responsibility, but had also spread the rumor that the demonstrators intended to storm the Brandenburg Gate. If they did so—although fortunately we did not know that on November 4—the required measures had been taken to prevent it. Thus it came about that one brother, a member of the People's Army, lay hidden, armed with live ammunition, not far from where another brother was taking part in the street demonstration. Stories of this kind came out afterward.

On the evening before the demonstration, Berlin was crammed with rumors. It was said that one million tickets to our city had been sold in the Federal Republic, and that trains carrying "demonstrators" of an undefined sort, disguised as workers, were on the way to the capital; and what would happen if they all joined their numbers to the demonstrators already in Berlin? Warned to be on the alert, I went over my speech once more that night to eliminate any provocative language. I did not feel calm until the next morning, when setting out too early through the empty downtown streets, we met quiet,

* Used to denote East Germans who found it easy and profitable to switch their allegiance to the West.

friendly peacekeeping volunteers walking in pairs, wearing their orange-and-green caps with the inscription: "No violence!" Among them were many colleagues of mine from the theater. This was the most beautiful moment I experienced that November 4—a day which many people talk about now as if they were remembering a long-ago happy event which they can hardly bring themselves anymore to believe really happened.

On November 21, when I was lecturing at the Karl Marx University in Leipzig, I ended my talk with the sentence: "I know that the revolutionary changes in our country are in good hands, insofar as they are in the hands of the people of Leipzig." My audience immediately corrected me. On Monday of that week, the character of the demonstrations in Leipzig had changed. This proved to be an index to the switch in mood and opinion which then ensued in other East German cities. *"Deutschland, einig Vaterland!"*—the call for a united Germany. There were reasons for this change of attitude, a couple of which I try to suggest in these essays. The Leipzigers I spoke with at that time seemed to be in a state of shock and were asking for support. They were looking for an avenue to express their views, because there was no longer a way to do this in the street demonstrations. That was when I began to receive letters from readers in West Germany. People I had never met warned me urgently that capital-rich parties in the Federal Republic were already searching for ways to buy up land and property in the GDR.

Responding both to pleas from the Leipzigers and to warnings from West Germans, I finally decided to join the "Save Our Country" campaign, although I secretly feared it was too late. It *was* too late. That same evening, West German Chancellor Kohl announced his Ten-Point Program for the reunification of Germany. That was something we could not have anticipated. We had launched our campaign just at the moment when the facts were coming out about the gross abuse of power in East Germany, about the true state of our economy and old town districts; about the environmental pollution; and just at the moment when many East Germans were able, for the first time, to see the cities and the consumer goods that were available in the other Germany. The critics were right: the word "socialist" had lost its appeal for many people. After hours of discussion, we had used it only once in the declaration we prepared, and even then it was, of course, redefined—in the phrase "the socialist alternative." The very term made many people angry and aggressive. No doubt they were also afraid that even using it once could delay our receiving the financial aid which we so urgently needed from the Federal Republic. Nor did they wish to take part in any more experiments: they preferred to adopt a policy which appeared to have proved itself already. Letters about our initiative kept piling up on my desk. Interestingly, people took offense at only a few of the well-known names on our long list of signatories. But I could see that they also disapproved of the either/ or tone of our statement; many found it simplistic. The choice we faced was no doubt less simple than we made it appear. Yesterday I received my first letter from a woman who asked herself and me whether by now we have not in fact arrived at the "or."

Next to this first pile of letters, a second pile kept growing relentlessly, made up of answers to the two articles of mine which had appeared in *Die Wochenpost* [*The Weekly Post*]. There were almost three hundred letters in all—many of which are now being published by Volk and Wissen under the title *Fitting in or Being Independent?*—and they taught me a great deal about the attitudes of my countrymen. What had made me think that oppressed people such as teachers would welcome freedom from this oppression? They were (and still are) suffering from its psychological aftereffects and preferred to deny rather than confront them. They fought off a voice which seemed responsible for making them suffer, as they had never fought their oppressors. I began to understand something more about the origins of the hatred, and of the need for revenge, which was now being shouted out on the streets. Perhaps I also learned more about the motives behind the sudden rage for German reunification, the unconscious motives behind the more superficial, material ones. And more, too, about the unconscious motives of the East Germans who had continued to leave the country. People whose sense of identity has been severely damaged cling to those whose identity is, or seems, intact. The appeal to stay here—launched quickly by grass-roots movements whose members wanted to go on working for change from within our own country—was doomed to fail.

From today's perspective, that appeal seems naïve, like so much of what happened back in that time of credulity, inexperience, and illusions. We will forget this, too, eventually. Maybe we want to forget it. How emotionally churned up people were, how improperly they behaved, how contrary to the rules. How people we had never laid eyes on smiled at us on the street. How customers and salesclerks got involved in discussions about urban and government affairs, as if we were in the middle of Brecht's play about the Paris Commune. People were already beginning to regard all this as normal. (Although, besides these, there were the others, the disoriented ones who drew up huge plans for our rescue and salvation, and felt that their day had come at last. Their plans made another big pile of paper on my

334

desk. Or those who felt they had to confide secret information about
the government and the economy, and insisted on the strictest security
measures while doing it. They could force you to read their tiny notes
covered with incomprehensible data, and then to tear the notes into
even tinier pieces while they watched, and throw them into the
wastebasket . . .)

Meanwhile, week by week, there was the constant factor of the
investigating commission assigned to look into the violent incidents
which had occurred in Berlin on October 7 and 8. The commission
which I and many others had called for had now begun its work. Was
it really "a school for democracy"? Yes, that is how I look at it. Three
dozen people of every political persuasion who in varying ways and
in varying degrees took part in our former political structures, or who
had consciously opposed them for some time, with varying results:
almost forty people, who found it hard to get along in the beginning,
yet learned to work together unconditionally, and to value and support
each other so that we could bear the things we were discovering—
the "true face of power"—and at least hold ourselves together for this
work in the universal crisis which embraced us all. Perhaps there is
hope for the future in the fact that models like these are not immediately being erased by the all-dominating drive to economic efficiency. In these past few months, what saved me were my many
meetings with people who had been caught up in the police actions
—their simplicity and humanity. Most of them were very young. Their
testimony about their experiences will make a unique historical
document.

And so a fourth tall stack of paper started growing on my desk.
But, in exchange for all this paper, for months on end there were no
books, no music, no theater. Only newspapers, the flood of letters,
the live TV news bulletins. A time of exceptional emotions.

Meanwhile, the signs tell me that this phase of my life is over.
Already I can talk about it from a certain distance, and not without
self-irony. What were changes are already changing again, and the
changers are changing with them. Or at least some of them are. It's
time to stand on the solid ground of facts. Only now the ground we
stand on is in a different country. It is no small feat to do what we
must do. But better be high divers and hanging gymnasts now than
be hung up later on the new realities. Once again, many people are
afraid. But these are different fears, and to some extent they are also
different people. And, once again, it requires courage to voice certain
opinions. In part they are the same opinions which we were not allowed
to voice before; and in part they are different opinions. I am just

335

beginning to receive the first in a new batch of letters—although these will never grow into a pile—which ask me: "Why aren't you telling us what you think?"

The politicians and the economists have the floor now. The political parties have the floor again. To some extent they are different parties than they used to be, and to some extent they are mirror images of parties in the Federal Republic, already looking to the day of reunification. I can see that all these people—politicians, economic managers, party officials—need a fatherland to carry on their enterprises. There is no motherland in sight, no more than before. An interview I recorded in June 1987 and October 1988 ["Unresolved Contradictions"]—long before the autumn of 1989—ends with a question: "Have you noticed how our recent history—the history of our own lifetimes and the history of this country—is full of unresolved contradictions and unsettled conflicts, which are just starting to pound right under the surface? That could turn out to be interesting." If that polity with its history no longer exists—that polity which, if people will only accept it, was a branch of the history of *Germany*—will this pounding heartbeat still be of interest to anyone? Will it beat more and more softly, and finally stop all by itself? And is that what people—many people—really want?

February 1990